THE PREHISTORY OF BRITAIN AND IRELAND

Sited at the furthest limits of the Neolithic revolution and standing at the confluence of the two great sea routes of prehistory, Britain and Ireland are distinct from Continental Europe for much of the prehistoric sequence. In this landmark study, Richard Bradley offers an interpretation of the unique archaeological record of these islands. Highlighting the achievements of its inhabitants, Bradley surveys the entire archaeological sequence over a 5,000-year period, from the last hunter gatherers and the adoption of agriculture in the Neolithic period, to the discovery of Britain and Ireland by travellers from the Mediterranean during the later pre-Roman Iron Age. His study places special emphasis on landscapes, settlements, monuments, and ritual practices.

This edition has been thoroughly revised and updated. The text takes account of recent developments in archaeological science, such as isotopic analyses of human and animal bone, recovery of ancient DNA, and more subtle and precise methods of radiocarbon dating.

Richard Bradley is Emeritus Professor in the Department of Archaeology, University of Reading. A Fellow of the British Academy and Honorary Fellow of the Society of Antiquaries of Scotland, he is the author of *The Use and Reuse of Stone Circles* and *The Idea of Order*, among many other publications.

CAMBRIDGE WORLD ARCHAEOLOGY

The *Cambridge World Archaeology* series is addressed to students and professional archaeologists, and to academics in related disciplines. Most volumes present a survey of the archaeology of a region of the world, providing an up-to-date account of research and integrating recent findings with new concerns of interpretation. While the focus is on a specific region, broader cultural trends are discussed and the implications of regional findings for cross-cultural interpretations considered. The authors also bring anthropological and historical expertise to bear on archaeological problems and show how both new data and changing intellectual trends in archaeology shape inferences about the past. More recently, the series has expanded to include thematic volumes.

RECENT BOOKS IN THE SERIES

ANTONIO SAGONA, *The Archaeology of the Caucasus*
D. T. POTTS, *The Archaeology of Elam*
ROBIN CONINGHAM AND RUTH YOUNG, *The Archaeology of South Asia*
CLAUDIA SAGONA, *The Archaeology of Malta*
FRANCES F. BERDAN, *Aztec Archaeology and Ethnohistory*
PETER MAGEE, *The Archaeology of Prehistoric Arabia*
KOJI MIZOGUCHI, *The Archaeology of Japan*
MIKE SMITH, *The Archaeology of Australia's Deserts*
A. BERNARD KNAPP, *The Archaeology of Cyprus*
LI LIU AND XINGCAN CHEN, *The Archaeology of China*
STEPHEN D. HOUSTON AND TAKESHI INOMATA, *The Classic Maya*
PHILIP L. KOHL, *The Making of Bronze Age Eurasia*
LAWRENCE BARHAM AND PETER MITCHELL, *The First Africans*
ROBIN DENNELL, *The Palaeolithic Settlement of Asia*
CHRISTOPHER POOL, *Olmec Archaeology and Early Mesoamerica*
SAMUEL M. WILSON, *The Archaeology of the Caribbean*
RICHARD BRADLEY, *The Prehistory of Britain and Ireland*
LUDMILA KORYAKOVA AND ANDREJ EPIMAKHOV, *The Urals and Western Siberia in the Bronze and Iron Ages*
DAVID WENGROW, *The Archaeology of Early Egypt*
PAUL RAINBIRD, *The Archaeology of Micronesia*
PETER M.M.G. AKKERMANS AND GLENN M. SCHWARTZ, *The Archaeology of Syria*
TIMOTHY INSOLL, *The Archaeology of Islam in Sub-Saharan Africa*

View of Ireland from the coast of south-west Scotland, emphasising the short sea crossing between them.
Photograph: Aaron Watson.

THE PREHISTORY OF BRITAIN AND IRELAND

Second Edition

RICHARD BRADLEY

University of Reading

 CAMBRIDGE
UNIVERSITY PRESS

CAMBRIDGE
UNIVERSITY PRESS

University Printing House, Cambridge CB2 8BS, United Kingdom

One Liberty Plaza, 20th Floor, New York, NY 10006, USA

477 Williamstown Road, Port Melbourne, VIC 3207, Australia

314–321, 3rd Floor, Plot 3, Splendor Forum, Jasola District Centre, New Delhi – 110025, India

79 Anson Road, #06-04/06, Singapore 079906

Cambridge University Press is part of the University of Cambridge.

It furthers the University's mission by disseminating knowledge in the pursuit of education, learning, and research at the highest international levels of excellence.

www.cambridge.org
Information on this title: www.cambridge.org/9781108419925
DOI: 10.1017/9781108419925

First published 2007
Second edition 2019

Printed in the United Kingdom by TJ International Ltd. Padstow Cornwall

A catalogue record for this publication is available from the British Library.

Library of Congress Cataloging-in-Publication Data
Names: Bradley, Richard, 1946– author.
Title: The prehistory of Britain and Ireland / Richard Bradley.
Description: Second edition. | Cambridge, United Kingdom; New York, NY:
Cambridge University Press, 2019. | Series: Cambridge world archaeology |
Includes bibliographical references and index.
Identifiers: LCCN 2019000687 | ISBN 9781108419925 (hardback) |
ISBN 9781108412476 (paperback)
Subjects: LCSH: Prehistoric peoples – Great Britain. | Prehistoric peoples – Ireland. |
Excavations (Archaeology) – Great Britain. | Excavations (Archaeology) – Ireland. |
Antiquities, Prehistoric – Great Britain. | Antiquities, Prehistoric – Ireland. |
Great Britain – Antiquities. | Ireland – Antiquities.
Classification: LCC GN805.B6954 2019 | DDC 936.1–dc23
LC record available at https://lccn.loc.gov/2019000687

ISBN 978-1-108-41992-5 Hardback
ISBN 978-1-108-41247-6 Paperback

CONTENTS

PREFACE TO THE SECOND EDITION

This book takes the place of a volume published a decade or so ago. Why was a revision needed, and how does it differ from its predecessor? The first question is perhaps the easier one to answer. The last few years have seen a massive increase in the number of field projects undertaken in Britain and Ireland, and significant developments in the dissemination of the results. During the same period work in archaeological science has shed new light on questions that had exercised prehistorians for years. The clearest indication of the increasing pace of research is provided by the bibliography. Rather to my surprise, I find that 50 per cent of the references are to sources that became available after the first edition appeared. Not surprisingly, that account is no longer accurate or up to date.

The new book has a different structure from that first edition and to some extent it draws on different sources of information. The version published in 2007 was unusual in emphasising the results of development-led archaeology. Its preparation involved visits to numerous fieldworkers and regional archives, as it was the only way of discovering what information was available. Over ten years later many significant projects have achieved final publication and information is widely disseminated through the internet. Like the original version, this book has a substantial bibliography, but it is still the case that more information is available from some regions than from others.

In 2007 I evoked the timescale of insular prehistory by scaling the accounts of different periods to the number of years involved; I devoted approximately 2,000 words to each century of the overall sequence. This was not a good idea, as it meant that my account of the later Bronze Age and Iron Age was unduly compressed. In the revised edition I have abandoned that scheme, dividing the main part of the text between five main chapters of approximately equal lengths. In this version the Chalcolithic and Early Bronze Age periods are discussed separately from the Late Neolithic. The narrative ends with Caesar's invasions of southern England in 55 and 54 BC, and the brief coda that discussed the Late Iron Age in the original version has been omitted. One feature that has been retained is the format of the maps, which divide the study area into twenty-six separate regions. Within each of these areas individual places are listed in the captions.

This revision has been more radical than I envisaged when I offered to write a new edition, although some of the original drawings and photographs have been retained or revised. As before, they are by Aaron Watson. I am very grateful to him for the skill with which he undertook the work and for his extraordinary visual flair. I must also thank Courtney Nimura for her help in preparing the final text.

Since this is really a new book it requires its own dedication. And there can be only one candidate. Alison Sheridan read and commented in detail on the first edition; she has contributed to most of my projects in Scotland; and her research features in many parts of this text. In its new guise this study is for her.

CHAPTER 1

THE OFFSHORE ISLANDS

THE VIEW FROM FAR AWAY

The existence of Britain and Ireland posed a problem for the geographers of the Classical world (Fig. 1.1). Their experience was limited to the Mediterranean where they had devised a scheme which saw the cosmos as a circular disc with the sea at its centre. For Hecataeus of Miletus, the land extended northwards into what is now Europe, southwards into Africa, and to the east as far as India, but beyond all these regions there was a river, Oceanus, which encircled the earth and marked the outer limit of the world (Fig. 1.2). Only the dead could reach its farther shore; for Procopius writing in sixth-century Byzantium Britain was a land of ghosts (West 2007: 390). There were two routes communicating directly between the inner sea and the most distant margin of the land. One was by the Arabian Gulf, whilst the second led through the Straits of Gibraltar into the Atlantic (Cunliffe 2001a: 2–6).

Strictly speaking, the two islands studied in this book were beyond the limits of the world and so they could not exist, yet, as often happens, theory came into conflict with practical experience. Long before the expansion of the Roman Empire there were reasons for questioning the traditional cosmology. Not long after 4000 BC axes made in the western Alps were distributed as far as the north of Scotland (Pétrequin et al. 2012. It is no longer believed that Stonehenge was designed by a Mycenaean architect, but there seem to have been some connections between Britain, Northern Europe and the Aegean during the second millennium BC (Kristiansen and Larsson 2005). In the first millennium, contacts between the Mediterranean and these outer islands intensified during what is known as the Atlantic Bronze Age (Ruiz-Gálvez Priego 1998), and, later still, there are ceramic vessels of Greek origin among the finds from the Thames and other English rivers where they occur in similar contexts to metalwork of local manufacture and must have been deposited during the Iron Age (Bradley and A. Smith 2007).

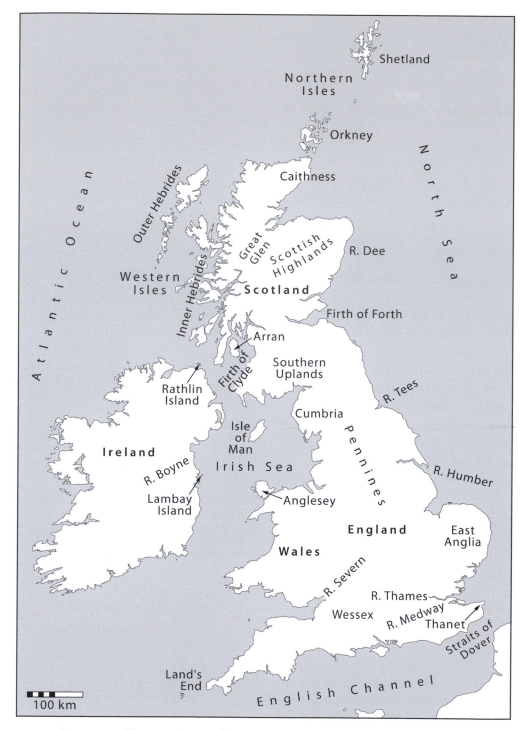

Figure 1.1 Places, regions, and rivers mentioned in Chapter 1.

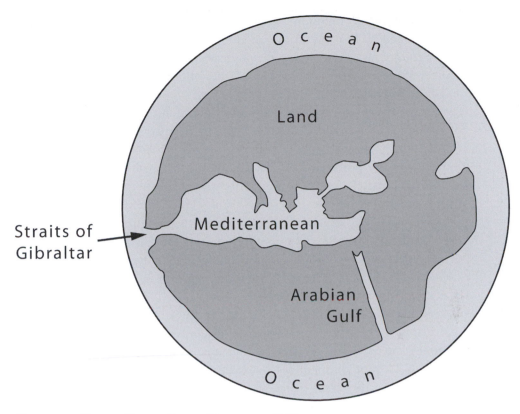

Figure 1.2 The world according to Hecataeus of Miletus.

   The paradoxical status of Britain and Ireland became even more apparent during the mid-first century BC when Julius Caesar twice invaded southern England, and again after the Roman Conquest which took place almost a century later. It was a source of political prestige to have annexed territory on the outermost edge of the world. Perhaps that is why the Roman general Agricola was so anxious to subjugate Orkney, the archipelago off the northern tip of Scotland, and even made plans for an invasion of Ireland (Fitzpatrick 1989).

   The very existence of Britain and Ireland seemed impossible to conceive, and yet they had actually been known to travellers for some time. Pytheas explored the Atlantic seaways about 320 BC, but his account was not always believed (Cunliffe 2001b). It was in AD 85 that the Roman fleet circumnavigated the entire coastline of Britain and first established that it was an island (Rivet and C. Smith 1979: 93). Even then, people were unsure of its location, and a popular view placed it somewhere between Spain and Gaul. The Greek geographer Strabo supposed that Ireland was further to the north. Still more distant was Thule, a frozen landmass that had been described by Pytheas. This was probably Iceland, but it became identified with the Shetland Islands because they seemed to represent the furthest point where human settlement was possible (Cunliffe 2001b).

Many of these confusions were not resolved until Britain and Ireland were mapped by Ptolemy in the middle of the second century AD. This was a scientific project which drew on observations assembled from a variety of sources. Ptolemy's map revealed the outlines of both islands, prominent capes and headlands, the mouths of important rivers, and the positions of certain mountains and forests, but it was never his intention to document the pattern of settlement (Rivet and C. Smith 1979: ch. 3). Apart from three important features, the map was basically correct (Fig. 1.3). Following earlier practice, Ireland was still positioned too far to the north. Smaller islands were also located inaccurately and were sometimes shown further from the mainland than was actually the case. Part of Scotland seemed to extend along an east–west axis, where the experience of early sailors showed that it should have run from south to north. Rivet and Smith have suggested that this arose because of confusion between two different locations represented by the same name, Epidium (1979: 111–13). In their view the map can be reoriented to give a better approximation of the coastline.

Such early accounts provide evidence of the original names of the largest islands. Britain was first known as 'insula Albionum', the island of the Albiones. Later, that was replaced by Pretannia, which soon became Britannia. Ptolemy's account distinguishes between Megale Britannia (Great Britain) which refers to the larger island, and Mikra Britannia (Little Britain) which describes Ireland. Elsewhere he refers to them as Alvion and Hivernia, respectively. Ireland was better known by the Greek name Ierne (the holy island) or its Latin equivalent Hibernia (Rivet and C. Smith 1979: 37–40).

Ptolemy's map of the islands was conceived as a scientific exercise, but accounts of their inhabitants took a different form. Although these texts are sometimes characterised as ethnography, they were conceived within a literary genre which stressed the important differences between the civilised populations of Greece and Rome and the barbarians with whom they came into contact. Such accounts were composed according to well-established conventions (Hustwit 2016). Little they said was based on first-hand observation, and many of their contents, including the writings of Caesar, disagree with the findings of modern archaeology. If Britain and Ireland existed after all, it was important to emphasise that in cultural and geographical terms they remained extremely remote.

THE IMPORTANCE OF BRITISH AND IRISH PREHISTORY

Ireland and Britain were at the limits of the Roman world, but they were also placed on the outer rim of Europe. Much of lowland Britain was eventually incorporated in the Roman Empire, but Ireland remained outside it altogether, and so for significant periods of time did the area occupied by Scotland today.

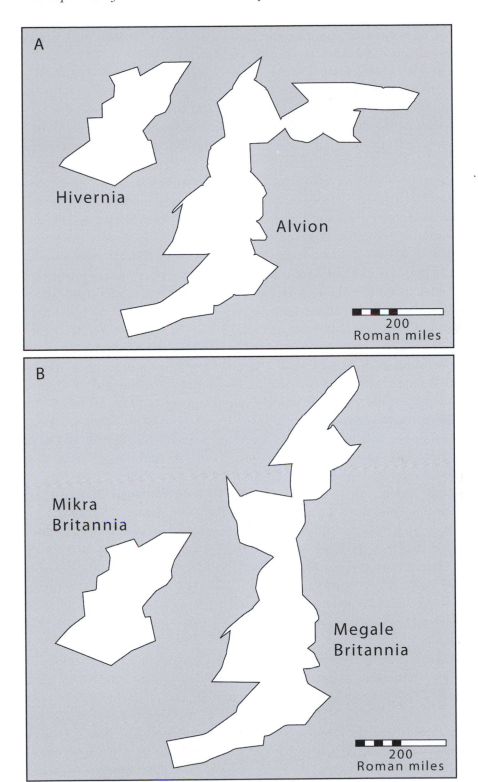

Figure 1.3 A: Ptolemy's map of Britain and Ireland. B: Ptolemy's map as reorientated by Rivet and Smith (1979).

Given their marginal position, what can the prehistory of these small islands contribute to a series concerned with world archaeology?

There are several answers to this question, and they will serve to introduce some of the main themes of this book. The first point follows from what has been said already. The inhabitants of Britain and Ireland do not seem to have experienced the drastic changes that characterised other parts of prehistoric Europe, and they remained largely beyond the influence of societies in the Mediterranean (Bradley et al. 2016a: ch. 8).

Certain periods and regions have featured in wider discussions of theoretical archaeology. The artefact record has supplied some influential case studies concerned with production and exchange. Hodder (1982) investigated the distribution of Neolithic axes, and the contents of certain exceptionally rich burials in Wessex are considered in discussions of prehistoric chiefdoms by Renfrew (1973) and Earle (1991: 80–98). During later periods the production and distribution of metalwork provided the basis for Rowlands's (1980) influential study of kinship, alliance, and exchange in the ancient world. It also plays a part in Kristiansen's and Larsson's (2005) book *The Rise of Bronze Age Society*.

The early monuments of Britain and Ireland have also inspired studies with a wider application. These include Renfrew's (1973; 1979) accounts of monument building and social organisation in southern England and in Orkney. Tilley (2010) has published widely quoted interpretations of prehistoric landscapes in Wales and England. Julian Thomas (2015a) has discussed Levi-Straus's notion of a 'house society' in relation to prehistoric Britain, and Kelly (2015) uses the archaeology of Stonehenge as a case study in her account of *Knowledge and Power in Prehistoric Societies*.

These examples are well known, but each has been selected to illustrate a particular thesis, and there is a risk of viewing them in isolation. Thus the archaeology of Stonehenge and the surrounding landscape may be familiar, but it is rarely considered in relation to the other developments that happened during the same period. It is equally true of the archaeology of megaliths, whether these are the passage tombs of the Boyne Valley in Ireland, the monuments on the Scottish island of Arran, or their counterparts in Orkney. Such studies were concerned with theoretical issues and simply drew on Britain and Ireland for examples.

There is another way of thinking about their distinctive archaeology. It has four outstanding features which deserve investigation in their own right. The first is the extraordinary abundance of monumental architecture in both islands. Structures like Newgrange, Maeshowe, Avebury, and Stonehenge are very famous, and the same applies to later monuments like Navan Fort or Maiden Castle, but they are rarely considered in their local settings. Instead they are treated as instances of a wider phenomenon and investigated in terms of general processes. These may involve such apparently practical issues as prehistoric engineering, territorial organisation, and ancient warfare, or more abstract ideas about the importance of ancestors, cultural memory, cosmology, and ritual. The megaliths of Neolithic Ireland have featured in a Darwinian model of mating behaviour, on the one hand (Aranyosi 1999), and a discussion of shamanism, on the other (Lewis-Williams and Pearce 2005: ch. 8). The Bronze Age hillforts of Ireland have featured in both a study of ancient warfare (O'Brien and O'Driscoll 2017) and a collection of papers concerned with 'costly signalling' – a concept developed in evolutionary biology (Conolly ed. 2017). Sometimes it is the details of these structures that have attracted the most attention. The chambered tombs in the Boyne Valley contain roughly half the megalithic art in Western Europe (G. Eogan 1986), and the layout of Stonehenge and allied monuments has been studied by archaeoastronomers for a hundred years (Ruggles 1999).

A second feature of prehistoric Britain and Ireland is their exceptional material wealth. This is partly due to the distribution of natural resources – copper is quite widely available, there is tin in south-west England, and gold occurs in some quantity in Ireland and can be found elsewhere (Timberlake 2016). Archaeologists have studied the distinctive manner in which finished artefacts were deposited (Bradley 2017a). Discoveries of high-quality metalwork do not provide a representative sample of the artefacts that were once available, for their raw material could easily be recycled. Instead these objects were deposited in graves and in natural locations such as rivers and bogs. That is why they have survived to the present day. Nor were all these objects of local manufacture, for many were made from foreign ores and deposited far from their sources. The Thames, for example, is nowhere near any deposits of copper or tin, yet it includes one of the highest densities of prehistoric weapons anywhere in Europe. Both Britain and Ireland participated in the circulation of metalwork over considerable distances, and they are not alone in containing an exceptional number of votive deposits. It is the range of contacts illustrated by these finds which makes them so remarkable.

A third element is the product of an exceptionally long history of landscape archaeology in these islands. In Britain, this began with the work of such antiquarians as John Aubrey and William Stukeley (Sweet 2004), and, in Ireland, it intensified with the topographical records collected by the Ordnance Survey a hundred and fifty years ago (Waddell 2005: 97–103). Both countries shared a tradition of documenting surface remains, especially those of earthworks. This first drew attention to a feature that still distinguishes their archaeology from that of other regions. It seems as if the landscape was subdivided by fields and boundaries on a larger scale and at an earlier date than in many parts of prehistoric Europe. In the late nineteenth century the tradition of topographical survey extended to settlement excavation, and the early twentieth century saw the development of aerial survey. In England, this revealed new features of the prehistoric landscape at a time when similar methods were rarely used in other countries.

The final characteristic of Britain and Ireland is the most obvious of all, for both are islands located some distance from Continental Europe. Each is accompanied by a series of much smaller islands with a distinctive archaeology of their own (Fig. 1.4). Some of them played a specialised role in maritime exchange, including Thanet which commands the route between the Channel and the Thames Estuary, and 'Ictis' where Pytheas recorded that traders obtained tin from the inhabitants of south-west England. A number provide important evidence of prehistoric activity, such as in the axe quarries at North Roe in Shetland and on Rathlin and Lambay Islands off the Irish coast. The Isle of Man midway between Ireland and England is noted for its distinctive chambered tombs (F. Lynch and Davey 2017), and Anglesey in north-west Wales was supposedly sacred to the Druids. Just as important are archipelagos where monuments and settlements survive in unusual numbers. They include the Inner and Outer Hebrides to the west of Scotland, and Orkney and Shetland which are usually referred to as the Northern Isles. The list could be longer, but in each case the archaeological record has some unusual features.

This raises a wider issue, for it is sometimes supposed that island societies develop a peculiar character of their own. They can build extraordinary field monuments. From the early work of Sahlins (1955) this argument plays a major role in Pacific archaeology and has been equally influential in the studies of the Mediterranean (Broodbank 2013). It could certainly account for such remarkable phenomena as the megalithic tombs of Neolithic Orkney or the Iron Age towers of the Hebrides, the Northern Isles, and the north mainland of Scotland, but on a larger scale it might also characterise Britain and Ireland as a whole, for they include unusual forms of architecture which are not known in Continental Europe.

Two observations help to set the limits of this account. In a sense this study cannot commence until both these regions were islands. Before that time the area occupied by England, Wales, and Scotland was continuous with Continental Europe and must not be considered on its own. This investigation begins when their geography assumed more or less its present form. This is also an account of their prehistory, and, although it is not a satisfactory term, it helps to define where the account should end. It concludes with their discovery by travellers from the Mediterranean and their incorporation in a wider world that culminated in Caesar's invasions of southern England.

THE SENSE OF ISOLATION

Britain and Ireland did not assume their present forms simultaneously, and this had serious consequences for their ecology and for the hunter gatherers who lived there. Ireland was cut off by the sea at a time when Britain was still attached to the European mainland (Sturt 2015). That happened well before

Figure 1.4 The offshore islands of Britain and Ireland.

Figure 1.5 Models for the changing coastlines of Britain and Ireland between 9000 and 5000 BC. Information from Sturt, Garrow, and Bradley (2013).

Ireland had any inhabitants and certainly before a number of animal species could have become established (Mitchell and Ryan 1998: table 4), among them cattle, elk, red deer, and roe deer. None formed part of the native fauna. Britain, on the other hand, was continuously settled from the end of the Ice Age and had already been colonised by these species before it was separated from the Continent (Montgomery et al. 2014).

Because Britain was cut off from the mainland quite late in the development of postglacial vegetation, it had more plant species than its western neighbour. The time interval is extremely significant. It seems as if Ireland became detached from south-west Scotland by a narrow channel. This had happened by about 12,000 BC as the polar ice cap melted and sea levels rose (Sturt 2015). The English Channel had formed by 8000 BC, and the fertile plain that linked what is now eastern England to northern France, the Low Countries, and Denmark was gradually reduced in size between about 10,000 and 6000 BC, when Britain was completely cut off from the Continent (Fig. 1.5). Finds from the bed of the North Sea show just how important this area had been, and new research has begun to map what must once have been an extremely productive landscape which is sometimes referred to as Doggerland (Gaffney, Thomson, and Fitch 2007).

The earliest settlement of Ireland seems to have taken place by boat around 8000 BC (Woodman 2015: ch. 7). By this stage the North Sea plain was already threatened by rising water, but it was before large areas of territory had been lost. The Isle of Man was separated from Britain and Ireland and was colonised by sea by about 8000 BC (Sturt 2015). Some of the islands off the west coast of Scotland were also used from an early date. Orkney was eventually settled by hunter gatherers, and there are other early sites in the Shetland Islands.

Ireland was obviously colonised long after any land bridge had been severed, and there are points in common between the material culture of its first inhabitants and the artefacts found in Britain. That connection seems to have been quite short-lived, and in time their histories diverged. Significantly, there is no evidence for the movement of raw materials between these islands. In fact, the Irish Mesolithic developed a distinctive character of its own which it shared to some extent with the Isle of Man (Woodman 2015: 198). It had a distinctive settlement pattern, too. The occupation sites of the later Mesolithic period concentrate along rivers and the shoreline, and there are indications that fishing was important. That is hardly surprising since wild pigs were the only large animals that could have been hunted.

The material culture of Mesolithic Ireland gradually diverged from that found in England, Scotland, and Wales. A similar process seems to have affected relations between Britain and Continental Europe, and again new artefact types came into use. Ballin (2016) suggests that this resulted from the formation of the English Channel and the loss of a land bridge joining Britain to the mainland. Recent work has produced convincing evidence for contacts between the Scilly Islands and Belgium during the Late Mesolithic period (Garrow and Sturt 2017: ch. 3), but with that exception it was the first time when Britain had a distinctive character of its own.

This introduces another theme of the book. To what extent were developments in prehistoric Britain independent from those in Continental Europe, and how far were they simply a continuation of them? How much evidence is there for the establishment of local identities in different parts of both islands, and, in particular, did events in Ireland and Britain follow a different course from one another? One way of defining local practices is to compare the archaeological records on either side of the Irish Sea.

THE LIE OF THE LAND

Such local traditions first emerged during the lengthy period in which Britain and Ireland were separated, first from one another, and then from Continental Europe. They were also influenced by the physical character of both islands and the pattern of communication within them.

At this point it is essential to say more about their geography. That immediately raises the problem of names. It would be easy to write this account in terms of current political boundaries, which divide the two islands between England, Scotland, and Wales, on the one hand, and Northern Ireland and the Irish Republic, on the other. That would be misleading. Although England, Wales, and Scotland occupy almost the same territories as they have since the Middle Ages, a similar argument does not apply to Ireland. Six of the modern counties form part of the United Kingdom, whilst the remainder comprise a separate nation state. As Ulaid, Ulster was one of the ancient kingdoms of Ireland, but it was more extensive than the area under British rule today. Thus it is best to refer to Ireland as a whole except where the archaeological evidence requires a different procedure. The other geographical unit is the island of Britain which was accepted as a distinct entity from the time of the first explorers. In recent years, Scotland and Wales have achieved a measure of political autonomy, and in this account they are treated simply as topographical units. There is nothing to suggest that they possessed any cultural cohesion during the prehistoric period.

The two main islands have a different physical structure from one another (Fig. 1.6). Britain has been divided by prehistorians into a Highland Zone towards the north and west and a Lowland Zone to the south and east (Fox 1932). That does not do justice to the complexity of the situation. Even within the Lowland Zone, there are significant differences of elevation which have had a major impact on the distribution of settlement; and large tracts of land which form part of the Highland Zone include sheltered, well-drained soils as capable of supporting farmers as regions further to the south. For example, many areas along the east coast of Scotland have the characteristics conventionally associated with southern Britain. In the same way, some of the exposed chalkland along the English Channel coast may have been less hospitable than low-lying parts of northern England. Human activity often focused on the valleys of major rivers, extending up the east coast from the Medway to the Dee and along the west coast from the Severn to the Clyde. This was not recognised by archaeologists until aerial survey extended into these regions.

That is not to say that the distinction between upland and lowland regions was unimportant, but it could be expressed in a better way. England and the southern part of Scotland are bisected by a spine of hills and mountains which run from south to north before they broaden out into larger areas of raised ground, the Southern Uplands and the Scottish Highlands, respectively. They are separated from one another by a system of valleys extending across country between the Forth and the Clyde; still further to the north the Great Glen connects the east and west coasts. There are other regions of high ground along the shores of the Atlantic and the Irish Sea. Western Britain is often more exposed than the land along the North Sea, and this difference may have had more influence over the distribution of early settlement than the conventional division between Highland and Lowland Zones. In fact a new study of the historical geography of England favours a different scheme and distinguishes between an eastern zone, a 'Central Province', and a western zone (B. Roberts and Wrathmell 2000). These divisions were based on map regression but are clearly reflected by the results of a new study of Late Iron Age and Roman rural settlement which illustrates similar divisions (Fig. 1.7; A. Smith et al. 2016; cf. Blair 2018: 6–8; Rippon 2018: 15–17).

Just as Fox wrote of *The Personality of Britain*, Estyn Evans studied *The Personality of Ireland* (E. E. Evans 1973). Instead of the distinction between a Highland Zone and a Lowland Zone, in Ireland discontinuous areas of high

Figure 1.6 Land over 200 m in Britain and Ireland.

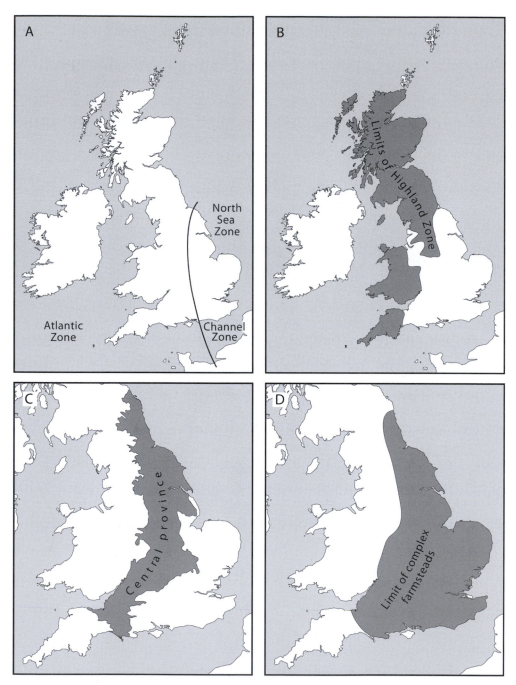

Figure 1.7 Four possible schemes for defining regional variation within England or the island of Britain. Information from (A) Cunliffe (2015); (B) Fox (1932); (C) B. Roberts and Wrathmell (2000); and (D) A. Smith et al. (2016).

ground extend around considerable sections of the coast and enclose the Central Lowland, parts of which contain poorly drained raised bogs. Although there are exceptions, the best land is found to the south and east, and much of the poorest is towards the north and west. A band of particularly favourable soils follows the coastline of the Irish Sea. The west coast is exposed to the full force of bad weather from the Atlantic. These distinctions are clearly illustrated by the sizes of modern farms, which are generally larger to the east and south. Again there are a number of fertile river valleys.

There are important differences between land use in the two islands. They are largely the result of differences of temperature and rainfall. In Britain, southern England experiences the most sunshine; northern and western Scotland have the least. Today the areas with lower precipitation are more suitable for growing crops. This permits cereal growing across most lowland regions and allows it to extend up the North Sea coast into Scotland (Coppock 1976a and b). By contrast, rainfall is rather higher to the west of the mountains which divide the island in half, and here there is a greater emphasis on livestock. A similar distinction can be observed in the pattern of settlement, with larger groups towards the east and south, and smaller, more dispersed settlements to the north and west, with a distinctive pattern of nucleated settlement in the Central Zone defined by Roberts and Wrathmell (2000).

To a large extent the same is true in Ireland, where there are similar contrasts in natural conditions (Aalen, Whelan, and M. Stout 1997). The main areas suitable for growing crops are towards the south and east coasts which experience more hours of sunshine than other regions. Dairy farming is important in the north and west of the island. The character of settlement varies, but again it is more dispersed towards the west where conditions are cooler and damper.

Having said this, another observation is important. The Classical authors quoted at the beginning of this chapter emphasised the remote position of Britain and Ireland. They made such claims because early travellers could establish their locations by the position of the sun. It is true that in terms of modern geography, Land's End is on the same latitude as Newfoundland, and Edinburgh is as far north as Moscow, but such observations are deceptive because of the effects of the Gulf Stream which warms the land from south-west England to the Northern Isles and makes it considerably more hospitable than would otherwise be the case.

The natural environment changed during the postglacial period (Bell and Walker 2004). A few species were present from the outset, notably hazel, birch, and pine. Oak began to colonise England and Wales by about 8500 BC and was present in Ireland by 8000 BC. The latter period also saw the appearance of elm in England and Wales, and over the next thousand years it established itself in Ireland and then in Scotland. After that, other species, including alder, assumed an increasing significance. Lime became important in Wales and England from approximately 5000 BC, and ash appeared roughly simultaneously.

This might give the impression that what had been an open landscape was colonised by dense woodland, and this is a stereotype which has been hard to eradicate. In his famous book *The Personality of Britain* Cyril Fox (1932: 82) declared that:

> Southern Britain presented an illimitable forest of "damp oakwood", ash and thorn and bramble, largely untrodden. The forest was in a sense unbroken, for without emerging from its canopy a squirrel could traverse the country from end to end.

That may not be true. There are several reasons for believing that the vegetation cover was much more varied. It is clear that it formed a complex mosaic which was sensitive to the local topography, climate, and soils. There were regional differences in its composition even over quite small areas, and different species predominated from one region to another. For example, by the end of the Mesolithic period only the southern half of Scotland was actually dominated by oak. Parts of the North Sea littoral and much of the west coast had a significant component of hazel, and this pattern extended as far as the Inner Hebrides. The Outer Hebrides, Caithness, and the Northern Isles were dominated by birch, whilst pine flourished in the mountainous interior (Tipping 1994a).

There were many breaks in the canopy. The most obvious were at the coast and beside lakes and rivers, but there were regions that were above the treeline altogether. They included high ground in Wales, northern England, and the north of Scotland. In each case the more open conditions would have attracted concentrations of grazing animals which could have had a further impact on the vegetation. The same was true along the paths they followed through the landscape and in areas where animals congregated. Other breaks in the cover might have formed quite naturally as trees died or as areas of woodland were affected by storms or lightning strikes (T. Brown 1997). Once it had happened, these clearings could have been kept open or enlarged by herbivores. Naturally created breaks in the forest cover might also be maintained by burning, but there is uncertainty whether it was always deliberate. Robinson (2014) has suggested that during the Neolithic period areas of woodland were occupied in the course of forest grazing, after which they grew over again. Then the vegetation had a different composition. Following the work of Vera (2000) he identifies a characteristic cycle of clearance and regeneration. This idea is supported by analysis of the insects in earlier prehistoric woodland which has identified species that could not have lived in a closed environment (Whitehouse 2006). Recently developed algorithms for analysing the results of pollen analysis lead to the same conclusion: the landscape was more open than was originally believed (Fyfe et al. 2013).

Other areas were used for growing crops. Recent work on the English chalk suggests that some regions were never colonised by trees in the way that had always been supposed (M. Allen and Gardiner 2009). They have even been characterised as 'prairies'. That finding is particularly important since they include some of the largest Neolithic monuments in England, including Avebury and Stonehenge.

At the same time there is evidence of local and more general climatic fluctuations, some of which will play an important part in later chapters. The problem is that such evidence is so diverse. It draws on an unusually wide variety of sources which include the climatic records preserved by speleothems, the development of peat bogs, the widths of tree rings identified by dendrochronology, the accumulation of sand dunes, and the changing character of lake sediments. Other sources include episodes of flooding in major rivers. These schemes have been compared with reconstructions of ocean temperatures but result in the identification of very different patterns. To give just one example, Charman (2010) suggests the onset of wetter weather in Britain and Ireland during eight separate phases between the beginning of the Early Bronze Age and the end of the pre-Roman Iron Age. He relates them to the 'Bond cycles' which occur at roughly five-hundred-year intervals and are identified by evidence of ice rafting. Macklin and his colleagues have studied an even longer sequence and recognise seven widespread episodes of flooding between 3780 and 330 BC (Macklin, Johnstone, and Lewin 2005). Bevan et al. (2017) favour a simpler scheme in which the onset of cooler and wetter conditions occurred towards the middle of the fourth millennium BC and the early first millennium BC. These schemes do not agree in detail, but share the premise that climatic fluctuations affected the character of settlement.

It is important to consider the evidence one case at a time. To take two obvious examples, in the Northern Hemisphere there seem to have been especially severe changes of climate around 2200 BC and 800 BC. The first was extremely widespread and had a catastrophic impact in Egypt, but there is no agreement whether it can be recognised in the evidence from Irish bogs (Roland et al. 2014). In Britain the only archaeological 'event' that can be identified at this time is the alloying of copper with tin to make bronze. It can hardly have been determined by environmental change. By contrast, climatic deterioration in the first millennium BC did have serious consequences, and in Ireland little evidence can be found for Early Iron Age settlement and land use (Plunkett 2007).

It can be difficult to relate climatic episodes directly to an archaeological timescale which is less precise. Indeed there is a danger of becoming trapped in a circular argument by which developments in the pattern of settlement are explained by those in the natural environment and changes in local conditions are dated according to archaeological interpretations. In 2012 Tipping and a number of colleagues tried to compare the 'moments of crisis' in the Scottish environment with the findings of prehistorians and showed how difficult it is to bring this evidence together (Tipping et al. 2013). Schulting (2010) came to a similar conclusion in his study of agricultural origins in North-west Europe. In any case accounts of climate change take no account of human decision-making. Perhaps ancient populations were better able to come to terms with natural events than many scholars suppose. In the past people might have shown more resilience than is commonly assumed. These questions are considered at appropriate points in later chapters.

THE WATERWAYS

How did people travel through the landscape? Grazing animals may have moved along the rivers. The same must surely apply to the paths followed by the inhabitants of Britain and Ireland, and yet this simple idea is seldom taken seriously. There is a long-standing assumption in the archaeology of southern England that the main patterns of communication followed what are known as ridgeways: long-distance routes extending across the higher ground. It is difficult to appreciate how tenacious such ideas can be. Avebury, for example, was thought to be located at one end of a long-distance path that extended to the flint mines of eastern England. Hillforts of later date were built at roughly equal intervals along this track.

Some of these routes did play a role as drove roads during the historical period, but their relevance to prehistoric archaeology is somewhat doubtful. They are cut by ancient boundary ditches which take no account of their existence. The same applies to early field systems and to excavated settlements. There is a simple reason why this idea became so popular. Before much was known about the natural environment of Britain, archaeologists had assumed that the hills were free of vegetation and that the lowlands were forested and sparsely settled (Fox 1932). Nothing could be more misleading, but it was true that many low-lying monuments had been levelled by the plough whilst their counterparts on the higher ground survived. In the end it took the development of aerial photography to redress the balance.

The same approach may be less relevant to mountainous regions in the north where the lower ground was vulnerable to flooding after heavy rain or snow. Otherwise it was the major valleys that saw most activity. It also suggested that the rivers would provide a more likely system of communication than a network of upland paths. That was also implied by numerous finds of logboats. In his discussion of river transport in prehistoric Britain Sherratt (1996) postulates two sources of origin for these patterns of communication. One was the Thames Estuary and the other was the south coast of Wessex. By following major rivers, travellers might have been able to avoid some of the most difficult waters off the shore and pass safely from the Channel to the Irish Sea. A third major focus must have existed in north-east England and linked the Humber Estuary to the Midlands and the west coast of Britain. Carleton Jones (2009) has taken a similar approach to prehistoric Ireland. Here some of the major rivers may have been less suitable for transport than their British counterparts and again areas of higher ground were important because large areas were covered by blanket bog. In fact the wetlands of the Irish midlands separate parts of the north and the south with very different archaeological records. Fig. 1.8 combines these schemes so that they link eastern England to the Atlantic.

These routes were only a part of a wider pattern. Sherratt (1996) observes that one of their sources, the Thames Estuary, was ideally placed for contacts with Continental Europe by the Rhine and the Seine (Fig. 1.9). He suggests links not just between western Britain and the east of Ireland, but also between parts of southern England and northern France. Other areas are within 200 km of one another, suggesting potential connections between the entire coastline of southern England and the area between Finistère and the Rhine. That zone also extends northwards into East Anglia. Towards the Atlantic, it links western England, Wales, and south-west Ireland. There are other potential connections between the north of Ireland and the west coast of Scotland. The 'Stepping Stones' project has highlighted the special role of islands off the west coast at the time when Britain was settled by farmers (Garrow and Sturt 2017).

Different regions of Britain and Ireland could have been in contact with parts of mainland Europe that had few connections with one another. The principal contrast is between an axis based on the English Channel and the North Sea, and another which extended from Britain and Ireland into Atlantic Europe. The first linked England and Scotland to an enormous area extending from France to south Scandinavia. The second joined south-west England, Wales, and Ireland to western France and the Iberian Peninsula.

Sherratt's scheme did not take into account the practicalities of travelling by water, but there have been important studies of ancient routes across the Channel (McGrail 1997: 207–22 and 265–88). A little-known paper by Margaret Davies (1946) took a similar approach to navigation in the Irish Sea, and a study of travel along the western seaways was based on computer modelling following similar principles to those used in Polynesian archaeology (Callaghan and Scarre 2009).

McGrail's research was specifically concerned with the sea routes documented by Classical writers in the immediate pre-Roman period. This is important because it explains some of the premises of his argument. It is concerned with trade in bulky commodities and presupposes that ships were equipped with sails; it is likely that earlier boats were rowed or paddled. He confines his attention to the routes suggested in written accounts and compares their suitability for long-distance voyages in relation to sea conditions, visibility, prevailing winds, and currents.

McGrail concludes that the most dependable sea routes were those crossing the English Channel towards its narrowest point at the Straits of Dover. They were a little more reliable than the passage between Normandy and Wessex,

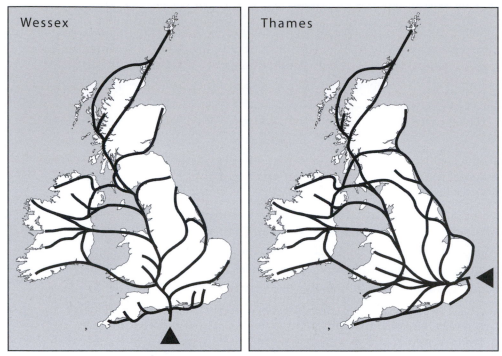

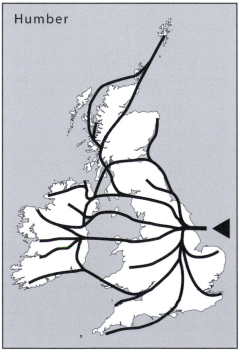

Figure 1.8 Riverine connections extending from the coast of Wessex, the Thames Estuary, and the Humber Estuary. Information from Sherratt (1996) and C. Jones (2009), with additions.

Figure 1.9 Sea routes between Continental Europe, Britain, and Ireland. Information from C. Fox (1932), M. Davies (1946), and McGrail (1997).

yet all of them were significantly better than the crossing from Finistère to the south-western peninsula of Britain. McGrail suggests that a sensible procedure would have been to use one of the easier routes from the Continent to Britain and then to sail along the coast (1997: 285–7). Callaghan and Scarre (2009) consider a similar model and suggest that boat crews may have landed at several points in the course of longer journeys. That is especially likely if they were navigating between Brittany and Ireland or from the west of Scotland to Orkney. But there is another problem. By their very nature such studies depend on a kind of risk assessment which cannot take into account the prestige that could be won by undertaking perilous voyages, yet this principle is familiar from ethnographic sources (Bradley 2014).

McGrail's analysis does not extend far beyond the English Channel, and other regions raise different possibilities. Like the Mediterranean, the Irish Sea is partly enclosed. It is rather more open to the south, but to the north it is entered through a narrow channel (Waddell 1992). There are powerful tides which converge on the Isle of Man from both directions. Thus they provide a series of routes from north-west and south-west Wales and create potential links between Ireland, south-west Scotland, and Cumbria. There is slack water from the southern tip of the Isle of Man westwards towards the Irish coast, and it would have made that region particularly accessible by sea.

There were certain hazards to avoid. They included whirlpools and eddies in the areas with strong tides. On the other hand, in good weather travellers in these waters would never have been out of sight of land, for the Irish Sea is ringed by a series of distinctive peaks which can be recognised from the water. All were more than 600 m high, which means that even the lowest could be identified under optimum conditions from a distance of 90 km (E. G. Bowen 1972). Further to the north, navigation would have been much easier since it was possible to travel from one offshore island to another without venturing far into open water. The same could have been true along the less sheltered west coast of Ireland. People could also have travelled up the North Sea, between estuaries like those of the Humber and the Tees and the drowned valleys known as firths along the Scottish shoreline.

Two further elements need to be considered here. The first is the chronology of seagoing vessels (Cunliffe 2017). The earliest plank-built vessels to leave any trace date from the earlier second millennium BC: a time when there is clear evidence for contacts between Britain, Ireland, and Continental Europe. Before then long-distance voyages may have been less frequent and were probably undertaken in skin boats (Van de Noort 2011). There is little evidence of pre-Roman harbours, but it seems as if a series of enclosed estuaries at important river mouths provided shelter for travellers from the Mesolithic period until at least the Early Bronze Age. Here it was possible to take advantage of the protection provided by islands or coastal bars. These places were associated with concentrations of non-local artefacts and raw materials, and

Figure 1.10 Sheltered water on the shoreline of Findhorn Bay. In the prehistoric period it was a maritime haven sheltered by the Culbin Sands. Photograph: Aaron Watson.

specialised artefacts were sometimes made there (Fig. 1.10). Because sea levels changed during the postglacial period such evidence is restricted to the area of isostatic uplift in the north of Britain and Ireland where the original shoreline still survives. A recent study identified such locations as 'maritime havens' where it was safe to beach light craft (Bradley et al. 2016b).

THE MENTAL MAP

This account raises important questions of perception. Are Britain and Ireland to be regarded as extensions of Continental Europe which were readily accessible by water? If so, which of these routes was most important, and did the pattern change at different times? Were the strongest links between particular parts of Britain and Ireland and separate regions of the Continent, or were there periods in which either or both of these islands were unaffected by outside contacts? Is it correct to study their prehistory as that of two areas of land, or would it be more appropriate to think of them in relation to the sea?

All too often the prehistory of both islands is written in terms of modern political divisions. This tendency can be identified at a variety of scales and has made the work of archaeologists unnecessarily difficult. It is normally done for convenience, but the question is rarely asked whether these distinctions had any relevance to social identities in the past. The main division is between books on Britain (for instance Pryor 2003; Pollard 2008; and Darvill 2010) and books about Ireland (Waddell 2010 and Mallory 2013). Few studies consider both the islands together. That is extraordinary when they can be seen from one another and the geographical distance between them can be as little as 30 km.

That procedure makes it doubly difficult to think in terms of other regional alignments. For example, during the second millennium BC there may have been closer connections between Ireland and the north and west of what is now Scotland than there were between the Scottish Highlands and the southern part of that country. Nor is it necessary to limit these connections exclusively to Britain and Ireland. Between about 1500 and 800 BC south-east England had strong links with northern France, and in the Iron Age there were many features in common between Brittany and south-west England (Cunliffe 2001a).

At the same time prehistorians in both islands have exhibited a sense of cultural insecurity. There are different reasons for this. One is purely methodological. Before the advent of radiocarbon dating, insular archaeologists were entirely dependent on chronologies developed on the mainland. Normally these were based on events in the Mediterranean or Egypt. Such schemes could be extended to the outermost margins of Europe only by emphasising connections between these areas. There was no alternative to this procedure, but it raised a problem, for it was necessary to say why those connections were possible and how they had occurred. They were generally explained by the movement of people and ideas from the complex societies of Southern and Central Europe towards the edges of the Continent. It was a method that had its strengths and weaknesses. Thus Piggott (1938) could suggest what still seem to be plausible links between artefacts from Bronze Age burials in southern England and those in the shaft graves of Mycenae. Almost twenty years later Atkinson (1956) took the view that Stonehenge had been designed by a Mediterranean architect, a theory which was never credible and has been rejected in the light of radiocarbon dating.

This approach had unexpected side effects. One was the assumption that Britain and Ireland occupied such a peripheral position in Europe that artefacts of Continental affinities would have been adopted only after a significant interval of time. That is why so many phenomena have proved to be significantly older than was first supposed; there have been few chronological adjustments in the opposite direction. The other feature was a predilection for naming insular phenomena after well-defined sites or cultural groupings on the Continent. This process seems to have operated in only one direction, and, with the exception of the 'Wessex Culture', British and Irish terminology was rarely employed on the mainland. The influence of this way of thinking is illustrated by the title of one of the most famous books on insular prehistory, Cyril Fox's monograph *The Personality of Britain* (Fox 1932). Its subtitle is especially revealing, for it considers *Its influence on inhabitant and invader in prehistoric and early historic times*. It concludes with a list of twenty propositions. Among the most important are these statements:

> The position of Britain adjacent to the Continent renders her liable to invasion from any point on some five hundred miles of the European coast ...

> The portion of Britain adjacent to the continent being Lowland, it is easily overrun by invaders and on it new cultures of continental origin tend to be *imposed*. In the Highland, on the other hand, these tend to be *absorbed* ... [emphasis in the original]

> There is greater *unity* of culture in the Lowland Zone, but greater *continuity* of culture in the Highland Zone ... [emphasis in the original] (Fox 1932: 77–8)

Although his ideas were first published in 1932, Fox's book was reissued in successive editions for more than a quarter of a century. It blends artefact studies and historical geography so adroitly that it is difficult to remember why so many migrations were postulated in the first place. It was because arguments about chronology had become entangled in questions of explanation. Writing in 1966, Grahame Clark questioned the usefulness of the 'invasion hypothesis'. It was used uncritically and had been applied to almost every archaeological problem.

Irish archaeologists had experienced the same difficulties in working out a chronology, and resorted to similar methods to those of their British colleagues, but in this case there was another problem. This was because of the origin myth set out in *Lebor Gabála Érren, The Book of the Taking of Ireland*. It describes five successive invasions which were responsible for the settlement of the country. Champion (1982) has pointed out that some of their sources come from the Bible and others from universal histories composed in the late Roman period. The invaders appear to have originated in Greece and the east Mediterranean. Although this account was rarely taken literally, it had an influence on the way in which Irish prehistory was studied, and it is surely significant that its translator and editor, Robert Macalister, was the professor of archaeology at University College, Dublin. Like the British scholars criticised by Grahame Clark, Irish archaeologists were tempted by the invasion hypothesis, and it was not until 1978 that its usefulness began to be questioned (Waddell 1978).

There were two ways of resolving this confusion. The more radical was simply to assert that the present-day notion of Britain and Ireland as self-contained entities was anachronistic. It had no relevance to the prehistoric period, and the differences between separate communities may have been less clear-cut in the past. For example, Caesar records that the same kings ruled territories on either side of the English Channel (*De Bello Gallico* II, 4, 6–7). Campbell (2001) has expressed a similar idea in discussing the relationship between early medieval Ireland and the kingdom of Dalriada on the west coast of Scotland. The sea may not have been a barrier but a connecting link.

Another approach was to explain the movement of artefacts and ideas by an ill-defined notion of 'trade', but again this raised some problems. It seems likely that the exchange of artefacts had at least as much to do with diplomacy as economics (after half a century the clearest statement remains Sahlins 1972). The exchange of goods and services may have been a way of forming and maintaining alliances, but once that possibility is raised, prehistorians face another problem. People were always on the move. Researchers may be captivated by the diffusion of fine pottery and metalwork, but such evidence may be only the visible residue of a much more important exchange of personnel. Instead of a long-distance trade in swords and spears, they might think about the institution of fosterage and the circulation of marriage partners. The question is how frequently this happened and how many settled in new places as a result. Much of the trouble is created by the language of insular archaeology. The movement of people overland is seen as settlement or migration; their relocation by sea is regarded as an invasion. That is hardly appropriate when the island of Britain is nearly a thousand kilometres long and is separated from northern France by a twentieth of that distance.

Only recently has it been possible to take the argument further, and it is unfortunate that, for all its promise, this work is in its early stages. It exploits new methods of analysing human remains. Individual remains are investigated for evidence of mobility since the isotopes recovered from bones, usually teeth, allow researchers to identify the regions where particular people had lived at different points in their lives. These markers accumulated over time and retain evidence of the local groundwater in those areas. This method raises new questions. Did people spend their entire lives in the same environment, or did they move from place to place? Were their bodies deposited in the areas where they had lived, or were they taken somewhere else for burial? How many of the occupants of a particular barrow or graveyard belonged to the local population? Did they include outsiders, and did the men who were represented have a different history from the women in the same cemetery? It can be difficult or impossible to pinpoint a single source of origin, but already this method has proved its value. It is likely to provide even more information in the future as new work extends this method of analysis from unburnt to cremated bones (Snoeck et al. 2016). In the case of human remains it has already shown how many people moved between different areas during the Early Bronze Age (Parker Pearson et al. 2016). Its application to livestock has been equally informative, and it has demonstrated that people travelled long distances with their animals to attend ceremonies at important monuments (Craig et al. 2015; Madgwick et al. 2017).

Isotopic archaeology is necessarily the study of individuals and their histories, although this method is often applied to the occupants of entire cemeteries or settlements. A still more recent approach is the extraction of ancient DNA from excavated bones. This provides genetic information taken directly from ancient material. In principle the evidence obtained from any one individual should shed light on all that person's ancestors (Reich 2018). On the other hand, sample sizes are necessarily so small that it is hard to be certain that the entire population is represented by the results. For example, the composition of the Irish population was worked out on the basis of only four individuals, three of them from the same Early Bronze Age cemetery; the other was of Neolithic date (Cassidy et al. 2016). Sample sizes are increasing so rapidly that any summary of the results would be out of date by the time this book is published, but at the moment the science seems to be more sophisticated than the archaeology. There is also a temptation to make premature claims (Vander Linden 2016). Some of these may be the result of sample bias: only a small proportion of the ancient population might have been buried, and there were substantial periods in the prehistory of Britain and Ireland when bodies were cremated, making them unsuitable for this approach. In spite of all these misgivings this method has already given some remarkable results. It suggests that the first farmers in Central Europe were the descendants of migrants from the Near East (Brandt et al. 2013; Szécsényi-Nagy et al. 2015; Reich 2018: ch. 5). They were not related to local hunter gatherers, as was once believed. This method has not been confined to the Neolithic period, and it seems as if the first metalwork was introduced to these islands by settlers from Continental Europe (Haak et al. 2015; Brace et al. 2018; Olalde et al. 2018; Reich 2018: ch. 5).

In each case the implication is the same. Britain and Ireland were not as isolated as many scholars had supposed. It is ironic that the new interpretations suggested by isotopic analysis and ancient DNA are so like those favoured by Childe (1942) over seventy years ago. The difference is that archaeologists no longer place so much weight on the evidence of portable artefacts, and the new methods of analysis are more rigorous. There are likely to be important developments over the next few years.

OBSERVING WHAT HAS VANISHED

There are many ways of writing about the prehistory of these two islands. What does this version have to offer?

The first point to make is that it attempts to cover the prehistory of Britain and Ireland on equal terms, and in each case it is informed by the results of development-led archaeology as they enter the public domain. They represent a new resource for scholars, and one which only now is being taken seriously (Bradley et al. 2016a). At many points they have provided information which is radically different from conventional wisdom about the past. They have identified new kinds of monuments and have extended the work of archaeologists into areas that had hardly been investigated before. They also suggest unexpected links between developments in different regions.

Some difficulties still remain. When the first edition of this book was written more than ten years ago it was difficult to access the small circulation reports ('grey literature') on projects that were undertaken as part of the planning process and funded by commercial developers. Outside Scotland, where public archaeology was better managed, it was necessary to consult paper copies at a variety of local archives. The situation has improved since then as many organisations make their results available online through the Archaeology Data Service (www.archaeologydataservice.ac.uk), but, understandably, major projects which are still being prepared for publication are less often represented. In Ireland, however, a different system is used. Although a growing number of excavations achieve final publication in monographs, articles, or on the internet, there remain some notable gaps. It means that in this account important findings may have been overlooked.

The emphasis of this book is on settlements, monuments, and landscapes rather than portable artefacts. To some extent this is a matter of personal taste, but it is more than that. For many years the prehistory of Britain and Ireland had been studied through material culture, even though little was known about its original contexts. The work of recent years has helped to redress the balance so that the deposits of valuables which had normally been discovered by chance can be investigated in relation to other less spectacular phenomena.

Chronology is less of a problem than it was a decade ago, but difficulties will remain until the dating of individual seeds or bones becomes a standard feature of every significant project. It is important to extend current programmes concerned with the analysis of individual objects, but contexts which lack diagnostic artefacts are generally under-represented. That is unfortunate as the dating of unaccompanied burials has had unexpected results. One is the recognition of a tradition of Middle Neolithic flat graves that ran in parallel with the use of long barrows. Another is the identification of Late Bronze Age human remains among the material found in settlements, while a more dramatic development is the identification of Iron Age inhumation cemeteries in lowland England.

An important initiative is the 'Bayesian' analysis of groups of radiocarbon dates which can be used where samples are in stratigraphic relationship to one another. Each date is really an estimate at a specified confidence level of the chances that the true age will fall at any particular point within a range of possibilities. This depends on calibrating the results from the laboratory by comparing them with the dates for tree rings that have been studied by dendrochronology, but it means that some estimates will be more likely than others. Where there is information on the chronological relationship between the items selected for analysis – for example they may have been deposited in sequence – the range of possibilities can be constrained, so that the final estimates of date range are significantly reduced. In ideal cases they may be as short as a human generation (Bayliss 2015). This method has been applied to a number of significant problems – the lifespan of individual long barrows, for example, the dating of Neolithic enclosures, or the phasing of a major hillfort – but it has certain limitations which need to be resolved in the future. Some contexts do not provide suitable samples for this method of analysis; there are plateaus in the calibration curve which means that some estimates cover a longer time span than others; and so far these methods have been restricted to a small range of well-funded projects, while the dating of other contexts is less precise.

These difficulties are exacerbated by questions of terminology. Wherever possible, this account refers to calibrated radiocarbon dates, as the period labels that are in common use were devised during the nineteenth century at a time when the importance of technological innovation was taken for granted. It would be helpful if the terms Neolithic, Bronze Age, and Iron Age could be abandoned altogether, but that would lead to problems of communication, especially when using older sources. In any case attempts to devise more flexible schemes have not been altogether successful. For example, in his book *The Age of Stonehenge* Colin Burgess defined a series of periods named after excavated sites, but there were problems with this procedure. Some of those excavations had not been published at the time and one of the sites has since been redated. Burgess (2001) admitted this when the book was reprinted twenty years later, but, unwisely, he did not change its contents.

In this book the chapter divisions do not follow the conventional framework laid down by the Three Age Model. Thus the end of the Mesolithic period is considered together with the first part of the Neolithic. The Late Neolithic is treated separately. The Bronze Age is also divided between two chapters, as major changes happened halfway through that phase. This is acknowledged by treating the later part of this period in a chapter on its own. The same applies to the earlier pre-Roman Iron Age.

Lastly, this book is only one account of a series of remarkable phenomena and is organised as a narrative rather than a manual. It aims to be theoretically informed but is not committed to any orthodoxy. The archaeological literature is overwhelmingly descriptive, whether it consists of accounts of artefacts, field surveys, or excavations, and it is essential that the student master the details of this material. But it is even more important to achieve a sense of perspective, and this has been difficult because so many studies are limited to particular areas and periods of time. There is a need for a bolder treatment, even if it proves to be mistaken. That risk is well worth taking, and it applies not just to this particular version, but to every attempt to come to terms with the past.

CHAPTER 2

A NEW BEGINNING

TWO MODELS

This chapter discusses the beginnings of the Neolithic period in Britain and Ireland and is concerned with the time between approximately 4000 and 3000 BC (Figs. 2.1, 2.2). That simple statement raises many problems.

In order to work out when the Neolithic started, it is necessary to establish what that term stands for today (Robb 2013; A. M. Jones and Sibbesson 2013; Ray and J. S. Thomas 2018). It is a period label which has been inherited from the past and has had rather different connotations from one generation to another. The adjective 'Neolithic' was originally devised to describe a particular kind of technology based on the use of ground and polished stone, although it was soon appreciated that the finished artefacts were often found with ceramics. This definition became less important once it was discovered that these innovations occurred at the same time as the adoption of domesticates. Childe (1942) even spoke of a 'Neolithic Revolution', a term which he intended to evoke the important social and economic changes associated with the development of farming. Still more recently, attention has extended to the idea that the Neolithic period also saw profound changes in human attitudes to the world and that these were reflected in the construction of monuments and the use of a more complex material culture (J. S. Thomas 2013; Ray and J. S. Thomas 2018).

Each of these definitions has a certain validity. The problem is how their different components fit together (Robb 2013; A. M. Jones and Sibbesson 2013). The oldest characterisation of the Neolithic period works well in England and Scotland, but in Ireland, and parts of Wales, ground stone artefacts had already been made by hunter gatherers (Woodman 2015: 146–8; David 2007: 150–4). Monuments do seem to be a largely new development, but again they cannot characterise the entire Neolithic phenomenon. In most regions they were not built at the very beginning of this period, and there are some areas in which they were never adopted on a significant scale. For example, in the south of Ireland,

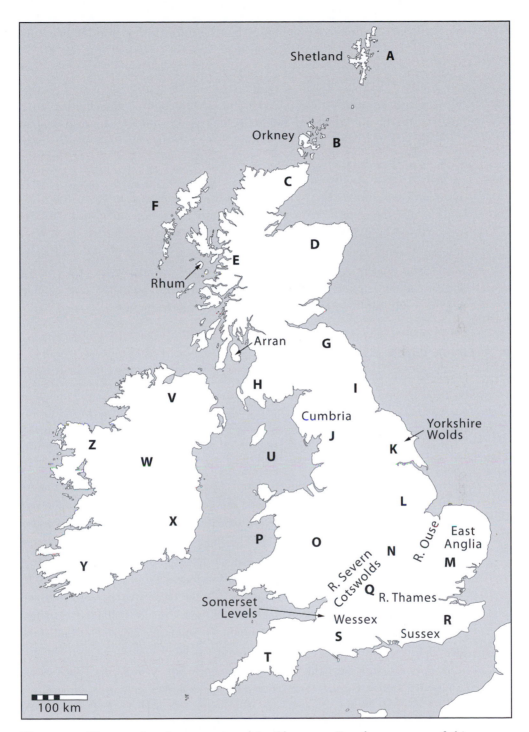

Figure 2.1 Places and regions mentioned in Chapter 2. For the purposes of this map Britain and Ireland have been divided into twenty-six areas and the individual sites are listed according to these divisions. A: Shetland; B: Orkney (Calf of Eday, Knap of Howar, Knowe of Ramsay, Smerquoy, Stonehall); C: Northern Scotland;

there is evidence for Neolithic houses, but the full range of stone-built tombs is missing, and part of the population may have been buried in caves (Dowd 2015: ch. 5; Ó Floinn 2011. That also happened in regions like northern England and south Wales which had a tradition of building mortuary monuments (Barnatt and Edmonds 2002; Meikeljohn, Chamberlain, and Schulting 2011; Leach 2015). In the same way, fieldwork in Ireland, and to a lesser extent in Scotland and Wales, has produced convincing evidence of houses and cereal growing (Smyth 2014), but in England this remains relatively rare (J. S. Thomas 2013). It seems as if different definitions of the Neolithic period apply to each of these islands, and yet their material culture shares many features in common. In particular, the ceramic sequence begins with a series of finely made undecorated vessels which were used until about 3500 BC (Sheridan 2010). Rather different technologies were favoured along the east coast and in western Britain and Ireland (Pioffet 2015), but the development of regional styles of decorated pottery did not happen on a significant scale until later. Similarly most parts of Britain and Ireland include the same kinds of stone artefacts.

Figure Caption 2.1 (*Cont.*)

D: North-east and Central Scotland (Balneaves, Crathes, Garthdee); E: Western Scotland (Achnacreebeag); F: Outer Hebrides (Bharpa Carinish, Eilean Domhnuill); G: Scotland on either side of the Firth of Forth (Auchenlaich, Carsie Mains, Claish; Cleaven Dyke, Douglasmuir, Littleour); H: South-west Scotland (Lochill); I: the English/Scottish borderland (Street House); J: North-west England (Carrock Fell, Pike o' Stickle); K: North-east England and the Peak District (Callis Wold, Duggleby Howe, Liff's Low, Lismore Fields, Rudston, Star Carr, Towthorpe, Whitegrounds); L: Eastern England from the Humber and the Fenland (Etton, Maxey, Haddenham, Hurst Fen); M: East Anglia (Brampton, Eynesbury, Fornham All Saints, Freston, Kilverston, Roughton, Spong Hill); N: The English Midlands (Briar Hill, Church Lawford, Godmanchester, Grendon, Husbands Bosworth, Northampton, Raunds, St Albans); O: the English/Welsh borderland (Gwernvale, Pipton); P: North and West Wales (Carreg Samson, Garn Turn, Rhuddlan); Q: the Thames Valley, Cotswolds, and South Midlands (Abingdon, Ascott-under-Wychwood, Crickley Hill, Eton, Hazleton, Hillingdon, Horton, Radley, Stanwell, Yarnton); R: South-east England including the Thames Estuary and the South Downs (Ashford, Blackwall, Coldrum, Court Hill, Isle of Sheppey, Orsett, Springfield, St Osyth, Whitehorse Stone); S: Wessex (Blick Mead, Coneybury, Dorset Cursus, Hambledon Hill, Larkhill, Maiden Castle, Normanton Down, Portland, Rybury, Stonehenge, Winchester, Windmill Hill); T: South-west England and South Wales (Aveline's Hole, Carn Brea, Helman Tor); U: the Isle of Man; V: Northern Ireland (Edenmore, Tievebulleagh); W: the Irish Midlands and the east coast (Cohaw, Hughstown, Spinans Hill); X: South-east Ireland (Corbally, Kilshane, Tullahedy); Y: South-west Ireland (Ferriter's Cove); Z: the Irish west coast (Ballyglass, Creevykeel, Poulnabrone).

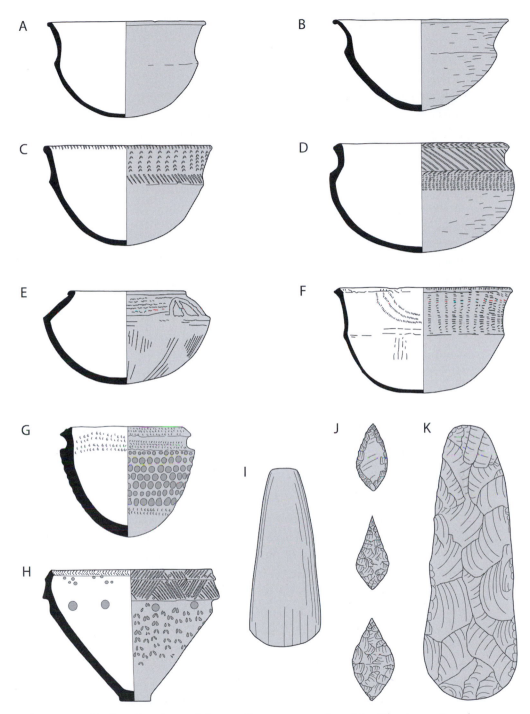

Figure 2.2 Outline drawings of the artefact types mentioned in Chapter 2. A and B: Early Neolithic carinated bowls; C–H: Middle Neolithic decorated pottery; I: ground stone axe; J: leaf-shaped arrowheads; K: unpolished axe.

A more serious problem involves the question of explanation. How did the insular Neolithic begin? Did it originate among the indigenous hunter gatherers who are described in the conventional terminology as 'Mesolithic'? How was it related to what was happening during the same period in Continental Europe, and to what extent did it develop a distinctive character of its own?

In many ways the evidence from Ireland comes closest to the accepted definition of the Neolithic period. Here there were changes in the nature and distribution of settlement and in the character of material culture (Cooney 2000; Carlin and Cooney 2017). Substantial houses are widely distributed and are associated with cereals and the remains of domesticated animals (Smyth 2014; McClatchie et al. 2016; McLaughlin et al. 2016; Whitehouse et al. 2014). Over the northern half of the island there is a dense distribution of mortuary monuments. In southern England, on the other hand, the situation is less clear (J. S. Thomas 2013). There are local differences between the distributions of Mesolithic and Neolithic occupation sites, but this is not always the case. In regions like the wetlands of the Somerset Levels, wild resources were still exploited (B. Coles and J. Coles 1986: ch. 4), and there may have been some continuity in the ways in which stone artefacts were made. In the south the evidence for domestic buildings is very limited (J. S. Thomas 2013; Cummings 2017). Cereals are usually found in small quantities along with evidence of wild plant foods (Robinson 2000).

Such stark contrasts do not extend into every area, but they gave rise to an important debate between the proponents of an 'Irish/Northern British' model which saw the Neolithic period as a radical break with the past (Cooney 2000: ch. 7), and a 'Southern English/Wessex' model which stressed continuity, acculturation, and a mobile pattern of settlement (J. S. Thomas 1988; J. S Thomas 2013). Scottish prehistorians have resisted the influence of the English interpretation and have taken exception to the idea that whatever happened in the archaeology of the south and east must have established the pattern for both islands (G. Barclay 2001).

These differences extend to the ways in which the archaeological record has been interpreted. Irish prehistorians consider that at the start of the Neolithic period an agricultural economy was introduced by settlement from overseas. Every aspect of the archaeological record changed quite rapidly, suggesting that the indigenous population soon adopted a new way of life. This model is the same as that applied in most parts of Europe. There that process had been checked in the early fifth millennium BC, but later it could have resumed (Bradley et al. 2016a: ch. 2). To the west it proceeded without a break, and it may be significant that there is a general resemblance between the first megalithic monuments in Ireland and along the Atlantic facade of Britain and those in northern and western France (Sheridan 2010). Although their chronologies overlapped for only a short period (Scarre 2015), these areas may have been among the sources of a new population.

By contrast, the 'Wessex' model was influenced by research in Northern Europe, where the Neolithic period began at virtually the same time as it did in Britain. Again it involved the creation of impressive monuments to the dead, but in this case the remains of houses do seem to have survived. Economic changes took place more gradually, and in South Scandinavia it was thought that the settlement pattern was initially based on domesticated animals. Arable farming on any scale did not appear until later. The early exploitation of domesticates ran in parallel with the continued use of wild resources. A common suggestion was that the indigenous people adopted elements of a new way of life through a long period of contacts across the agricultural frontier to the south (Fischer 2002). It was implied by the presence of pottery and imported axes on Mesolithic sites. In this case the movement of ideas might have been as important as the movement of farmers. Every part of that interpretation has been questioned in recent years (Sørensen and Karg 2014; Shennan 2018, ch. 7).

The southern English model (J. S. Thomas 1988) was explicitly based on analogy with the sequence in Scandinavia, and for a while it appeared that the Neolithic of these regions had some features in common: an initial emphasis on mobility; a settlement pattern which resulted in the survival of insubstantial houses; the formal deposition of artefacts in pits; and the construction of various kinds of earthwork monuments. The problem is that these comparisons applied to the Neolithic end of a longer sequence. How did the British and Irish Mesolithic compare with its Northern European counterpart?

The Scandinavian model depended on several key features: a long period of contact with areas to the south, shown by the movement of non-local artefacts and the adoption of an unfamiliar technology; reduced mobility and possibly the year-round occupation of certain favourable locations; increasing evidence of social complexity suggested by the development of cemeteries and votive deposits; and the introduction of small quantities of cereals and domesticates to settlements whose economy was otherwise based on hunting, gathering, and fishing. These processes seemed to have been vital to the adoption of agriculture and to the changes that went with it.

As Rowley-Conwy has observed, there are few signs of any of these features in the Mesolithic of Britain and Ireland (2004; 2011). The best evidence for social complexity comes from the beginning of that phase, and the largest domestic buildings belong to the early Mesolithic period (C. Waddington 2007), as does the one convincing cemetery at Aveline's Hole with radiocarbon dates in the ninth century BC; the same applies to most other finds of human bones (Meikeljohn, Chamberlain, and Schulting 2011). The only place with much evidence of ritual activity is the early site at Star Carr

(Conneller 2004; Milner, Conneller, and Taylor 2018: ch. 5), although there was a row of massive posts of comparable date on the site of the later monument at Stonehenge (Cleal, Walker, and Montague 1995). The only indications of a complex material culture are provided by a series of decorated artefacts like those from Rhuddlan which also date from the first part of this period (Quinnell and Blockley 1994: ch. 11). At present there is a single site, Ferriter's Cove in south-west Ireland, where domesticated animals have been identified in a secure Mesolithic context dating from about 4300 BC (Woodman, Anderson, and Finlay 1999), yet the first evidence of cereals is significantly later (McClatchie et al. 2016; Stevens and Fuller 2012). Sherratt argued that the earliest traces of cultivation with the primitive plough known as an ard occur between about 3500 and 3250 BC (1997: fig. 3.2), but a recent discovery in Scotland puts the date back to the thirty-eighth or thirty-ninth century BC (*Current Archaeology* 318: 11). Still more important, the settlements which do contain a mixture of Mesolithic and Neolithic material culture are largely found along a restricted section of the Scottish coastline, and it is not always clear whether both assemblages were in use simultaneously (Wicks, Pirie, and Mithen 2014). There is a similar problem in Ireland (Woodman 2015: 330–5; M. Lynch 2017). These observations cannot support any model with a wider application.

Indeed, there may be signs of discontinuity at the end of the fifth millennium BC and the beginning of the fourth. One of the features supposed to indicate greater control over the environment during the later Mesolithic period was deliberate firing of the natural vegetation. It might have increased the food supply and could certainly have helped to concentrate game animals in particularly favourable locations. It is clear that this was being done from the beginning of the Mesolithic. If it happened increasingly often, that would be expected as the landscape was invaded by trees. It can no longer be thought of as a 'pre-adaptation' to farming (Simmons 1996), and Kevin Edwards (1998) suggests that at the beginning of the Neolithic this practice came to an end. A more recent study favours a longer history of upland grazing and burning (Garton 2017). Nevertheless its intensity may have been reduced.

There is important evidence of diet from the analysis of human remains found near the sea. This work suggests that during the Mesolithic period coastal communities had made significant use of marine resources, but at the beginning of the Neolithic their representation was significantly reduced. From that time onwards greater use was made of terrestrial plants and animals. The sample is limited because few Mesolithic bones survive, but similar results have been obtained along the Atlantic coastline from Portugal to Brittany and also in south Scandinavia (M. Richards 2004; Cramp et al. 2014).

There is another revealing trend in the environmental record. To a large extent the beginning of the Neolithic period corresponds with a decline in the amount of elm pollen. It no longer seems as though this is the result of a specific economic practice, like ring-barking growing trees or collecting leaf fodder. It is more likely that the phenomenon results from the spread of a disease which attacked this particular species (Girling and Grieg 1985). At one time the 'Elm Decline' was used as a chronological marker, but this may be misleading (Batchelor et al. 2014). On the other hand, it does seem likely that the spread of the disease was facilitated by the movement of people on an increasing scale. It may have been accelerated by the creation of more areas of open ground.

The earliest radiocarbon dates for Neolithic artefacts are between about 4050 BC and 3700 BC and come from south-east England (Whittle, Healy, and Bayliss 2011: ch. 14). After that time there is more evidence from other regions, but these estimates raise certain difficulties. This was a period where the calibration of radiocarbon dates is not precise, meaning that the true ages of particular samples have a wide distribution. The direct dating of carbonised cereals in Ireland suggests that they first appear between 3720 and 3680 BC (McClatchie et al. 2016). Another difficulty is in deciding when Mesolithic material culture went out of use. There are too few dates to shed much light on that process, but they do suggest that in England the use of microliths extended into the very beginning of the fourth millennium BC and most probably down to the fortieth or thirty-ninth centuries (Griffiths 2014; Innes, Blackford, and Rowley-Conwy 2013).

The number of radiocarbon dates obtained from Britain and Ireland rises sharply after 4000 BC. This has been treated as a proxy for the population of these islands, suggesting that it grew remarkably quickly after the adoption of agriculture. In fact the increase was so steep that it was believed to document a period of immigration (Collard et al. 2010; Woodbridge et al. 2014). Of course, there are problems with this approach as the frequency of available dates depends on the selection of samples for analysis; the archaeology of certain periods may attract more interest than that of others. Nevertheless virtually the same pattern has been recognised in Continental Europe, and in each case the number of dates falls sharply after a few hundred years (Shennan 2013); in Britain the peak began about 4000 BC and lasted until 3300 BC (Shennan 2018, ch. 8). Current research may amplify these arguments by documenting the genetic composition of the British and Irish populations (Brace et al. 2018), but it will be a problem comparing samples of Neolithic human bone with those from Mesolithic sites, as they are very rare. Even so it suggests that the first farmers were immigrants who settled in these islands from at least two separate sources: the near-Continent towards the south and east, and the Atlantic coastline of Europe. A new study favours a greater contribution from the latter region (Brace et al. 2018).

However this evidence is interpreted, the British and Irish Neolithic drew on at least two sources. There are various links between the insular record and the evidence from Continental Europe. Perhaps this has been obscured because scholars have been looking for a single origin for insular Neolithic artefacts. It has never been found, although there are connections between the undecorated Neolithic pottery of northern France, Belgium, and the southern Netherlands and the earliest pottery in Ireland and Britain, just as there may have been further connections with north-west France (Pioffet 2015). It is less clear how the insular flint industries are related to those on the Continent, but in this case some of the variation may result from the use of different raw materials, although the use of mines began at the beginning of this period (Shennan et al. 2017). Far more important are two other elements whose significance is not disputed. The main domesticated animals of the British and Irish Neolithic were cattle, sheep, goats, and pigs. There were no cattle in Ireland during the Mesolithic phase, and, in Britain, the native wild cattle were quite distinct from the animals that first appear in the Neolithic, which have more in common with those in mainland Europe (Tresset 2003). The origins of domesticated pigs are controversial, but there are no wild progenitors for sheep or goat on either island. The same applies to wheat and barley. These staples must have been introduced from across the sea, although no traces of seagoing vessels survive.

The second component is monumental architecture, which seems to have become an established feature of the landscape from an early stage of the Neolithic, although it may not have happened immediately. Again it is unwise to seek a single source of inspiration for any of these structures, but the tradition of long mounds or 'long barrows' that is so widespread in Britain and Ireland was distributed along the edges of the Continent as far east as Denmark and Poland and as far west as Brittany (Bradley et al. 2016a: 69–78 and 87–91). Some of the insular structures contained stone chambers of forms that are not unlike those in Atlantic Europe, although they went out of use around the end of the fifth millennium BC (Sheridan et al. 2008; Sheridan 2010; Scarre 2015). In the same way, distinctive earthwork enclosures defined by an interrupted ditch had a wide distribution on the Continent, reaching from Bornholm to the east to Ireland to the west. They are particularly common in Denmark, northern Germany, Belgium, and the north of France. Many of these monuments look remarkably similar to one another, but radiocarbon dating shows that they were built at different times (Whittle, Healy, and Bayliss 2011: ch. 15). They bear a particularly strong resemblance to those in southern Britain and may have been used in the same ways. In these islands they were first built some time after the earliest long barrows.

Since such connections are widely accepted, why has it been so difficult to define the sources of the British and Irish Neolithic? Perhaps this is because of the islands' distinctive geography, which allowed them to form links with regions of the European mainland that would not have been in regular contact with one another. That may be why the insular Neolithic was so distinctive. It drew on many different sources of inspiration. The problem for future research is not to discover the source of the insular Neolithic but to explain how so many diverse influences were drawn together in a new synthesis over a short period of time.

Why did Britain and Ireland 'become Neolithic'? It is certainly true that this process happened simultaneously across a considerable area. It affected southern Scandinavia at the same time as these two islands. Since there is no evidence for contacts between Britain and Northern Europe during the Late Mesolithic period, it suggests that the initial impulse must have begun on the Continent. Several models have been proposed, and, logically, they should apply not just to Britain and Ireland but to Denmark, Sweden, and The Netherlands as well.

The first is that in each of these areas indigenous hunter gatherers were well aware of farming communities and their practices but were reluctant to change their way of life. That reluctance might have been because of deep-rooted reservations about Neolithic systems of belief (Bradley 1998a: ch. 2), or it could have been because the local environment was so productive that there was little need to experiment with new ways of producing food. In the first case, their growing exposure to Neolithic customs and material culture might have encouraged internal tensions. If so, the adoption of farming could have been a way of gaining social position (Fischer 2002). The second possibility is that the adoption of domesticates was the result of adverse circumstances as the economic prosperity of local hunter gatherers was threatened by failures of the food supply (Zvelebil and Rowley-Conwy 1986). Each argument is plausible in itself, but neither seems to have a direct bearing on the prehistory of Britain and Ireland. There is little evidence for contacts between insular hunter gatherers and Continental farmers, and there are no signs of social complexity in the insular Late Mesolithic. Rather, Ireland became isolated from Britain and Britain became isolated from the mainland.

In Northern Europe the territory occupied by early farmers had remained much the same over a long period of time. Why were they so reluctant to settle larger areas? Perhaps the reason that the initial expansion of agriculture seemed to falter was that it had reached the limits of the land where it could produce a dependable supply of food. Beyond it there were regions with unfavourable weather and poorer soils. Bonsall and his colleagues have observed that the expansion of farming into those areas seems to have occurred as the climate changed, so that it would have been possible to practise the same economy over a more extensive territory (Bonsall et al. 2002). Similar evidence is discussed by Hinz (2015), who observes that the amelioration was comparatively short-lived and ended with the onset of cooler conditions by 3550 BC. It suggests an incentive for expansion that had been lacking before. Although this analysis has been questioned by Schulting (2010) and Tipping (2010b), at present it seems to be the only model which explains developments in Britain and Ireland as well as those in Scandinavia.

For a time colonisation by sea was an unfashionable option, and it did not account for every aspect of the insular Neolithic. There are also a number of features that could be more closely linked to a Mesolithic way of life (Ray and J. S. Thomas 2018: 57–66). The most important may also be the most intangible. Neolithic material culture was adopted remarkably quickly over large parts of Britain and Ireland. Perhaps this was influenced by existing knowledge of insular geography. Extended journeys along the rivers and around the coastline must have drawn on the accumulated experience of the indigenous population. That could explain why some of the Neolithic ceremonial monuments were built in places which had already fulfilled an important role in an older pattern of communication and why artefacts dating from both phases occur at the same sites on the coast (Bradley et al. 2016b). It applies to the siting of certain enclosures and tombs in locations that had been used before, but, provided clearings were maintained by grazing animals, it need not presuppose an unbroken sequence of activity.

That is less of a problem on those coastal sites where shell middens continued to accumulate after 4000 BC, but this was a local phenomenon, confined to western Scotland, the Inner Hebrides, Shetland, and possibly Ireland (Wicks, Pirie, and Mithen 2014; Woodman 2015: 330–5; M. Lynch 2017). Another intriguing convergence is represented by the use of raw materials. It seems clear that in a number of regions, including parts of the southern English chalk and the Scottish islands of Arran and Rhum, stone sources first used in the Mesolithic period were exploited on a more intensive scale during the Neolithic. In the same way, coastal hunter gatherers in north-west England had worked small pieces of a distinctive kind of tuff which they probably collected from stream deposits. During the Early Neolithic period the parent outcrop was discovered in the Lake District mountains and became one of the largest sources of polished axes. It is unlikely that this happened by chance. People may well have traced these pebbles to their point of origin, using the same techniques as recent mineral prospectors (Bradley and Edmonds 1993).

There is more to say about the spread of portable artefacts, for here there was not only continuity but change. It seems as if one of the first developments of the Neolithic period was the establishment of flint mines close to the English Channel coast in Sussex and Wessex. They were in operation by the early fourth millennium BC and work there may have started even sooner (M. Barber, D. Field, and Topping 1999; Baczkowski and Holgate 2017). The methods of extracting the stone were very similar to those employed at equivalent sites in the Continent, yet they could only have been devised through a long period of trial and error. Given the early date of the English examples, it is obvious that these methods of working were introduced in their developed form from the European mainland (Baczkowski 2014). The English sites seem to have been devoted to the production of axes and were located beyond the limits of the settled land. It is especially interesting that these mines originated at such an early date since adequate raw material could have been found in surface deposits – as it obviously was during the Mesolithic and again in the Late Neolithic period (Gardiner 1989). Not everyone may have had access to mined flint, and it could be that certain objects took on a special significance.

That is even more obvious from the distribution of Alpine axes made of jadeite which date from the very beginning of the Neolithic period in these islands. They had been made in remote and dramatic locations in the western Alps, and many were of such high quality that they could not have been ordinary work tools (Pétrequin et al. 2012. Their introduction must have been the inspiration for major axe quarries in highland areas, some of which – Pike o' Stickle, Tievebulleagh, and Graig Llwyd – were in similar places (Fig. 2.3). The stone source on Scafell Pike is within a short distance of the highest point in England. Radiocarbon dates from Langdale in north-west England suggest that the Cumbrian quarries were used at the same time as the early flint mines in the south (Bradley and Watson in press). It could apply to other distinctive materials which were used for making artefacts. Portland chert had been employed since the Mesolithic period, but in the Neolithic period it was used for making high-quality arrowheads (R. Stewart 2017). The dissemination of Arran pitchstone was another new development. It was highly distinctive, as it resembles obsidian. It was obtained on an island off the west coast of Scotland and used on a limited scale by local hunter gatherers, but it became more important during the Early Neolithic period and was eventually distributed as far as Ireland, Orkney, and the north of England (Ballin 2009).

It is always easier to document the movement of objects than the spread of ideas, but there were also certain social practices that may have retained their importance from the Mesolithic to the Neolithic period. One was the use of caves for the deposition of human bones (Meikeljohn, Chamberlain, and Schulting 2011; Dowd 2015; Leach 2015). This is especially interesting since disarticulated human remains are also found in chambered tombs. Cummings and Whittle (2004) have drawn attention to the close relationship between some of these structures in Wales and striking features of the natural topography, suggesting that places with a long-established significance in the landscape may have been monumentalised.

So far this account has employed two traditional terms, 'Neolithic' and 'Mesolithic', and has considered their connotations. Other terms have a more straightforward chronological significance. For the purposes of this study, the Neolithic period is divided into three main phases. The Early and Middle Neolithic are considered here, and the Late Neolithic in Chapter 3. The commonest division is between an 'Early' Neolithic (about 4000–3500 BC),

Figure 2.3 The Langdale Pikes where stone axes were made in remote locations during the Early and Middle Neolithic periods. Photograph: Aaron Watson.

when monumental structures first developed, and a Middle Neolithic phase (approximately 3500–3000 BC) with a more varied ceramic tradition and an increasing variety of mortuary monuments and earthwork enclosures.

HOUSES AND SETTLEMENT PATTERNS

The Neolithic took different forms in different areas. In England, the number and size of extraordinary monuments support Julian Thomas's notion that the period is characterised by a particular way of thinking about the world. In Ireland, it also involved the rapid adoption of agriculture.

One of the most striking results of field archaeology has been the discovery of Neolithic houses in Ireland and to a smaller extent in Scotland and north-west Wales (Smyth 2014). This contrasts with their rarity in England (Fig. 2.4; Cummings 2017). It can hardly be a result of differential survival. Many of the structures found in Ireland were in areas that had experienced a long history of cultivation, just as some of the projects carried out in England have examined well-preserved deposits.

Different kinds of Neolithic archaeology are represented by work in these two countries. In Ireland, a long period of research concerned with megalithic tombs was followed by investigations of occupation sites. In England, on the

Corbally

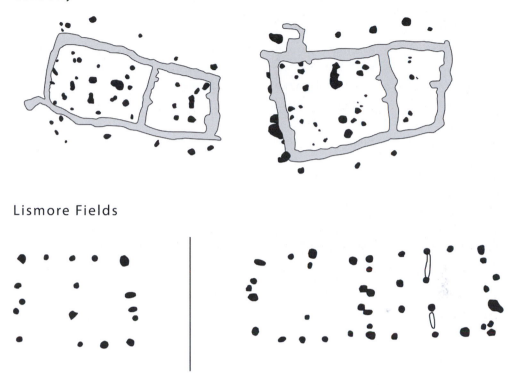

Lismore Fields

10 m

Figure 2.4 Plans of Early Neolithic wooden houses at Corbally, in the east of Ireland, and Lismore Fields, in northern England. Information from Purcell (2002) and Darvill (1996).

other hand, attempts to locate substantial settlements by field walking have largely gone out of fashion. Either the most promising candidates proved to be more specialised structures like earthwork enclosures, or the remains of living places were so ephemeral that they encouraged prehistorians to devote more attention to monuments. In Ireland, Scotland, and Wales, fieldworkers have been able to study settlements and tombs, but only in Orkney is it possible to treat both on equal terms (C. Richards and R. Jones 2016).

Such variations reflect certain realities. In Ireland and in northern and western Britain, the house and the individual settlement seem to have provided a focus for domestic life, even when they were complemented by specialised monuments. In England, and especially in the south and east, the sheer scale of some of these monuments draws attention to the very limited evidence for everyday activities. Again this may reflect priorities in the past as well as the biases among fieldworkers in the present.

It is hard to escape assumptions drawn from the archaeology of Continental Europe. They are influenced by the material remains of a much earlier period and relate to a time up to a thousand years before the period in question here. They refer to a remarkably stable pattern of settlement typified by massive domestic buildings, but this was coming to an end in the mid-fifth millennium BC, and by 4000 BC no trace of it remained (Bradley et al. 2016a: 58–73). Around the rim of Continental Europe the evidence is very like that in Britain and Ireland, and the remains of occupation sites are less apparent. Often they are reduced to scatters of artefacts and pits, and the presence of well-preserved dwellings is exceptional.

Ireland, Wales, and Northern Britain

There are further contrasts that need to be explored. The longhouses of the sixth and earlier fifth millennia BC in Continental Europe had been organised into hamlets or even small villages. It seems likely that the first Neolithic dwellings in Britain and Ireland had a more dispersed distribution. To some extent the pattern may be changing as a result of recent fieldwork. Some of the Neolithic houses in Ireland form part of a wider distribution, with more than one nucleus where several houses occur together. There is evidence that structures were replaced in the same positions (Smyth 2014). Without a much finer chronology it provides virtually the only evidence of sequence, and at present it is impossible to tell how many other buildings were in use together. It was originally suggested that this pattern was established around 4000 BC, but radiocarbon dates on short-lived samples limit the currency of the Irish examples to about a century and a half between 3750 and 3600 BC (McLaughlin et al. 2016).

There were regional differences in the forms taken by Early Neolithic houses on both islands, although all the securely dated examples were rectangular, oval, or square (Sheridan 2013). In Ireland their walls were commonly set in trenches, making them easy to identify in modern excavations. In England, on the other hand, they are usually identified as a setting of postholes (A. Gibson 2017) and their traces can be less obvious. Some distinctions emerged with the passage of time. Most structures were built of wood, but rather later stone houses with a similar ground plan have been identified at Eilean Domhnuill in the Outer Hebrides (Armit 2003a) and in the Orkney settlements of Knap of Howar, Smerquoy, and Stonehall (C. Richards and R. Jones 2016).

Despite these distinctions, a number of houses shared features in common. Their contents can be unusual. Those in Ireland include significant quantities of fine pottery but few other artefacts. In some cases, objects seem to have been placed in their foundations, and others have produced significant quantities of burnt grain (Smyth 2014: 62–70). These finds have led to confusion.

On the one hand, the exceptional character of such deposits encouraged the view that the buildings were used in rituals and ceremonies. On the other, it suggested that if large quantities of grain are found inside them, this should have been standard practice at Neolithic settlements. Both these observations may be misleading. The artefacts in the postholes and wall trenches might have been offerings made when the building was erected (Smyth 2014: 57–62). The exceptional collections of pottery may have been placed there when those structures were abandoned and destroyed, in which case neither group of objects need have been associated with the occupation of the houses themselves. The discovery of carbonised grain can also be confusing, for in common with other Neolithic buildings, some of these structures were burnt down. A similar process happened at so many sites of the same date that it seems to have been intentional (Noble 2006: ch. 3). These finds may shed light on the rituals associated with the occupation of houses, but they do not transform the dwellings into some kind of specialised monument. It is possible that Neolithic longhouses in parts of Continental Europe were abandoned when one of the occupants died (Bradley 1998a: ch. 3). That interpretation may also be relevant here, not least in those cases where the remains of earlier settlements were buried under mounds or cairns.

The idea that certain rituals centred on domestic buildings may also explain the exceptional structures built in Scotland at this time (Fig. 2.5; Ray and J. S. Thomas 2018: 105–13). At first sight they share the attributes of the Irish houses, but they are considerably larger. These structures were rectilinear with rounded ends; some were divided into several compartments; and again they were associated with fine pottery and deposits of burnt grain (Brophy 2007). They had been built on a massive scale, and yet the separate rooms were so small that circulation about the interior would have been very difficult (Debert 2016). Still more revealing, they might be burnt down and replaced on at least one occasion. The features of an ordinary dwelling were apparently reproduced on a monumental scale, but people would still have understood the reference to domestic architecture. On the other hand, these sites have certain exceptional features. Again the artefact assemblage contains significant quantities of ceramics, but few lithic artefacts (G. Barclay, Brophy, and MacGregor 2002). The buildings are apparently isolated from ordinary dwellings, yet pollen analysis shows that the example at Crathes had been built in an area of agricultural land (H. Murray, C. Murray, and Fraser 2009: 25–9). Similar structures can be found near to specialised earthwork monuments of the kinds described later in this chapter.

A revealing comparison is between two timber buildings on Deeside in north-east Scotland. Both were of the same date and were excavated by the same people. The small domestic building at Garthdee was only 95 m² in extent but included thirty-four ceramic vessels and no fewer than 400 lithic artefacts

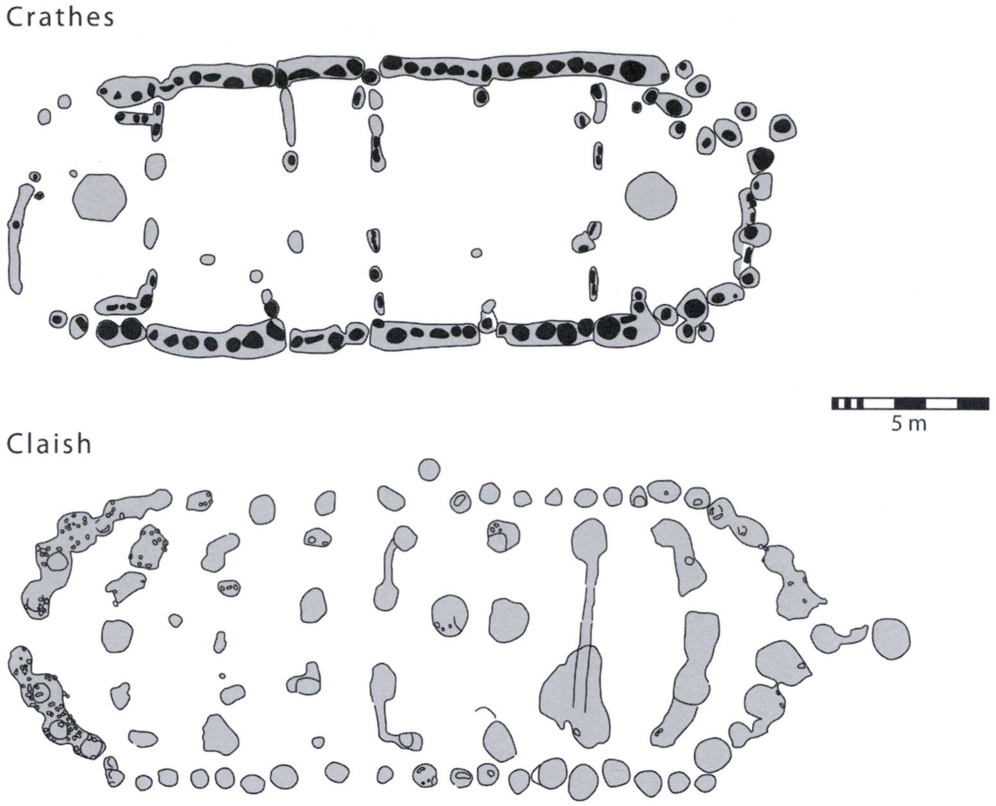

Crathes

Claish

Figure 2.5 The ground plans of timber buildings interpreted as Early Neolithic halls at Crathes, north-east Scotland, and Claish, central Scotland. Information from Barclay, Brophy, and MacGregor (2002) and Murray, Murray, and Fraser (2009).

(H. Murray and C. Murray 2014). The 'hall' at Warren Field, Crathes, only 20 km away, had almost twice that floor area. It is associated with up to fifty pots but included only fifty pieces of worked stone (H. Murray, C. Murray, and Fraser 2009). Both buildings contained carbonised grain, but they may have been used in different ways.

The Scottish and Irish buildings have been used to counter the idea that the Neolithic settlement pattern was based on mobility and the use of wild resources (Sheridan 2013). Although domesticated animals provided food and secondary products, it is the cereals from these sites that have attracted most attention for discoveries of this kind have been less abundant in southern England where Neolithic houses are rare (Robinson 2000). These discoveries call into question some of the tenets of the new interpretation, but it is important to see them in perspective, for buildings of these kinds were quite short-lived and do not represent the normal pattern for the Neolithic period. Many were erected during the early fourth millennium BC, and after that time they disappear, to be replaced by more ephemeral dwellings. That is true of most of the well-preserved structures in Ireland (McLaughlin et al. 2016), but it does not apply so clearly to the Scottish sites. From approximately 3500 BC the settlement pattern in different regions seems to have been rather more homogeneous. Cereals are less often recovered and almost everywhere houses become more difficult to identify. Stevens and Fuller (2012) even suggest that cereal growing was abandoned. Although this can be disputed, crops may sometimes have failed. Hinz (2015) has recognised a similar process on the near-Continent and suggests that it was associated with climate change around 3550 BC.

Hinz's interpretation is supported by recent work in Ireland. Here it seems as if the first Neolithic settlements made a significant impact on the environment. Pollen analysis has identified a series of major clearings at the beginning of the Neolithic period. They are associated with the appearance of cereal pollen. It is revealing that, after a brief phase of expansion during which substantial houses had been built, some of those clearings became overgrown. From then on, there are more indications of pastoral farming (O'Connell and Molloy 2001; Whitehouse et al. 2014). Rather similar claims have been made at a number of sites in Britain where clearings were either abandoned around 3300 BC or reverted to less intensive land use (Stevens and Fuller 2012; Woodbridge et al. 2014), but in this case there seems to have been greater regional and chronological variation, and the next significant impact on the landscape did not come until the Chalcolithic period around 2300 BC. It is not clear why these changes happened, but Dark and Gent (2001) have made the interesting observation that the first cereals introduced to these islands would probably have been protected from crop pests. That immunity would have broken down over time, meaning that the earliest crops could have been unusually productive.

Lowland England

The environmental record from lowland England does not follow quite the same trajectory as its Irish counterpart, and the evidence for earlier Neolithic settlement takes a very different form. There is no shortage of pit deposits containing the distinctive kinds of material associated with well-preserved settlements (Garrow 2007; Anderson-Whymark and J. S. Thomas 2012) and in the Thames Valley there are even the remains of open-air middens (T. Allen et al. 2013); they would have been so fertile that they may well have been cultivated (Guttmann 2005). There is not much evidence, even from extensive excavations, that several houses existed together on the same sites. In England and Wales very few buildings on the scale of the Scottish 'halls' have been found. There were exceptionally large examples at Yarnton in the Middle Thames (Hey, Dennis, and Robinson 2016: 51–62) and Whitehorse Stone in Kent (Booth et al. 2011: 63–94), but they may have consisted of two smaller structures built end to end, probably in sequence.

There are two possibilities. The first is that settlements really were insub-stantial and short-lived. That might be suggested by the small size and limited contents of most of the artefact scatters and by the restricted number of pits associated with many of these sites. This is reflected by the rarity of carbonised cereals in these contexts, compared with the remains of wild plants (Robinson 2000). On the other hand, it is not inconceivable that rectilinear houses had once been more widely distributed and that they were built in a way that did not leave subsoil features behind. Waterlogged wood from the Somerset Levels shows that people employed sophisticated carpentry techniques, including the use of planks, from the Early Neolithic period (B. Coles and J. Coles 1986). Other structures could have been built of turf, cob, or even mud brick. One indication that more houses existed in England is provided by exten-sive excavations at settlements along the east coast which are characterised by groups of pits whose contents could be refitted (Garrow, Beadsmoore, and Knight 2005). Traces of structures might not have survived, but there are empty areas in between these features which are of roughly the shape and dimensions of the domestic buildings of this date. Other arcs or clusters of pits may have been inside the houses themselves. This view was taken by the excavators at a site in the Thames Valley where several timber structures and a 'house void' of similar proportions were recorded in the course of fieldwork (Fig. 2.6; Chaffrey and Brook 2012).

A persistent feature of these occupation sites is the presence of pits whose contents could be carefully organised as they were placed in the ground (Lamdin-Whymark 2008). They could include pottery, lithic artefacts, querns, and animal bones that seem to have been taken from middens, but occasion-ally they contained disarticulated human remains. It was once argued that such pits were grain silos, but it seems more likely that they were dug specifically to receive their contents. The same kinds of deposits were in the hollows left by fallen trees, and this may have been the origin of such a distinctive practice (C. Evans, Pollard, and Knight 1999). It seems possible that this material was care-fully buried when occupation sites were abandoned (Healy 1987). That prac-tice has worrying implications for field archaeology. In those parts of England where flint is readily available it can be difficult to recognise concentrations of surface finds dating from this period.

Studies of carbonised seeds and animal bones have provided some informa-tion on the character of early Neolithic settlement, but the largest collections of faunal remains come from the excavation of specialised monuments, whilst the main groups of cereals are associated with structures that could have been set on fire. New research on crop remains has had two important outcomes. Isotopic analysis has established that manuring was employed in Britain from the beginning of Neolithic farming in these islands. It was a well-established technique and must have been introduced from outside; there is no evidence of an experimental phase (Bogaard et al. 2013). Another study concerns the

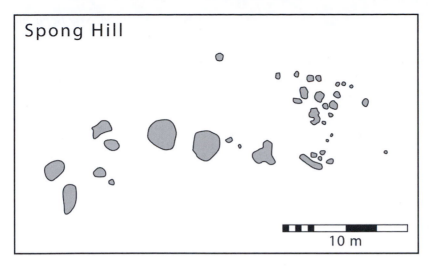

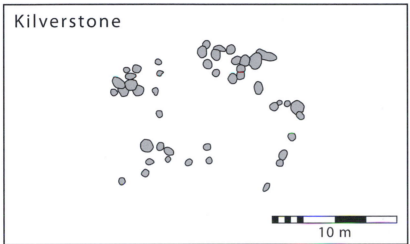

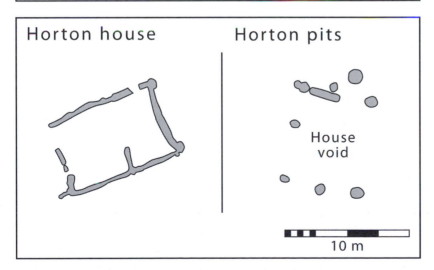

Figure 2.6 Groups of pits enclosing 'house voids' on two sites in East Anglia, plus a similar feature at Horton in the Thames Valley. An excavated house plan at Horton is included for comparison. Information from Healy (1988), Garrow, Beadsmoore, and Knight (2005), and Chaffrey and Brook (2012).

weeds associated with the first cereals. Despite accounts of the Early Neolithic period that emphasise mobility and the use of wild resources, Bogaard and Jones (2007) have shown that the proportion of weeds in British samples is the same as it is in the Linearbandkeramik, when settled farmers had lived in enormous longhouses.

Serjeantson (2014) has studied the faunal remains dating from the same period and makes an equally striking observation. Apart from the contents of an exceptionally early pit at Coneybury in Wessex, they do not include more than 5 per cent of wild animal bones: a revealing contrast with the evidence from the Late Mesolithic period, for example that from Blick Mead a short distance away (Jaques, Lyons, and Phillips 2017). It is obvious that domesticated animals were introduced to these islands, and Serjeantson comments that not only were sheep absent from the native fauna, they were poorly suited to the British environment at this time.

Perhaps more direct evidence of human diet will be obtained by other methods of analysis. Just as the evidence of stable isotopes suggests a drastic change from a marine to a terrestrial diet at the start of the Neolithic, there seems to be evidence for a major emphasis on animal products during this period (M. Richards 2004; 2008). That is not to imply that every community practised the same economy. Human remains from individual tombs provide very similar signatures to one another, but there are important contrasts between the samples taken from different monuments of this kind, suggesting that there was a range of variation and that some people ate more meat than others. In the same way chemical analysis shows that certain ceramic vessels contained milk or dairy products (Cramp et al. 2014). The use of secondary products was fundamentally different from the practice of hunter gatherers who exploited their prey for its meat.

MORTUARY MONUMENTS

What of the earliest monuments? Most accounts of the Neolithic period provide a commentary on a series of separate types. Understandably, those associated with human remains dominate the discussion, not least because so many mounds and cairns can still be seen today. This raises several problems. First, it suggests that prehistoric people were building these structures according to a series of prescribed templates when excavation has shown that the final forms of such buildings provide little indication of their internal construction. There is evidence of improvisation as well as changes of plan (McFadyen 2007). Superficially similar forms of mound or cairn may have developed along radically different lines. Secondly, there is a tendency to treat all the component parts of such monuments as a unitary conception whereas recent fieldwork suggests that many could be found on their own. A third problem is that closer attention to the sequence at individual monuments reveals that the mound or cairn which provided the main focus for discussion was the last element to be built and normally brought the use of that site to an end.

In fact it seems as if some of the earliest monuments may have taken a distinctive form. Two elements are particularly important here and in some ways relate to similar ways of utilising components of the natural landscape. For the most part they have different distributions from one another. Along the coastline of the North Sea and the English Channel timber 'mortuary houses' are quite common, although this term does not do justice either to their distinctive form or to the material associated with them. Their distribution hardly overlaps with that of 'portal dolmens' which occur in areas to the west (Fig. 2.7).

Excavation of the 'mortuary houses' has identified settings of D-shaped postholes of considerable proportions. Usually they occur in pairs, although other configurations are found. Work at the well-preserved site of Haddenham in eastern England confirmed what was long suspected, that these are the remains of tree trunks which had been split in half (C. Evans and Hodder 2005). Many of these sites are associated with human remains. There are examples beneath barrows or cairns, but they were usually built after these posts had been set in place, and there are even cases where such structures were never covered by a mound. Sometimes the posts decayed before human remains were introduced, in which case these structures were considered as monuments in their own right (Noble 2017: 153–9). They are particularly interesting since there is evidence that at the beginning of the Neolithic period the holes left by fallen trees held offerings of cultural material. Perhaps these components of the native woodland were thought to be especially significant.

In upland areas, especially in Ireland and western Britain, a comparable process may be evidenced by portal dolmens. These are usually classified as megalithic 'tombs', although it is not certain that they were originally associated with human remains. Nor is there much evidence that they were covered by cairns. In fact they seem to have been intended as closed 'boxes' covered by a disproportionately massive capstone which could be higher at one end than the other. Some monuments resemble natural rock formations, and in certain cases it seems as if the massive covering slab had been obtained on the site itself (Whittle 2004). Their chambers were raised above shallow pits, which may have been the quarries from which the capstone was taken (Cummings and Richards 2016). Analysis of charcoal found in one such feature at Garn Turne in Wales confirms that 'portal tombs' were among the earlier mortuary monuments, with dates between 3780 and 3650 BC (Cummings and C. Richards 2014). Those from Poulnabrone on the west coast of Ireland are even older (Fig. 2.8). They suggest that the site was first used about 3885–3720 BC (A. Lynch 2014a).

Lochhill

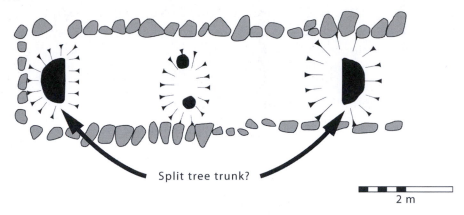

Split tree trunk?

2 m

Carreg Samson

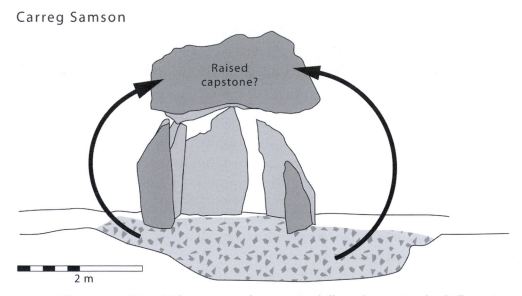

Raised
capstone?

2 m

Figure 2.7 (Upper) The mortuary house at Lochill, south-west Scotland, illustrating the use of a split tree trunk in its structure. (Lower) The chambered tomb at Carreg Samson, south-west Wales, illustrating the raising of a massive rock for use as its capstone. Information from Masters (1983) and Richards (2004).

Closed chambers of other kinds may belong to the beginning of the Neolithic sequence in Britain and Ireland, as they do in western France where a number of sites were originally associated with monumental cists (Sheridan 2010; Scarre 2015). The interior did not become accessible until a later phase. It is likely that a similar process took place in Britain and Ireland. Among the more convincing examples are the 'rotunda graves' of the Cotswolds which were incorporated into later long cairns (Darvill 2004: 60–3), and a remarkable site at Achnacreebeag in the west of Scotland which has been compared

Figure 2.8 The portal tomb at Poulnabrone in the west of Ireland. Photograph: Aaron Watson.

with a series of monuments in the west of France dated between 4200 and 3800 BC (Sheridan 2010). The Carrowmore cemetery on the west coast of Ireland provides another example of this development, for here massive stone chambers were erected within circles of boulders (Cummings and C. Richards 2016). In this case the cemetery developed into a group of passage tombs. That development is discussed in Chapter 3.

There are other ways in which the Irish Neolithic is distinctive, for here the remains of domestic dwellings seem to have been closely associated with mortuary monuments, which often take the form of elongated mounds or cairns. At Ballyglass in the west of the country one of these overlies the remains of a wooden structure (Ó Nualláin 1972; 1998). The same happened at a neighbouring monument, but in this case excavation exposed the plans of three separate houses, two of which overlapped. It is clear that the layout of the tomb was influenced by the organisation of the older settlement.

Similar links have been inferred in other areas. At Bharpa Carinish in the Outer Hebrides the exiguous traces of another dwelling were found only 30 m from a chambered tomb and may have shared the same alignment as that monument (Fig. 2.9; Crone 1993). In England and Wales, there are cases in which a chambered tomb overlay the remains of earlier dwellings. This was clearly demonstrated at Gwernvale (Britnell and Savory 1984: 50–2), but slighter domestic structures also seem to have preceded the well-excavated

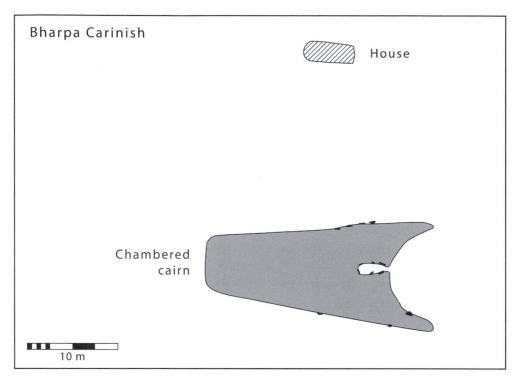

Figure 2.9 The relationship between a chambered cairn and a Neolithic house at Bharpa Carinish, Western Isles. Information from Crone (1993).

cairns at Ascott-under-Wychwood (Benson and Whittle 2007) and possibly Hazleton (Saville 1990). The two houses discovered at Whitehorse Stone in south-east England are not far from a distinctive group of stone-built tombs (Booth et al. 2011: 84–94), one of which, at Coldrum, is associated with exceptionally early radiocarbon dates (Wysocki et al. 2013). The connection between domestic structures and monuments perhaps goes even further. The stone houses at the island site of Eilean Domnhuill were approached through an impressive stone setting which the excavator compares with the forecourt of a megalithic tomb (Armit 2003a). Elsewhere in the Hebrides there may have been similar sites based on a foundation of stones similar to the crannogs of later periods (*Current Archaeology* 325: 9).

In Orkney, the comparison between houses and more specialised architecture extends to the internal structure of the tombs described as 'stalled cairns' which feature a series of compartments, linked by a central corridor. Colin Richards has argued that the architecture of these tombs refers to the characteristic form and organisation of domestic dwellings at sites like Knap of Howar (Fig. 2.10). It seems appropriate to consider such monuments as the houses of the dead, but he suggests that the tombs might have been the source of inspiration for the dwellings rather than the reverse (C. Richards and

Knap of Howar

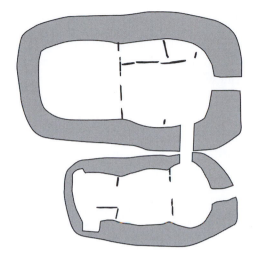

5 m

Calf of Eday

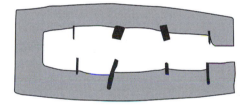

5 m

Knowe of Ramsay

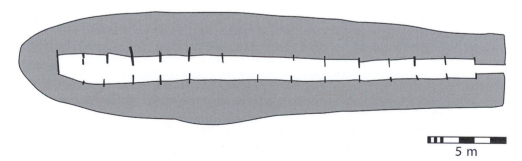

5 m

Figure 2.10 Plan of the stone houses at Knap of Howar, Orkney, compared with two chambered cairns featuring comparable divisions of space. Information from A. Ritchie (1983) and Davidson and Henshall (1989).

R. Jones 2016). A new study suggests that in fact their histories overlapped (Bayliss et al. 2017b).

These monuments can also be studied on a larger scale, but this work often focuses on the evidence for regional variation. Minor architectural details can easily assume a life of their own until any wider patterns are obscured. This is particularly true when megalithic tombs are considered one class at a time, for it presupposes that prehistoric people intended to build particular 'styles' of monuments in the first place. That is by no means obvious. Two issues seem to be particularly important: the relationship between the external appearance of different tombs and the organisation of the features found within them; and the structural sequences that led to these monuments assuming their present forms.

The first point needs careful consideration, for it is clear that there is no consistent relationship between the shape of the mound or cairn and the layout of any structures inside or underneath it. Long mounds, oval mounds, and round mounds all cover similar features and the outward appearance of these monuments disguises the fact they might have achieved the same form by different means (Fig. 2.11).

The second point highlights an important difference between Irish monuments and those in Britain. Apart from portal tombs, the earliest style of monument in Ireland was probably the 'court cairn'. It has this name because the internal chambers are approached through a curvilinear walled enclosure or 'court' that remained open to the elements (Figs. 2.12 and 2.13). Although many monuments have been damaged, these features were normally associated with long mounds or cairns. A recent project dates them between about 3800 and 3500 BC, but there are some outliers (Schulting et al. 2012). The most obvious characteristic of these sites is their diversity, and yet it seems that many of them had been constructed in a single operation or developed over a restricted period of time. The mound or cairn normally took the same form, but there are variations in every other element. They concern the nature of the court itself – it could occur singly or in pairs, and individual examples could be more or less enclosed; they might concern the number of chambers and their relationship to one another; or they might be related to differences of scale or accessibility between the separate parts of these tombs. The reasons for their creation are rarely discussed. Powell (2005) makes the interesting suggestion that these different configurations reflect the complex patterns of kinship and alliance between different segments of the local population. The tomb plans with their bewildering variety of chambers acted like a genealogy, expressing the connections between different groups of people and enshrining those arrangements in a lasting architectural form. If so, then a single tomb might represent more than the individual household. Rather, the combinations of different courts and chambers might provide an idealised image of social organisation across a wider landscape.

Figure 2.11 Long cairn at Camster, northern Scotland, incorporating the positions of earlier circular monuments. Photograph: Aaron Watson.

In Britain, there are other problems in approaching megalithic tombs, or their equivalents constructed in less durable materials. It has been easy to suppose that mounds and cairns were meant to contain burial chambers in the way that seems to have happened in Irish court tombs. That was not always the case, and, pace Kinnes (1992), it is difficult to identify any overarching scheme. These structures had certain clearly defined elements, but not all of them were present on every site. They include:

- An earthen barrow or cairn which could be rectangular, oval, trapezoidal, or circular (elongated monuments were usually higher towards the east);
- A monumental forecourt or facade in front of the entrance;
- Ditches or quarries which extend along the sides of long barrows and sometimes enclose the entire structure. In the case of oval or round barrows they extend around the perimeter but may have been broken by an entrance;
- A chamber or chambers which are approached through the forecourt or located in the side of the structure (they include the settings of split tree trunks described earlier);
- A blocking of timber or stone introduced when a monument was closed.

There are also ditched or fenced enclosures with a similar ground plan where the other elements do not occur. In the literature they are called 'mortuary enclosures'.

Nearly all these elements can be found on their own (Fig. 2.14). Thus wooden 'mortuary houses' are recorded as isolated structures, or they may be recognised inside open enclosures. There are timber forecourts which were not associated with mounds or burials, and there are mounds which may

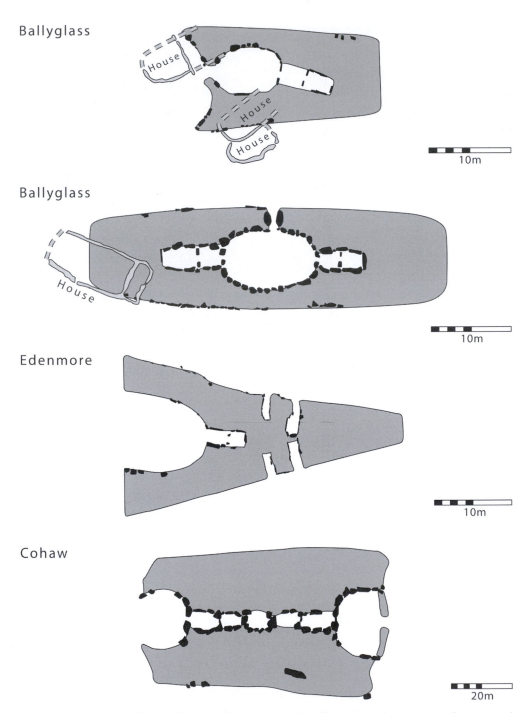

Figure 2.12 Plans of four Irish court tombs, illustrating the variety of court and chamber plans. Those at Ballyglass overlie older houses. Information from ÓNualláin (1972) and De Valera (1960).

Figure 2.13 The court tomb at Creevykeel, in the west of Ireland. Photograph: Aaron Watson.

never have included any human remains. The classic form of the long barrow could encapsulate the positions of older structures, including round barrows or round cairns, and the entire scheme may have been conceived on a modest scale, or it might have required a greater amount of labour. In the south these monuments were usually sealed or allowed to decay, whilst those in northern England and eastern Scotland were often set on fire (Kinnes 1992). There never was an ideal conception of how that sequence should end. Rather, there were many local variations which may have been influenced by the status of particular individuals or communities.

With all these qualifications in mind, there is a dominant pattern in Britain which contrasts with what has been said about monuments in Ireland (Fig. 2.15). Whereas court tombs exhibit a wide variety of ground plans, their architecture makes use of a few recurrent features that were combined in different ways. This process seems to have taken place over a limited time and did not involve any drastic changes to the configuration of the monuments. The British evidence suggests that individual examples developed from many different starting points. In this case monuments were modified, extended, and even changed their shapes, and parts of the structures may have been replaced. The only consistent feature of the larger sites was that in the end some of them assumed the same form.

It follows that these constructions were not an integral part of such sites until a final phase. In the case of non–megalithic long barrows it seems unlikely

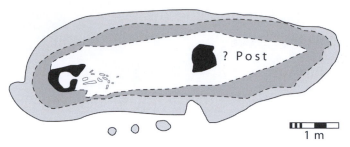

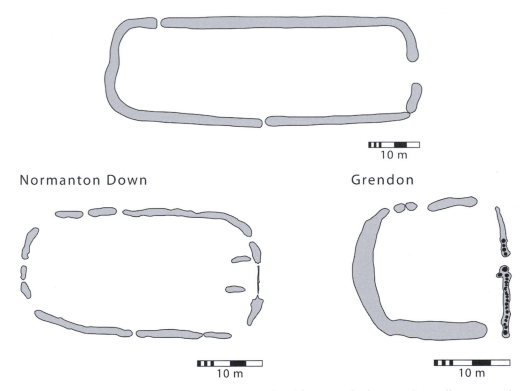

Figure 2.14 Mortuary structures and related features which are traditionally associated with long barrows but can also be found in isolation. The structure at St Albans was probably an isolated 'mortuary house'; Dorchester on Thames features an open 'mortuary enclosure'. A similar structure was recorded as a standing earthwork on Normanton Down. The monument at Grendon resembles the forecourt of a barrow, but is not associated with a mound. Information from Niblett (2001), Whittle et al. (1992), Vatcher (1961), and Gibson and McCormick (1999).

Street House

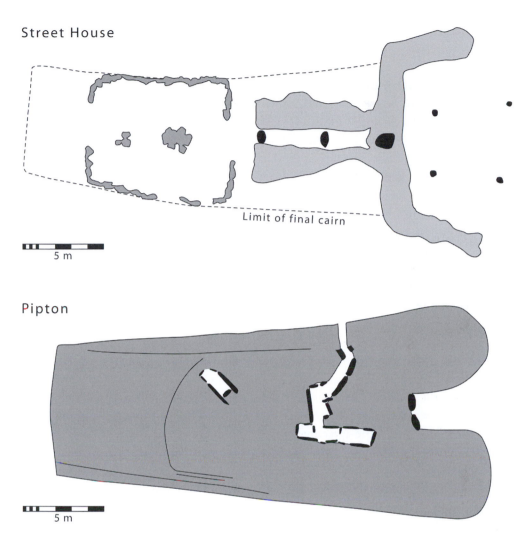

Limit of final cairn

5 m

Pipton

5 m

Figure 2.15 The long cairns at Street House, north-east England and Pipton, South Wales. The cairn at Street House overlay three older structures: a square enclosure, a 'mortuary house', and a timber forecourt. The long cairn at Pipton seems to have covered a variety of older structures with their own burial chambers. Information from Vyner (1984) and Savory (1956).

that the 'chambers' were covered by mounds until those sites went out of use. Otherwise barrows or cairns may have been constructed at the same time as the stone chambers in order to ensure their stability. In each case the mounds sealed the features created during earlier phases and cut them off from the living. It may be why the building of these earthworks could happen during a phase when such structures were set on fire. This was not a cremation rite in the way that is often claimed (Kinnes 1992). Like other Neolithic monuments, the use of these places concluded by people burning them and covering them over. It happened particularly often in north-east England and eastern

Scotland, but in western Britain the equivalent was the closing of megalithic tombs with a deposit of rubble (Darvill 2004: ch. 7). Although the construction of long mounds and related monuments was spread over at least three hundred years, there is little to suggest that individual sites lasted for more than a few generations, and sometimes they went out of commission even sooner (Bayliss and Whittle 2007). It raises an intriguing problem. Until comparatively recently long mounds and causewayed enclosures were considered as the typical monuments of the Early or Middle Neolithic phases in Britain, and it was assumed that they were built and used over a long period of time. In fact barrows of strikingly similar types were not built simultaneously, and many were employed over surprisingly short periods. As a result their histories did not overlap.

It is important to emphasise the complexity of the situation, for it has been customary to compare the forms of long mounds and long cairns with those of Neolithic dwellings which share their rectilinear ground plans. This raises several problems. If the configuration of these barrows was intended to recall Continental longhouses occupied many generations before the settlement of Britain and Ireland, it would not explain why oval and circular monuments were constructed at the same time and why mounds of all these shapes were associated with the same kinds of structures. A closer comparison might be with the 'halls' and other large buildings excavated in recent years; they could even share the same monumental facades (J. S. Thomas 2015a). The connection becomes even more apparent with the discovery of exceptionally large timber buildings in Scotland. The longest at 30 m or more recalls the dimensions of mortuary monuments in the same region. Perhaps the strongest link between the living and the dead was with such specialised buildings rather than ordinary dwellings. It is unlikely that everyone had the same status in life or in death, and the evidence of human remains suggests that comparatively few people were commemorated.

SETTLEMENTS AND TOMBS

Why was it that such buildings suggested the appearance of the tombs? A useful starting point is the work of Lévi-Strauss (1983) on what he calls 'house societies'. He is most concerned with kinship organisation and the emergence of hierarchies, but his work is particularly important because it shows how the idea of the 'house' extends to the occupants of the building and the members of a wider community. It is in this sense that the term is used in a paper by Helms (2004), who discusses the different worldviews of mobile hunter gatherers and early farmers. One might almost say that it is by the construction of houses, both real and metaphorical, that particular groups distinguish themselves from others and define their membership. Their composition is less fluid than that of hunter gatherer groups and is maintained for a longer period of time. Such concerns are particularly relevant when people are exploiting unfamiliar terrain, and the new arrangement may reflect the labour requirements of early agriculture. Perhaps that is one reason why houses are such a conspicuous feature at the beginning of the Neolithic period (Sheridan 2013).

A pertinent observation comes from a paper by Carsten and Hugh-Jones (1995) introducing an edited volume devoted to Lévi-Strauss's ideas. They observe how common it is for houses to be regarded as living creatures and thought of in the same terms as human beings, who are born, grow old, and die. Like people, houses have biographies of their own.

> Houses are far from being static material structures. They have animate qualities; they are endowed with spirits or souls, and are imagined in terms of the human body … Given its living qualities … it comes as no surprise that natural processes associated with people, animals or plants may also apply to the house. (Carsten and Hugh-Jones 1995: 37)

Perhaps the reason why the British and Irish evidence poses so many problems is that the histories of the buildings in which people had lived were reflected in their relationship with mortuary monuments. There is an obvious contrast between the regions where houses are common and those in which they are rare. In lowland Britain, where pit deposits are particularly frequent, the artefact assemblage occasionally contains human bones. It seems possible that relics circulated in the same manner as the objects with which they were found. That is consistent with the evidence from mortuary monuments which not only included the remains of complete corpses but could also feature certain body parts to the exclusion of others (Whittle and Wysocki 1998: 151–8; Ray and J. S. Thomas 2018: 106–22, 130–40, and 201–24). Although deposits of pottery are associated with some of these monuments, many excavated mounds in the south provide little evidence of portable material culture.

The preservation and circulation of human bones was a particular feature of southern England, although it seems to have extended across a wider area. It is here that there is most evidence for the deployment of unburnt corpses which might be arranged according to age, gender, or different parts of the body. Artefacts are not common at most of these monuments. It seems possible that the residues of older settlements were permitted to decay and were dispersed in the same manner as human remains (Pollard 2004). In Ireland, where houses are much more common, the residues of domestic occupation might have been deposited in tombs together with the remains of the dead. In this case a few of the bodies were burnt, but there is little to suggest that this was the principal mortuary rite, as radiocarbon dating has shown that some of the cremations associated with court tombs were Early Bronze Age secondary burials (Schulting et al. 2012; Cooney 2014).

A high proportion of the Irish houses had been destroyed by fire. Although this might have been a result of warfare, the evidence is ambiguous. In a sense the careers of particular people and the histories of their houses were the same. The house was a living creature and its life had to be extinguished at the same time as the human body. That may be why, in Ireland, what are apparently domestic assemblages accompanied the dead person to the tomb – they might even have been the contents of a settlement. By contrast, in southern England, the remains of settlement sites were dispersed along with human remains. The bones were deposited in tombs where finds of artefacts are uncommon.

This is not to imply that formal burials were restricted to monuments. Two of the earliest radiocarbon dates for Neolithic activity in southern England are for isolated inhumations, one at Blackwall on the Thames floodplain (S. Coles, Ford, and Taylor 2008) and the other at Winchester (Lewis and Preston 2012). The Blackheath grave contained a flint knife and is dated to 4230–3970 BC. It has been discussed in some detail, but the example found in Wessex, which has a date of 4082–3971 BC, has attracted less attention. Flat graves of the same kind are recorded from other places and are not uncommon on those projects where unaccompanied human remains are submitted for radiocarbon dating. The majority are assigned to the Middle Neolithic period, when long barrows and causewayed enclosures eventually went out of use. Their frequency has probably been underestimated. Cremation burials are also represented, but they are rare.

The same applies to the human remains found in caves. It happened in areas where mortuary monuments are uncommon but is also represented in regions in which such structures are well known. Many of them were chance finds and were not recorded in much detail; in this case the deposits were often disturbed and out of context. Again radiocarbon dating provides the vital information. In this case the deposition of unburnt human remains took place discontinuously and the Early and Middle Neolithic phases feature particularly strongly in the results of recent research. Those in north-east England are dated between 3600 and 3300 BC (Leach 2015).

DEVELOPMENTS IN THE SOUTH: CAUSEWAYED ENCLOSURES AND RELATED MONUMENTS

It has long been recognised that mortuary monuments can cluster around the positions of a distinctive kind of enclosure. It is an accident of history that the characteristics of the British Neolithic were first defined by the excavation of a causewayed enclosure, so that the earlier part of this period took its name from Windmill Hill, an earthwork on the Wessex chalk (Whittle, Pollard, and Grigson 1999). Now it is apparent that monuments of this form have a limited distribution across the two islands and were not among the first monuments built there. Rather, their use on any scale commenced about 3650 BC (Whittle, Healy, and Bayliss 2011: ch. 14). Many were short-lived. They are often found in southern and midland England, but are rarer in the north, in Scotland, and in Wales (Ray and J. S. Thomas 2018: 140–51). Similar enclosures have only recently been identified in Ireland, although some may have taken rather different forms from the other sites, and that at Magheraboy which produced some exceptionally early dates now appears to be contemporary with the remaining examples (Carlin and Cooney 2017). They include the newly identified enclosures at Hughstown and Spinans Hill (O'Brien and O'Driscoll 2017: ch. 7). Another enclosure at Kilshane has an unusually late date of 3645–3390 BC and was associated with the bones of forty to fifty cattle (Fitzgerald 2006). It has been interpreted as a henge but lacks the circular ground plan of that kind of monument.

The construction method was distinctive (Fig. 2.16). Causewayed enclosures are so called because they are defined by interrupted ditches. It is not always clear whether the positions of the causeways correspond to gaps in the bank, but it is obvious that this was more than a technique of construction. Some of the enclosures are approximately circular or oval, but this is not always the case. A study of the English sites draws together much of the research on earthworks of this kind (Oswald, Dyer, and M. Barber 2001).

Two points need making at the outset. These monuments were first identified from surface remains and were subsequently recognised on air photographs, but there are other structures which may have been closely related to them. They are found in western Britain and are typified by the excavated enclosures at Carn Brea (Mercer 1981a) and Helman Tor (Mercer 1997) in Cornwall. They were built on granite and were defined by drystone walls as well as earthworks. They are of the same date as the more conventional sites, but took a different form. Often the perimeter extended between a series of prominent natural outcrops, and at Carn Brea the rubble walls were interrupted at intervals and the entire complex was bounded by an earthwork bank and a discontinuous ditch. Similar monuments have been claimed in north-west England and the west of Ireland, but remain unexcavated.

On the Continent, palisaded enclosures are known whose perimeters were broken in a similar manner (Whittle, Healy, and Bayliss 2011: 878–85). An enclosure at Orsett in the Thames Estuary had both an earthwork and a fence (Hedges and D. Buckley 1978), but on the important Irish site of Tullahedy a conspicuous glacial mound was enclosed by a discontinuous palisade associated with the remains of several timber buildings (Cleary and Kelleher 2011). It was associated with almost seventy arrowheads and over a hundred stone axes. There may have been a similar monument at Knowth in the Boyne Valley, where two concentric palisades were found with the remains of wooden houses (G. Eogan 1994a: 291–327).

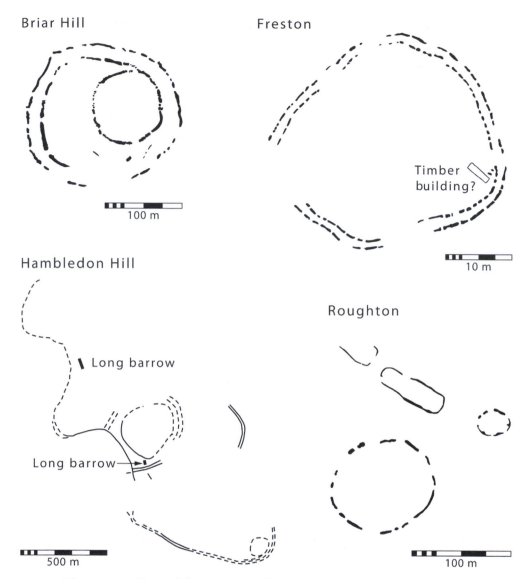

Figure 2.16 Plans of four causewayed enclosures in England, illustrating their relationship to other earthworks. Information from Oswald, Dyer, and Barber (2001).

It has always been supposed that causewayed enclosures and their equivalents had a single function. That is very doubtful. Their Continental counterparts went through a lengthy history extending from the late Linearbandkeramik to the Copper Age: a period of well over a thousand years (Whittle, Healy, and Bayliss 2011: ch. 15; Shennan 2018: 146–50). Whilst the earthwork perimeter retained its characteristic form, the sites seem to have been used in different ways from one period to another. There is evidence for regional variation. Individual examples extend along a continuum from enclosed settlements or even hillforts to ceremonial centres. Some sites were associated with buildings, pits, and specialised deposits of artefacts, but others were almost empty. It comes as no surprise that the same should be true in Britain. Thus a walled enclosure like Carn Brea was associated with wooden houses, defences, and areas of cultivated ground (Mercer 1981a), whilst the earthwork monument at Etton in eastern England contained placed deposits of artefacts, animal bones, and human remains (Pryor 1998). Although it was especially well preserved, it did not include any buildings. The site was liable to flood and would probably have been inaccessible for part of the year. In the same way the natural mound enclosed by the palisade at Tullahedy was cut off from its surroundings by an area of wetland (Cleary and Kelleher 2011).

This does not imply that individual enclosures in Britain and Ireland were either ceremonial centres or settlements, although opinion has certainly oscillated between these two extremes. There are grounds for caution. They date from the period when substantial houses were no longer built, and even at monuments from which structures seem to have been absent the excavated material has a similar composition to the finds from domestic sites. It seems as if the pottery is in the same styles, and a study of the worked flint from these monuments failed to identify any features which distinguished it from the assemblages in settlements (Saville 2002). A similar argument applies to the animal bones from these locations (Parmenter, E. Johnson, and Outram 2015). Both settlements and enclosures can be associated with pits containing carefully selected groups of cultural material. Each provides abundant evidence of burning, and human bones are recorded from enclosures as well as the places where people lived. There are some exotic items from the earthwork monuments, but they can be found elsewhere. The main distinction between causewayed enclosures and open settlements is the greater formality with which artefacts and other items were deployed (J. S. Thomas 2016).

This had several aspects. There was the formality that was inherent in the very design of these earthworks. They comprised one or more circuits of bank and ditch interrupted at regular intervals by causeways and sometimes by more formal entrances. The perimeter was entirely permeable. There were individual monuments with several concentric earthworks where different activities may have taken place in different areas, and this has been claimed at Windmill Hill where the character of the deposits seems to have changed as one moved towards the innermost enclosure, but even here these separate components developed over a period of time (Whittle, Pollard, and Grigson 1999). It appears that the outer part of the monument was associated with deposits of cultural material and human remains, mainly those of infants. Craft production, butchery, and the deposition of meat joints were associated with the next sector of the enclosure, whilst it was the innermost space that was most obviously linked with the domestic world. At Etton, which had only one ditch, the internal space was divided in half. One part included a series of deposits associated with the activities of the living, whilst the other contained imported artefacts and burnt human and animal bones (Pryor 1998).

The enclosure at Etton is revealing in another way, for the excavator has questioned the conventional assumption that this monument was conceived as an enclosure in the way that archaeologists had supposed. He suggests that it is better thought of as an arrangement of separate pits, not all of which were dug or maintained simultaneously. Rather than forming a continuous (or discontinuous) bank, the excavated soil was spread around the rims of these features to provide a vantage point from which people could view their contents. The separate pits or ditch segments contained a wide variety of deposits which had been carefully placed there, including human skulls, meat joints, axeheads, and complete pots. They could be laid out in formal patterns then covered over. Individual sections of the perimeter were repeatedly recut, allowing the original offerings to be inspected and further material to be added.

Certain monuments changed their form and character over time. They may have been rebuilt at a late stage in their development, and it was then that most of the causeways in their ditches were removed, creating a continuous barrier. It seems possible that the banks were reconstructed with vertical outer walls or timber revetments, and formal entrances may also have been established. This has not been observed at many sites, but it does raise the possibility that some of the earthworks were changed into defensible enclosures. It may be no accident that among them were Hambledon Hill and Crickley Hill, both of which occupied positions that were reused as Iron Age hillforts (Whittle, Healy, and Bayliss 2011: 716–19), and that examples in Ireland were originally investigated as later prehistoric defended sites (O'Brien and O'Driscoll 2017). It is particularly interesting that several of the English enclosures include unusual concentrations of arrowheads, suggesting that they had been attacked. The bodies of two men who had been killed by arrows were found in the ditch of the Stepleton enclosure at Hambledon Hill (Mercer and Healy 2008: 760). There may have been a high level of violence during this period, but the evidence has often been overlooked (Schulting and Wysocki 2005). It is certainly consistent with the injuries shown by human bones found in other contexts in Britain. A recent study suggested that between 4 and 8 per cent of the Neolithic skulls examined showed signs of injuries. Most had healed, but in 6 per cent of the cases this had not happened (Schulting and Fibiger 2014).

Just as causewayed ditches could be rebuilt as defensive earthworks, entire enclosures could be duplicated. There are sites where at least two of these monuments were built close to one another or even side by side. Examples include Hambledon Hill and Rybury, where they are located some distance apart, and Hembury, Court Hill, Fornham All Saints, and Etton, where the two structures were adjacent to each other (Oswald, Dyer, and M. Barber 2001). Only at Hambledon Hill is there evidence that they were built at different times and had different contents (Mercer and Healy 2008: ch. 4 and table 11.5). Enclosures could also extend their area, and Oswald, Dyer, and Barber (2001) have suggested that a number of examples with several concentric circuits may have developed over a significant period of time; this view was based on surface observation, but since they put it forward their interpretation has been supported by radiocarbon dating. In most cases enclosures seem to have been enlarged, and, as it happened, they might assume a more regular ground plan. These authors comment on a number of examples which look approximately circular to anyone inside them or encountering them from a distance. At the same time some enclosures seem to have been constructed to command views in particular directions. That certainly applied to a pair of neighbouring monuments on the Isle of Sheppey at the entrance to the Thames Estuary (M. Allen, Lewis, and C. Ellis 2008).

Early fieldwork at causewayed enclosures was concerned with investigating their credentials as the first Neolithic settlements in lowland England. Although they produced what seemed to be 'domestic' assemblages, it soon became apparent that there were too many anomalies for this interpretation to be warranted. Instead of the general scatter of animal bones that might be found at a living site, substantial meat joints were committed to the ground and sometimes entire animals were buried there. As well as the remains of animals there were human bones, sometimes burials but more often disarticulated fragments similar to those associated with long barrows. All this material was placed in the ground with some deliberation, and normally it was carefully covered over. It seemed more likely that these deposits resulted from specialised events which may have included episodes of feasting, the sacrifice of animals, offerings of food, and the celebration of the dead. There is even evidence of opium poppy from the enclosure at Etton (Pryor 1998: ch. 10). These ideas received powerful support from excavation at Hambledon Hill which showed that in the enclosure ditches there had been a large number of human skulls, mostly those of young people (Mercer and Healy 2008: ch. 7).

Similar anomalies soon became apparent among the excavated material from these monuments. At Hambledon Hill there was processed grain which must have been introduced from outside (Mercer and Healy 2008: 469–76). At Windmill Hill there were few large vessels suitable for storage and many small bowls that could be used for serving food and drink (Howard 1981). Similarly, the presence of non-local artefacts raised an interesting problem. From the early years of the excavation of Windmill Hill it had been apparent that stone axes from distant regions of Britain were distributed on and around the site, and for that reason the enclosure, and others like it, were identified as nodal points in a Neolithic 'axe trade'. The argument was illogical since these objects had been brought to these sites but never left them again. Closer attention to their contexts showed that they had been deposited there together with the other material discussed in this section. At Etton, it even seems as if they were destroyed by working them down and placing the resulting fragments in pits together with burnt bone (Pryor 1998: 260–8 and 271–2). The walled enclosure at Carn Brea may have been linked with the production or distribution of pottery and axeheads in the surrounding area, and what may be a similar site on Carrock Fell in north-west England was located on a mountain top close to a Neolithic axe quarry (Fell and Davis 1988; Pearson and Topping 2002). Such connections made it even less likely that these were ordinary settlements. Perhaps they were aggregation sites where public events took place.

There are good reasons for accepting this view. The development of causewayed enclosures happened during a period which saw significant changes in the nature of material culture. After an initial phase in which pottery had taken a similar form throughout most parts of Britain and Ireland, there are the first signs of regional diversity, reflected by the adoption of more local styles of decoration. There were also axes from a variety of distant sources. If the artefact assemblage seems to have been more diverse, so was the population associated with these monuments. Mike Richards (2004) has shown that the bones from individual tombs show less varied dietary signatures from those in the enclosure complex at Hambledon Hill (see also M. Richards 2008). The people who were represented there had lived in a wider range of environments or engaged in different methods of food production.

In recent years more attention has been paid to the setting of these monuments. It is clear that whilst some enclosures included enormous collections of Neolithic artefacts, they were actually set apart from the ordinary settlements of the same period. They might be located in isolated positions towards the margins of the settled landscape and could sometimes be seen from a distance. A few sites commanded an extensive view, and others were intervisible with the places where flint axes were made, yet environmental evidence suggests that certain examples had been located in woodland clearings (K. Thomas 1982). Far from being the 'central places' of this period, they occupied neutral locations in between the main concentrations of population. That even applies to an enormous monument complex like Hambledon Hill.

One result of fieldwork in the vicinity of causewayed enclosures has been the recognition that the distribution of pits and artefact scatters can extend beyond the limits of these earthworks. This is most obvious at Etton in eastern England where a large number of pits have been found. They have the same range of contents as the deposits associated with the enclosures themselves, although others date from the Late Neolithic period (Medlycott 2011: 9). At Husbands Bosworth in the east Midlands there was a possible 'mortuary house' of the kind associated with barrows (R. Buckley and George 2003: fig. 3). At Eton in the Thames Valley extensive and well-preserved midden deposits have been discovered in between the sites of two causewayed enclosures, but in this case they may predate the monuments altogether (T. Allen et al. 2013). Perhaps they result from assemblies that had taken place well before these earthworks were built.

DEVELOPMENTS IN THE NORTH: CURSUS MONUMENTS, BANK BARROWS, AND ROUND BARROWS

Long Enclosures

Events took a different course in northern Britain and, to some extent, in Ireland. In both regions considerable rectangular buildings played a significant role as domestic dwellings and possibly as public buildings (Fig. 2.17). They included the timber 'halls' discussed on page 45. Their siting is particularly revealing. The excavated examples at Claish (G. Barclay, Brophy, and MacGregor 2002), Littleour (G. Barclay and Maxwell 1998), and Carsie Mains (Brophy and G. Barclay 2004) are all located within a short distance of enormous earthwork monuments.

Both Claish and Littleour are close to an exceptionally long mound of the kind which is sometimes described as a bank barrow. In each case that earthwork seems to have developed out of one or more burial mounds of conventional proportions. The Auchenlaich long mound, which is close to the hall at Claish, contained a megalithic chamber (G. Barclay, Brophy, and MacGregor 2002), whilst detailed survey at Cleaven Dyke near to Littleour suggests that it began as a conventional burial mound which was gradually extended until it eventually ran for 2 km. Excavation suggests that a developed stage in the sequence can be dated to the early or mid-fourth millennium BC (G. Barclay and Maxwell 1998).

The surviving earthwork at Cleaven Dyke poses another problem. For most of its length it consists of a central mound in between two widely spaced ditches, but towards one end those ditches may have defined the limits of an open avenue or enclosure. That raises a question of definition, for elongated mounds of this kind are usually classified as bank barrows, whilst extended rectilinear enclosures are generally known as cursuses (Loveday 2006). Cleaven Dyke is not the only composite monument of this kind, and field survey in a different region of Britain has shown that these two classes of field monument are closely associated with one another (Bradley 1983). They are based on the same principle of extending a rectangular or oval monument on a significant scale.

Are there similar indications from other areas? With the possible exceptions of the bank barrows at Stanwell in the Thames Valley (Lewis et al. 2010) and Scorton in the north–east (Speed 2009), none of the English monuments seems to have had a timber precursor, nor have any post-defined monuments been identified. Other bank barrows are found along the east coast and extend into the southern Pennines, the Thames Valley, and Wessex, but none attains

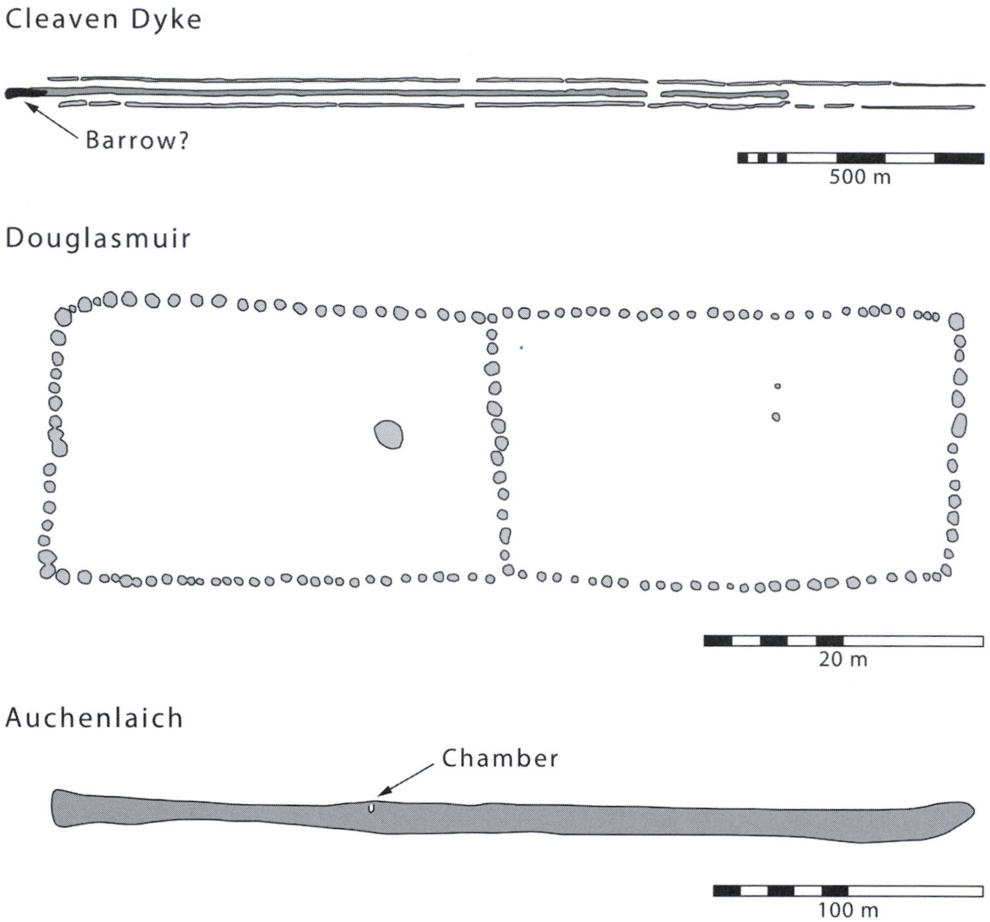

Cleaven Dyke

Barrow?

500 m

Douglasmuir

20 m

Auchenlaich

Chamber

100 m

Figure 2.17 An elongated timber enclosure at Douglasmuir, together with outline plans of Cleaven Dyke and the bank barrow at Auchenlaich. All three sites are in eastern or central Scotland. Information from Kenrick (1995), Barclay and Maxwell (1998), and Barclay, Brophy, and MacGregor (2002).

the remarkable length of the principal Scottish examples. The Irish evidence is even more limited. Although a few promising candidates have been recognised, the cursuses in that country have not been firmly dated (Corlett 2014). This is significant as their characteristics overlap with those of the ditched roadways leading to important sites used in the Iron Age, like Tara and Loughcrew. That might not apply to the remaining candidates which occur in seeming isolation and may be of Neolithic date.

The chronology of cursuses and bank barrows is very important, as it seems as if the idea of elongated timber and earthwork monuments originated in the north of Britain during the currency of Neolithic halls (J. S. Thomas 2006; Millican 2016; Brophy 2016). They experienced a similar cycle of deliberate burning and rebuilding. This is a feature which they share with domestic dwellings in Ireland. Major earthwork cursuses seem to be later in date and most were probably constructed between about 3650 and 3350 BC (A. Barclay and Bayliss 1999).

Although the English cursuses may have originated after those in the north, they eventually grew to enormous proportions. In their final form they consisted of elongated enclosures with an internal bank and an external ditch. These earthworks were occasionally breached by causeways, but were rarely provided with formal entrances at the terminals. Individual examples incorporated existing structures in their paths – long barrows, round barrows, or 'mortuary enclosures' of various sizes – and they might also be aligned on earlier earthworks. In the Ouse Valley in eastern England Malim (2000) suggests that they were associated with small territories and distributed at intervals of about 6 km. It was relatively common for a cursus to lead towards (or extend from) an older rectilinear enclosure or even a long barrow, but other arrangements have been recognised. At Springfield close to the Thames Estuary there was a timber circle in this position (D. Buckley, Hedges, and N. Brown 2001).

Some cursuses were built in comparative isolation, but there are also instances in which they seem to have been constructed incrementally, as one of these enclosures was added on to the end of another. Alternatively, they could run side by side, they might converge on certain focal points, or their positions may have overlapped. The two largest cursus complexes illustrate some of these patterns (Fig. 2.18). At Rudston in north-east England no fewer than five of them focused on the tallest monolith in Britain. The terminal of one of the monuments was enlarged to resemble a long barrow. Taken together, these cursuses ran for about 10 km (Stoertz 1997: 25–30).

The other major complex is known as the Dorset Cursus in southern England, although, properly speaking, it consisted of two, and possibly three, such monuments built end to end (Barrett, Bradley, and M. Green 1991: 35–58). Again their combined length is 10 km. It would have taken half a million worker hours to complete the entire structure. They incorporated burial mounds in their path, and further monuments of the same kind were aligned on the ends of these earthworks. As at Rudston, one of the terminals was built on a massive scale, as if to echo the characteristic form of two adjacent long barrows. At its northern limit, the Dorset Cursus ran up to another mound which was subsequently lengthened to form a kind of bank barrow. An elongated enclosure was built alongside it (M. Green 2000: fig. 37). The earliest section of the Cursus was aligned on the midwinter sun as it set behind a long mound incorporated in its path. According to radiocarbon dates, this was one of the last examples to be built, most probably between about 3360 and 3030 BC.

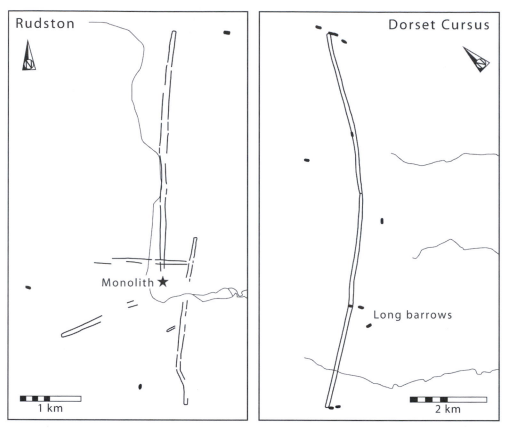

Figure 2.18 Outline plans of the Rudston Cursus complex, north-east England, and the Dorset Cursus, Wessex, showing their relationship to watercourses and long barrows. Information from Stoerz (1997) and Barrett, Bradley, and Green (1991).

Such monuments are interpreted as avenues or processional ways, although it is not known whether the construction of the earthworks monumentalised an existing path or represented a new development (Fig. 2.19). In the same way, because certain examples led between mortuary mounds, it may be that such routes were intended for the dead rather than the living. Human bones have been found in the excavation of cursuses, and the idea that they were intended primarily for the deceased might also account for the interplay between these monuments, which are open structures, and bank barrows, which are solid mounds. It would certainly help to explain why there were so few points of access to the interior. There has been little discussion of the fact that these putative paths were blocked at both ends. That would surely have impeded access, and yet it was only from inside the enclosures that anyone would have been aware of the alignments they created. One possibility is that these structures were originally open and that, like many of the long barrows and long cairns described in this chapter, they were closed during a subsequent phase. In

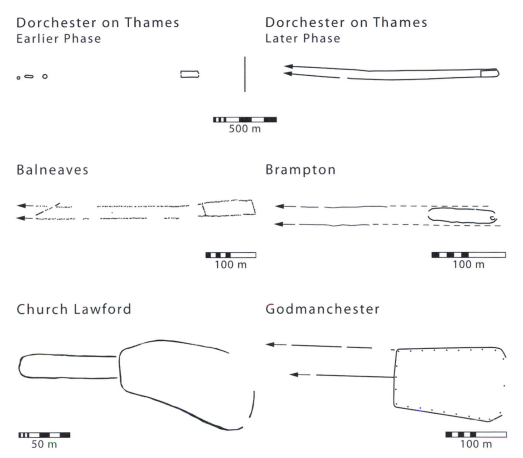

Figure 2.19 Plans of five cursus monuments and the enclosures associated with their terminals. The plan of Dorchester on Thames summarises its sequence of construction. Balneaves is in eastern Scotland and the other sites are in the English Midlands. Arrows indicate that the earthworks extended further. Information from Bradley and Chambers (1988), Brophy (2016), Malim (1999), Palmer (2009), and McAvoy (2000).

their original form they might have resembled a so-called 'avenue' at Raunds (J. Harding and Healy 2007), but they were constructed on a larger scale.

Celestial alignments like that in Dorset are uncommon, but have been recognised at Dorchester on Thames where they were associated with both the summer and winter solstices (Bradley and Chambers 1988; Gill Hey pers. comm.). Similar claims have been made for a cursus monument at Godmanchester in eastern England, but its main characteristic is that it led into a large trapezoidal enclosure with dates between about 3900 and 3300 BC (McAvoy 2000). There was a similar monument at Church Lawford in the west Midlands where the enclosure was associated with a sherd of Early Neolithic pottery and two radiocarbon dates. They did not agree with one another, but both fell in the mid- or late fourth millennium BC (Palmer 2009: 22–31 and 56–9).

Fieldwork has shown that most cursus monuments and bank barrows were integrated with features of the local topography. Two particular arrangements are widely recognised. The first is where they extended across valleys so that their terminals were visible from one another and commanded an extensive view over the lower ground. Alternatively, they cut across the contours so that any people travelling along them would have experienced a sequence of changing vistas at different points in their journey. It is not always obvious how much of the surrounding landscape would have been clear of trees, but pollen analysis undertaken close to the two largest monuments, the Dorset Cursus and the Rudston complex, produced unexpected evidence of an open landscape (French et al. 2007: ch. 2; Bush 1988).

A second arrangement is perhaps more common. This is where the configuration of cursuses or related monuments seems to follow the course of a nearby river. Sometimes the same principle extends to the siting of several monuments within the same small area. The flowing water might have provided a metaphor for life itself: an association that is found in many societies (C. Richards 1996). In Britain the only direct evidence for a connection of this kind comes from ceramics, axeheads, and human bones deposited in the Thames during the Middle Neolithic period (Lamdin-Whymark 2008). Along its banks there are a number of cursuses.

For many years such cursuses were dated to the Late Neolithic period, and even now it is difficult to appreciate the implications of the new chronology. Two points are of fundamental importance. The first is that linear monuments of the kind considered here may have originated in northern Britain, where the earliest examples were probably wooden structures, rather than the earthwork monuments that are more familiar in the south (J. S. Thomas 2006). The sites which attracted most attention from archaeologists were among the last ones to be built. It is small wonder that they have been so difficult to interpret. In lowland England they are associated with long barrows and allied monuments, but their northern prototypes seem to form part of a still broader pattern which had extended to other large timber buildings. A second point is even more important. Cursus monuments and bank barrows are unlike other monuments in being an entirely insular development.

Round Barrows

The round barrows in the north raise even more problems. Again the final form of these mounds provides no clues to the structures concealed beneath them; nor do they shed any light on the rituals that were carried out there. There are several points to consider. Many of these earthworks were built over several phases, and the prominent mounds that survive today can be secondary additions to a smaller monument, as was the case at Duggleby Howe on the Yorkshire Wolds (A. Gibson and Bayliss 2009). Another complication is that some of the Neolithic 'round barrows' excavated in the same area during the nineteenth century have proved to be only the most prominent parts of denuded long barrows. This has been established by fieldwork and is also apparent from air photography (Stoertz 1997). To add to the confusion, in this region the distribution of Neolithic round barrows largely avoided that of long barrows (J. Harding 1996). To some extent the same phenomenon occurred in and around the Upper Thames Valley (Benson and Whittle 2007: fig. 15.2).

In fact the earliest features found beneath the northern round mounds are strikingly reminiscent of those associated with long barrows. They include pairs of D-shaped postholes which probably held split timbers, and the monument at Callis Wold even included a timber facade like those associated with those monuments (Fig. 2.20; Coombs 1976). Still more important, these structures were commonly set on fire, so that early accounts of both long barrows and round barrows refer to 'cremation trenches'. The few radiocarbon dates for these structures suggest that they were in use at the same time, and the human remains associated with both kinds of earthwork were treated in the same ways.

By the middle of fourth millennium BC there are indications of a new development as intact bodies were buried beneath round barrows, accompanied by a selection of grave goods. That contrasts with their general absence during earlier phases. The main items were flint arrowheads and ceramic vessels, which could be accompanied by animal bones. They might be laid out on the surface, as happened at Callis Wold, but at the best studied of these sites, Duggleby Howe, they were buried in sequence within a deep chalk-cut shaft (A. Gibson and Bayliss 2009). It remained open for a considerable period of time and the pit was only covered by a mound long afterwards. Then further individuals were buried on the site.

The sequence is especially important as it sheds light on other discoveries from poorly documented excavations. The earliest burials at this site date to about 3500 BC and were associated with worked flints and decorated pottery. Duggleby Howe can be compared with the barrow at Wold Newton with a date between 3600 and 3400 BC and with another at Towthorpe which included the remains of six bodies, flint arrowheads, and pottery (A. Gibson and Bayliss 2010). These discoveries contrast with the later graves at Duggleby which have dates between 3300 and 2900 BC and include a wider variety of offerings: finely worked arrowheads, a flint adze, a polished knife, beavers' incisors, and a series of boars' tasks (A. Gibson and Bayliss 2009). Similar structures include the circular monument at Whitegrounds, where an inhumation dated between 3500 and 3000 BC was associated with an adze and another belt ornament (Brewster 1984), and Liff's Low in the Peak District which included an even wider range of grave goods – flint arrowheads, two flint axes, an

Callis Wold

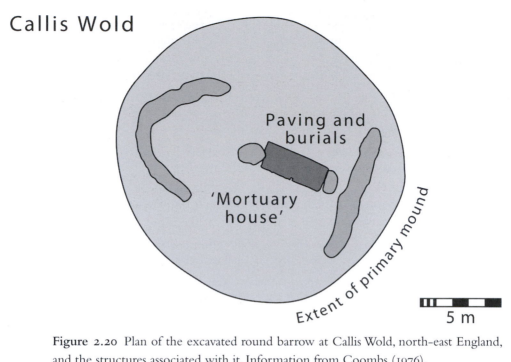

Figure 2.20 Plan of the excavated round barrow at Callis Wold, north-east England, and the structures associated with it. Information from Coombs (1976).

antler macehead, polished knives, and a decorated pottery vessel. In this case it is dated between about 3300 and 3100 BC (Loveday and A. Barclay 2010). Although most of this information comes from antiquarian excavations it suggests that the use of these sites became increasingly important from 3500 BC and possibly earlier and that the practice of individual burial with grave goods was mainly a feature of the time between 3300 and 3000 BC. The contrast with earlier practices could not be more apparent. Important problems remain. Did the new approach to the dead really begin in northern England, or is the evidence distorted by the large number of excavations carried out at standing mounds on the Yorkshire Wolds during the nineteenth century? They had largely escaped agricultural damage, and it remains to be seen whether similar structures once existed in lowland areas. This question is considered in the following section.

WIDER RELATIONSHIPS

Having distinguished between some of the developments in the north and those taking place in the south, how were the cursuses related to causewayed enclosures, and how were both kinds of structure related to Neolithic round mounds?

It has long been accepted that some causewayed enclosures are linked to the positions of long barrows, but this statement needs qualification. They were first built after the earliest mortuary monuments, and while a few examples are located close to burial mounds of the orthodox type, they are also paired with more specialised earthworks of the kind first identified in northern Britain. These are usually oval or round barrows associated with the distinctive burial rite described in the previous section. It happened in the Thames Valley at Abingdon where a low mound was built outside a causewayed enclosure but postdated it by at least three hundred years (Bradley 1992). It contained two inhumation burials which shared the same grave and were associated with a flint arrowhead, a polished knife, and shale or jet belt fitting. In this case there was a flat cemetery nearby. The graves were not covered by any kind of mound, and their chronology was only established by radiocarbon dating. There was also an elongated pit containing the disarticulated bones of a number of different people. Again there was no evidence of any monument and it was broadly contemporary with the other burials (A. Barclay and Halpin 1999: 28–34).

The relationship between causewayed enclosures and cursus monuments raises further problems. The dates of the early timber cursuses in northern Britain should overlap with those from causewayed enclosures during the second quarter of the fourth millennium BC, but to a large extent their distributions did not coincide. The later cursuses, however, were more considerable structures and are found throughout the distribution of lowland enclosures, forming a distinct zone which extends across country from north to south; this observation is considered further in Chapter 3. There seem to be two principal relationships between these traditions of earthwork building. In parts of the Thames Valley, for instance, cursus monuments seem to avoid the places where causewayed enclosures had been built, so that it is possible for both to have been used simultaneously (compare Hey et al. 2011: figs. 12.26 and 12.30). In other cases it is clear that a cursus or related monument cut across the position of an existing causewayed enclosure, suggesting that it had fallen out of use.

The clearest examples of this relationship are at Etton in eastern England, and Maiden Castle in the south (Fig. 2.21). At Etton two cursuses were constructed running more or less parallel to one another following the former course of the River Welland. The Maxey cursus ended alongside the enclosure, whilst the Etton cursus, which may have continued the axis established by its neighbour, crossed the position of that enclosure, cutting it in half. In principle, that should have involved a drastic transformation, but it is intriguing that the older earthwork had already been divided in two, one part associated with deposits connected with daily life and the other containing human and animal remains. The new division followed a different course but may have maintained the same concept (Pryor 1998: fig. 4). This is less likely to have happened at Maiden Castle, where it seems that a long barrow had been built just outside another enclosure. The same relationship is found at other sites, but in this case the mound was extended at both ends so that in one direction

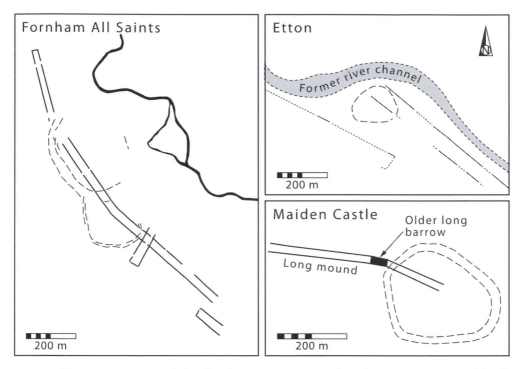

Figure 2.21 The relationship between causewayed enclosures, cursuses, and bank barrows. At Fornham All Saints, East Anglia, a cursus cuts across two of these enclosures and runs parallel to a river. At Etton, also in eastern England, two cursuses follow the course of another river and one of them cuts across a causewayed enclosure. At Maiden Castle, Wessex, a long barrow built just outside a similar enclosure was lengthened at both ends. Information from Oswald, Dyer, and Barber (2001) and Bradley (1983).

it ran straight across the existing monument and, in the other, continued for a considerable distance beyond it (Bradley 1983; Sharples 1991: fig. 33). Something rather similar may have happened at Fornham All Saints in eastern England where two causewayed enclosures had been built side by side, one of them as an annexe to the original monument. The same axis was followed by a cursus which cut across both earthworks along a path parallel to the River Lark. Nearby there were two more monuments of the same kind, one of them running past an older enclosure and perhaps extending to the river bank (Oswald, Dyer, and M. Barber 2001). It seems clear that an important transformation of the landscape was under way.

In other cases the spatial relationship between such structures is more apparent than their chronology. For example a cursus at St Osyth in the Thames Estuary is orientated on the position of a causewayed enclosure, but that monument may have gone out of use before the alignment was established (Germany 2007). In the same way a similar enclosure has recently been identified at Larkhill on Salisbury Plain. It is on the axis of the Lesser Cursus in the Stonehenge complex, but this does not mean that they were used concurrently (Thompson, Leivers, and A. Barclay 2017). Not far away, the Stonehenge Cursus, which is broadly comparable, was built at least a hundred years after the construction of that enclosure.

Although cursuses and causewayed enclosures could have coexisted for a time, it was the linear monuments that retained their significance for longest. That is not to say that the sites of older enclosures were necessarily deserted, for many of them produce artefacts of Late Neolithic, Chalcolithic, and Early Bronze Age dates. Nor were these places entirely without more recent monuments, but it was rare for the original structure to be refurbished during these episodes of reuse. It seems more likely that attention shifted towards the positions of the newly established cursuses.

The Causes of Confusion

One reason why cursuses have been dated to the Late Neolithic was the fact that they remained the focus for deposits of distinctive artefacts which might be placed in and around their earthworks. There are even cases in which the ditches were recut. The problem was made much worse by the character of the pottery associated with these monuments, or with smaller structures nearby. It belongs to a loosely defined tradition of decorated ceramics known as Peterborough Ware or Impressed Ware, although it can be subdivided into a number of regional styles. Although decorated vessels came into use during the currency of long mounds and causewayed enclosures, the greater part of the Peterborough tradition had been assigned to the Late Neolithic period, and it was usually supposed that it did not go out of fashion completely until the Early Bronze Age. Radiocarbon dating shows that this scheme was incorrect and that pottery of this type may have been current at a significantly earlier date than was once supposed. In fact it originated about 3600 BC and by 3400 BC it was widely distributed (Ard and Darvill 2015). It went out of use around 3000/2900 BC soon after the Late Neolithic period started. It means that monuments which had been dated to the third millennium must have been built much earlier.

These rather technical arguments affect a series of earthworks which are frequently associated with cursus monuments, although it cannot be established that they were of exactly the same dates as one another. They also raise questions of terminology and interpretation (Fig. 2.22).

Round Barrows and Hengiform Enclosures

The problem of terminology needs to be considered first. Two problematical categories commonly appear in archaeological literature: round barrows and 'hengiform' enclosures. Round barrows are simply circular mounds and are

Radley

Hillingdon

Etton

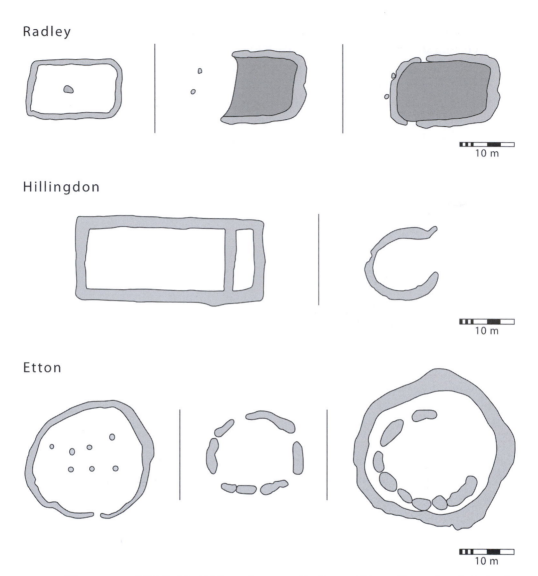

Figure 2.22 Middle Neolithic enclosures at Radley and Etton, illustrating their development over time. At Radley an open enclosure was replaced by two successive oval mounds. At Etton three circular enclosures, two of them with segmented ditches, were built in sequence. The excavated monuments at Hillingdon share some of these characteristics. Here the rectangular structure was aligned on the circular enclosure. Information from Bradley (1982), French and Pryor (2005), and Powell et al. (2015).

usually delimited by a ditch. They were built and used throughout the Early and Middle Neolithic phases, but changed their character during that time (Kinnes 1979). As the evidence from northern England has shown, the first examples might be associated with timber 'mortuary houses' like those identified beneath long mounds, while the later examples featured intact bodies accompanied by distinctive grave goods. The significant point is that this tradition of building round barrows was entirely separate from practice in the early Metal Age when similar ideas were reintroduced from the Continent (Healy 2012). The incorrect dating of Peterborough Ware had allowed researchers to suppose that round barrow burial continued without a break from the middle of the fourth millennium BC to the middle of the third.

For a while Irish archaeologists confronted a similar problem. It concerned what they called Linkardstown cists. They were individual inhumation burials placed within massive stone coffins and buried beneath substantial round cairns. These burials were quite distinct from the main classes of megalithic tomb, and were inaccessible once the monument had been built. Again there was the same temptation to interpret these burials in the light of superficially similar practices during the Early Bronze Age, but radiocarbon dating has shown that in fact they belong to the period between about 3600 and 3300 BC (Brindley and Lanting 1990). They predate passage tomb cemeteries in Ireland, but, like them, they occur in a restricted zone crossing the middle part of the island from east to west. They seem to be of similar date to the first of their British counterparts.

Neolithic round mounds are particularly difficult to identify where they have been levelled by the plough, with the result that in most cases only a ditch survives. To add to the confusion some of these sites have been described as hengiform enclosures (Wainwright 1969). The term is particularly unhelpful for it implies that they are miniature versions of the henges built during the Late Neolithic period, but the morphological argument is not convincing, for in some cases they are simply circular earthworks with one or more entrances; others had causewayed ditches. The chronological argument is on even weaker ground, for the link with henge monuments was postulated at a time when it was believed that the currency of Peterborough Ware extended well into the third millennium BC. Now that seems unlikely, meaning that the currency of these two kinds of monument need not have overlapped. Again the conventional terminology conceals some dangerous assumptions.

Most 'hengiforms' have been identified from crop marks or by excavations on sites levelled by cultivation. For that reason it is often uncertain whether they were the remains of circular enclosures that were originally open at the centre, or ploughed-out mounds of the kind already described. Moreover, one of the defining characteristics of a henge monument is the presence of an external bank and an internal ditch. In many cases it is impossible to reconstruct the form of the original earthwork. All that is clear is that the ditch was repeatedly recut and sometimes the monument increased in area as the perimeter was rebuilt.

In fact a number of small circular monuments do contain Neolithic burials with grave goods. At one time this tradition was considered as a particular feature of northern England, but the results of development-led fieldwork have shown that this is not the case. The excavations of the last twenty years have established that similar graves can be found much more widely. They have been identified in East Anglia, Wessex, the Thames Valley, the English Midlands, and the Welsh Marches. A recent discovery is a massive deposit of human bones from a triple ring ditch at Northampton. It dated from the end of the fourth millennium BC and included the remains of an estimated 130 people (A. Yates et al. 2012).

Oval Barrows and Enclosures

There is another problem, too. In their desire to fit excavated monuments into well-established 'types', fieldworkers have exercised some latitude in their identification of round barrows and ring ditches, for a number of these monuments were not circular in the first place. That provides an important clue, for it is already apparent that Middle Neolithic mortuary monuments included a number of oval mounds. Until recently they seemed to represent the end of the tradition of building long barrows, but there is reason to be more cautious now. Although certain examples are associated with individual burials with grave goods, others include more complex arrangements of human bones. A few were rebuilt to a circular ground plan during a secondary phase, but, as so often happens, an unnecessarily rigid typology conceals what was probably a continuum.

Oval mounds were built on various scales, from the substantial structures found at the southern terminal of the Dorset Cursus (Barrett, Bradley, and M. Green 1991) to smaller and lower mounds like the example associated with the Abingdon causewayed enclosure (Bradley 1992). Even so, they share one important characteristic, for in most cases the earthwork was flanked by a ditch on three sides. On most sites that open space was closed during a subsequent phase, so that the completed structure had a continuous perimeter, although it could be interrupted by narrow causeways. Such monuments are commonly found close to cursuses and may even share the same axis as those monuments. Cursuses can extend up to earthworks of this kind and may even incorporate them in their terminals. A good example of these relationships may be found at Eynesbury in eastern England where a U-ditched barrow seems to have been built on the same alignment as a nearby cursus (Fig. 2.23; C. Ellis 2004). An even shorter mound of similar type was located beside that earthwork with its axis at right angles to it. At some stage the larger barrow seems to have been lengthened and was enclosed by a second cursus. The smaller mound was closed by excavating a narrow ditch across its open end.

Again the evidence is rather ambiguous. On most sites the excavated remains are reduced to features cut into the bedrock, and it is not always clear whether they were associated with a mound or whether some monuments were open at the centre. Oval mounds certainly survive, but low platforms and enclosures have also been recorded as standing earthworks. This may reflect the amount of human labour that could be invested in their creation, but it is just as likely

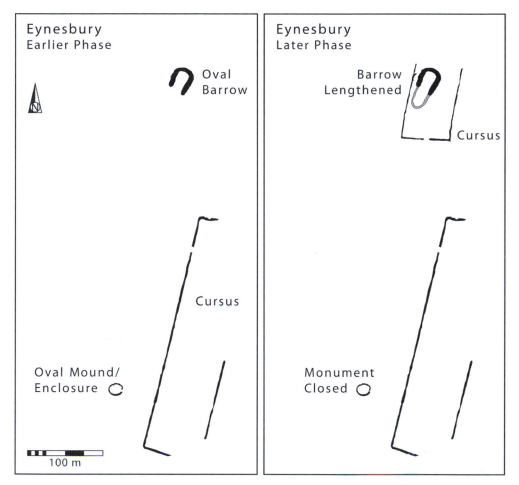

Figure 2.23 The possible sequence at Eynesbury, East Anglia, where two cursuses are associated with oval or circular mounds, each of which was modified in the course of its history. Information from Ellis (2004).

that a mound might be composed largely of topsoil and turf. In that case nothing would survive a long period of ploughing. The argument is especially troubling as it is known that some of the surviving long mounds, among them examples of considerable size, were built in exactly this fashion. Despite these uncertainties, it seems likely that oval mounds or enclosures were used during the same period as Neolithic round barrows and long barrows. They were associated with similar rituals, but it is not clear when they went out of use.

Such developments were widespread. To quote two recently excavated examples, a similar U-ditched monument at Hillingdon in West London was built on the same alignment as a rectangular enclosure associated with Impressed Ware. A second enclosure of the same type dated between 3270 and 2940 BC (A. Powell et al. 2015: fig. 2.3). At Ashford in south-east England, a Neolithic ring ditch, which may also have originated as an oval monument, was reconstructed as a circle of posts or pits and incorporated into another cursus (Carew et al. 2006). Again it was associated with sherds of Impressed Ware, but in this case it dated between the thirty-sixth and thirty-third centuries BC.

One characteristic connects several of these developments. By their very nature cursuses and oval enclosures have a clearly defined long axis. So do those Neolithic ring ditches which were provided with an entrance. It had an obvious precedent. Causewayed enclosures were sometimes sited to command views in one direction, while long barrows and long cairns were generally directed towards the position of the morning sun: a pattern that has been documented in detail in northern Scotland (D. Scott 2016). What was largely new is that Middle Neolithic (and later) structures could also be aligned on one another, forming a striking link between earthworks built at different times and used in different ways. A good example is the monument complex at Raunds in the east Midlands (J. Harding and Healy 2007).

CONCLUSION

This chapter has compared developments in northern and southern Britain as the character of Neolithic culture became increasingly diverse. According to Stevens and Fuller (2012) this was when arable farming became less significant, and Woodbridge et al. (2014) suggest that the population numbers fell and the amount of cleared land was reduced from about 3300 BC (Shennan 2018: 192–8). One possibility raised by new studies of human bone is that life was becoming more violent (Schulting and Fibiger 2014). An increasing proportion of the human remains from barrows and enclosures shows evidence of serious or fatal injuries. It is hard to interpret this observation. Did people who had died in conflicts have preferential access to these monuments? Is it a reflection of increasing strains in Neolithic society as more of the landscape was settled and the initial phase of cereal growing came to an end? The climate may have been cooler and wetter at this time and farming might have been more difficult (Bevan et al. 2017). It is too soon to tell.

What is clear is that the initial distinction between north and south helps to characterise the early years of the Neolithic period in Britain, just as developments in Ireland, which are discussed in Chapter 3, set the course for the Late Neolithic. At its simplest the available evidence has two separate strands. One links Britain and Ireland to Continental Europe and is most clearly evidenced in the south, towards the Channel coast. Its widest manifestation is the adoption of long barrows and allied monuments, some of them with stone chambers, but it is also shown by the use of causewayed enclosures whose distribution is densest towards the south and east, and sparsest in the north and west. These monuments were used in very similar ways to their counterparts on the European mainland.

By contrast, the development of cursus monuments which eventually became so important in Neolithic Britain seems to have been an entirely insular phenomenon which began in the north, at the farthest remove from the Continent where comparable structures have never been found. Their development provides one of the first indications that indigenous societies had diverged from their European neighbours and that the insular Neolithic was acquiring a distinctive identity of its own. Those contrasts became even more pronounced during the Late Neolithic period, which is considered in Chapter 3.

CHAPTER 3

NORTH, SOUTH, EAST, AND WEST

TIME AND SPACE

Chapter 3 considers a much shorter sequence and reviews developments in the two islands between approximately 3000 and 2400 BC (Figs. 3.1, 3.2). During that time – the Late Neolithic period – links with Continental Europe may have lapsed. In their place there were stronger connections between different parts of Britain and Ireland. Those new alignments are summed up by the title 'North, South, East, and West'. The situation did not change significantly until the adoption of metals, which is considered in Chapter 4.

Chapter 2 was mainly concerned with the ways in which unfamiliar practices were adopted in both islands. They included new ways of living, new methods of food production, novel attitudes to the dead, and, most of all, the creation of a distinctive range of monuments. These buildings provided the clearest indication of a fresh way of thinking about the world. There were certain changes during the crucial period between 4000 and 3000 BC, and yet these local differences seemed less important than more general trends.

If the first mortuary monuments suggest that personal differences were played down, that was eventually to change. From the mid- to late fourth millennium BC there were individual burials in Britain, the later examples in ring ditches, or in round and oval mounds. Such monuments were widely distributed, and by 3000 BC they were associated with a distinctive range of grave goods. The importance of individual burials seems to have increased as the process of monument building reached its limits. At the same time, these graves are often found close to earthworks of long-established forms, including causewayed enclosures and cursuses, or were even added to existing mortuary monuments like those at Whitegrounds (Brewster 1984) or Biggar Common (D. Johnston 1997). Only recently has it been recognised how many deposits included the remains of people who had been injured or killed in violent conflicts (Schulting and Fibiger 2014). The changes registered in the archaeological record may not have gone unopposed.

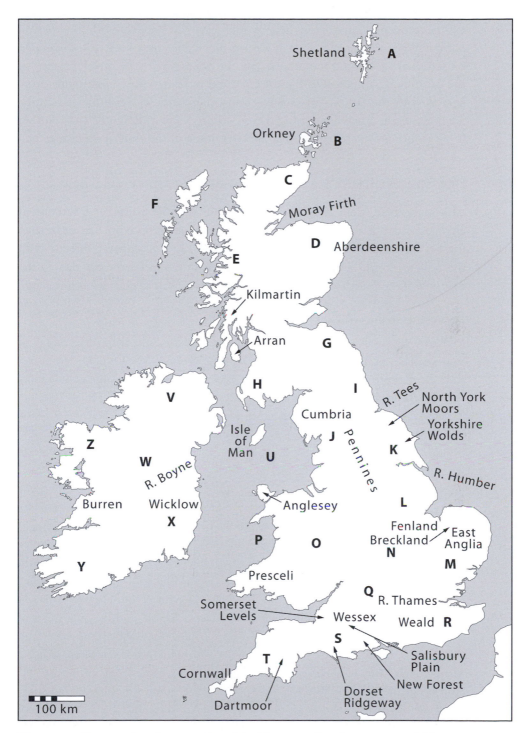

Figure 3.1 Places and regions mentioned in Chapter 3. For the purposes of this map Britain and Ireland have been divided into twenty-six areas and the individual sites are listed according to these divisions. A: Shetland; B: Orkney (Barnhouse, Crantit, Crossiecrown, Cuween, Ha'breck, Howe, Isbister, Links of Noltland, Maeshowe,

The processes considered here would have overlapped with the period considered in Chapter 2. That is almost inevitable since so much depended on regional variation. From about 3300 BC there were new developments in the north and west, especially in Orkney and Ireland, whose beginnings overlapped with the last use of cursuses and other Middle Neolithic structures. They represent a new beginning whose origins were in different areas and set in motion important changes that affected much of the third millennium BC.

HOUSES AND THE CHARACTER OF SETTLEMENT, 3300–2400 BC

Although there were new kinds of monument, the pattern of settlement changed too. The clearest evidence of this transformation comes from Ireland, for it is here that the nature of these settlements can be compared directly with the pollen record (Whitehouse et al. 2014). As noted in Chapter 2, during the first half of the fourth millennium BC there was a peak of clearances associated

Figure Caption 3.1 *(Cont.)*

Midhowe, Pierowall, Quanterness, Quoyness, Ring of Brodgar, Skara Brae, Stones of Stenness, Taversoe Tuick, Wideford); C: Northern Scotland (The Ord); D: North-east and Central Scotland (Broomend of Crichie, Greenbogs, Littleour, Loanhead of Daviot); E: Western Scotland (Kilmartin, Machrie Moor, Temple Wood); F: Outer Hebrides (Calanais, The Udal); G: Scotland on either side of the Firth of Forth (Balfarg, Forteviot, North Mains); H: South-west Scotland (Dunragit, Glenluce Sands); I: The English/ Scottish borderland (Blackshouse Burn, Meldon Bridge, the Milfield Basin); J: North-west England (Copt Howe, Langdale, Long Meg and her Daughters, Mayburgh, Shap); K: North-east England and the Peak District (Arbor Low, Catterick, Dishforth, Duggleby Howe, Ferrybridge, Fylingdales Moor, Rudston, Thornborough, Whitegrounds); L: Eastern England between the Humber and the Fenland (Maxey, Over); M: East Anglia (Flixton, Grimes Graves); N: the English Midlands (Biddenham, Briar Hill, Catholme); O: the English/Welsh borderland (Dyffryn Lane, Hindwell, the Walton Basin); P: North and West Wales (Barclodiad Y Gawres, Bryn Celli Ddu, Llandegai); Q: the Thames Valley, Cotswolds, and South Midlands (Devil's Quoits, Dorchester on Thames, Rollright Stones); R: South-east England including the Thames Estuary and the South Downs (Beachy Head, Heybridge, Ringlemere); S: Wessex (Amesbury, Avebury, Bluestonehenge, Crouch Hill, Dorset Cursus, Durrington Walls, Greyhound Yard, Knowlton, Marden, Marlborough, Maumbury Rings, Monkton up Wimborne; Mount Pleasant, Silbury Hill, Stonehenge, the Sanctuary, West Kennet, Woodhenge); T: South-west England and South Wales (Priddy, Stanton Drew); U: the Isle of Man; V: Northern Ireland (Ballynahatty, Giant's Ring, Lyles Hill); W: the Irish Midlands and the east coast (Balregan, Dowth, Knowth, Loughcrew, Newgrange, Tara); X: South-east Ireland (Knockroe); Y: South-west Ireland (Ballynacarriga, Island, the Grange); Z: the Irish west coast (Carrowkeel, Carrowmore, Knocknarea, Mullaghfarna, Tonafortes).

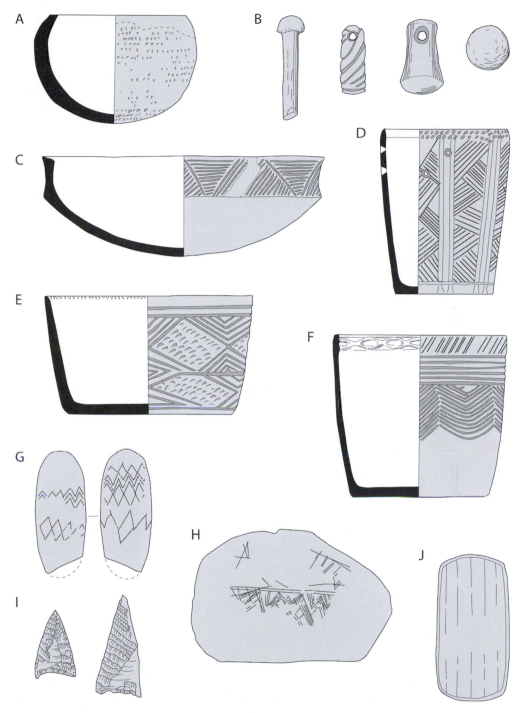

Figure 3.2 Outline drawings of the artefact types mentioned in Chapter 3. A: Carrowkeel Ware; B: bone pin, two pendants, and stone ball of the kind found in Irish passage tombs; C: Unstan Bowl; D–F: Grooved Ware; G and H: decorated stone plaques; I: oblique arrowheads; J: polished flint knife.

with cereal pollen. The same phase saw the building of substantial rectangular houses, whose remains are being discovered increasingly often. After that time the evidence takes a different form. New clearings are known, but there is less direct evidence of crop cultivation and in some areas human activity made a smaller impact. O'Connell and Molloy (2001) suggest that there may have been more emphasis on stock raising. Something similar may have happened in Britain where the importance attached to cereal growing was reduced around 3300 BC (Stevens and Fuller 2012). The amount of cleared land may also have been smaller (Woodbridge et al. 2014). The situation did not change significantly until the end of this period.

The character of domestic dwellings changed too, for by the Late Neolithic period the comparatively robust buildings discussed in Chapter 2 had been superseded by ephemeral and rather smaller oval and circular structures, although slight rectangular houses have also been identified which date from the earlier third millennium BC (Smyth 2014). So have less regular structures with recessed floors a little like Anglo-Saxon Grübenhauser which are represented in the Middle and Late Neolithic periods in northern England (Darvill 1996: 105; Fenton-Thomas 2009). Buildings of all these kinds are more difficult to recognise than their predecessors. Excavation at Knowth in the Boyne Valley has shed some light on this problem. It has defined a sequence which runs in parallel with important changes in material culture (G. Eogan and Roche 1997). The first phase is characterised by undecorated pottery of the kind which is found throughout these islands during the earlier fourth millennium BC. It is associated with a series of rectilinear or slightly oval buildings and two discontinuous palisades. Some of these structures had been disturbed by later land use, but others were preserved beneath a series of tombs.

The main passage tomb at Knowth also sealed the remains of circular stake-built structures associated with decorated pottery which was probably an Irish counterpart of Impressed Ware (Fig. 3.3). These buildings overlapped one another and not all of them survived intact, but they were so much slighter than their predecessors that no trace of them remained beyond the limits of the mound (G. Eogan and Roche 1997: 51–70). Since that earthwork reached its final form about 3200–3000 BC, it follows that this kind of architecture must have been established by then.

It seems possible that the structures identified at Knowth formed only part of a more extensive settlement. That is suggested by the remains of circular buildings associated with two of the other concentrations of passage tombs in Ireland. A series of rather ephemeral roundhouses has been identified close to those on Knocknarea (Bergh 1995 and 2015), and well over a hundred houses or stone enclosures have been identified at Mullaghfarna, just below the cemetery at Carrowkeel. It is not known how many of the structures were used at the same time, nor is it certain how they were related to the tombs, but some of these buildings are associated with radiocarbon dates in the Middle

Knowth
Earlier houses

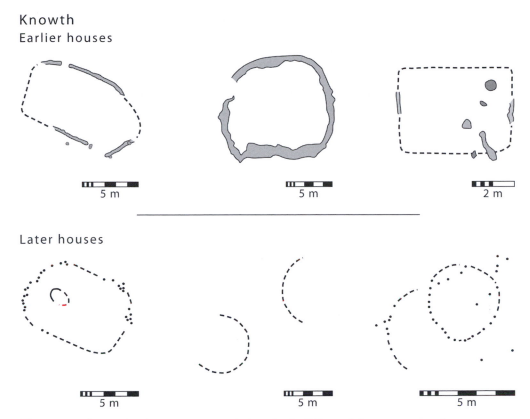

Later houses

Figure 3.3 Successive house types predating the building of the passage tombs at Knowth. Information from Eogan and Roche (1997).

Neolithic period (Bergh 2015). They may have been used by visitors to these cemeteries, but the best comparison could be with settlements in Orkney where the development of circular or oblong houses took place in the late fourth millennium BC. Here there were small villages the best known of which is Skara Brae (C. Richards and R. Jones 2016). The excavated settlement of Barnhouse is perhaps most relevant to the argument, for it was established by 3100 BC and was located only a short distance away from the passage tomb of Maeshowe (C. Richards 2005; C. Richards et al. 2016).

Neolithic houses are commonly preserved in Orkney. The earliest structures, at Ha'breck on Wyre and Wideford on Mainland, were built of wood (C. Richards and R. Jones 2016), but Late Neolithic houses were of stone. Their timber counterparts are difficult to identify in other areas, yet a few examples have now been recognised on the Scottish mainland and also in England and Wales. The earliest circular dwellings are associated with Impressed Ware and others are found with Grooved Ware, the ceramic tradition that eventually replaced it. Although there were still some oval and rectangular structures, circular buildings have been discovered in increasing numbers by excavations in both islands.

Such houses were used throughout the period considered in this chapter, and their forms did not change completely with the introduction of metals. Some were defined by rings of post sockets and a few examples were so small that they may have played a specialised role. The surviving evidence usually consists of hearths, and circles or arcs of stake holes. There are also pairs of isolated postholes which face south-east. They may be all that remains of the porches of insubstantial buildings which, like so many others, had been directed towards the sunrise. All these structures are accompanied by pits.

It is difficult to consider more than a small sample of well-preserved settlements because the structural evidence is so easily destroyed, but in areas with an abundant supply of raw material another source of information is provided by the results of field walking. This has been a particular feature of southern England where flint is widely available. This method can define occupation areas only in the broadest terms, but again there is a striking contrast with the period discussed in Chapter 2. The occupation sites of the Early and Middle Neolithic periods have not been easy to define because little material remains on the surface. That is probably because the contents of individual settlements were buried when a site was abandoned (Healy 1987). Although later settlements do include many pits, their positions are marked by more extensive spreads of artefacts. They cover very large areas, and it can be difficult to decide where one concentration ends and another begins (Bradley 1987), although recent fieldwork at Biddenham in the east Midlands has identified a series of distinct concentrations within a wider distribution in the topsoil (Luke 2016: fig. 3.1). In the south the inhabitants seem to have made profligate use of the available flint and generated large quantities of debitage during the course of occupation. They also employed a greater variety of artefacts than their predecessors, who had favoured a small number of lightweight multi-purpose tools (Bradley 1987). That may suggest that certain areas were used more intensively and perhaps for longer periods. The largest lithic scatters may have been the sites of settlements as extensive as those in Ireland.

Such observations have not been made in isolation, for in Britain larger areas were occupied. This is indicated by the distribution of artefacts, and it suggests that a wider range of environments were being used. It was certainly the case in East Anglia where Garrow (2007) has investigated the distribution of pits associated with diagnostic pottery. Some existing clearings may have been quite short-lived, but it seems as if activity increased in the uplands. Recent work around major ceremonial centres in Wessex indicates that they had been built in an open landscape (French et al. 2007: ch. 2).

Similar evidence is provided by a series of rock carvings made between about 3000 and 2000 BC (Fig. 3.4). They were mainly a feature of Northern Britain and Ireland. Their distribution is revealing (Bradley 1997: ch. 6). Although they

Figure 3.4 Open-air rock art at Cairnbaan in the west of Scotland. Photograph: Aaron Watson.

can cluster around the ceremonial monuments of the Late Neolithic, they can be as closely related to the wider pattern of settlement. They are found in the vicinity of lithic scatters, as well as on higher ground which overlooks the occupied area. In the west of Ireland they are associated with passes providing routes across the uplands. They are often found around springs and waterholes, and in Scotland they occupy the sheltered basins used by summer farms in the historical period. A few are found by sheltered harbours on the coast. In northern Britain rock art may focus on valleys leading through the wider land-scape (A. M. Jones et al. 2011). Although such places must have been visited during the Early Neolithic period, this evidence suggests that larger areas were being used than before. It also raises the possibility that travel between different regions became increasingly important.

Crop cultivation continued on a reduced scale, but little is known about methods of food production, as most of the excavated evidence comes from ceremonial sites. It seems likely that the subsistence economy did become more diverse and cereals played a more restricted role, but there is no evidence that arable farming had failed or been abandoned (Stevens and Fuller 2012). That was certainly not the case in Scotland where Late Neolithic plant remains have been studied in detail (R. Bishop 2013). It would be wrong to suppose that the increase in pastoralism documented by pollen analysis in Ireland extended throughout Britain as well.

HOUSES, TOMBS, AND ARENAS: IRELAND, ORKNEY, AND NORTHERN BRITAIN

Passage Graves

Like its predecessor, Chapter 3 is biased towards the archaeology of monuments. Again the initial development began beyond these islands. The previous chapter considered one of the main styles of mortuary monuments and its origins. If the development of long mounds might have commemorated rectangular domestic buildings, another tradition of mortuary monuments developed along the western coastline of Europe. In this case practically all the structures were of stone. These are the megaliths known as passage tombs (Scarre 2015; Schulz Paulsson 2017: ch. 12).

They are so called because they have two distinct elements. An entrance passage leads to a chamber which is generally situated beneath the centre of a mound. Most sites observe a clear distinction between these two components; the passage restricts access to the interior and may be low and narrow; the chamber, on the other hand, can be unexpectedly large and is sometimes spanned by a high corbelled roof. A number of these sites were decorated by abstract pecked designs (Shee Twohig 1981; Robin 2009). Irish passage tombs are usually associated with circular cairns, and the distribution of such monuments extends as far as the Northern Isles. It was in Orkney that some of the largest examples – those of Maeshowe type – were built in the years around 3000 BC (Schulting et al. 2010).

Although there are many variations among these monuments, two points seem to be established. These structures have so many features in common that they can be treated as a single architectural tradition. It is no longer possible to argue that different regional groups developed entirely independently of one another (Schulz Paulsson 2017). At the same time, it is clear that the oldest of these monuments are found on the Continent. Among the areas in which they developed were Brittany and the Iberian Peninsula (Scarre 2015). By the time they were in widespread use in Britain and Ireland their original importance on the European mainland had been lost, although some of them were reused.

Ireland

The Irish evidence is especially striking. It seems as if the first passage tombs are probably those at Carrowmore in the west of the country (Fig. 3.5). The monuments consist of above-ground megalithic chambers, enclosed by a ring of boulders, and may never have been covered by a cairn. In some cases there are signs of a rudimentary entrance passage, but the tombs could have been open to the elements as their chambers were revisited at various times after their construction.

Bone and antler pins were found within the chambers and have recently been dated. They focus on the period between 3600 and 3200 BC (Bergh and Hensey 2013; Hensey 2015: ch. 1), but it is impossible to say whether they were associated with the original construction of these monuments or with a later stage in their histories. Only one of the structures excavated to date was accompanied by a cairn. This is Tomb 51, which is the focal point of the complex. It is the largest monument and occupies the highest ground. It is also the only one decorated with pecked designs. It was not built until about 3550 BC (Sheridan 2003a). Most of the other dates for Irish passage tombs come from the Boyne Valley, near the east coast where much larger monuments were constructed around 3000 BC (A. Lynch 2014b; G. Eogan and Cleary 2017: ch. 4). The Mound of the Hostages at Tara was built and used between 3350 and 2900 BC (M. O'Sullivan 2005). It is possible that passage tombs were adopted through a gradual process of competitive emulation: successive monuments increased in size and the labour required to build them (Sheridan 1986; Hensey 2015).

It would mean that in the late fourth millennium BC earlier passage tombs replaced the court cairns discussed in Chapter 2. This development has a wider significance as the earliest examples must have been inspired by contacts along the Atlantic seaboard of Europe, whilst court tombs reflected a different axis with its emphasis on areas to the east in Scotland. Passage tombs soon became the dominant element in the Irish landscape, and are mainly in the north and

Figure 3.5 A stone chamber located inside a circle at boulders at Carrowmore in the west of Ireland. The mountain of Knocknarea can be seen in the background. Photograph: Aaron Watson.

centre of the country where their distribution focuses on a zone extending between Drogheda to the east and Sligo to the west (G. Eogan 1986); it is not unlike the distribution of the earlier Linkardstown cists. Taken together, they are close to the limit of the northern part of Ireland identified in Chapter 1; similar structures are almost entirely absent beyond the poorly drained midlands. The main concentrations of these monuments are in a series of cemeteries, of which Carrowkeel, Loughcrew, and the groups of monuments in the Boyne Valley are perhaps the best-known examples (Figs. 3.6 and 3.7). In each case one massive monument is surrounded by a series of smaller tombs, but that configuration may be repeated several times (Cooney 2000: 152–73). Thus it applies to at least three different clusters of chambered tombs at Loughcrew; there were distinct concentrations of monuments at Carrowmore and on the nearby mountain of Knocknarea (Bergh 1995); and a similar arrangement may once have existed with two of the large tombs in the Boyne Valley: Newgrange (Fig. 3.8) and Knowth. Within any one cemetery the tombs were carefully located in relation to one another, and at Knowth they surrounded the space that was eventually occupied by the largest monument; here the entrances of the satellite tombs were directed towards that focal point (G. Eogan and Cleary 2017: fig. 10.4). Such cemeteries could even incorporate structures of other kinds. On a still larger scale it seems as if groups of monuments in

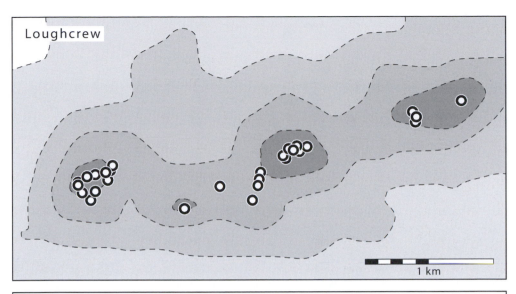

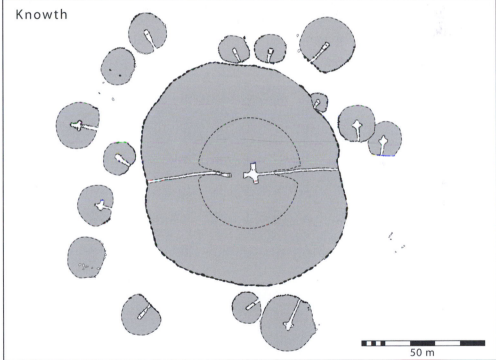

Figure 3.6 (Upper) Plan of the cluster of passage tombs on the high ground at Loughcrew in the east of Ireland. (Lower) Outline plan of the cemetery at Knowth, Boyne Valley. Note how the central tomb was enlarged after its initial construction. Information from Cooney (2000) and Eogan and Cleary (2017).

Figure 3.7 Detail of the Irish hilltop cemetery at Loughcrew. Photograph: Aaron Watson.

Figure 3.8 Distant view of the restored mound at Newgrange. Photograph: Aaron Watson.

different places might have been aligned on one another. Thus those on the mountaintop at Carrowkeel acknowledge the position of a similar cemetery on the summit of Knocknarea (Bergh 1995). Those sites are intervisible, yet some of the passage tombs at Loughcrew seem to be orientated on similar sites in the Boyne Valley, although they cannot be seen (Patrick 1975).

It has been difficult to work out a chronology for these monuments because they were permeable structures. They could be entered and their contents supplemented or removed over a considerable period of time. That raises a problem, yet the contents of Irish passage graves were strikingly consistent, and so were the practices associated with them. Many of the remains were of adults whose bodies had been cremated, but it is possible that unfleshed bones were also exposed to fires (G. Eogan and Cleary 2017: ch. 5). There were smaller numbers of children; most of them were unburnt. Some of the cremations might be placed in stone basins inside the main chamber or a series of side chambers, where other finds include a specialised group of bone artefacts such as pendants and pins, and a style of profusely decorated pottery which takes its name from the cemetery at Carrowkeel. Other portable artefacts may have been especially significant. The carved stone basins found in some of these monuments have been considered as symbolic querns and may highlight the importance of fertility (McQuillan and Logue 2008). The same monuments contain small stone balls which are sometimes compared with marbles. They may be equivalent to the pebbles associated with rock art in Britain or with similar objects made from fired clay or chalk which can be found in Late Neolithic settlements and enclosures. In north-east Scotland stone balls were lavishly decorated; a few related artefacts have been recognised in Orkney (Sheridan 2014). In Ireland, stone ard shares, which may have been associated with the productivity of the land, were deposited as offerings in rivers, but in this case it is not known when it happened (Simpson 1993).

There is some evidence that Irish tombs were rebuilt or refurbished during their period of use. According to George Eogan (2009) the great chambered tomb at Dowth in the Boyne Valley was reconstructed and enlarged on at least two occasions. That would explain why its chambers and passages are poorly integrated with the mound that is visible today. As was the case at Newgrange and Knowth, it may have been accompanied by smaller monuments of the same kind (Fenwick 2017).

The character of these structures changed over time. Eriksen (2008) suggests that the great mound at Newgrange was modified on at least two occasions, and Robin (2009) has identified panels of pecked decoration that had obviously been recycled from older structures; some were erected upside down. Other monuments were treated in an even more drastic manner. Work on the main passage tomb at Knowth has established that many of the orthostats were reused from another structure; they had been taken down and moved, and sometimes the original decoration was discovered on the backs of the stones

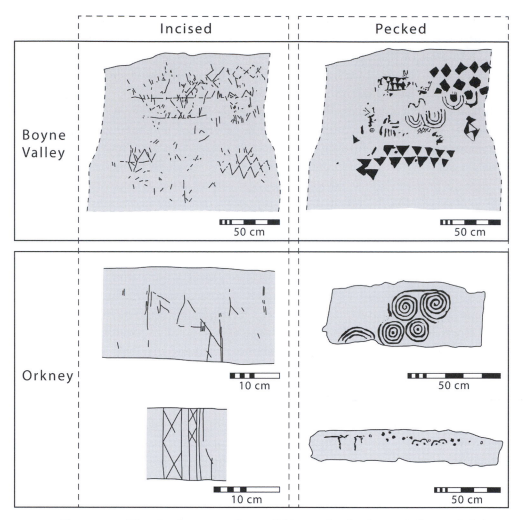

Figure 3.9 The development of megalithic art in the Boyne Valley and Orkney. In Ireland incised decoration precedes the creation of pecked designs on the same surfaces. Both techniques were used in Orkney, but here the sequence is conjectural. Information from Eogan (1997) and Bradley at al. (2001).

(G. Eogan and Cleary 2017: 73–7). It is not known where the dismantled building had been, but the final mound there was so large that its remains could still be buried beneath it. At Newgrange and Knowth it is clear that the pecked designs had been renewed and changed on more than one occasion. George Eogan (1997) has identified several overlays on some of the uprights at Knowth, leading him to suggest that the earliest designs were incised linear motifs and that the pecked circles and spirals that are often associated with the Boyne Valley may have been a later development (Fig. 3.9).

Hensey (2015) offers an interesting interpretation of the architecture of Irish passage tombs. Drawing on the evidence of comparative religion, he suggests that the earliest structures – those in the west – embodied a journey to the world of the dead. The monuments at Carrowmore were open to the elements and the interior was clearly visible, but the passage leading to the central chamber rarely extended as far as the outer limit of the monument. It may not have been used by the living, and in any case those chambers were too small for people to have entered them.

That contrasts with the next structures to be built which included the earliest passage graves in regions further to the east. Now the interior was hidden by considerable cairns, some of which were on prominent hilltops. The passage, a 'roofed tunnel' leading into these structures, was low and narrow and must have made access difficult. Space was equally restricted inside the central chamber. It must have been almost permanently dark. In Hensey's terms these places were associated with 'retreat' and 'seclusion'. He suggests that they were used by a few people who made special journeys to visit the dead in what he describes as a kind of vision quest (Hensey 2015: ch. 2).

That is very different from the activities associated with the latest and largest passage tombs in Ireland, and it is unfortunate that they have received so much attention at the expense of earlier constructions. Sometimes their passages were more accessible and their chambers could accommodate significantly more people. There was a new emphasis on the exterior, and in the Boyne Valley a series of smaller monuments surrounded the largest tombs. The mounds and cairns could be augmented by platforms, small stone settings, or timber circles, and excavation shows that large numbers of artefacts were deposited in the surrounding area. At Newgrange there is evidence of feasting (Mount 1994; Carlin 2017). Hensey (2015: ch. 6) concludes that these structures can be thought of as temples. In contrast to earlier monuments they attracted large numbers of visitors.

Megalithic art plays an important role in his interpretation. The decoration of Irish passage tombs could have had two distinct aspects. Those who were permitted to enter the chamber and passage would have viewed a particular selection of motifs, but the very structure of the monument meant that they had to inspect them in sequence (Bradley 2009a). At the same time, people who were not allowed to go further than the perimeter of the cairns would have been aware of a different selection of images. Once again they would have seen them in a prescribed order as they moved around the kerb.

These conventions may have changed over time, for most Irish passage tombs do not have decorated kerbstones (Fig. 3.10). They are a special feature of monuments in the Boyne Valley, and even here there may be evidence of a complex sequence. At Knowth the principal passage tomb was enlarged and both its passages were extended (G. Eogan and Cleary 2017: fig. 2.2). It seems as if the decorated kerb was the last part of that structure to be built. The designs could have been inspected by people who were not allowed inside the tomb. The distribution of quartz may follow a similar pattern, for Bergh has

Loughcrew Cairn L

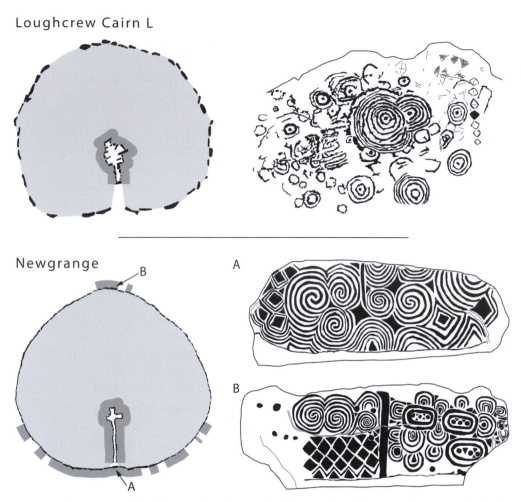

Figure 3.10 The changing locations of the decorated surfaces in Irish passage tombs. At Loughcrew in the east of the country most of the designs are confined to the chamber. At Newgrange, in the Boyne Valley, they extend to the outer kerb. Information from Shee Twohig (1981), O'Kelly (1982), and Robin (2009).

suggested that it was originally deposited inside the chambers of Irish passage tombs (1995: 156). Only in the latest of these sites did it embellish the exterior (Hensey and Shee Twohig 2017). Again it seems as if different features were directed towards different audiences. In contrast to the chambers and passages at Knowth, the kerb of the central mound made use of more than one kind of stone. Both there and at Newgrange the raw materials deposited outside the largest monuments were introduced to the site from an area extending as far as the coastline 50 km to the north (Mitchell 1992). They seem to provide a model of the wider landscape, yet many were simply small pieces of distinctively coloured rock. This practice may show how far people travelled to visit the tombs.

Certain individuals might have been allowed to observe phenomena that were denied to others. This is most apparent from the celestial alignments associated with Irish tombs (Prendergast et al. 2017). Their full extent is uncertain because some of the monuments are poorly preserved or were restored without an adequate record. It is accepted that the entrance passage at Newgrange is aligned on the midwinter sunrise, although the light actually travels down a specially constructed channel above the entrance of the tomb. The passages at Knockroe were aligned on the midwinter sunrise and sunset, respectively. One of the decorated monuments in the cemetery at Loughcrew was orientated on the midwinter sunset.

Several points are important here. These arguments apply to 16 per cent of the Irish passage tombs with adequate preservation, and all the convincing alignments are concerned with the movements of the sun (Prendergast et al. 2017). There does not seem to have been the same interest in the moon. At the same time these effects could be seen from the interior of these monuments and would have been lost on spectators who were excluded from the chamber. Few people could have watched them, for if too many were present they would have obscured the only source of light. Alternatively, these effects were directed exclusively to the dead.

It seems possible that the use of passage tombs involved other experiences that were restricted to a small number of participants. Jeremy Dronfield (1995) has argued that some of the abstract designs associated with Irish megalithic art refer to the visual images associated with altered states of consciousness. In Hensey's interpretation they might have been sought during visits to the most secluded chambers. A potential problem is that such ideas explain why certain designs assumed a special importance; but there was nothing to prevent them being copied from one decorated surface to another until they lost their original associations. There is also some experimental evidence that the peculiar form of this kind of structure, with its narrow entrance passage and high central chamber, creates unusual acoustic effects (Watson and Keating 1999). They may even have helped to generate the mental and physical conditions described by Dronfield.

It is thought that the mounds covering Irish passage tombs were modelled on the layout of circular houses, as they were in Atlantic Europe (Laporte and Tinévez 2004). That is especially likely since the cemetery at Knowth overlay the remains of what may have been a series of such dwellings. That is not the only link between them, for the circular ground plan of houses and tombs is echoed in other media, in particular the curvilinear decoration with which some structures were embellished. It is mirrored by small settings of pebbles outside the monuments themselves; others were created on their mounds, or even buried underneath them (Bradley 1998a: fig. 33). It seems unlikely that they were used in marking out the structures before they were built, and they are better regarded as geoglyphs. Similar designs extend to the decoration of natural rock exposures in Britain and Ireland. Both are found at Loughcrew where fragments of already decorated stone were probably built into the monuments (Shee Twohig et al. 2010).

The adoption of the largest passage tombs created restrictions of access that would have been less apparent before. Space was very restricted within the chambers and side chambers, and here there were rather different designs from those around the exterior. In the same way, only a small number of people would have been able to appreciate the solar alignments that had been built into the architecture of these buildings. Others would have been excluded. Perhaps the monuments were associated with a smaller section of society than the court tombs that preceded them. It seems as if the knowledge and ability needed to plan these buildings may not have been generally available, even though their actual construction required an enormous workforce. Alison Sheridan (1986) is surely right to suggest that the construction of passage tombs was a source of prestige. Different communities attempted to outdo one another in mounting these ambitious projects. The same should apply to the separate clusters of passage graves within the larger cemeteries. That is surely significant as similar cemeteries are not associated with tombs of this kind in Scotland and Wales.

There were few burials inside the monuments, and there is little to suggest that particular individuals were provided with grave goods, although this evidence may have been affected by later disturbance to the sites. Even so, there are signs that social divisions were acknowledged in architectural form, as the tombs within the individual cemeteries varied so greatly in size. It is equally significant that there were three separate cemeteries in the Boyne Valley. There the passage tombs had decorated kerbs that would have been accessible to larger audiences than the chambers concealed behind them. It marks a largely new development. The closed spaces of those chambers eventually lost some of their importance, and the surrounding area was occupied by new kinds of architecture. At the same time the curvilinear decoration which is such a feature of the exterior of these monuments was echoed by simpler designs in the wider landscape.

There are various clues to this development in Ireland. It seems possible that the exterior of these tombs became more significant with time (Fig. 3.11). This is most apparent on Knocknarea where Stefan Bergh (1995) has identified a series of low platforms built around the flanks of several passage tombs. They could have accommodated a larger audience than the chambers. There is another example at the decorated tomb of Knockroe (M. O'Sullivan 2004), and something similar may have happened outside the kerbs at Newgrange and Knowth where excavation has found many artefacts. They have been interpreted as evidence of ordinary domestic activity, but that seems rather unlikely as they include the remains of feasts (Mount 1994). They could have

Knocknarea

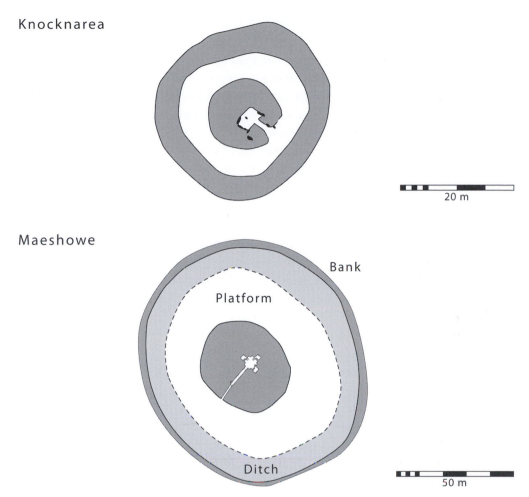

20 m

Maeshowe

Bank

Platform

Ditch

50 m

Figure 3.11 The relationship between internal and external features at two passage graves. One example at Knocknarea in the west of Ireland is surrounded by a bank. The monument at Maeshowe, Orkney, is situated on an earthwork platform bounded by a ditch and bank. Information from Bergh (2000) and Davidson and Henshall (1989).

been deposited by visitors to the tomb. Much of this material accumulated after the construction of these monuments and, in the case of Newgrange, the hearths, gullies, and postholes around the entrance recall the ephemeral buildings preserved beneath the bank of the henge at Durrington Walls in Wessex (Parker Pearson 2007). Two of the hearths are at the centre of square settings of postholes (O'Kelly, Cleary, and Lehane 1983: plates 3 and 7), while others may have been enclosed by gullies or arcs of stakes. They also resemble a series of circular and sub-circular structures at a recently excavated site at Ballynacarriga which dates from the Late Neolithic period (Tierney 2009).

Orkney

It seems as if similar monuments emerged in the Hebrides and Orkney towards the end of the fourth millennium BC. Again they were transformations of the domestic dwellings of the same period. On one level the houses of Late Neolithic Orkney form part of the general tradition of circular or oblong dwellings considered at the beginning of this chapter. On another, they are idiosyncratic. It may be because they are exceptionally well preserved, but they have a number of unusual features which are echoed in monumental archi-tecture. Among them are their entrance passages, the presence of intramural compartments, and the use of decorated stones (M. Richards 2004). They changed their internal organisation over time, and it is the earlier phase of these buildings that has the closest connection with passage tombs (Fig. 3.12; C. Richards and R. Jones 2016).

The first of the houses had a roughly cruciform interior and a circular external wall, so that they combine elements of older and newer ways of organising space. The circular structures had one entrance facing a central hearth. There might be recesses set into the thickness of the walls, but the main focal point was at the back of the dwelling (Fig. 3.13). Such buildings could be grouped together into small villages. Those at Skara Brae were connected by a series of low passageways. In this case important thresholds were marked by incised motifs (A. Thomas 2016). Similar designs are also found on the portable artefacts associated with these sites, including the decorated pottery known as Grooved Ware (Garwood 1999; Ray and J. S. Thomas 2018: 242–55). It is likely that the incised patterns inside these buildings were emphasised by the use of pigment.

Many of these elements are represented in the passage tombs of the same period (Davidson and Henshall 1989: ch. 5). The chamber had a complex layout. It utilised some of the same elements as the domestic dwellings, but it also exaggerated them. In the Maeshowe tombs the main chamber was farthest from the exterior, and each of the side chambers had to be accessed separately. Indeed, there are cases in which the side chambers led to further cells, each with a narrow passage of its own. These subdivisions are similar to the recesses that were built into the houses at Skara Brae (C. Richards and R. Jones 2016). The importance of the thresholds inside these tombs is emphasised by panels of incised decoration very like those within the dwellings (A. Thomas 2016). This comparison is important, for such images resemble the earliest motifs found in the Boyne Valley but are completely different from the pecked designs in the Irish tombs which Dronfield (1995) suggests could have referred to altered states of consciousness.

How were these monuments used? Excavation at Quanterness found that the chambers and side chambers contained large amounts of unburnt human bone. The excavator suggested that these monuments housed the bodies of

Barnhouse

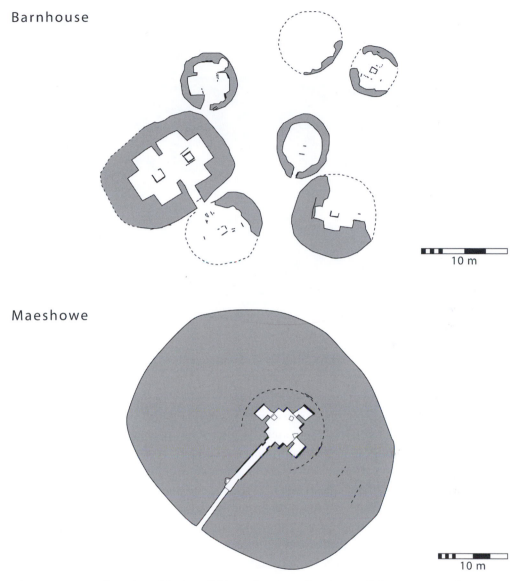

Maeshowe

Figure 3.12 Outline plan of the Neolithic settlement at Barnhouse, Orkney, compared with that of the nearby chambered tomb of Maeshowe. Information from C. Richards (2005).

entire communities (Renfrew 1979), but Colin Richards (1988) argued that the Maeshowe-type tombs included some of the body parts that had been removed from older stalled cairns. This idea has been rejected in the light of a new study of the excavated material, supported by radiocarbon dates (Schulting et al. 2010). In any case both kinds of monuments may have been used at the same time (Bayliss et al. 2017b).

Maeshowe tombs are not only elaborations of the basic plan of a dwelling; they are located close to the living sites themselves. In some cases these tombs

Figure 3.13 The interior of a well-preserved house at Skara Brae, Orkney.
Photograph: Aaron Watson.

seem to be paired with individual settlements. This applies to the relationship between the passage grave on Cuween Hill and the excavated houses
at Stonehall, but the same pattern connects the passage grave on Wideford
Hill to a nearby living site, and the famous tomb at Quanterness to another
settlement at Crossiecrown (C. Richards and R. Jones 2016). In other cases
the monuments may have been built over the sites of older dwellings. This
probably happened at Howe (Ballin Smith 1994: 10–14), and the same relationship has been postulated at Maeshowe (C. Richards 2005: ch. 9). There
may also have been a link between that tomb and the Late Neolithic buildings
at Barnhouse and the Ness of Brodgar. Barnhouse included a stone decorated
with a complex pattern (C. Richards 2005: fig. 4.29). A piece with exactly the
same motif had been built into the foundations of the chamber at Maeshowe.

In another way the sequence in Orkney is similar to that in Ireland. Sharples
(1985) has made the point that the earlier Orcadian tombs were entirely
focused on the interior space: that is where the human remains are found, and
there are few artefacts anywhere else. Later tombs had a different character.
Whilst they included more bones, there were further deposits outside them.
In a few instances it seems as if special structures were created for the purpose.
Maeshowe is particularly relevant, for the chambered tomb was built on an
earthwork platform enclosed by a ditch and possibly a wall which must have
been contemporary with the building of the mound (C. Richards 2005: ch. 9).
At two other Orkney monuments, Quoyness and Taversoe Tuick, a platform

was built around the perimeter of an existing passage tomb, restricting access to the interior (Davidson and Henshall 1989: 154–8 and 160–3). At Quoyness this structure included pottery and animal bones. At Isbister and Midhowe walled enclosures may have been built on to the original construction although it is not clear when that happened, and on Sharples's own site at Pierowall another platform was constructed against the collapsed perimeter of the cairn. In every case it is as if the monument was turned inside out so that in time the exterior assumed more importance than the interior. It recalls the evidence from Ireland where platforms were constructed outside the tombs on Knocknarea and where the kerb at Newgrange became the focus for deposits of cultural material and a series of hearths and timber buildings.

Maeshowe contributes to this discussion in other ways (Fig. 3.14). The tomb is most unusual because the corners of the burial chamber are defined by four tall pillars, whilst another four frame the entrance passage (Davidson and Henshall 1989: 142–6). Although they are undoubtedly impressive, they do not contribute to the stability of the monument. Since they had been quarried some distance away, why were they there at all? A possible answer is provided by a substantial socket cut into the earthwork platform (C. Richards 2005: 242–4). Is it possible that these stones had been taken from another structure on the same site? If so, they could have been reused, like the decorated orthostats incorporated in the principal passage grave at Knowth. An alternative is that they include six of the monoliths originally destined for the Stones of Stenness not far away. Here a ring of enormous uprights was encircled by a ditch associated with radiocarbon dates between 3020 and 2890 BC (Fig. 3.15; J. N. G. Ritchie 1976). The monument may never have been completed. There could have been a direct link between both the structures in Orkney as it is generally agreed that Maeshowe assumed its present form around 3000 BC.

At the same time the plan of the chambered tomb at Maeshowe resembles that of the latest structures in the nearby sites of Barnhouse and the Ness of Brodgar, which are of similar age (C. Richards 2005; C. Richards et al. 2016; Towers, Card, and Edmonds 2017; Card 2018). Again their outer walls were supplemented by a platform. One of the characteristics of such buildings is that they contained two massive stone-lined hearths. There is a similar hearth in the centre of the Stones of Stenness (J. N. G. Ritchie 1976).

Colin Richards (1996b) argues that all these constructions – the house, the tomb, and the stone circle– referred to one another at the same time as this complex provided a microcosm of the surrounding landscape. The area with so many monuments was in between two lochs and reinforced by a horizon of hills, some of them with standing stones. There were important contrasts between these sites. Whatever its origins, the preserved structure at Maeshowe was some kind of tomb. It might have been augmented by an earthwork platform and enclosed by a ditch that probably held water, but it lacked an impressive facade. Thus the monument was closed to the wider world. Both Maeshowe

Figure 3.14 Internal view of the chamber of Maeshowe, Orkney, showing one of the pillars defining the limits of the structure and the entrance to a side cell. Photograph: Aaron Watson.

Figure 3.15 The Stones of Stenness, Orkney. Photograph: Aaron Watson.

and Newgrange were orientated on the midwinter sun, but that had to be observed from the chamber. A stone circle, on the other hand, was a largely permeable structure, and Richards himself emphasises the visual relationships between the monoliths at Stenness and more distant areas of high ground. The enclosure was an open arena and could have accommodated a large number of people. The nearby monument of the Ring of Brodgar provides some indication of the wider significance of such monuments, for recent work suggests that it had been built out of raw materials introduced from different sources (J. N. G. Ritchie 1998; C. Richards 2013). It was constructed several centuries later than its neighbour, around 2500 BC (C. Richards 2013).

Since these monuments were investigated there has been a dramatic development in the archaeology of Neolithic Orkney. On the neck of land in between these two henge monuments an unusually well-preserved 'settlement' is being excavated at the Ness of Brodgar (Towers, Card, and Edmonds 2017; Card 2018).

Work is still in progress and has focused on the interior of an enclosure of considerable proportions. To date seven stone buildings have been excavated (Fig. 3.16). Geophysical survey shows that their distribution extended further, and the entire area within the walled perimeter could have been occupied by substantial buildings. Not all of them were contemporary with one another and deposits of midden material built up to such an extent that until recently the site was interpreted as a natural mound. The buildings were of

Figure 3.16 Excavated buildings at the Ness of Brodgar, Orkney. Photograph courtesy of Hugo Anderson-Whymark.

considerable proportions. Two of them resembled the largest structures at the nearby settlement of Barnhouse, but the others were even bigger. They were generally oval in plan with massive stone-lined hearths like the example inside the Stones of Stenness. A series of piers divided the interior of Structure 8 into four rooms, each with its own hearth. There is little sign of smaller circular or oblong houses like those in the settlements of Barnhouse and Skara Brae. Instead it seems as if the site contained a series of public buildings. A possible comparison is with two timber structures at Balfarg close to the east coast of Scotland (G. Barclay and Russell-White 1993). They seem to have been associated with the same style of pottery as the Orkney sites and one was eventually buried beneath a shallow mound. Although these timber buildings have been interpreted as open enclosures, they are the same size as the structures in

Ness of Brodgar
(Structure 8)

Balfarg
(Structure 1)

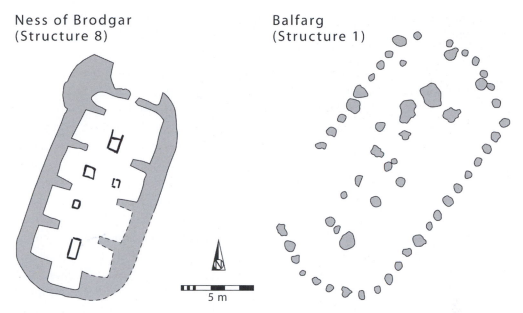

5 m

Figure 3.17 Structure 8 at the Ness of Brodgar, Orkney, compared with a timber building of similar date at Balfarg, eastern Scotland. Information from Towers, Card, and Edmonds (2017) and Barclay and Russell-White (1993).

Orkney and probably could have been roofed (Fig. 3.17; Tanja Romankiewicz pers. comm.).

The exceptional character of the Ness of Brodgar is apparent in four ways. Despite the complex structural sequence it was not used for a long time (Card et al. 2017). The stone structures were provided with tiled roofs. Some of the walls carried painted decoration and the boundary of the site was defined by a stone wall. Two of these elements can be recognised on other sites, but this particular combination may be unique. Much smaller walled enclosures have been identified at the Links of Noltland and incorporate cattle skulls in their fabric (H. Moore and Wilson 2011). Similar enclosures are evidenced by geophysical survey on other sites in Orkney. It seems possible that some of the clusters of domestic buildings formed a solid structure bounded by an outer wall (C. Richards and R. Jones 2016: 247–53). At the same time the distinctive non-figurative motifs associated with the structures at the Ness of Brodgar also occur at Skara Brae and feature inside local passage graves, particularly the great monument at Maeshowe (A. Thomas 2016).

Grooved Ware, Stone Circles, and Henges

Similar designs have been recognised on portable artefacts from Orkney and most especially on Grooved Ware, the decorated pottery associated with all these sites (Garwood 1999; Sheridan 2004). It probably originated in the north but its distribution soon extended to Ireland in one direction and southwards to other parts of Britain. A new study shows that it was first made during the later fourth millennium BC and that massive stone buildings of the kind associated with the Ness of Brodgar and Barnhouse were used between about 3000 and 2800 BC; smaller houses which shared some of the same architectural features were built until about 2300 BC (Bayliss et al. 2017b).

Quite different issues arise with the Irish monuments where a few of the latest passage tombs are associated with this style of pottery (Carlin 2017). Newgrange presents some problems of its own. Here the main passage tomb is enclosed by a series of monoliths. They are not concentric with the kerb but emphasise the position of the entrance and the section of the perimeter which had been enhanced by blocks of quartz (Cooney 2006). The original excavator took the view that the chambered tomb and the stone setting were contemporary with each other, but a more recent study suggests that the monoliths were not erected until the mound had collapsed (G. Stout and M. Stout 2008: 84–92). Stone circles are associated with chambered tombs at other sites in Ireland, and the Mound of the Hostages was surrounded by a series of 'fire pits' dated between 2030 and 1690 BC (M. O'Sullivan 2005). To judge from archive photographs of the original excavation these might have been the sockets for upright stones that have since been removed. In northern Scotland, monuments of superficially similar character were enclosed by stone circles during the Early Bronze Age (Bradley 2000a).

The stone circle is not the only structure outside the principal monument at Newgrange, for a large enclosure was built beside the mound and was formed by concentric rings of pits or, more likely, postholes. It occupied virtually the same amount of space as the passage tomb itself and was associated with fragments of burnt animal bone (Sweetman 1985). This structure was built long after the tomb and apparently underlies one of the monoliths of the Great Circle (G. Stout and M. Stout 2008: 84–92). It dates from the later third millennium BC.

Other enclosures in Ireland were built of wood (Fig. 3.18). A well-preserved monument is found not far from the Giant's Ring near Belfast and, like its counterpart at Newgrange, it seems to have formed only one component of a more extensive complex, including a series of 'megalithic cists' (Hartwell 1998). These were miniature passage tombs which were built inside shallow pits, and, like their full-size prototypes, were associated with Carrowkeel Ware. Again the principal enclosure was defined by two parallel circuits of posts. They enclosed the position of a timber circle with a massive square setting at its centre. The wooden structures at Ballynahatty are associated with Late Neolithic Grooved Ware and with a quantity of animal bones which are perhaps the remains of feasts. The enclosure and the timber circle were both burnt to the ground. Afterwards, the positions of the posts in the circular building were indicated by cairns.

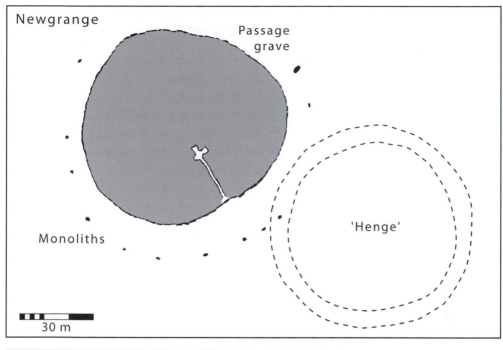

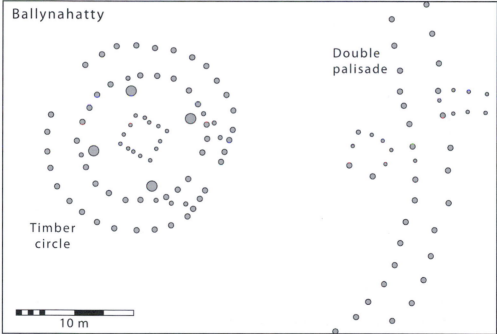

Figure 3.18 (Upper) The relationship between the main passage tomb at Newgrange and the adjacent post circle which has been interpreted as a henge. (Lower) The excavated area of the palisaded enclosure at Ballynahatty, northern Ireland, and the timber circle inside it. Information from Bradley (1998) and Hartwell (1998).

The evidence from Ballynahatty is particularly relevant to the argument, as a similar but smaller circle was constructed outside the east entrance to the principal tomb at Knowth (G. Eogan and Roche 1997: 101–201). Again it was associated with placed deposits of cultural material, including sherds of Grooved Ware. They should be contemporary with at least some of the features in front of the entrance of Newgrange, and not far away were the sockets of another ring of posts (Sweetman 1987). Anna Brindley has identified the positions of two more in a similar position to the wooden structure at Knowth (1999: fig. 3.6). Monuments with similar associations have been found in the course of development-led excavations in Ireland.

Many circular enclosures in Ireland were built by excavating soil from the interior and using it to construct a bank (G. Stout 1991) and, as this book goes to press, aerial photography during the summer of 2018 has located a series of enormous timber and earthwork enclosures near to the principal passage tombs in the Boyne Valley. They have not been excavated, but a related example at Monknewtown included a cremation associated with Carrowkeel Ware (Sweetman 1976). Much more is known about the Giant's Ring at Ballynahatty in northern Ireland which may have been laid out around the position of an existing passage tomb (Hartwell 1998). Such earthworks are usually compared with Late Neolithic monuments in Britain, and the link with megaliths certainly suggests that their histories might have overlapped. A recently excavated example at Balregan close to the east coast was associated with Grooved Ware (Ó Donnchadha and Grogan 2010). It had two concentric ditches and may once have been associated with a large stone circle. Excavation of the Grange at Lough Gur provides a similar result (Cleary 2015). Although it had been assigned to the Late Bronze Age, new fieldwork shows that the original structure was constructed during the earlier third millennium BC. Sherds of Grooved Ware found there date between 2950 and 2850 BC and samples from the bank and the old land surface provided three more results between about 3000 and 2550 BC. Another henge monument at Tonafortes close to the west coast has produced a date in the mid-third millennium: 2460–2140 BC (Danaher 2007: ch. 4). The evidence of Irish henges is limited but broadly consistent.

Across the Sea

To summarise, megalithic tombs on either side of the Irish Sea seem to have developed through a process of competitive emulation among different communities until these monuments grew to enormous proportions. At the same time there was a gradual change in the audiences who used the monuments. Space would always have been restricted inside a passage tomb, but it seems as if the areas outside these buildings acquired a growing significance. The building of external platforms, timber settings, or earthwork enclosures continued a process that was already well advanced, and by the time that these structures enhanced the original importance of the tombs, it seems likely that social relations were changing. There may have been the same emphasis on the supernatural, but the significance of mortuary rites might have been gradually reduced.

One connection is especially important. Grooved Ware apparently originated in Orkney and could have been introduced to Ireland some time before Carrowkeel Ware went out of use (Carlin 2017). The earliest Grooved Ware in Orkney had incised decoration, and similar material has now been identified on the other side of the Irish Sea. The same kind of decoration is found in other media and illustrates a network of contacts at the turn of the fourth and third millennia BC (J. S. Thomas 2010). Some of the main divisions of space inside the Maeshowe tombs were indicated by incised motifs. They are entirely absent from the earlier tombs in Orkney, but have an exact counterpart in the first phase of decoration in the passage graves of the Boyne Valley (G. Eogan 1997; A. Thomas 2016). Similar designs were added to stone artefacts in Late Neolithic Orkney and in other parts of Britain, and again they have counterparts in other regions. The most obvious are several stone plaques found on the Isle of Man. There is a similar object from an axe quarry in North Wales and a series of decorated objects from sites in lowland England including a ditched enclosure in the south-west (A. M. Jones, Díaz-Guardamino, and Crellin 2016).

Most of these objects carry incised decoration of the kind associated with houses in the north, but larger pieces were occasionally embellished using the same technique. They could be incorporated in the structures of later monuments. This was probably the case at Lyles Hill in northern Ireland (E. E. Evans 1953: 30–2) and Fylingdales Moor in north-east England (Vyner 2011). In both cases the motifs are very like those from Skara Brae and the Ness of Brodgar, and it is possible that they had been taken from buildings that no longer survive.

That would not apply to other pieces of stone which carry pecked decoration similar to that in Irish tombs. Again they can be well outside the distribution of passage graves. One was discovered at Over in the East Anglian Fens (C. Evans 2016: 68–70), and another was a massive chalk block from Monkton up Wimborne in Wessex which was decorated in the same style as the passage graves at Loughcrew. It was near the bottom of a shaft surrounded by a circle of pits that were probably dug at the end of the fourth millennium BC (French et al. 2007: 112–21 and 378–9). A third example comes from the Kilmartin complex in the west of Scotland where the motifs were on both sides of a finely worked slab (A. M. Jones et al. 2011: fig. 9.4 and 257–60). Again it may have been reused from some kind of structure.

Although such arguments are tenuous, there are obvious links between the monuments on either side of the Irish Sea. It has long been argued that the characteristic form of Maeshowe makes a direct reference to the passage tombs of the Boyne Valley, but radiocarbon dating suggests that Quanterness could be slightly older (Schulting et al. 2010). Other monuments in Britain are still more obviously related to those in Ireland. They include two decorated passage tombs on Anglesey; further links have been suggested with individual sites in the Hebrides and the Isle of Man. Similar connections may even extend to megalithic cists of the kind found at Ballynahatty, for they are like structures found in Orkney, including one from Sand Fiold (Dalland 1999) and a recently published example at Crantit (Ballin Smith 2014).

It is easy to make too much of the evidence of megalithic art, for whilst it is a common feature of the later tombs in Ireland, in Britain it is rare. The incised decoration of the Maeshowe tombs may have close affinities with the early designs found in the Boyne Valley, but the pecked motifs that are also known in Orkney have their closest parallels along the west coast of Britain. They extend from an early stone circle, Temple Wood in western Scotland (J. Scott 1989), and the passage tomb of Barclodiad Y Gawres in north-west Wales (T. Powell and Daniel 1956; F. Lynch 1991: 70–8) to a Grooved Ware vessel in the Upper Thames Valley (A. Barclay and Halpin 1999: fig. 4.33). There are other links between distant areas. A number of chambered tombs in Scotland and Ireland had platforms built outside them during, or even after, their main phase of use. They include those at Ord North (Henshall and J. N. G. Ritchie 1995: 119–24) and Quoyness (Davidson and Henshall 1989: 154–8). Similarly, Newgrange, Maeshowe, and Knockroe are aligned on the midwinter sun (Prendergast et al. 2017).

The first henges and stone circles were shared between regions on either side of the sea, and sometimes their structures suggest a direct connection between British and Irish monuments. Whatever the origin of the stone circle at Newgrange, this would be consistent with the dates for the Stones of Stenness where the structure was associated with Grooved Ware (J. N. G. Ritchie 1976). At Llandegai on Anglesey, an early henge monument may have been of similar age (F. Lynch and Musson 2001). It was associated with Peterborough Ware and is believed to date from about 3200–3100 BC, but in this case the enclosure is unusual because its bank is placed inside the ditch; an alternative suggested by Alex Gibson (2018) is that this was an enclosed Iron Age settlement. Whatever the solution, the earliest earthwork at Stonehenge which dates from 2900 BC also had an external ditch and so did several others which have been described as 'formative henges' (Burrow 2010a). Among them are the Priddy Circles in south-west England, one of which is associated with radiocarbon dates of 2930–2870 BC and 2780–2550 BC (Lewis and Mullin 2011). At Llandegai a second circular enclosure was built around 2700 BC, but in this case the earthwork adopted the conventional form with an external bank and an internal ditch (F. Lynch and Musson 2001). It seems possible that the perimeter of Stonehenge was rebuilt to conform to the same configuration, but it is not clear when that happened (Parker Pearson et al. 2009: 29–31). Something similar occurred inside the henge at Durrington Walls where a timber building had been enclosed by a circular earthwork with the ditch on the outside (J. S. Thomas 2007a). Again it was reconstructed in a more orthodox format.

A number of other monuments could have been built at the beginning of the third millennium BC. The large stone circle at Long Meg and her Daughters in north-west England illustrates the same relationship, for here an outlying stone is embellished with the characteristic repertoire of Irish megalithic art (Burl 1994). It also establishes an alignment on the midwinter sunset. In this case the monoliths seem to have replaced an earlier earthwork related to a causewayed enclosure. Radiocarbon dating has shown that smaller stone circles at the Scottish site of Balbirnie (J. N. G. Ritchie 1974; A. Gibson 2010a) and the Welsh site of Bryn Celli Ddu were built at about the same time (Burrow 2010b). Both were associated with cremated bone.

Calanais in the Outer Hebrides is of special importance (Ashmore 2016). Here a stone circle with unusually tall monoliths was built during the early third millennium BC. It was erected in a place which had already been settled and cultivated. In a subsequent phase a clay platform 6 m in diameter was constructed inside the circle and provided the foundation for a small wooden building associated with sherds of Grooved Ware. The monument was approached by no fewer than four alignments of monoliths which were laid out at right angles to one another and converged on the centre of the circle. Inside the ring a tiny passage tomb was built on the site of the timber structure (Fig. 3.19). The chambered cairn was associated with Bell Beaker pottery of the kind considered in Chapter 4 and dates from 2400 to 2300 BC.

The stone circle at Calanais has been compared with the Stones of Stenness which were enclosed by a ditch. Colin Richards has suggested that there was once a building inside the ring of uprights at Stenness (2013: 86–78). It was associated with a stone-lined hearth that still survives. He argues that this structure had been encased in an earthwork platform like those at the nearby settlement of Barnhouse (C. Richards 2005). The small building inside the stone setting at Calanais suggests a similar arrangement. In lowland Britain structures of similar proportions were preserved beneath the bank of a henge monument at Durrington Walls (Parker Pearson 2007). Again they were associated with Grooved Ware. They can also be compared with the more fragmentary structures recorded around the entrance of Newgrange (O'Kelly, Cleary, and Lehane 1983).

Timber circles provide another illustration of long-distance connections during this period. They come in a variety of sizes, from small post settings

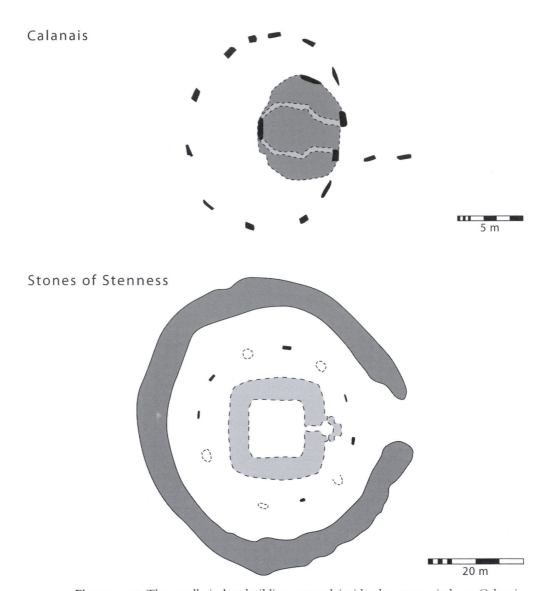

Figure 3.19 The small timber building erected inside the stone circle at Calanais, Outer Hebrides, compared with a larger structure postulated by Colin Richards inside the Stones of Stenness, Orkney. Information from Ashmore (2016) and C. Richards (2013).

indistinguishable from ordinary houses to grandiose structures that were probably specialised buildings (Pollard 2009; Noble, Greig, and Millican 2012; Laidlaw 2017). The smaller could easily be roofed, but it would have been difficult with the largest examples. The important point is that these buildings form a continuum and that structures of quite different sizes observe the same organisation of space. A particularly striking pattern is exemplified by the circle at Ballynahatty which encloses a central square of large posts (Hartwell 1998).

The same design is found very widely and extends from Ireland to southern England. It occurs outside the passage grave at Knowth (G. Eogan and Roche 1997), but the same arrangement was followed on the island of Arran, off the Scottish coast (Haggarty 1991), at the Udal in the Outer Hebrides (Ballin-Smith 2018: fig. 2.15), at Durrington Walls on the Wessex chalk (Parker Pearson 2007), perhaps at the Rollright Stones on the Cotswolds, and, according to antiquarian sources, the Mayburgh henge in north-west England (Lambrick 1988: figs. 25 and 27; Topping 1992). Most of these structures were associated with Grooved Ware. In some ways they raise the same problems as the halls discussed in Chapter 2. Perhaps they were public buildings whose form was modelled on that of the domestic dwelling. They come in a variety of sizes just like enclosures and tombs, and it may be that, like those monuments, the escalating scale of construction was one way in which different groups of people competed in a process of conspicuous consumption. That term seems especially appropriate since some of these places provide evidence of feasts.

Finally, there is a more general relationship to observe between Late Neolithic Ireland and the same period in Britain. For the most part local communities drew on distant areas as a source of ideas which they employed in idiosyncratic ways. In certain cases these geographical connections may have focused on small regions with concentrations of Late Neolithic monuments at the expense of their wider hinterland. All of them included significant concentrations of Late Neolithic monuments. To some extent that was true of Orkney, and it certainly applied to Cumbria in north-west England (Watson and Bradley 2009) and Kilmartin Glen on the west coast of Scotland (Cook, C. Ellis, and Sheridan 2010). The same idea might apply to Anglesey, with its decorated passage graves and the henge monument(s) at Llandegai (F. Lynch 1991). All these places shared features with Neolithic Ireland. Perhaps that is not surprising, for they were on the coast and yet were cut off from inland areas. Cumbria and Anglesey were isolated by high mountains, Orkney and Kilmartin by water. The Isle of Man, on the other hand, shared elements with Ireland and Scotland and had distinctive features of its own, in particular a series of cremation cemeteries (Burrow 1997).

The evidence for such connections takes many forms: particular types of field monuments, unusual portable artefacts, decorated tombs, and rock art. What matters is that they bear a stronger resemblance to features of Irish archaeology than they do to the repertoire of the British Late Neolithic. A telling example is a pair of enormous decorated boulders at Copt Howe in Cumbria which command a direct view of the Langdale Pikes where large numbers of stone axes had been made during the Early and Middle Neolithic periods; it is not clear if the quarries remained in use after that. It was decorated in the same style as Irish megalithic art and, like the passage of Irish tombs, a cleft in the rock commanded a dramatic view of the midsummer sunset (Bradley and Watson in press). One of the major henges in the same region, Mayburgh, lacks the customary ditch and is an embanked enclosure of Irish type (Topping 1992). It seems as if people living in north-west England developed stronger links with their neighbours across the water than they did with communities on the other side of the Pennines. A similar argument may apply to south-west Wales where at least one henge of Irish form has been identified (G. Williams 1984).

Such connections may be acknowledged by two exceptional monuments: the passage tombs of Maeshowe (Davidson and Henshall 1989: 142–6) and Barclodiad Y Gawres (T. Powell and Daniel 1956; F. Lynch 1991: 70–8). Both are particularly similar to monuments in Ireland. That applies to their architecture and to their characteristic decoration. At the same time, they diverge from the predominantly eastern orientation of such sites. Maeshowe faces south-west and is aligned on the midwinter sunset. Barclodiad Y Gawres faces north-north-west and so it could not be aligned on either the sun or the moon. What they do have in common is that both are directed towards Ireland. It is impossible to be sure that this was intended, but, given the evidence that Irish Neolithic cemeteries were orientated on one another, the idea should be taken seriously.

THE CURIOUS CHARACTER OF HENGES

Timber Circles and Stone Circles

It may seem unusual to devote so much space to the archaeology of Ireland and Scotland, when some of the most famous monuments of the Late Neolithic are in southern Britain, but it is impossible to understand them in terms of local developments.

There is a problem in studying these monuments. In the absence of excavation, virtually all the attention has been paid to their earthwork perimeters, with the result that the sites are classified according to their size and the number of entrances. That procedure cannot take account of any internal features. Moreover the timber circles and stone circles that are sometimes inside them are also found in isolation, suggesting that the earthwork perimeter was not an essential component of these sites.

For that reason it seems wise to begin this discussion with freestanding rings of posts and stones. That has one advantage, for ditches can be cleaned or recut and banks can be rebuilt. It may be difficult to find material associated with their original construction. On the other hand, the wooden uprights were sometimes charred when they were set in the ground. As a result, they provide a reliable source of dating evidence, although individual posts could have been replaced. Alex Gibson (2005) has studied their chronology in relation to the scale on which these monuments were built. The earliest were of modest proportions and were built as early as 3000 BC; good examples are the

Scottish site of Littleour (G. Barclay and Maxwell 1998) and a ring of posts at Ferrybridge in north-east England (I. Roberts 2005: 197–9). They became much larger in the period around 2500 BC, when some of them adopted a more complex layout. They include two adjacent structures on Machrie Moor on the island of Arran (Haggarty 1991). During the second millennium BC their size diminished. Much less is known about stone circles, but to a limited extent they may have followed a similar pattern (Bradley and Nimura 2016). Among the earlier examples were the small stone setting at Balbirnie (A. Gibson 2010a) and the more substantial structures at the Stones of Stenness (J. N. G. Ritchie 1976) and Calanais (Ashmore 2016), but again some of the largest monuments date from the mid- to late third millennium BC. After that time they decreased in size. Since stone structures sometimes replaced those of timber, it is not surprising that these trends should overlap.

A growing number of post settings have been found in isolation (Fig. 3.20). A typical example was at Flixton in East Anglia (Boulter 2012). Others have been located outside the earthworks of major monuments, as they were at Ferrybridge. This has important implications, for the distribution of Late Neolithic ceremonial sites is essentially a distribution of earthworks, which sometimes occur together in groups. They can be identified from the air. Certain regions have always stood out because such features are unusual. The results of development-led excavation and especially of aerial photography (Millican 2016) raise the possibility that timber circles were much more widely distributed. It was the practice of bounding these structures by a bank and ditch that varied from one region to another.

Two features of these sites are especially revealing: their spatial organisation and their development over time. Timber circles were not necessarily isolated. Nor were henges; more than one example could be built on the same site, and some of them were approached by wooden avenues, comprising two rows of posts. The best example is the 'droveway' which connects a series of monuments in the Milfield Basin in north-east England; Clive Waddington has shown that it was defined by lines of timber uprights, rather than shallow ditches as was previously thought (Passmore and C. Waddington 2009: 183–5). Elsewhere in northern England similar features are associated with radiocarbon dates between 2800 and 2500 BC (Tavener 1996). At Kilmartin an avenue of the same kind was built between about 2900 and 2500 BC (Cook, C. Ellis, and Sheridan 2010).

The Northern Circle inside the earthwork at Durrington Walls illustrates the same point. It took the characteristic form of a square within a circle, and was approached by two rows of close-set timbers which provided access through a wooden screen just outside the monument (Wainwright and Longworth 1971). A similar phenomenon is recorded at palisaded enclosures like Meldon Bridge (Speak and Burgess 1999), Dunragit (J. S. Thomas 2015b), and Forteviot (Noble and Brophy 2011). It is also found at stone settings, for example two of

Wyke Down   Greenbogs   Machrie Moor   Ballynahatty

Mount Pleasant

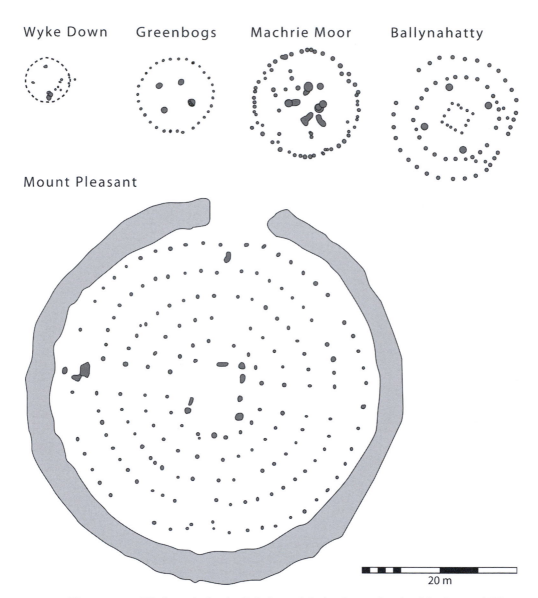

20 m

Figure 3.20 Timber circles in Britain and Ireland associated with Grooved Ware. Information from Noble et al. (2012) and Bradley at al. (2016a).

those at Stanton Drew in south-west England which are approached by short alignments of paired monoliths. Geophysical survey suggests that they were built on the sites of circular timber buildings, one of them with a rectilinear post setting at its centre (David et al. 2004).

Each of these circles had at least one entrance, meaning that they also possessed a distinctive orientation. Sometimes it emphasised the position of a natural landmark or another monument, but celestial orientations were important too. In southern England a good example is the timber setting at Woodhenge where the structure was directed towards the position of the midsummer sunrise (Pollard and Robinson 2007). In other cases the cardinal points appear to have been more significant.

The internal organisation of the timber circles varies from single rings of posts to more complex patterns. The largest monuments involved the erection of as many as six concentric rings, and the setting revealed by geophysical survey beneath a stone circle at Stanton Drew may have had nine (David et al. 2004). Something similar could have happened at the timber setting at Balfarg in eastern Scotland (Mercer 1981b; Needham, Parfitt, and Varndell 2006: fig. 20). A visitor to such monuments might have expected to pass through the entrance and to proceed to the centre, but this was not always possible, as the posts may have been linked by screens. The distribution of artefacts deposited inside Woodhenge certainly suggests that people had to move around the perimeter of the building, approaching the innermost space along a curving path that can be likened to a maze (J. Harding 2003: 74–81). Another monument, at Catholme in the English Midlands, was associated with radial lines of posts, extending out from the centre like the spokes of a wheel (Buteaux and Chapman 2009). Trial excavation shows that it dates from about 2500 BC and would have been contemporary with the largest henges in southern England.

Different parts of these buildings were associated with different kinds of archaeological material. For example, at Durrington Walls the distributions of pottery and flint artefacts in the Southern Circle avoided one another (C. Richards and J. Thomas 1984). Sometimes it seems as if such deposits could have been placed there in sequence. At Woodhenge, the groups of wild animal bones were closer to the entrance than those of domesticates (Bradley 2000b: table 6). A similar contrast has been recognised between deposits of pig bones and those of cattle. Such conventions also extended to portable artefacts. Fragments of stone axes occurred in the outer part of the building, but, apart from one example made of chalk, none was found towards its centre.

It is not clear how these deposits were related to the individual posts. Had they been placed around them whilst they were still intact, and were they buried in the hollows left when the timbers decayed? Were they placed in pits when those uprights had already rotted, like the cairns built over the postholes in the circle at Ballynahatty (Hartwell 1998)? Recent excavation at the Sanctuary at Avebury even suggests that on some sites the individual timbers were replaced soon after they were erected, implying that the act of setting them up was more significant than the overall design (Pitts 2001).

There were also composite monuments in which both materials were used together.

At the Sanctuary, close to Avebury, the interior of a timber circle was hidden by placing upright stones in between adjacent pairs of posts (Pollard 1992). This was executed so precisely that it seems likely that those posts were erected at the same time. The stone circle closed off part of the building rather like the chamber in a passage grave. Another composite monument may have been the Devil's Quoits in the upper Thames where a considerable stone circle enclosed the position of a smaller ring of posts (A. Barclay, Gray, and Lambrick 1995).

Sometimes the organisation of the structures was even more complex. The principal post setting at Mount Pleasant was structured around four corridors laid out at right angles to one another (Wainwright 1979). To the north and south, the passages were of even width; the other two became narrower as they approached the centre of the circle. Although the excavator suggested that this building was replaced by a series of standing stones, it seems more likely that these features were contemporary with one another and that the monoliths functioned as barriers screening the centre from view. Taken together, the posts and monoliths conform to the familiar design of a square within a circle.

Something similar is suggested by geophysical survey inside the southern circle at Avebury where Alexander Keiller excavated the positions of an enigmatic stone setting together with the socket of an enormous standing stone (the 'Obelisk)'. He also found part of a small wooden building which he associated with the medieval village on the same site. It is much more likely that this had been the central part of a Neolithic structure like those at other monuments. Comparison with a building inside the nearby monument at Marden suggests that it might have been bounded by a ring of posts (Amanda Clarke pers. comm.). It seems as if the structure at Avebury was commemorated by a larger stone setting with a similar plan. The Obelisk indicated the position of the 'house', and a square setting of monoliths was built around it. In turn it was enclosed by a stone circle (*Current Archaeology* 330: 8).

In other cases the replacement of timber monuments in stone might have fossilised their characteristic form and protected them from decay. Successive monuments occupy exactly the same area of ground, and may be the same size as one another. It happened at Temple Wood in the Kilmartin complex (J. Scott 1989), but the clearest example of this relationship was at Machrie Moor on the island of Arran (Haggarty 1991). At times stone circles take up details that were present in the wooden buildings. They respected their orientations, and even the timber avenues may have been replaced by monoliths. The connection with wooden monuments may be emphasised in other ways, as several of the uprights at Avebury had previously been used to polish stone axes (Drisse 2017).

Just as timber structures might be replaced in a more durable medium, the rarer wooden avenues had their equivalents in stone (Fig. 3.21). The best-known example is the West Kennet Avenue at Avebury which links the henge to the Sanctuary, but another avenue extended from the western entrance of the monument and cut across the remains of an older enclosure – perhaps a 'formative henge' (Gillings et al. 2008: chs. 2 and 3). There may have been an

Stanton Drew

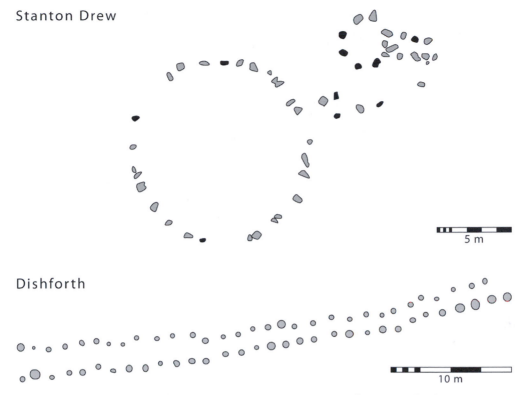

Dishforth

Figure 3.21 Stone and timber 'avenues'. At Stanton Drew, south-west England, two short avenues approach stone circles which are suspected to overlie timber monuments. The timber setting at Dishforth, north-east England, is associated with Late Neolithic pottery and radiocarbon dates. Information from Burl (2000), David et al. (2004), and Tavener (1996).

alignment of standing stones linking the Stones of Stenness and the Ring of Brodgar on Orkney (C. Richards 2013: 215–18). Another large stone circle which once possessed a stone avenue was at Shap in Cumbria (Clare 1978). They are not the only examples, yet little is known about how these structures were used. If one avenue at Avebury communicated between two different stone circles, its counterpart seems to have been decommissioned, and at one stage it was apparently closed by a row of monoliths.

Some of the monuments are enormous and their construction must have involved more labour than the timber settings that preceded them. That is particularly true when the source or sources of the stone were some distance away. It was obviously important to use materials taken from particular places, and the Ring of Brodgar, which was constructed in the mid-third millennium BC, was built out of materials assembled from different parts of the Orkney Mainland where fieldwork has identified one of the principal quarries (C. Richards 2013: ch. 5). The same may have happened at Stanton Drew (Lloyd Morgan

1887), and it even seems possible that stones were taken from older buildings in the way that had happened at Knowth and possibly Newgrange (G. Eogan and Cleary 2017). Parker Pearson and Ramilsonina (1998) draw attention to the physical properties of the raw materials employed on these sites. Wood is an organic substance and comes from living trees. Stone, on the other hand, stays the same for longer – and apparently forever. They compare this evidence with contemporary practice in Madagascar, where wood is associated with the living, and stone monuments with the dead. Commentators have taken exception to this use of ethnographic analogy (Barrett and Fewster 1998), but that interpretation is consistent with the archaeological evidence from Britain. The timber structures found in henges can be associated with a rich material culture, including deposits of pig bones which may result from feasting. The stone monuments, on the other hand, have few associated artefacts. They are found with human remains but with little else. It seems as though places which had once been connected with the living were now devoted to the dead.

Palisades

Timber circles and stone circles might have had similar histories and could almost have been interchangeable. Just as there were composite monuments at Mount Pleasant and the Sanctuary, the short avenues of monoliths at Stanton Drew resemble the post alignments leading into wooden monuments. In the same way the massive palisaded enclosures of the Late Neolithic period may have played a similar role to earthwork henges (Fig. 3.22).

The history of these timber enclosures is far from clear, but new work at Durrington Walls shows that the bank of the famous henge monument replaced a setting of enormous posts which followed the same alignment (*Current Archaeology* 319: 6–7). It contained a variety of circular buildings, but timber circles were also built inside the great palisade at Forteviot which was never replaced by an earthwork (Noble and Brophy 2011). There are other sites where it is possible to compare these palisades with earthwork monuments, but the sequence is not always obvious. At Mount Pleasant the excavator claimed that a great palisade was erected during the Bell Beaker period inside an existing earthwork associated with Grooved Ware (Wainwright 1979: 327–45). His view was based on radiocarbon dating, but finds of diagnostic artefacts, including carved stone balls which come from more secure contexts, would favour a different interpretation in which the timber enclosure preceded the bank and ditch. Not far away, at Greyhound Yard in Dorchester, there was a freestanding palisaded enclosure of similar proportions. Grooved Ware was the only style represented there (P. Woodward, S. Davies, and Graham 1993: ch. 2). In northern Britain palisaded enclosures of the same kind have been identified by excavation at Dunragit (J. S. Thomas 2015b) and Meldon Bridge (Speak

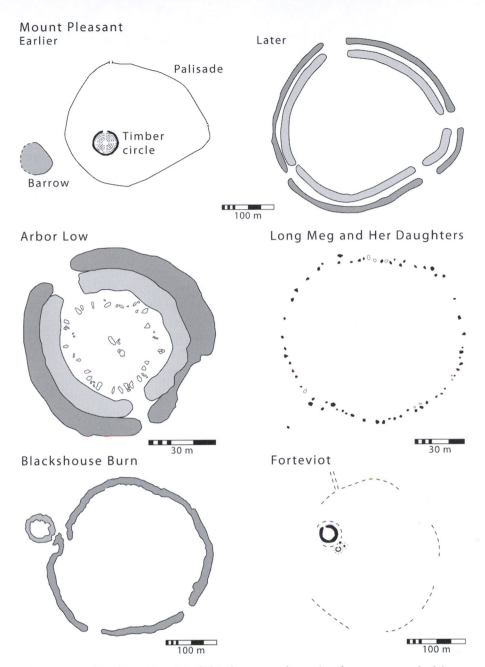

Figure 3.22 Five large Late Neolithic henges and associated monuments. At Mount Pleasant, Wessex, a palisaded enclosure may have been replaced by an earthwork monument. A round mound was built outside it. At Arbor Low the enclosure seems to have been built around an older stone setting. The stone circle of Long Meg and her Daughters, north-west England, overlay the edge of an earlier ditched enclosure. At Blackshouse Burn, southern Scotland, a timber enclosure was overlain by a rubble bank. A smaller enclosure was built outside one of its entrances. At Forteviot, central Scotland, other small monuments were built inside a large palisaded enclosure approached by a short 'avenue'. Information from Wainwright (1979), Burl (2000), Lelong and Pollard (1998), and Noble and Brophy (2017).

and Burgess 1999). At Dunragit, a ring of enormous uprights was surrounded by a palisade associated with Grooved Ware. It has radiocarbon dates in the twenty-ninth to twenty-seventh centuries BC. At Catterick (Hale, Platell, and Millard 2009) two concentric palisaded enclosures associated with Grooved Ware resemble a structure with similar associations at Ballynahatty in the north of Ireland (Hartwell 1998).

It is difficult to reconstruct any of these monuments from subsoil features, but two characteristics stand out. The palisades were very high and their entrances were exceptionally narrow. These monuments were generally between 5 and 10 ha in extent, but the largest, at Hindwell in Wales, enclosed 36 ha (A. Gibson 1999; N. Jones and A. Gibson 2017). Apart from two exceptionally early examples at West Kennet (Whittle 1997; Bayliss et al. 2017a), they seem to have been constructed during the first half of the third millennium BC. The individual posts must have been between 5 and 9 m in length and would have hidden whatever was happening behind them. The entrances add to this effect, for they are very narrow, and in certain cases people had to pass through them in single file. At Dunragit, Forteviot, Walton, and Meldon Bridge they are approached by short avenues of paired uprights, but they do not share a common orientation.

Banks and Ditches

Henges are generally characterised as enclosures with an external bank and an internal ditch. Those with a single entrance may be earlier than the others, but it was not always the case. It is questionable whether the same term ought to be applied to structures of such different sizes. Their diameters can extend from under 10 m to more than 400 m. In the same way some contained settings of posts or monoliths, but others were seemingly empty.

Not all the monuments identified as henges conform to these criteria. This account has already shown that the relationship between the bank and ditch can be reversed, and some of the largest examples were provided with more than two entrances. There were even exceptions to the circular ground plan, and a site at which one of the entrances was blocked. As Chapter 2 explained, there can be problems distinguishing the smallest henges from the remains of round barrows when they are levelled by the plough. Indeed the very name 'henge' is inappropriate since it is the Old English word for a gallows and referred to the stone lintels at Stonehenge rather than the earthwork enclosure on the same site (A. Reynolds 2009: 210–11). A still more serious problem is that it can be difficult or impossible to determine the chronological relationship between the bank and ditch and the features they appear to enclose.

This account begins with some of the smaller structures, for their comparative simplicity helps to define the questions that have to be resolved. Some recently excavated monuments are especially informative. A good starting point is provided by a structure at Heybridge close to the Thames Estuary (Roy and Heppell 2014). It was only 6 m in diameter and had a single entrance. It was approached by a narrow avenue bounded by stakes or hurdles. The filling of the ditch contained both Impressed Ware and Grooved Ware, and a complete Grooved Ware vessel had been placed in the ditch terminal. The site was associated with burnt human bones. More cremated bone was deposited in a pit together with a flint arrowhead of a specialised Late Neolithic form. The earthwork perimeter was reinforced on the inside by a circle of small posts. Unfortunately, there was little evidence of sequence because, like many others, the site had been levelled by the plough. This gave rise to the difficulties discussed towards the close of Chapter 2.

Further information is provided by two small henges on Wyke Down in Wessex (Barrett, Bradley, and M. Green 1991: 92–102; French et al. 2007: 83–94). They were not far apart, and despite some minor differences – their ditches were dug using different techniques; they may have been constructed or used in sequence; and they were not quite the same sizes as one another – they have many features in common. Both date from the period between 2930 and 2600 BC and were associated with deposits of Grooved Ware, animal bones, and lithic artefacts. Each included a small quantity of unburnt human bone. Their entrances were directed across a shallow valley towards a conspicuous section of the Dorset Cursus. Close to what may have been the earlier structure were circular houses of the same date.

Some indication of what might have been lost to the plough comes from a rather larger monument at Ringlemere in south-east England (Parfitt and Needham in press). In this case the enclosure had been buried beneath a later round barrow with the result that its interior was better preserved. It retained evidence of a more complex sequence than the other sites, and is particularly important in showing that the enclosure ditch was not a primary feature. It was dug after at least one of the principal structures had been built. The earliest seems to have been a horseshoe-shaped post setting associated with Grooved Ware, but at different stages it also contained curving arcs of stakes, a trapezoidal structure, several fence lines, and a series of hearths and pits. Again the main association was with Grooved Ware, but some of the later features did contain Beaker pottery. As Chapter 4 will show, Ringlemere retained its importance into the Early Bronze Age when gold and amber artefacts were buried there.

Similar developments took place at many other sites but were particularly obvious where small henges and related structures were found together in groups, as happened on Wyke Down. An example of this arrangement is the monument complex at Dorchester on Thames (Bradley and Chambers 1988; Whittle et al. 1992). Here a whole series of small ditched enclosures were built in relation to the remains of a Middle Neolithic cursus. When it was originally constructed it was associated with at least two 'mortuary enclosures' and probably with some circular mounds. During the Late Neolithic period several small henges were added, as well as freestanding timber circles. These structures shared some common elements. Radiocarbon dating has shown that both types were constructed and used between 2900 and 2600 BC. They were associated with substantial numbers of cremation burials which were usually deposited in secondary contexts, including the hollows left as posts decayed. Some of these structures were located inside the earlier cursus and others were just outside it, but they emphasised its continuing importance by following the same orientation so that the entrances to these monuments were directed along the axis of the older earthwork.

Two distinctive monuments were different from the others. One was a ring ditch enclosing a square setting of four posts (Whittle et al. 1992: fig. 15). It was associated with sea shells and a stone axe from south-west England; both would normally be found with Grooved Ware. The published plan suggests that this distinctive earthwork may have had a blocked entrance following the outer boundary of the cursus. It recalls two enclosures inside Durrington Walls which contained timber buildings (Fig. 3.23). The example at Dorchester on Thames was buried beneath the bank of Big Rings, the only large henge at the site, and it is clear that the imposition of such a massive structure changed the character of this complex. Its layout made no reference to the remains of the cursus or the small monuments that had been erected along its course. Instead its entrances established a new orientation for the site.

The large henge at Dorchester on Thames is a little unusual because no structures were discovered inside it, but in another way it conforms to a wider pattern. While the smaller enclosures and post circles do seem to have been closely related to the earlier tradition of cursus monuments, the creation of the largest henge monuments may have involved their rejection. Structures of both types could be superimposed, as they were at Maxey in East Anglia (Pryor et al. 1985) and Thornborough in north-east England (J. Harding 2013). They might avoid one another, as happened in Cranborne Chase where the large henge monuments at Knowlton might have replaced those on Wyke Down and were located several kilometres away from the Dorset Cursus (French et al. 2007). In the same way the Rudston Cursus complex is remarkable for including only one small structure of this type. Larger henges were in the Vale of Mowbray a considerable distance further to the west (J. Harding 2013). Of course this did not happen in every instance, but the evidence suggests that a significant rupture occurred in the organisation of the Late Neolithic landscape.

There is no doubt that the largest henge monuments really were distinctive. Their earthworks possess a distinctive character which has given rise to much discussion. The same applies to the considerable stone and timber settings found within them. How should they be interpreted?

Dorchester on Thames

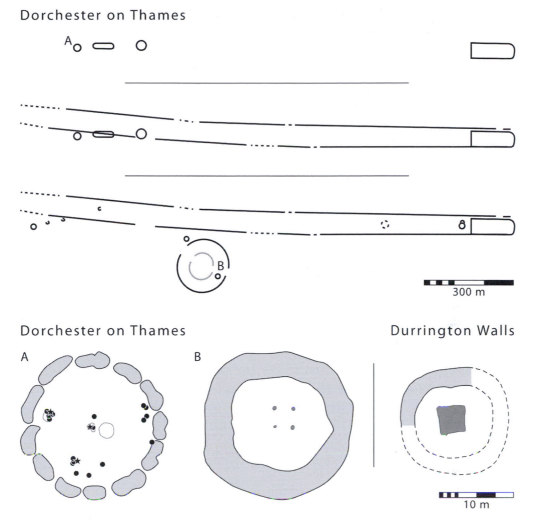

Dorchester on Thames   Durrington Walls

Figure 3.23 Outline plan showing the sequence of enclosures built within, and around, the cursus at Dorchester on Thames. One of them (B) is shown in detail and had four posts at its centre. It was buried beneath the bank of a large henge monument, Big Rings. It is compared with one of the internal structures within the main enclosure at Durrington Walls. Information from Whittle at al. (1992) and J. S. Thomas (2007a).

It is often supposed that they were like amphitheatres, allowing a large number of people to watch the events taking place inside them (Fig. 3.24). The banks would provide an excellent view, and yet on the British sites they were separated from the interior by a ditch. The basic format was the same whatever the extent of the enclosure and whether or not there were any structures within it. In principle, this would suggest that large numbers of people participated in the use of these places, but the architecture of the monuments might also have emphasised the distinction between those who were allowed into the

Figure 3.24 The henge monument at Avebury, Wessex, showing the position of the ditch, a section of the Outer Circle, and, in the background, the position of the Southern Circle. Photograph: Aaron Watson.

enclosures and an audience on the bank. The contrast is particularly obvious considering the enormous communal effort that went into building them. The earthwork at Durrington Walls may have taken half a million worker hours to construct (Startin and Bradley 1981).

Another way of looking at this evidence is to suggest that the banks of the larger henge monuments were intended as barriers or screens (A. Gibson 2010b). They actually concealed events from the greater part of the population. That may be why they were sometimes higher at the entrance. One reason for taking this view is that some of these earthworks may have replaced the timber enclosures considered earlier. Those palisades were so high that they must have hidden the interior from view. A possible interpretation is suggested by comparison with the royal centres of the Irish Iron Age and early Middle Ages. Warner (2000) argues that their external banks and internal ditches provided a kind of defence in reverse. These were powerful places where one could communicate with otherworldly forces. They might be a source of danger and those powers had to be contained.

Pit Circles

Not all the sites described as henges were above-ground structures. Another way of defining a circular space was by digging a ring of pits. The smallest were the same size as the simpler timber circles, whilst the largest was at Maumbury Rings in southern England (Bradley 1975). This was an enclosure with an external bank, but, instead of the usual post settings, a ring of deep shafts was excavated in the bottom of its ditch. There were approximately forty-five of them, each dug about 10 m into the chalk. It is clear that the shafts had been filled in deliberately. It is known that the process took place in stages, and that each episode had been accompanied by the deposition of artefacts and bones. Carved chalk objects and deer skulls were in the middle filling of the shafts and finds of human bones were towards the surface. A similar sequence was identified at one of the small enclosures on Wyke Down, 40 km away, where the earliest deposits included carved chalk objects and antlers. There followed a series of flint implements and animal bones, whilst the latest material included sherds of Grooved Ware, human cremations, and part of an unburnt skull (Barrett, Bradley, and M. Green 1991: table 3.12).

Human bone is so common in pit circles that they have been interpreted as cremation cemeteries, but that was not the only function of these sites (Kinnes 1979; Noble and Brophy 2017). The best-known evidence comes from Stonehenge where the deposits in the Aubrey Holes have radiocarbon dates between about 3000 and 2500 BC (Parker Pearson et al. 2009; Willis et al. 2016). Often the deposits of human remains were secondary to the monuments at which they were found, so those structures cannot have been built specifically for the disposal of the dead. Similar evidence has been recognised on other sites, including the upper levels of the Neolithic round barrow at Duggleby Howe, but in this case the monument had been associated with the dead from the outset (A. Gibson and Bayliss 2009).

Relationships

Having considered the components of a series of Late Neolithic monuments, how were they related to one another? It is clear that these sites saw a complex sequence of activity, and Alex Gibson (2010b) has argued that in certain cases the earthwork perimeter was the last feature to be built. It might have been impossible to erect the circles inside it because of the presence of a ditch; sometimes it is poorly aligned with the internal structures; and in one case part of a post circle must have been buried by the bank. He suggests that this sequence was followed at a number of major monuments. His argument is supported by work on the Scottish henge at North Mains, for here a timber circle was associated with radiocarbon determinations in the Late Neolithic period, but a cremation burial sealed beneath its bank dated from the Early Bronze Age (G. Barclay 1983). Comparable sequences have been established by excavation at Ringlemere in south-east England (Parfitt and Needham in press), the Welsh henge monument of Dyffryn Lane (A. Gibson 2010b), and Broomend of Crichie in Scotland (Bradley 2011). Gibson (2010b) suggests that

Figure 3.25 Silbury Hill, Wessex. Photograph: Aaron Watson.

far from providing a monumental setting for the buildings inside them, the construction of the earthwork might have brought their use to an end.

A few earthwork or palisaded enclosures were also associated with mounds. Whilst these are often thought of as barrows or mortuary monuments, that may not have been their purpose, and excavation at the largest of them, Silbury Hill in Wessex, showed that it was originally conceived as a ditched enclosure (Fig. 3.25; Leary, D. Field, and Campbell 2013). Another enormous mound of Late Neolithic date was inside the Wessex henge of Marden (Leary and D. Field 2012), and there was one beside the River Kennet at Marlborough (Leary et al. 2013). Although they are poorly dated, they might be considered as raised platforms which would provide a vantage point from which a small number of people could observe activities that were otherwise concealed. It is true that Silbury Hill commands a view into a Grooved Ware complex at West Kennet, just as the building of Conquer Barrow at Mount Pleasant might have allowed people to see into the palisaded enclosure that preceded the henge on the same site (Wainwright 1979). The same could have happened elsewhere, although another function of these platforms might be to raise certain people above the level of those inside the monuments. It is usually supposed that these practices were peculiar to southern England, but that need not be true. There was another earlier prehistoric mound on the axis of the entrance at Dunragit (J. S. Thomas 2015b), and viewers could have overlooked the

Late Neolithic timber enclosure at Newgrange from the raised area on top of the largest chambered tomb where there may once have been a standing stone (O'Kelly 1982: 26).

MAKING CONNECTIONS

Although this account has dealt separately with timber circles and stone circles, earthworks and palisaded enclosures, it is clear that these elements overlap and were to some extent interchangeable. There seems no point in regarding them as separate 'types', for not only do the categories cut across one another, structures of ostensibly different forms are often found in the same complexes. They might juxtapose open sites and enclosures, large monuments and much smaller ones. In the same way, some of them are associated with considerable numbers of artefacts, whereas others have very few. This weakens any classification based on their architecture and implies that certain places were used in very different ways from others. Particular structures may have been visited infrequently; others may even have been inhabited, whatever their more specialised roles.

Nonetheless certain tendencies can be identified amidst so much variety. In some cases these monuments increased in size until they reached a peak in the middle and late third millennium BC, after which they were constructed on a smaller scale. Wooden structures that were subject to decay were sometimes replaced in stone, and when this happened the activities associated with them seem to have changed their character so that a site which had originally been used for feasting became a place for the dead. Even when it did not occur it seems that at a late stage in their history, some of these monuments were screened off – and possibly closed – by an earthwork.

That was not the case in every area. Many timber and stone circles were never conceived on an elaborate scale. Nor were their positions emphasised by the construction of enclosures. Some of the regions in which henge monuments are apparently rare include Neolithic post circles which are not associated with any earthworks. That contrast between larger and smaller monuments is found in many parts of Britain and may reflect important differences in the ways in which societies were organised or their capacity to mobilise workforces for the building of monuments. In Wessex, the Thames Valley, north-east England, central Scotland, Orkney, and the Boyne Valley large monuments were the norm, but in East Anglia and the English Midlands smaller structures may have played the same roles. It was the less elaborate monuments that were sometimes associated with older cursuses. It seems as if the largest henges of the Late Neolithic period took less account of the past.

A striking feature of the biggest sites is the way in which individual monuments or groups of monuments increased in scale in parallel with one another. Within the limits of radiocarbon dating it happened over a restricted period of time, and a number of these developments could have taken place simultaneously in different regions. They required the participation of large workforces, and monuments like Durrington Walls preserve evidence of extravagant feasts. Other events were marked by deposits of special artefacts. Some were extremely lavish but others are easily overlooked, like the small pieces of Welsh bluestone from the excavation of Silbury Hill (Leary, D. Field, and Campbell 2013: 212). Neither process was confined to the interior of these monuments, as similar material was buried in pits in the areas around them. Not all these assemblages were distinct from those at settlements, but they were created with greater formality and had a wider range of contents. The position of one of the pits outside Woodhenge was marked by a cairn (Stone and Young 1948), and at Crouch Hill on the English Channel coast a midden with similar contents seems to have been enclosed by a ditch (Gardiner 1987). A group of Grooved Ware pits close to the site of the Rudston Cursus included deposits of animal bones that might have resulted from feasting (Rowley-Conwy and Owen 2011), and the same applies to similar features beside the Dorset Cursus (Barrett, Bradley, and M. Green 1991: 75–84). Those monuments obviously remained important long after they had been built.

Sometimes the closest connections seem to be between regions that were long distances apart. For example, the oval stone settings described as 'coves' are found inside a small number of stone circles but are distributed from Scotland to Wessex (Burl 1988a). A timber structure of the same form was erected inside an older causewayed enclosure at Briar Hill in the Midlands (Bamford 1985: 43–4), and again it was associated with Grooved Ware. So were lines of posts or pits subdividing larger monument complexes. They are recorded in north-east England and in Wessex (Miket 1981; Thompson and Powell 2018). Another connection between the north and south is illustrated by double-ditched henges, among them a site considered on page 133: Big Rings at Dorchester on Thames (Whittle et al. 1992). If communities were seeking to emulate each other's achievements, that process was geographically extensive. It seems to have extended from Orkney to southern Britain and drew in people on either side of the Irish Sea. What is quite remarkable is that after the demise of passage tombs, it does not seem to have involved any reference to Continental Europe.

Monuments are the embodiment of particular ideas, and there will always be room for doubt over the strength of such connections. Fortunately, they are evidenced in other media, among them artefacts which had moved a long way from their sources. During the Early and Middle Neolithic periods this had been the case with stone axes, but after 3000 BC, fewer sources remained in use; north-west Wales, the west of Cornwall, and the mines at Grimes Graves in East Anglia were the main examples. More significance was attached to the use of high-quality flint. Some of the most elaborate artefacts – polished knives and finely flaked arrowheads – were made in workshops near to the north-east coast of England (Manby 1974; Durden 1995), whilst similar raw material was extracted by mining close to the Fen Edge (Mercer 1981c). It seems likely that the finest of their products were distributed along the North Sea littoral from north-east Scotland to the Thames Estuary and probably as far as Beachy Head where some of them were made (Ballin 2011; Gardiner 2008). The same most likely applies to finely crafted maceheads.

Such connections are equally apparent from the distribution of Grooved Ware. This ceramic tradition seems to have developed in Orkney, where it has features in common with the designs on houses, passage graves, and stone artefacts, but it was soon adopted in other parts of Britain and Ireland (Carlin 2017). There is no reason to suppose that it appeared later in southern England. This ceramic tradition is peculiar to these two islands, and yet it is widely distributed within them. In that respect it contrasts with the kinds of decorated pottery that developed from the mid-fourth millennium BC. British and Irish Grooved Ware can be divided into a series of sub-styles, but the main source of variation seems to be chronological rather than regional. The styles also varied according to the contexts in which these vessels were used. Grooved Ware is a particular feature of Late Neolithic ceremonial centres, and it may be no accident that occasional vessels found at these sites are decorated with motifs that occur in megalithic art. The pots might be made locally, but such designs link them to widely distributed traditions of monumental architecture.

One way of explaining such connections is by studying where the main monuments are found. It might appear surprising that they should be situated so near to Roman roads or forts, or even close to the royal centres of early medieval Scotland and Ireland. The reason is that such places were especially accessible and that they were located on obvious routes across the landscape. These areas may have included Late Neolithic settlements, but that is not always apparent, and many of the places with most surface finds of the same period lack such monuments entirely. Henges and related structures can be found along the valleys leading through the uplands, near to navigable rivers and the places where they were easiest to cross. These would have been the ideal routes for later roads to follow and would have been well placed as power bases from which to oversee the local population.

One suggestion is that the ceremonial centres of the Late Neolithic were a focus for pilgrimage. This idea was advanced by Colin Renfrew (2000) to explain the concentrations of exotic artefacts found on and around these sites, but new work has extended to the animal bones recovered by excavation. Isotopic analysis has established that live animals, or possibly joints of salted meat, were introduced to these sites from environments some distance away (Craig et al. 2015). That work has focused on sites in Wessex where faunal remains are prolific and well preserved, but there is no reason to suppose that the pattern was restricted to that part of the country.

The strategic siting of such monuments is apparent at a more general level. Deposits of unusual or exotic artefacts are commonly found near them. Good examples are the concentration of such finds around the monument at Arbor Low which include flint from the Yorkshire coast (Barnatt and Edmonds 2014: 23–8 and 68–71), or the Thornborough complex which was also associated with a variety of non-local raw materials (J. Harding 2013: 149–73). The same happens in Wessex, where special artefacts were deposited in pits and were accompanied by a selection of animal bones and decorated pottery. A similar pattern is found in north-east England, although there some of the imported items may have been deposited in water (J. Harding 2013: 205–8).

In northern Britain and the north of Ireland there is a further relationship to consider. A mixture of fieldwork, museum study, and archive sources shows that a series of sheltered lagoons at important river mouths were associated with groups of exotic objects and evidence of craft production (Bradley et al. 2016b). They include finds of Grooved Ware. It is revealing that these maritime havens were offset from the ceremonial centres of the Middle and Late Neolithic periods, which were usually further inland; the two groups were connected by the river and were rarely more than 10 km apart. A good example is Dunragit in south-west Scotland where the monuments were on the opposite side of an estuary to an enormous collection of artefacts on the Glenluce Sands (J. S. Thomas 2015b; Bradley et al. 2016b; Bradley 2017b). Perhaps such places were used by different groups of people: the coastal landing places by strangers who had travelled there by boat, and large enclosures and other places by the local inhabitants and possibly pilgrims. That might explain why some of the most important monuments were offset from the coast itself. Thus in Ireland the Boyne tombs are 12 km inland from Drogheda where the river meets the sea, and Ballynahatty is 8 km inland from the harbour provided by Belfast Lough. The Kilmartin complex is 5 km inland from the Scottish coast, and the concentration of monuments in the Milfield Basin is 12 km from the North Sea, although they might have been accessed along the local rivers: a distance of 30 km.

Major henges are concentrated in a zone which divides an area of lowland extending eastwards towards the North Sea from a region with closer links to western Britain and Ireland (Parker Pearson et al. 2015: 45). This division is first apparent in the distribution of the cursuses considered in Chapter 2 and is best illustrated by two chains of large Late Neolithic monuments, one of which runs from the Channel coast at least as far as the west Midlands, and the other along the low ground in between the Pennines and the Yorkshire Wolds (J. Harding 2013). Parker Pearson argues that these were liminal areas in between different communities and that the henges provided neutral locations where assemblies took place. This idea is especially relevant to the southern English monuments since there is a growing body of evidence that contacts with the Irish Sea zone were important at this time. His interpretation also applies to the Stonehenge region which contains cursuses, henges, and stone circles. For that reason it is considered in the final section of this chapter.

Lastly, it was important to create these monuments in places with the right natural setting, for many henges used the surrounding topography in similar ways. From Avebury to Orkney, circular monuments were purposefully built at the centre of circular landscapes: places that were surrounded by a ring of higher ground (C. Richards 1996b). Sometimes the horizon merged with the enclosure bank, but in other cases it was concealed from view (Watson 2001a). Watson's fieldwork has demonstrated that such effects had been carefully contrived so that a particular monument might appear to occupy the centre of the world. Had it been sited anywhere else, those visual effects would have been lost (Watson 2004). If such a site were to provide a microcosm of the surrounding country, it was vital that it should command an uninterrupted view of the horizon. A number of enclosures were also aligned on prominent hills, valleys, or the position of the sun. That would certainly apply to sites in Wessex where there is environmental evidence that the chalk was never colonised by dense woodland during the postglacial period (M. Allen and Gardiner 2009).

It is obvious that major monuments were commonly located along rivers, but it is worth adding that some of the most significant places in the Late Neolithic were in places with springs and the sources of rivers. The obvious example is Silbury Hill at the source of the River Kennet (Leary, D. Field, and Campbell 2013), but the nearby henge at Marden incorporates a series of springs (Leary and D. Field 2012), and so does a large enclosure at Blackshouse Burn in southern Scotland (Lelong and Pollard 1998). Even more significant is the Walton Basin on the border between England and Wales where an extraordinary series of monuments – a causewayed enclosure, a cursus, small henges, and palisaded enclosures – focus on an important source of water, the Hindwell Pool (N. Jones and A. Gibson 2017). In Ireland it seems possible that the tombs and enclosures of the Boyne Valley were associated with 'ritual ponds', but it has still to be shown that they were deliberately constructed and so far only one has provided evidence of Neolithic date (M. O'Sullivan, Davis, and G. Stout 2012: 40).

Stonehenge

A good way of summarising many of these points is to consider the best known of all the prehistoric monuments in Britain, for it epitomises many of the processes that have been described so far (Darvill et al. 2012; Parker Pearson et al. 2015) (Fig. 3.26).

Figure 3.26 The outer setting of monoliths and lintels at Stonehenge, Wessex. Photograph: Aaron Watson.

In some respects Stonehenge is unique. It had an unusual structural sequence (Fig. 3.27); its architecture made use of techniques that were not found anywhere else; some of its raw materials were introduced from a great distance; and its scale was unprecedented. At the same time, each of these characteristics is related to more general trends during the Late Neolithic period and helps to define the issues that need discussing here.

The first enclosure at Stonehenge was one of the 'formative henges' discussed on page 120. It dated from about 2900 BC. Its ditch was interrupted at many points and had been deliberately refilled to cover a number of placed deposits, mainly of animal bones. The perimeter earthwork was precisely circular and may have had two or three main entrances. It was located in the centre of a circular landscape formed by a horizon of higher ground, but that effect was limited to the area immediately around the monument.

It is ironic that the enclosure at Stonehenge should have given its name to an entire class of sites, for it is a class to which the original structure did not belong. In contrast to the earthwork of a henge, its bank was inside the ditch, although it appears to have been reconstructed in the orthodox form during a subsequent phase. The rebuilt enclosure was probably associated with two structures, as well as an enigmatic setting of timber uprights in its northern entrance. None of these is exactly dated. At the centre of the monument there may have been a timber building, although its plan can no longer be recovered.

Aubrey Holes

? Post settings

Stone settings and Avenue

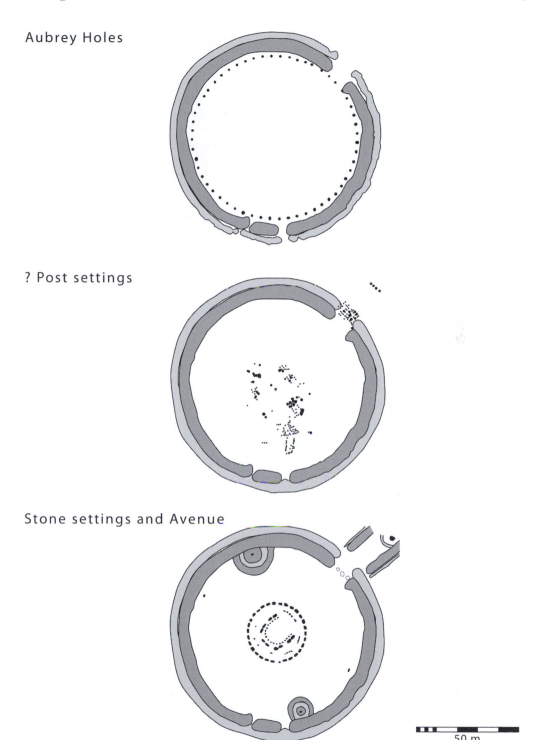

50 m

Figure 3.27 The principal structural phases at Stonehenge. Information from Cleal, Walker, and Montague (1995) and Darvill et al. (2012).

That is because its position is still occupied by standing stones, but also because it formed the principal focus for antiquarian excavations. Even so, it is known that post sockets existed in this area and that some of them were earlier than individual monoliths. The distribution of these postholes is confined to the zone occupied by the later stone circles, suggesting that one kind of structure replaced another, as happened on other sites.

A second structure consisted of two parallel rows of posts extending between another entrance to the monument and the central area just described. They seem to have formed a narrow avenue. Close to the centre of the site it was interrupted by a wooden screen. Although its date has been questioned, exactly the same arrangement is found at Durrington Walls, where its Late Neolithic context is well established. At Durrington, it led to the Northern Circle, a ring of upright posts associated with Grooved Ware (Wainwright and Longworth 1971: fig. 17).

The third component of this phase at Stonehenge was a series of pits concentric with the inner edge of the bank. They contained deposits of artefacts and cremated bone in their fillings. One reason for suggesting that some of them were later in date than the earthwork enclosure is that more cremation burials were found in features dug into the top of the bank and the upper levels of the ditch. Atkinson (1956) interpreted this as evidence of a cemetery, but some of these features had obviously been refilled before such deposits were made there. Most burials were of adults and can be compared with those from other monuments of this kind (Willis et al. 2016). These developments marked the closure of the original structure and provide evidence for an increasing concern with the dead. Another approach is to follow the idea of the original excavator, Colonel Hawley, who regarded the Aubrey Holes as stone sockets. He observed signs of friction on the edges of these features where uprights had been manoeuvred into place. They were of the right dimensions to have accommodated a series of monoliths. The most likely candidates are the 'bluestones' that had been introduced from south-west Wales where quarries of Neolithic date have been investigated by excavation (Parker Pearson et al. 2015). They may originally have been erected in a circle on the bank of the Avon a little over 2 km away. Although it is impossible to prove a link between this site and the more famous monument, the stone circle beside the river has become known as 'Bluestonehenge' (M. Allen et al. 2016).

The next development at Stonehenge typified a wider development in the late third millennium BC. This was the translation of the central timber monument into stone. It is not quite clear when it happened, and it may have been a complex process. At first there appear to have been two circles of uprights, arranged in pairs, although they may never have been completed. The form of the innermost stone setting raises problems, for the stones were later removed and erected in other positions. Nevertheless some of the reused monoliths had been shaped so that they could carry lintels. It is a moot point whether

Mount Pleasant

Stonehenge

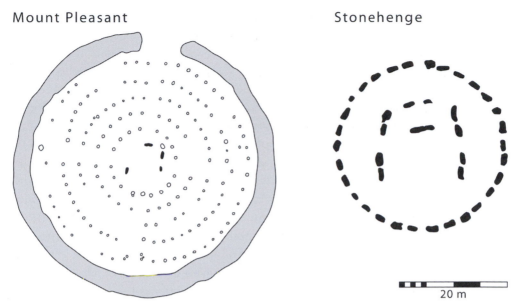

Figure 3.28 The layout of Stonehenge interpreted as a square within a circle, compared with the composite stone and timber monument at Mount Pleasant, Wessex. Information from Darvill (2016) and Wainwright (1979).

that plan was abandoned before the project was complete, or whether these stones had been brought from somewhere else, perhaps Bluestonehenge or even a dismantled structure nearer to the quarries in Wales. At all events it suggests that a deliberate attempt was being made to copy the characteristics of a timber building in a more durable medium. Such a scheme was to be executed during a later phase in the history of Stonehenge, but using a completely different raw material.

By 2400 BC the abandoned scheme seems to have been reinstated using sarsen, a local kind of rock. Two massive structures were built out of this material instead of bluestones. Although some of their elements were rearranged, that really represents the final form of the monument. It consisted of a massive circle of sarsens joined together by lintels enclosing a second setting composed of pairs of uprights linked in a similar fashion. Although it is often described as an oval, similar to the layout of a cove, Darvill (2016) has argued that this was more like the pairing of a circle with a square found at other monuments (Fig. 3.28). If so, this was by far its most grandiose manifestation. Whether or not this was the case, inside each of these circuits were low pillars of Welsh rock which seem to have been reused from an older structure. Each stone must have had its own history and the completed monument not only utilised raw material obtained on the Wessex chalk, it referenced another landscape over 200 km away. Perhaps this expressed the unification of two communities located in central Britain and the west respectively (Parker Pearson et al. 2015: 75).

During the same phase the perimeter of Stonehenge was modified, and now an earthwork avenue extended from the northern entrance of the enclosure to the site of 'Bluestonehenge' on the bank of the Avon. There were timber circles close to the river at Durrington Walls, where another avenue led to the water's edge (Parker Pearson 2007). There must have been a link between these different sites, for Stonehenge was very much a copy of a wooden monument. The sarsens had been shaped, and the lintels were secured in place using joints that would have been more appropriate in timber carpentry. The surfaces of some stones were treated so that they resembled carved wood, and later, in the Early Bronze Age, metal axeheads were depicted by carvings on five of the monoliths. In many ways this structure epitomises tendencies that have already been identified at other monuments. For example, the bluestone pillars are paired with the sarsen uprights in a similar fashion to the composite structures at Mount Pleasant and the Sanctuary. Still more striking, the finished building was obviously aligned on the sun. Looking north-eastwards, it rises at mid-summer over the course of the avenue. To the south-west, it sets at midwinter behind the tallest pair of standing stones. The rising ground along the final section of the Avenue enhances this effect. From this position the horizon is hidden from view, and behind the circle there is nothing but the sky. The layout of the monument can also be understood as a series of barriers screening an area in its centre which few people could have ever seen.

That hypothesis applies to many of the larger monuments constructed during the later third millennium BC, but the building and use of Stonehenge introduce some new elements. Although many finds are poorly documented, it seems clear that the monument was associated with an unusual quantity of human bones. Few have any contexts and by no means all of them have been accurately dated, but it adds weight to the interpretation proposed by Parker Pearson's and Ramilsonina (1998). Their case is all the stronger since radio-carbon dates suggest that the sarsen structure at Stonehenge could have been contemporary with the timber buildings at Durrington Walls and Woodhenge. Not only were the stone structures a more durable version of those timber monuments, their associations were entirely different from one another. The timber circles were associated with many portable artefacts and a consider-able quantity of animal bones: the result of feasts at midwinter. Stonehenge contained very few objects, and in their place there were human remains.

As the associations of such monuments changed, so did the scale on which they were built. Stonehenge must have made greater demands on human labour than any other building of its time, and yet it occupied a comparatively small area. Even the final sarsen circle was not much over 30 m in diameter. This chapter has considered the ways in which access to particular monuments came to be increasingly restricted. This structure took that process to its limits. A building that would have required more labour than ever before was impossible for large numbers of people to visit.

The crucial transition from a timber monument, less impressive than its neighbours at Durrington and Woodhenge, to a uniquely complex piece of architecture came at a special time in the archaeology of southern England, for this was when the first metalwork appears and when a new ceramic style, the Bell Beaker, is found in graves. Both these developments would have been impossible without renewed contacts with Continental Europe. The growing scale of these structures during the later third millennium BC suggests that competition within and between different communities must have intensified at this time. How appropriate that Beaker pottery should be associated with the transformation of Stonehenge and that it should be at Amesbury, only a short distance away on the opposite bank of the River Avon, that one of the earliest burials associated with these new forms of material culture should be found (Fitzpatrick 2011). This was not only one of the first of a new tradition of individual graves, it was one of the richest. Isotopic analysis suggests that the burial was that of an immigrant from the Continent. A Beaker mass grave was found nearby, and close to it there was yet another enclosure containing sherds of Grooved Ware (Fitzpatrick 2005). The growth of Late Neolithic monuments was sometimes associated with the promotion of long-distance relationships. Now that process extended beyond Britain and Ireland, and, long after the first introduction of farming, both these regions were drawn back into an international network.

CHAPTER 4

A WORLD ELSEWHERE

If Grooved Ware was an insular ceramic tradition, originating in the north but adopted in most parts of these islands, Bell Beakers represent a very different phenomenon (Figs. 4.1, 4.2). Their distribution is truly international and extends from Norway to North Africa. They are found as far east as Hungary and as far west as Portugal (Bradley et al. 2016a: fig. 4.4). This has raised many problems of interpretation, for they are often associated with early metalwork as well as new burial practices. It would be easy to argue that they represent a class of prestigious artefacts employed in social transactions, but that cannot supply the entire answer. Like Grooved Ware, Bell Beakers can be found in special contexts, but they also occur in settlements (Vander Linden 2006).

One important influence was the practice of individual burial with grave goods associated with Corded Ware in Central and Northern Europe (Fig. 4.3). Scholars have discussed its relationship with Bell Beakers, and for a long time it seemed most likely that these two ceramic styles were used in succession, so that the earliest Bell Beakers might have been in the north where they could have developed from the Corded Ware tradition. Now that looks improbable. The oldest radiocarbon dates for Bell Beakers come from Portugal, and it seems as if the earliest vessels have a distribution extending up the Atlantic coastline from the Iberian Peninsula (Salanova 2016; Bradley et al. 2016a). These finds are commonly associated with human remains, some of them in reused megalithic tombs (C. Gibson 2016), and with the earliest use of metal. The first Bell Beakers in Northern Europe are contemporary with vessels that were once taken as their prototypes.

The realignment poses a further problem. If Bell Beakers and Corded Ware were independent developments, how and why were elements of both traditions combined? Bell Beakers were closely associated with metalwork, including weapons and personal ornaments, and with archery equipment. Corded Ware was also associated with burials, but they contained a rather different assemblage in which stone battle axes and flint knives played a more prominent part (Bradley et al. 2016a: 121–5). Both groups were dominated by

Figure 4.1 Places and regions mentioned in Chapter 4. For the purposes of this map Britain and Ireland have been divided into twenty-six areas and the individual sites are listed according to these divisions. A: Shetland; B: Orkney (Ring of Brodgar); C: Northern Scotland (Balnuaran of Clava, Corrimony, Culbin, Dail na Caraidh, Littleferry, Strath Oykell); D: North-east and Central Scotland (Broomend of Crichie,

fine decorated pots which could have contained liquids, and some of those found in the Iberian Peninsula seem to have held fermented drinks (Guerra Doce 2006).

Those two groups were first linked together through a well-established exchange network based on the long-distance movement of Grand Pressigny flint from western France (Bradley et al. 2016a: 116). This distinctive honey-coloured material bore some resemblance to metal and was distributed over an enormous area extending along the Atlantic and Channel coasts as far as The Netherlands and reaching inland until it connected the distribution of early Bell Beakers to that of Corded Ware; it is not found in Britain or Ireland. In time the two traditions lost their separate identities, and it was during this second stage that further artefact types were introduced to both islands (Needham 2005). In contrast to the material culture of the Late Neolithic, they formed part of an international phenomenon. That development presents some problems of its own.

Chapter 1 discussed the 'invasion hypothesis' which had played such an important role in prehistoric archaeology during the mid-twentieth century, and the reaction that followed Grahame Clark's review of this concept in 1966. He took a minimal view of migrations during prehistory and attacked what he saw as an uncritical approach to the subject. He believed that there were only two cases in which significant numbers of people had settled distant areas. One was the introduction of agriculture, discussed in Chapter 2, and the other was

Figure Caption 4.1 (*Cont.*)

Skilmafilly); E: Western Scotland (Oban); F: Outer Hebrides (Calanais); G: Scotland on either side of the Firth of Forth (Balfarg, Cairnpapple, North Mains, Gullane, Tentsmuir); H: South-west Scotland (Glenluce); I: the English/Scottish borderland (Whitton Hill, Street House); J: North-west England; K: North-east England and the Peak District (Danby Rigg, Gardom's Edge, Gristhorpe, West Heslerton); L: Eastern England between the Humber and the Fenland (Over, West Row, West Whittlesey); M: East Anglia (Seahenge, Sutton Hoo); N: the English Midlands (Barnack, Biddenham, Catholme, Gayhurst, Lockington, Raunds); O: the English/Welsh borderland (Dyffryn Lane); P: North and West Wales (Bedd Branwen, Brenig, Great Orme, Stackpole Warren, Vaynor Farm); Q: the Thames Valley, Cotswolds, and South Midlands (Devil's Quoits, Dorchester on Thames, Radley); R: South-east England including the Thames Estuary and the South Downs (Mucking, Ringlemere, Thanet); S: Wessex (Amesbury, Avebury, Durrington Walls, Mount Pleasant, Silbury Hill, Snail Down, Stonehenge); T: South-west England and South Wales; U: the Isle of Man; V: Northern Ireland (Beaghmore, Clogherny Meenerrigal, Dundrum Sands); W: from the Irish Midlands to the east coast (Newgrange, Keenoge, Knowth, Tara); X: South-east Ireland; Y: South-west Ireland (Crumpane, Lough Gur, Ross Island); Z: the Irish west coast (the Burren, Roughan Hill).

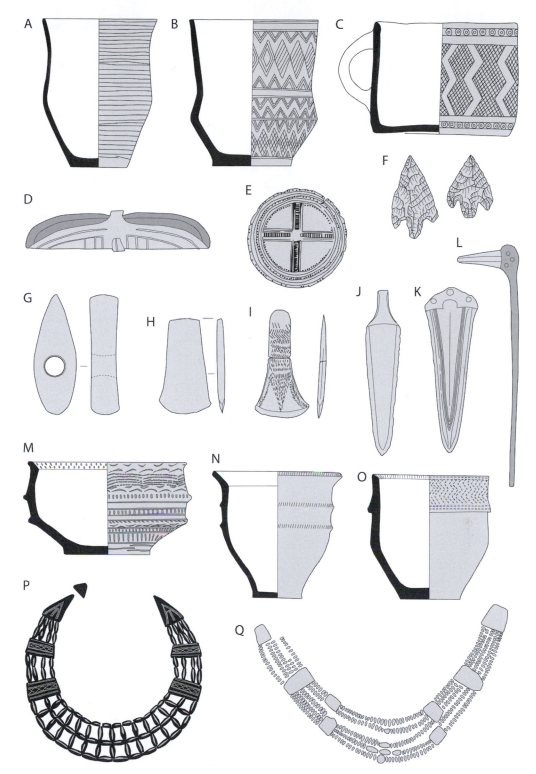

Figure 4.2 Artefact types mentioned in Chapter 4. A–C: Bell Beakers; D: gold earring or hair ornament; E: decorated gold disc; F: barbed and tanged arrowheads; G: battle axe; H and I: axeheads; J and K: daggers; L: halberd (shown as hafted); M and N: Food Vessels; O: collared urn; P and Q: spacer plate necklaces of jet (P) and amber (Q).

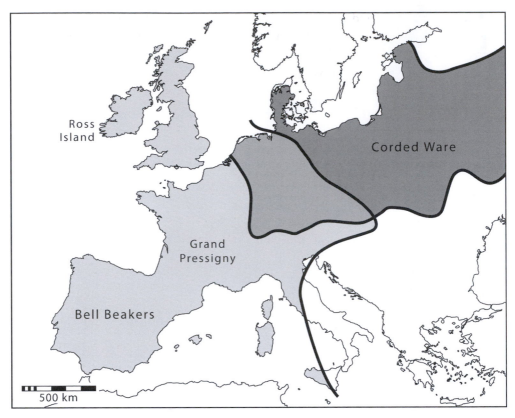

Figure 4.3 The complementary distributions of Bell Beakers and Corded Ware in Europe. Information from Cunliffe (2013).

the invasion, or invasions, of the 'Beaker Folk'. This was so much part of the framework accepted at the time that David Clarke (1970) suggested a greater number of episodes of Beaker settlement from the Continent than previous scholars in this field. Only recently has it been possible to devise more scientific methods for studying migration. One is based on the isotopic analysis of human bone. The first results do suggest a certain amount of mobility, but much of it could have been between different parts of these islands, although this method has identified some immigrants from the Continent (Parker Pearson et al. 2016).

A still more recent development is the analysis of ancient DNA. This method has been applied to the groups of human remains associated with Corded Ware and Bell Beakers. In the case of Corded Ware there is growing evidence of migration from the Yamnaya complex in south-east Europe. There seems to be similar discontinuity between the genetic evidence associated with Bell Beakers and human remains from the preceding period (Olalde et al. 2018; Reich 2018: 107–17). It is a pattern that extends across large parts of the Continent, but there is a serious problem in taking this approach to the evidence from Britain and Ireland. The Late Neolithic period in both islands lacks much unburnt human bone, and that is what is needed for this kind of analysis. Having said this, it is certainly true that the remains associated with insular Beakers compare with those from the mainland. It seems as if the model that was accepted for most of the last century was correct. One problem will be in assessing the number of incomers and their relationship with the indigenous population. Olalde et al. (2018) suggest that by the full Early Bronze Age as few as 10 per cent of the population were of indigenous descent, but this could be misleading as laboratory analysis has focused on the people whose bodies were associated with Beaker pots. Many others must have lived and died over the same period but they were not commemorated by formal burials.

Studies of the Bell Beaker phenomenon in Continental Europe have confronted other issues. Although this style of pottery might be associated with early metalwork and with a restricted range of funeral gifts, it was hard to identify the other elements needed to define an archaeological 'culture' (Bradley et al. 2016a: 131–5). There was no Beaker economy; these artefacts could be found with a variety of monument types; and, most important of all, Beaker settlements and houses assumed many different forms (Besse and Desideri 2005). More often than not, this distinctive material assemblage was associated with kinds of buildings that were already well established.

Again there were empirical and theoretical problems to overcome. A practical difficulty concerned Beaker chronology in Britain and Ireland. Clarke (1970) had postulated a series of migrations linking specific parts of Continental Europe to particular parts of these islands, identifying such connections on the basis of pottery types and their associations. Once the colonists had settled here, they made their pottery in more local styles which gradually changed their character over time. Continental scholars disputed some of the comparisons on which his interpretation was based and proposed a simpler scheme. The British and Irish sequence had apparently moved in parallel with well-documented developments in The Netherlands (Lanting and Van de Waals 1972).

It remained to test these ideas by a programme of radiocarbon dating. The initial work published in 1991 was unsatisfactory (Kinnes et al. 1991), but more radiocarbon dates have been obtained in recent years and a much clearer pattern has emerged. The overall date range has narrowed to 2400–1800 BC, and it seems as if the earliest Beakers are especially close to those found on the Continent; most later types represent insular developments. It is only with the earlier styles that long-distance migration can be postulated (Needham 2005).

What were the contexts of Beaker material in Britain and Ireland? They differ fundamentally. It is commonly supposed that fine Beakers are associated with burials, where they form part of a stereotyped assemblage associated with specific individuals. That rarely happened in Ireland (Waddell 2010: 119–23; Carlin and Brück 2012; Carlin and Cooney 2017). As this is the area with the earliest copper mines, it is the logical place at which to begin this account. Although it includes pottery with stylistic links to both Western and Central Europe, Ireland was directly connected to the Atlantic seaways and in an excellent position to participate in a network that originated in Iberia.

The introduction to this book touched on the problems of using a period framework based on technology. That is important as there is a contrast between the first use of copper in these islands and that of bronze. For that reason it is helpful to distinguish between a Copper Age or Chalcolithic and an Early Bronze Age in Britain and Ireland (Needham 2012). The Chalcolithic began about 2500 BC and the Bronze Age ran from 2200 BC. In some parts of Europe metalworking was adopted through a growing familiarity with the raw materials. Occasional items of metalwork might have been imported into what was essentially a Neolithic setting. This may not have happened in Britain and Ireland where the first adoption of metals is usually described as an event. On the other hand, surviving tool marks at the site of Durrington Walls may be those of metal axes introduced a little before the advent or acceptance of Bell Beakers. That is by no means certain, but it could explain the virtual absence of stone axe fragments at this extensively excavated site (Parker Pearson et al. 2017).

In other regions the adoption of metalwork marked the culmination of a process by which it was adopted in one society after another as the requisite knowledge became available. By 3000 BC, it had been taken up in North-Central Europe and across the Iberian Peninsula, and in the mid- to late third millennium its distribution expanded to Britain, Ireland, France, and south Scandinavia. The production of bronze artefacts involved the addition of tin, and across the Continent the adoption of this process took even longer. Moreover, the idea of doing so seems to have travelled in the opposite direction, so that it had happened by 2200 BC in Britain where local tin was available in the south-west, but did not reach Central and Northern Europe for at least another two centuries (Pare 2000).

How did these changes impact on indigenous communities who had experienced little or no contact with the Continent since the fourth millennium BC? There is a striking convergence between the earliest dates for Beaker ceramics and metalwork and the construction of enormous monuments of purely insular kinds. They include the largest henges in Wessex – sites like Durrington Walls and the principal setting of monoliths at Stonehenge – but the evidence extends to large mounds like Silbury Hill, to extraordinary post settings like those at Catholme, and even to the Ring of Brodgar in the far north.

Perhaps there was a direct connection between these two phenomena. The rapid escalation in the construction of monumental architecture might have been a deliberate reassertion of traditional norms at a time when their very existence was under threat. Massive buildings which lacked any counterparts in Continental Europe were erected in reaction to new ideas and new people whose first appearance threatened to undermine the norms on which communal life had been based (Bradley 2013a). If so, then the existence of two competing worldviews was comparatively short-lived and such enormous structures usually went out of use. It would not be until the first millennium BC that monuments on a similar scale were created in the insular landscape. At the same time links with the local past were not severed irrevocably, and during the Chalcolithic period, and sometimes the Early Bronze Age, similar but smaller buildings were created in many parts of both islands.

This was an important transition, but its true significance is all too easily masked by conventional period divisions. Henges, it is assumed, are a Late Neolithic feature, while Bell Beakers and their associations are Chalcolithic or Copper Age. In fact both these phenomena overlapped, and it is the abruptness of the changes that requires attention here.

THE FIRST METALWORK

The earliest Irish metalwork has always presented problems. It consisted mainly of axeheads, although there were also halberds and knives or dagger blades. All were made of a distinctive type of copper whose most likely origin was in the south-west of the country (O'Brien 2004a). Products from this source were distributed throughout the island and also occurred in Britain, particularly towards the west and north; in the south, metalwork was imported across the Channel. On chronological grounds all these artefacts should date from the same period as Beakers, but the different kinds of material were not found in association with one another. The problem was summed up by Case (1966) in an article entitled 'Were the Beaker-people the first metallurgists in Ireland?' Whether or not metalworkers had used this kind of pottery, where had they acquired such a specialised technology? Despite the reaction against prehistoric migrations, it was clear that such complex processes as metallurgy could not have developed spontaneously. They had to be taught and learnt.

Both problems were resolved by excavations at Ross Island in south-west Ireland (O'Brien 2004a). It had always been suggested as the site of early copper extraction, and here it was possible to investigate some of the mines where the raw material was obtained, and a work camp in which it was processed. That specialised settlement was associated almost exclusively with Beaker pottery. At last the beginnings of Irish metallurgy could be set in a wider context. The project shed some light on the processes followed at the mines and it permitted a tentative comparison between the technology employed at Ross Island and the procedures followed along the coastline between Normandy and Spain. The dates from Ross Island show that mining there commenced around 2400 BC and continued until about 1900 BC.

Apart from the settlement of Lough Gur, also in south-west Ireland, there are no other places where early metal occurs on sites with Beaker pottery. That is probably because they were deposited according to different conventions. As O'Brien (2004a) observes, the earliest metalwork is dominated by axeheads. They may have replaced their stone equivalents, and, like them, they are some-times found in hoards or votive deposits. In contrast, Beaker pottery may have taken on some of the existing roles of Grooved Ware (Carlin and Cooney 2017). Halberds, on the other hand, were deposited in different areas from Bell Beakers. This contrast is found throughout Ireland and Britain and is difficult to explain (Needham 2016).

Irish Beakers were associated mainly with settlements and monuments, although there can be problems in distinguishing between these kinds of site. The best known of these 'settlements' were at Newgrange and Knowth (O'Kelly, Cleary, and Lehane 1983; G. Eogan and Roche 1997: ch. 5). In both cases there seems to be the same link with an important structure from the past, and a small tomb at Knowth housed one of the few Beaker burials in Ireland. At Newgrange the supposedly domestic deposit was in front of the entrance to the tomb. Here Beakers were mixed with Grooved Ware, worked flints, and the enigmatic structures discussed in Chapter 3. The lithic industry included a series of arrowheads and discoidal knives of the kind associated with Grooved Ware, but Beaker forms were present in smaller numbers (O'Kelly, Cleary, and Lehane 1983). At the neighbouring monument of Knowth, however, Beaker ceramics were stratified above the levels containing Grooved Ware, but even here the excavated assemblage presents some problems. Again it was associated with concentrations of ceramics, flint artefacts, and hearths, but the Beaker pottery was unusual, for some of these groups included a high proportion of decorated vessels (G. Eogan and Roche 1997: ch. 5). In both cases it is possible that these artefacts were deposited by visitors to the monuments or even by pilgrims.

Beaker pottery was associated with another distinctive class of structure. This was the wedge tomb which had a wider distribution than any other type of megalith in Ireland (O'Brien 1999). These monuments will be considered later in this chapter, but at this point it is worth saying that similar patterns are found in Atlantic Europe, where many of the Beaker burials were associated with the reuse of megalithic monuments (C. Gibson 2016). In Ireland the decorated vessels were found with cremations, recalling those in Neolithic passage graves, and were not accompanied by any other grave goods. Radiocarbon dates suggest that wedge tombs were built during the late third millennium BC (Brindley and Lanting 1992). One example contained a small collection of metalwork (O'Brien 1999: 164–5).

The artefacts that were used as grave goods in Britain occurred in different contexts in Ireland (Waddell 2010; Carlin and Brück 2012; Carlin and Cooney 2017). That obviously applies to the Beakers themselves, but it is also true of the objects that one might expect to find with them. The characteristic arrowheads of this period were represented in wedge tombs, but they were also deposited in a hoard. The stone wrist guards that are associated with Beakers in British burials have sometimes been found in bogs. The tanged copper knife was another type that could occur in graves, but it did not happen in Ireland where some of these artefacts might have been associated with hoards and votive deposits. When a tradition of individual burial first developed in Ireland, as it did about 2200 BC, it was associated not with Beakers but with a different style of pottery, the Food Vessel (Brindley 2007).

Other kinds of metalwork were rarely associated with the dead either in Britain or Ireland. This is particularly true of axes, which seem to have been the main products of the Irish smiths. These were generally found in isolation or with other metal artefacts. Some were in dry land hoards, but often they were associated with water and placed in bogs, rivers, and lakes (Needham 1988). Even the single finds carried a special significance. They are considered later in this chapter.

The early beginning of copper working should not overshadow the use of native gold, for it also began during the later third millennium BC (G. Eogan 1994b). Three kinds of artefact were important. There were gold discs which were produced from about 2300 BC, as well as the distinctive artefacts which are often described as ear rings, although they were probably hair ornaments. Such trinkets are known from various parts of Europe and are associated with the earliest Beaker burials in Britain which date from approximately 2350–2150 BC. The other form was the lunula, which is interpreted as a kind of collar (Fig. 4.4). A few come from Britain and north-west France but in this case the gold may also have originated in Cornwall or Devon (Standish et al. 2015). They are usually single finds, and none was clearly associated with a burial. They were made during the currency of Beakers and shared their character-istic decoration. In lowland England the closest connections were probably across the Channel and between the east coast and The Netherlands. Some of the graves included the classic components of the Bell Beaker repertoire. Others contain battle axes whose forms referred back to the Corded Ware tradition, and yet their distributions overlapped.

Many of the same kinds of artefacts are found on both sides of the Irish Sea, but in Britain they are normally associated with burials in flat graves or small round barrows. During an initial phase between about 2400 and 2150 BC such mounds were usually small and associated with one inhumation burial, gen-erally a male, located in a central position beneath the monument (Garwood 2007). Some of the burials were associated with wooden chambers of a kind

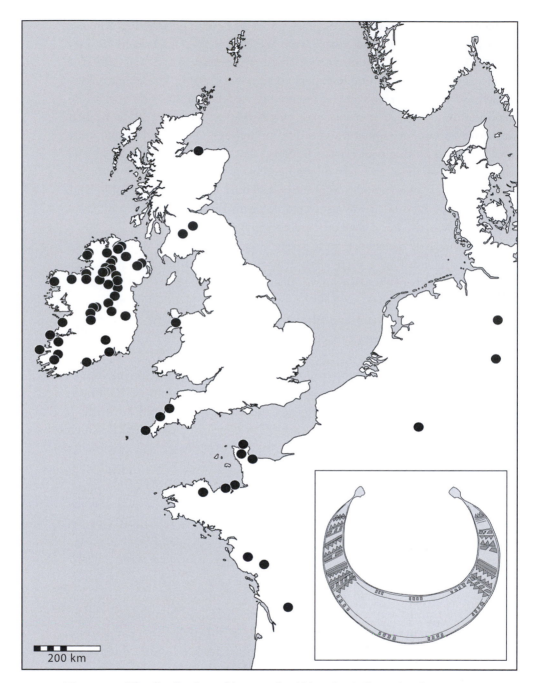

Figure 4.4 The distribution of decorated gold lunulae. Information from Eogan (1994).

represented on the Continent (Bradley et al. 2016a: 145–6). They included archery equipment, knives, daggers, awls, and a variety of personal ornaments. Although they were broadly contemporary with large henge monuments, they could be located a short distance away from them. For instance, the rich

Beaker burials excavated at Amesbury were over 1 km from Durrington Walls, although they were near a circle of pits or posts associated with Grooved Ware and dated between 2800 and 2500 BC (Fitzpatrick 2011). A similar pattern has been identified around the Devil's Quoits, a henge monument in the Upper Thames Valley (Lambrick and T. Allen 2004). In addition, a few burials were in small barrows of a kind associated with Corded Ware on the Continent. Their distribution extended from the English Midlands to western Scotland (Last 2007b: 166–73; Cook, C. Ellis, and Sheridan 2010: 175–7).

THE NEW LIFE

Beaker Settlement Sites

Beakers are found in settlements where they form the predominant, and sometimes the only, ceramic style. They are commonly associated with a distinctive range of worked flints. These sites are more common than they are in Ireland and seem to be a particular feature of the Western Isles and the North Sea coast (A. Gibson 1982). Some of the earliest vessels are from the maritime havens in the north and west discussed in earlier chapters (Bradley et al. 2016b). The vessels on domestic sites occurred in a wide range of sizes and fabrics and could represent a complete assemblage rather than a set of specialised equipment. For the most part the domestic ceramics were more robust than their equivalents in graves, suggesting that certain vessels were meant to withstand normal wear and tear, whilst others might be finely finished but were used only once (Boast 1995). The occupation sites are often ephemeral but include the same mixture of pits, middens, and circular and oblong houses as those associated with Peterborough Ware and Grooved Ware (Fig. 4.5). A few boat-shaped buildings were shared between the Hebrides and Brittany (Parker Pearson, Sharples, and Symonds 2004: 43–52; Pailler and Stéphans 2014). Otherwise there does not appear to have been a separate type of 'Beaker' house.

In southern England, some of the best-preserved evidence is sealed by deposits of hillwash in valley bottoms where there are traces of ard cultivation (M. Allen 2005). Similar evidence is found on sand banks and gravel bars beside the River Thames in London (Sidell et al. 2002). On the edge of the Fenland near Peterborough, there seem to be fence lines suggesting the existence of small plots or fields (Pryor and Bamforth 2010: fig. 3.10). Perhaps they can be compared with the shallow gullies associated with Beaker and later pottery beneath the early medieval cemetery at Sutton Hoo in eastern England (Carver 2005: ch. 11). There may be similar evidence from Snail Down in Wessex, where the earthworks of two field boundaries underlie a group of later barrows. A circular house was associated with the settlement at Sutton Hoo, but at Snail Down arcs of stake holes provide the only evidence of wooden buildings (N. Thomas 2005: 73–6). Similar structures associated with

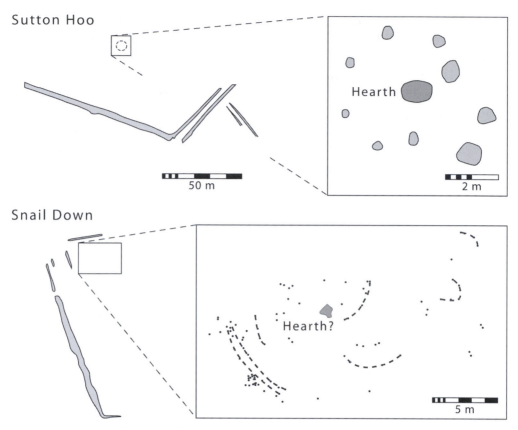

Figure 4.5 Plans of Bell Beaker settlements and structures at Sutton Hoo, East Anglia and Snail Down, Wessex. The site plans indicate the course of low banks or ditches, and the insets show settings of postholes, hearths, and stake holes. Information from Carver (1998) and N. Thomas (2005).

Beaker pottery have been identified during development-led excavations in Ireland (Tierney and Logan 2008).

An important link with traditional practice is found at some of the henges. Beaker pottery can be associated with the stone phases of these monuments, although this link is not always clear-cut. Sometimes it extended to the banks and ditches enclosing earlier structures. One way of viewing the connection is to suggest that the adoption of Beakers happened as those structures became more directly connected with the dead. The same idea might be expressed by graves in the vicinity, and at different times in the Early Bronze Age the interior of an older henge or stone circle could be buried underneath a barrow. It happened close to Stonehenge (Pitts 2018), at Ringlemere in south-east England (Parfitt and Needham in press) and at Dyffryn Lane in Wales (A. Gibson 2010b). Gibson suggests that it may also have occurred at the Scottish henges of Cairnpapple and Balfarg and even at Woodhenge.

A different development affected some of the megalithic tombs in Scotland, as they were selectively reused for Beaker burial (Wilkin 2016). There is little sign that their structures were modified, although certain architectural details may have been copied in building a new series of monuments (Bradley 2000a). The reused tombs contained human remains and pottery, but there were few other artefacts. Sometimes their entrances were blocked during this phase. Other monuments may have been 'closed' in a different way. This could have happened to some of the timber and stone circles which were surrounded by a ditch at a late stage in their history (Bradley 2011). In northern Scotland earlier structures could be closed by the erection of a ring of monoliths (Bradley 2000a and 2005). These sites are considered on page 194.

The Movement of Metals

If the first deposits of metalwork were in Ireland, by 2000 BC they were common in Scotland. There were fewer in England and Wales. That change is significant as it spanned the period in which bronze working developed in Britain. Some of the raw material was imported from Ireland, but now it was probably alloyed with Cornish tin (Needham 2004). The British metalwork was more varied than its Irish counterpart which was dominated by large numbers of axes known from hoards and single finds. It emphasises the point that during the Beaker ceramic phase one group of artefacts might be associated with the dead, whilst another was employed in a different sphere. Stuart Needham (1988) suggests that the deposits in graves were connected with particular people, and those in hoards with the wider community.

These new developments articulated with the practices discussed in Chapters 2 and 3, and there was no obvious change in the pattern of settlement, although cereal farming became rather more important (Stevens and Fuller 2012). Some people lived in insubstantial round or oval houses, as they had done for over five hundred years. In the same way, Beakers were associated with structural changes at British henges which perpetuated, and even enhanced, their traditional architecture. People formed new alliances to highlight their own positions, and in doing so they adopted a new technology. No doubt that process involved the movement and exchange of personnel (Vander Linden 2006), but it also drew on developments that extended into the past.

DISTANCE AND ENCHANTMENT

The Death Assemblage

These questions have been considered in some detail because the same issues are important in the Early Bronze Age. How was British and Irish material

Figure 4.6 The Cursus Barrows. Part of a linear cemetery close to Stonehenge. Photograph: Aaron Watson.

culture related to that in Continental Europe? What is the significance of the types of artefacts shared between these islands and the mainland, and does the evidence of burials and metalwork hoards provide an accurate picture of life during this period?

There can be little doubt that approaches to these problems have been influenced by the archaeology of a few areas and, in particular, Wessex. They have also placed an undue emphasis on the objects found in graves (Fig. 4.6). That was understandable in the development of Bronze Age studies, for it was only by identifying those objects with the widest distributions that there was any prospect of relating insular material culture to the historical chronology established in the Mediterranean. At the same time, a small selection of exceptional artefacts came to dominate the discussion for reasons which are explained by the history of fieldwork. Long before settlement excavation was considered possible or useful, well-preserved barrows were investigated for grave goods. Since early antiquarians did little to record the structures of the mounds, the contents of a biased sample of graves provided most of the material for study.

Their excavations were devoted to standing monuments which survived in great numbers on the chalk of southern and north-eastern England because both regions had been used as grazing land. In the nineteenth century, there were people with the financial means and social connections to conduct large numbers of investigations. For a long time research focused on the contents of their collections, and even now the results of their fieldwork provide a misleading impression of the Early Bronze Age.

Such biases can be remedied in several ways. More sophisticated excavations have treated individual mounds, and the areas outside them, as cemeteries that might contain a whole range of burials of different ages and types (Last 2007a). Other kinds of monument were discovered, too. Aerial photography and development-led excavation redress another imbalance in the record. It no longer seems as if the main concentrations of Bronze Age barrows were on high ground, as was once supposed. Rather, they are only the surviving part of a wider distribution of monuments associated with major valleys. Others have been obliterated by cultivation. Such work also shows that the great concentrations of burials long recognised in regions like Salisbury Plain, the Dorset Ridgeway, or the Yorkshire Wolds are like those in areas where few earthworks survive. For example, many round barrows are located along the rivers discharging into the Fenland (C. Evans and Knight 2000b), whilst the density of round barrows on the island of Thanet, which commands the route from the Channel to the Thames Estuary, is similar to that on the Wessex chalk (Perkins 2010).

In both the Beaker period and the Early Bronze Age finds of high-quality metalwork are known well outside the areas which have usually been studied. Among the discoveries in England are a group of gold ornaments associated with a palisaded enclosure at Lockington (Hughes 2000). There is a gold vessel from the reused henge monument at Ringlemere (Parfitt and Needham in press) and a number of other finds from Kent (Champion 2004). In the Midlands, two barrows, at Raunds and Gayhurst, are associated with enormous collections of bones, suggesting that hundreds of animals had been slaughtered and consumed at feasts (J. Harding and Healy 2007: 256–63; Chapman 2007). There is little to distinguish the most complex grave assemblages at lowland monuments like those at West Heslerton in northeast England from burials in the well-known cemeteries on the chalk nearby (Haughton and Powelsland 1999). The real difference is that these monuments did not survive above ground and had been protected from antiquarian activity.

There have been fewer new developments in Irish archaeology, but this is because some areas are poorly suited to air photography, although geophysical survey is making an important contribution. There has been a marked increase in discoveries as large areas of topsoil are stripped in the course of developer-funded excavations. Like the east coast of Scotland, Ireland contained many flat cemeteries in which the dead were buried in stone coffins or cists (Cahill and Sikora 2011, vol. 1). Here barrows or cairns were less often built. Some of the graves recently discovered in Scotland are just as noteworthy as the better-known examples in the south of England. Indeed, one result of new fieldwork has been the recognition of burials in pits and flat graves even in barrow-dominated landscapes.

Wider Worlds

The contents of Early Bronze Age burials pose several problems. It is obvious that unusual artefacts were obtained from a distance and that local products imitated exotic types. In the past this was explained in two ways. The first has proved especially tenacious. True to the intellectual climate of the time, Piggott's classic account of the rich graves of the 'Wessex Culture' drew on Continental parallels to postulate an invasion of southern England by an elite from Brittany (Piggott 1938). This was based on the similarities between the grave goods in these two areas. A similar relationship was proposed with the burials of the Únětice Culture in Central Europe (Fig. 4.7). It is true that, like Wessex, this region contains some exceptionally rich burials associated with round barrows, but in fact most of the graves are in flat cemeteries, and more artefacts were deposited in hoards (Steffen 2010; O'Connor 2010). There are stylistic links between the metalwork from this region and Britain, but long-distance connections are equally apparent from the distribution of Baltic amber (Vandkilde 2017: 140–5). Beads of this material are distributed from Britain and Scandinavia as far as the Mediterranean. Bronze axes of British forms are even depicted in the rock art of southern Sweden (Skoglund 2017).

A second approach was equally influential. For a long time, studies of the Early Bronze Age supposed that Britain and Ireland were on the outer edge of ancient Europe and that its core was in the Mediterranean (Childe 1940: ch. 8). This was taken as the ultimate source of inspiration for a number of new developments, from artefact types to the design of monuments. Some of those links were implausible – Irish passage tombs are Neolithic and cannot be compared with the tholos tombs of Greece – but it may be that the entire approach was wrong. Why should these islands have been dependencies of the European mainland? It is ironic that the closest link between the study area and the wider world involved movement in the opposite direction. Amber which may have been imported from Scandinavia was used to make jewellery in Britain, and a few of the finished artefacts were deposited in the shaft graves at Mycenae.

A useful perspective on such long-distance contacts is provided by the faience beads which were in use in Britain and Ireland between about 1900 and 1500 BC. They are also found in Greece, Central Europe, and south-west France (Sheridan and Shortland 2004). Might they provide more convincing evidence of international trade? It was once considered that the Mycenaeans were exchanging southern faience for northern amber. It is true that these beads were linked by a similar technology, but now it is obvious that it was the technology that was adopted in these different areas: its products were not

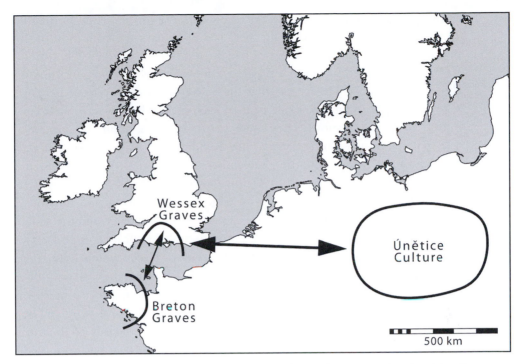

Figure 4.7 The triangular relationship between the Early Bronze Age burials of Wessex and those in Brittany and Central Europe.

exported from a single source, and the British examples made use of tin from south-west England (Sheridan and Shortland 2004). At the same time, there must have been contacts from one end of the island to the other, for some of the artefacts with this distinctive composition were made in the north of Scotland. The best evidence comes from the maritime haven at Findhorn Bay on the Moray Firth (Bradley et al. 2016b).

The same applies to the adoption of metallurgy, and here a core–periphery model is equally inappropriate. Ireland contains gold, and some of the objects produced there were exported to the Continent (G. Eogan 1994b). Copper mining was established in the south-west of the country from 2400 BC, and new sources were exploited when Ross Island went out of use (O'Brien 2004a). Around 1900 BC other mines were established in Wales and parts of northern Britain and remained in operation for about three hundred years, and in one case for even longer (Timberlake 2016). It is clear from metal analysis that Cornish tin and possibly gold were exploited from an early stage.

It seems more consistent with the evidence to suggest that the concentrations of richer burials in Europe are related to the proximity of metal sources or the routes along which the material was distributed. That would explain the prominent position played by southern Britain, Ireland, and north-west France. Similarly, the growth of the Únětice Culture might be related to the presence of tin; local communities could also access copper from the Alps (Vandkilde 2017). In the area of isostatic uplift there is early metalwork from most of the maritime havens around the coast of Britain and Ireland (Bradley et al. 2016b).

A study by Needham (2000) suggests a more satisfactory way of thinking about this evidence. He accepts that there were close connections between individual artefacts on either side of the Channel and that objects might have moved in both directions. They were particularly important because they referred to links with distant areas. They could also be made out of materials with unusual physical properties, like amber, gold, and jet (A. Woodward and Hunter 2015: 498). The work of Helms (1998) is particularly relevant here. She discusses the role played by knowledge of distant places and unfamiliar practices. Long-distance travel can be a source of social power, and the acquisition of exotic items may assume a cosmological significance. It is the fact that some of those connections were with remote places which leant them their special power. It may be why drawings of axeheads feature on a number of stone monuments in Britain, including cists in the Kilmartin complex on the west coast of Scotland (A. M. Jones et al. 2011: 257–60 and 317–21). They depict a similar selection of artefacts to the metalwork hoards of the same period. Links with Early Bronze Age Ireland were important, but from about 1950 BC there is particularly clear evidence of contacts across the Channel, illustrated by the distribution of vessels made from gold, amber, and shale. It extends from Cornwall to the Rhine. Most of the English examples were found near to the coast, and were outside the main concentrations of barrows (Needham, Parfitt, and Varndell 2006: fig. 38).

Boats and Boat Graves

The importance of sea-borne contacts was emphasised in another way as a few British graves contained coracles or dugout canoes (Fig. 4.8). In other cases their plan resembled that of a boat. Their chronological distribution seems to be confined to the Chalcolithic and Early Bronze Age periods; in contrast to the evidence from the Baltic, there were no monuments in the shape of a seagoing vessel during the later Bronze Age (Van de Noort 2011). The graves took two main forms (Bradley 2018). The majority contained tree trunk coffins which bear a striking resemblance to log boats. They date between 2200 and 1700 BC and can reproduce details of these vessels in their construction, although only two examples could have been used on water. One came from the west coast of Scotland near Oban and might have been a reused vessel. The other was found on the shoreline. Excavation has also identified a series of graves whose form resembled that of a small boat. Stone-lined cists adopted the same outline or were occasionally covered by a stone of similar size and shape (Bradley 2018).

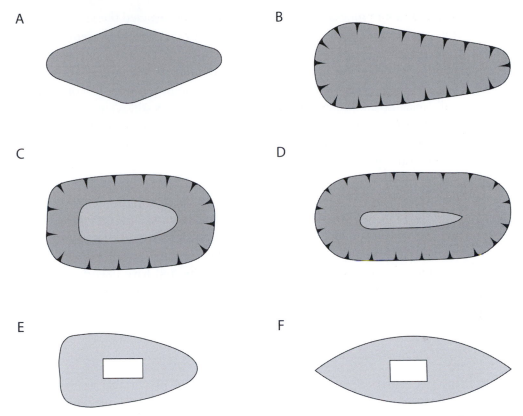

Figure 4.8 Outline plans of the main types of boat graves represented in the British Isles. They are not drawn to scale but are approximately the same sizes as one another. A: ship setting with pointed prow and pointed stern; B: boat grave with pointed prow and stern approximately at right angles; C: grave containing a small vessel similar in form to a coracle; D: grave containing a possible log boat with a pointed prow and its stern at right angles; E: cist grave covered by a massive capstone, pointed at one end; F: cist grave covered by a massive capstone pointed at both ends. Information from Bradley (2018).

Their distribution is revealing. Although a few were inland finds, others were discovered by sheltered bays. There were several on the Firth of Forth and two more by the Moray Firth. The well-preserved wooden coffin from Gristhorpe in north-east England came from a mound overlooking the North Sea (Melton, Montgomery, and Knüsel 2013), and there are reports of stone settings in the shape of small boats close to a bay on the Solway Firth (Bradley 2018). A similar structure was found in a cemetery beside the Clyde Estuary in the west of Scotland (Duffy 2007). It was defined by a setting of stones and the vessel was shown as if it was travelling towards the island of Arran which is notable for its prehistoric monuments.

That is not to suggest that these small structures depicted the kinds of vessel that ventured far out to sea. It was the idea of the boat that seems to have been important. The same applies to some of the artefacts associated with this group of burials. Thus the grave goods from a burial beside the Moray Firth included items whose distinctive style and composition refer to connections with Ireland (Bradley 2018). This evidence points to a still wider pattern. Like the precious cups in southern England, it is striking how many of the 'richest' Early Bronze Age burials along the North Sea coast were located near the shoreline compared with those further inland.

There is some evidence of change over time. The main periods in which the maritime havens of northern Britain were used were the Mesolithic, the Neolithic, and the first half of the second millennium BC. At several of these sites the sequence ended with the construction of mortuary cairns on or by the beach. It was most evident at the Glenluce and Gullane Sands, but urned cremation burials dating from the end of this period have been found more widely and are recorded at Culbin, Littleferry, and Tentsmuir in Scotland, and, in Ireland, from the Dundrum Sands (Bradley et al. 2016b).

Metal Analyses

Another source of information is the movement of portable artefacts. The findings of metal analysis are important here (Rohl and Needham 1998; Bray and Pollard 2012). After the discovery of Cornish tin, the inhabitants of southern Britain may have exported raw materials, both as native ores and in the form of bronze, but from about 1650 BC the occupants of these islands made less use of local metals and the European mainland provided a more significant source. That was especially true in the south. The sequence is consistent with studies of ancient seafaring. Before the first exploitation of copper and tin, travel across open water may have been dangerous and infrequent, and it is surely significant that it was not long before these changes happened that sewn-plank vessels seem to have developed. Their remains have been found in the Humber Estuary close to some of the richest burials in northern England (Van de Noort 2011).

RELATIONS WITH THE DEAD

At various points in this chapter the text has referred to 'single' or 'individual' burials. The terms have been used interchangeably, but that can be misleading.

On one level the notion of single burial was an artefact of early field-work (Fig. 4.9). Antiquarians thought that round barrows were memorials to important individuals (A. Woodward 2000). Each mound would cover a grave containing their remains, accompanied by a variety of artefacts. The first

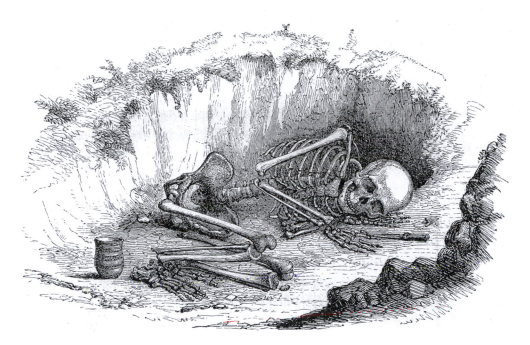

Figure 4.9 A typical 'single' burial as depicted in Canon Greenwell's book *British Barrows* (Greenwell 1877).

excavators targeted the centres of barrows and what was sometimes the earliest in a whole series of burials. If their finds were to be studied as a coherent assemblage, it was important that they had been deposited at the same time, and yet it is now known that any one grave can include the remains of several people. They could have been buried simultaneously, some bodies might be incomplete, or the grave might have been reopened for the reception of other corpses or groups of bones (A. Gibson 2016). Renewed excavation of these monuments shows that such features were often overlooked in early investigations. In any case there are too few graves to represent the entire population, and it is clear that isolated body parts continued to circulate, as they had during the Neolithic period.

Individual Burials, Single Graves

In Western thought the 'individual' carries specific connotations relating to identity and agency. Those ideas developed during the Enlightenment, and there are societies in which this approach is not appropriate: people are not thought of as autonomous entities but are defined in terms of their relationships with others (C. Fowler 2004). The idea of an individual burial might be equally misleading because the portrayal of the deceased created during the funeral was composed by the mourners who placed particular objects in the grave

(Brück 2004). It is not clear whether they had been the property of the dead person, and certain items may have been made for the occasion.

Some artefacts were so fragmentary that they must have circulated over several generations (A. Woodward and Hunter 2015: ch. 10). In the cases of necklaces different components could be combined in the same deposit, but not all the offerings had a lengthy history and the flowers found in Scottish graves must have been gathered specially for the funeral (Tipping 1994b). The corpse could not determine how it was to be displayed in death; the image encountered by the modern archaeologist reflects the relationships between the deceased and those who undertook the burial.

The Funeral as Negotiation

Perhaps the grave was an arena for negotiating relationships between the living and the dead, and funerals may have brought together mourners from distant places. That is not how the evidence has been understood, for more emphasis has been on the contrast between 'richer' and 'poorer' graves (A. Woodward 2000). The distinction between adult and child burials has also been studied, and so has that between men and women, although gender distinctions were inferred on the basis of grave goods as barrow diggers rarely retained the excavated bones. Only recently has their study been placed on a sounder basis (Rogers 2013). In each case the objective has been the same: to use the contents of the burials to reconstruct social organisation. Archaeologists have employed the grave assemblage to infer social status and to identify the activities associated with particular people in the past. In the eighteenth century William Stukeley identified Kings' Barrows and Druids' Barrows on Salisbury Plain, and more recent writers discussed the graves of warriors, archers, leather workers, smiths, and shamans. This approach makes too many assumptions. The dead were equipped by those who survived them, and the deceased might be accompanied by the material associated with more than one of these roles. Thus the man who has become known as the 'Amesbury Archer' might have been a hunter, but he was also portrayed as a warrior, a flint worker, and a smith, for his grave contained several sets of objects that might otherwise have been distributed between different burials (Fitzpatrick 2011).

Of course there were contrasts between the contents of these graves, but, taken as a whole, the British and Irish evidence seems surprisingly uniform. There are a few exceptional deposits, but the range of variation is comparatively limited considering how many have been excavated. The quantity of metal items even in the richest Continental graves is hardly impressive compared with the contents of major hoards (Hansen 2016), and it is overshadowed by the large number of objects consigned to rivers in Britain and Ireland during the Middle and Late Bronze Ages. Some burials were accompanied by a locally made pottery vessel, and even the necklaces of jet, faience, and amber might contain beads which were already worn or broken (Frieman 2012; A. Woodward and Hunter 2015: chs. 7 and 8). Of course there were occasional episodes of lavish consumption and display, but these were mainly concerned with mound building, the construction of cremation pyres, and with funeral feasts (Barrett 1994: chs. 4 and 5). Few burial mounds attained the proportions of the largest Neolithic monuments, and some Bronze Age barrows developed incrementally over long periods of time. There seems little justification for postulating a rigid social hierarchy.

The same point is illustrated by the distribution of mortuary monuments. Passage tomb cemeteries and large henges had been widely spaced across the landscape, as if they provided focal points for a large area around them. Early Bronze Age cemeteries occurred at smaller intervals, although they were some-times established close to older ceremonial monuments. They were so frequent, and their contents were so uniform, that most of them are best regarded as the burial places of local communities (H. S. Green 1974). If higher-status graves are to be identified, then they are more likely to be those associated with long-established sites like Stonehenge. Isotopic analysis has shown that about a third of the people represented by Early Bronze Age inhumations had lived in other areas (Parker Pearson et al. 2016). When they died it is possible that they were taken to places with special histories and associations. Not everyone was accorded this privilege.

The Forms of Mortuary Monuments

The first Beaker round barrows have been discussed already, but between about 2150 and 1850 BC burial mounds became more diverse, and many structures underwent a series of transformations. In particular, barrows might be associated with a larger number of deposits and a wider variety of people. They included a greater proportion of women's graves and those of chil-dren. There were more variations in the treatment of the body, and cremation became increasingly important (Garwood 2007).

This contrasts with the period between about 1850 and 1500 BC which saw the development of the major cemeteries that were once considered to char-acterise the Early Bronze Age as a whole. Although the mounds were often large and could assume specialised forms, they were frequently constructed in a single phase, and the central graves might contain only one body. The linear barrow cemeteries of the Wessex downland date from this period and are unusual in being organised in such a formal manner (Garwood 2007), but less regimented rows of barrows can be found in other areas (Havard, Darvill, and Alexander 2017: 48–55). Cremation was widely practised, and certain of the individual monuments contain the richest graves of this period.

A basic distinction is between the use of an individual mound for a whole series of burials (a cemetery barrow/cairn), and the development of barrow cemeteries, which are groups of barrows, associated with one or more interments. Both are considered here. The mortuary monuments of north-east England provide a good starting point, for any mound could include several graves and each might contain the remains of several people (Petersen 1972). Cemetery mounds occurred in other areas. In the south, for instance, well-excavated and well-preserved monuments in Wessex contained the remains of roughly fifteen people, while the cairn at Bedd Branwen on Anglesey included a similar number (F. Lynch 1971). Mounds in Ireland featured as many as nineteen (M. O'Sullivan 2005: 169–70), although the median was six (Waddell 1990). There was considerable variation between one region and another. The round barrows of central southern England contained an unusually wide variety of artefacts, but these sites cannot typify the entire range of mortuary practices found in these islands. English barrows were commonly organised into small groups, but in other regions, most obviously in Ireland, large mounds were often isolated (J. Eogan 2004).

There were ways of commemorating people without constructing any monument. In the East Anglian fens bodies might be placed in bogs or pools together with Early Bronze Age artefacts (Healy and Housley 1992). Across large parts of Ireland, areas of western Scotland, and along the North Sea coast from the River Tees to the Moray Firth there were cemeteries of flat graves which lacked any mound or cairn (Cowie and Shepherd 2003). Such variation is by no means unusual. Apart from the many people whose remains left no trace, the deposits found in graves include inhumations, cremations, and smaller groups of disarticulated bones. Although inhumation was favoured at an earlier stage than cremation, the use of both rites overlapped and deposits of both kinds can be found in the same grave.

The Treatment of Human Remains

There is a way of thinking about such evidence which combines several of the points made so far. Not all the graves described as 'individual' burials contained the remains of one person, although this was frequently the case (A. Gibson 2016). Male burials adopted a different body position from those of women, but within these deposits artefacts were associated with particular people and were often placed in specific places in relation to the corpse. The repetition of an agreed formula was important, and these conventions seem to have been strictly observed.

Sometimes the dead wore distinctive costumes, and it was in this guise that they may have joined the ancestors. The dressing of the dead must have been very important, but the crucial evidence rarely survives, and in the past small artefacts that were really parts of a funerary costume were treated in the same way as more obvious grave goods like ceramic vessels and their contents. They included pins, toggles, belt fittings, and beads. Other items attached to the body were equally important. Among them were hair ornaments, and studs that may have been associated with body piercings (Cahill and Sikora 2014; A. Woodward and Hunter 2015: 182–6). Only occasionally do organic remains survive, as they did in a recently excavated burial in Strath Oykell in the north of Scotland where the body of a woman had been wrapped in cattle hide and covered by a large piece of textile (Lelong 2014). The burial was inside a cist and was not accompanied by any artefacts that could be interpreted as offerings.

Another well-preserved grave was at Whitehorse Hill on Dartmoor (A. Jones 2016). It was inside another cist, but this time the body had been burnt. The bones were wrapped inside the pelt of a bear and were associated with the remains of a textile garment embellished with calf skin. In this case there were some portable artefacts, and a basketry container contained jewellery, including a set of beads. Other items would not have survived under normal conditions, including wooden studs worn through the lips or ears, and an arm band made from cattle hair.

The chance survival of furs and fabrics allows a very different perspective on Early Bronze Age burials. If it had happened frequently, it could have made a more striking impression on the mourners than the occasional pot or piece of metalwork, and it is revealing that the grave in Strath Oykell would not have attracted much attention if its contents had decayed. Only rarely does an artefact assemblage communicate as effectively as an ornately dressed body.

What was the relationship between burials that were found together? Sometimes there were connections between successive deposits in the same graves. Often the original excavation had been reopened (Garwood 2007). That means that its precise position was still known, but when it happened other features of the original burial were taken into account. Where the first burial was that of an adult man, the next interment was generally a woman or a young person who would be laid out on the same alignment as the previous burial or at right angles to it. The process might be repeated. At the same time where inhumations and cremations were found together, the unburnt corpse was usually the first one committed to the ground, and the cremation was generally placed in a subsidiary position or at a higher level in the filling of the grave (Mizoguchi 1993). At times it is clear that relics were removed. Not all the earlier skeletons are complete, and it is possible that some artefacts were taken away (A. Gibson 2016). For example, careful excavation showed that the central grave at Gayhurst Quarry had been recut on five occasions, allowing remains of the dead to be inspected at intervals (Fig. 4.10; Chapman 2007).

Gayhurst

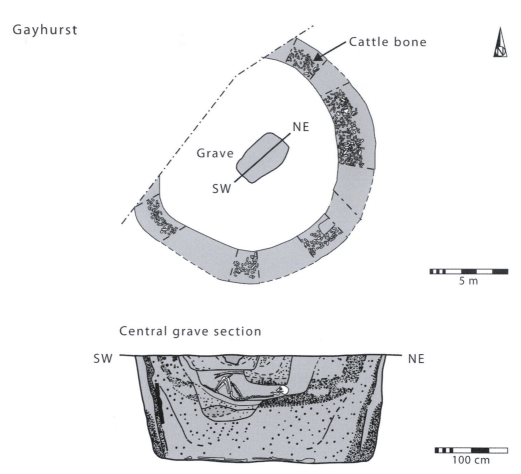

Figure 4.10 Plan of an excavated round barrow at Gayhurst, English Midlands, containing deposits of cattle bones in the surrounding ditch. The section of the central grave shows that it was reopened on several occasions. Information from Chapman (2007).

Positioning the Graves

Similar ideas apply to the siting of different graves. They may be juxtaposed, they can be aligned on one another, or their positions may respect one another with so much accuracy that it must have been intended. This would have required detailed knowledge, and such information even extended to the configuration of the corpse. This is clear from Last's analysis of the burials from a round barrow at Barnack in eastern England (Last 1998). Another example of these patterns is the cemetery at Keenoge in the east of Ireland which included a series of graves, most of them in pits or cists; the inhumations were often accompanied by cremations (Mount 1997). With few exceptions, the burials followed approximately the same alignment, but the bodies in adjacent graves tended to be organised in pairs, one with the head to the east and

Keenoge

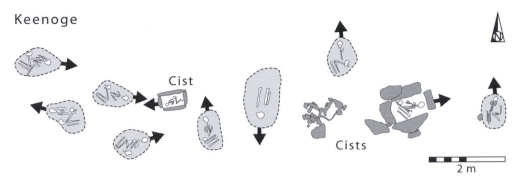

Figure 4.11 The Early Bronze Age flat cemetery at Keenoge in the east of Ireland, emphasising the orientation of the inhumation graves. Information from Mount (1997).

the other laid out in the opposite direction (Fig. 4.11). The only divergence from this pattern concerned a few graves with a north–south axis, but even then the inhumations were paired in a similar fashion. It resembles the process described by Last, but this time in a flat cemetery.

The same applies to groups of cremation pits. At Skilmafilly in north-east Scotland excavation revealed an extensive distribution of pits on a site where no trace of any monument was found (M. Johnson and Cameron 2012). Some deposits of burnt bone were inside Early Bronze Age pots, but others were unaccompanied. More pits contained charcoal, possibly taken from a pyre, but they were without any human remains. The cemetery was organised in a distinctive manner, with an arc of burials towards the north (Fig. 4.12). It might have respected the position of a mound, but it seems more likely that this had been an open enclosure since the cemetery was divided in half by two rows of pits, most of them containing charcoal. There was a cremation at its centre. The plan of the cemetery is strikingly similar to that of a roundhouse with its entrance towards the south-east (Pope 2015). The comparison cannot be taken too far but even extends to its size.

In several cases social relationships were expressed on an intimate scale, and newer burials could be related to those of the recently deceased. The same principle applies to people who had died long before, but it is more difficult to recognise. Perhaps the best evidence comes from earthwork monuments. For a long time it was assumed that they could be reduced to a few distinctive forms, so that there would be a consistent relationship between the appearance of any particular barrow and the character of the principal burial or burials found there. That was unduly optimistic as it is clear that, except in the late group of single-period barrows discussed by Garwood (2007), the shape of the mound is no guide to the deposits associated with it. Impressive earthworks may be found with sparsely furnished graves and more elaborate deposits can be covered by smaller mounds or can even be found outside them.

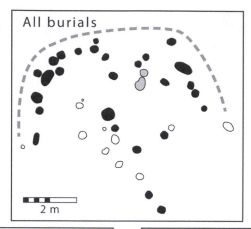

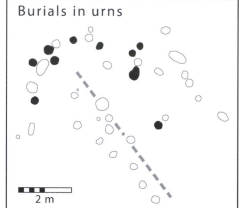

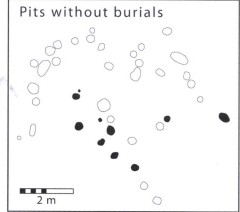

Figure 4.12 The organisation of the cremation cemetery at Skilmafilly, north-east Scotland, emphasising its curving perimeter and the line of features orientated on its centre. Information from Johnson and Cameron (2012).

That is because monuments were rebuilt or extended over time, so that in principle they might begin with an unmarked grave and pass through a series of structural stages during which they changed from one 'type' of monument to another. The outward appearance of any barrow marks the point at which that process stopped.

A similar process extended to the relationships between mounds in the same group (Figs. 4.13 and 4.14). Although the separate monuments could be placed some distance apart, it was quite common for them to be orientated on certain focal points or arranged in lines so that every barrow had its neighbour or neighbours. In that way one earthwork might refer to the position of another, and sometimes they were even combined as formerly discrete structures coalesced. Just as mounds could be linked together, they could also be kept separate, and Woodward (2000) has shown that some of the larger cemeteries can be subdivided into distinct clusters or rows of mounds. At Over

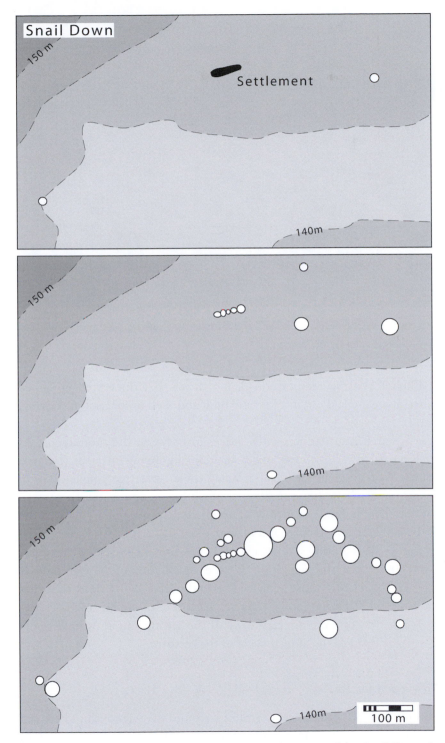

Figure 4.13 Three successive phases in the development of the Snail Down barrow cemetery, Wessex. The sequence begins with the Bell Beaker settlement illustrated in Figure 4.5 and ends with two lines of Early Bronze Age round barrows. Information from N. Thomas (2005).

Figure 4.14 Linear cemetery of large Early Bronze Age cairns at Kilmartin, western Scotland. Photograph: Aaron Watson.

in the English Fenland radiocarbon dating shows that three well-preserved round barrows were laid out in a line and built and used in succession (Garrow et al. 2014).

There is some information on the spaces in between the monuments. At sites in Kent barrow cemeteries might include alignments of posts (Bennett et al. 2008). At Radley in the Thames Valley, there were two parallel lines of round barrows orientated on the site of a Neolithic enclosure, but there were also flat graves, including a short row of urned cremations which followed the axis of the cemetery (A. Barclay and Halpin 1999: fig. 1.10). This is one of the barrow groups whose siting was influenced by the presence of an older monument, and it reinforces the suggestion that the organisation of these complexes was one way of relating those who had recently died to the dead of earlier generations. Paul Garwood (2003) suggests that a few of the linear cemeteries on the South Downs were directed towards the setting sun, thus linking the fortunes of the dead to the annual cycle of the seasons.

The Present and the Past

Early Bronze Age cemeteries were organised around the relationships between the dead themselves: not only those who had just died but also the burials of their forbears. The same idea is expressed by the circulation of older objects and their eventual deposition in the ground. The result was rather like a genealogy in which the placing of the grave, its orientation, and its contents located any particular person within a wider network of relationships extending into the past. That might be expressed quite informally in the organisation of flat cemeteries like Keenoge or Skilmafilly. It could also be set out on a more public scale through the development of a barrow cemetery.

The past remained as important as it had been during the Beaker phase. Newly built mounds were located close to the remains of henges and cursuses and might respect the alignments established by those structures even when the monuments were no longer maintained. For example, there was an important cemetery in and around an older henge at West Heslerton in northeast England (Haughton and Powelsland 1999), and round barrows in the same region were commonly superimposed on long barrows. In Ireland one of the largest groups of Bronze Age burials was in the mound covering the passage tomb at Tara (M. O'Sullivan 2005).

Similar links with the past are illustrated in other ways. One is the reuse of older rock carvings in the construction of Beaker and Early Bronze Age cists. The decorated fragments must have been of some antiquity as the pecked motifs were already worn. Others were truncated when these pieces were broken off an outcrop. They might have been treated as relics and introduced into new contexts (Bradley 1997: ch. 9). A still more striking example comes from the barrow cemetery at Raunds. A burial in Barrow 1 contained a boar's tusk which was between 420 and 990 years old (J. Harding and Healy 2007: 162). At Barrow 6 the disarticulated bones of two people who had died between 3360 and 3090 BC accompanied an Early Bronze Age inhumation dated between 2140 and 1890 BC (J. Harding and Healy 2007: 131–2).

Beyond Burial Mounds

Some cemeteries contained monuments that must have played a part in the staging of funerals. They included the low platforms described as saucer barrows (A. Jones and Quinnell 2014), and occasionally there were the remains of cremation pyres. At Biddenham in the English Midlands deep shafts were excavated on one edge of a cemetery and included the remains of wild animals (Luke 2016: 79–83). Sometimes circular enclosures were also associated with these complexes. A few had recessed interiors bounded by an earthwork bank and are described, somewhat confusingly, as 'pond barrows' (C. Evans 2016: ch. 5). There could also be palisades bedded in a continuous trench or other rings of posts or hurdles. Some structures did include human remains, especially the pond barrows which are associated with cremation burials, but all these features could be found around the barrows in a cemetery. Otherwise they might be buried underneath them.

It is surprising that the mounds are seldom considered in their own right. It is obvious that much thought went into their design and construction and into the choice of suitable materials for building them. Soils were brought from different locations to construct a composite monument, and the same was true of other materials (Owoc 2004). Both could have been selected for their distinctive colours and textures, and in south-west England their placing within the completed structure was influenced by the position of the rising or setting sun. Tilley (2017) has shown that in the same region small cairns and other structures were built from pebbles that were carefully selected for their distinctive character, including their sizes, colours, and textures. Although there is no evidence that these structures were associated with the dead, they are associated with radiocarbon dates in the Early Bronze Age.

Colour was equally important in the construction of barrows. When a mound was built in stages, its appearance would have changed. This might have been equally significant, and in southern England the sequence of construction generally involved a progression from dark to light. At the same time the first stage of barrow building frequently involved the use of turf, a living material stripped from the surrounding area and often inverted. After a hiatus it was capped by an inert deposit: usually gravel, chalk, or sand. Deprived of any nutrients, the vegetation soon decayed. In that way the monument went through a similar cycle to the human body (Bradley and Fraser 2010).

So far the account has been concerned with relationships of various kinds – relations between the contents of graves; relations between the burials in the same cemetery – but there is one which has not been considered here. That is the crucially important relationship between the dead and the places where they were buried. Topography played an important role, but their siting was influenced by the continuing attraction of monuments established during the Neolithic period. On the Wessex chalk where the barrows have been studied for nearly three hundred years, it is apparent that the largest examples were constructed in places with a distinctive history. These groups contained more mounds of specialised forms and were associated with an unusual variety of grave goods (Bradley and Fraser 2010). Such differences owed as much to the past significance of those places as it did to the status of the people buried there.

Lastly, there were features which fall outside these trends. They include prominent monuments that were built on exceptionally high ground, especially hills and mountains in the Welsh Marches, North Wales (Fig. 4.15), the Pennines, and north-east England. They are not always easy to identify from below, but commanded extensive views and some could be seen from one another; Johnson (2017) provides a recent study of this evidence. It raises important questions about the place of Early Bronze Age mounds and cairns in the wider pattern of settlement. They may have commemorated people with a special position in the community, but, in complete contrast, there were others that were not associated with any human remains. These structures present a special problem in south-west England (A. Jones 2005).

Figure 4.15 Montaintop cairn at Carnedd Fafydd, Snowdonia, North Wales. Photograph: Aaron Watson.

There were also flat cremation cemeteries which were not necessarily enclosed by formal monuments although their siting could have referred back to the structures of the past. One of the best examples is at Vaynor Farm in South Wales (A. Barber and Hart 2015). Here a henge monument had been built and used between about 2720 and 2340 BC. It was associated with a setting of posts or monoliths. Not far away was a large Early Bronze Age cemetery which contained a series of cremation burials which were mainly associated with Collared Urns. It should have been used at about the same time as Skilmafilly, but the two sites were towards opposite ends of Britain. Their discovery, and the recognition of other cemeteries like them, is a warning against placing too much weight on the monumental architecture of this period.

MONUMENTS AND THE SETTLEMENT PATTERN, 2000–1500 BC

Settlements and Cemeteries

It is frustrating that settlements can be difficult to find and that the candidates which are suggested are not always easy to date. For that reason more attention has been paid to the distribution of monuments, as this can shed some light on the areas people used in the course of their lives. Much of the difficulty arises because it is supposed that certain places were treated as 'ritual landscapes' and given over to the commemoration of the dead. That cannot be taken for granted.

In fact there is some evidence for the relationship between cemeteries and living areas, but it takes different forms in different regions. In the Upper

Thames, for example, it seems as if settlement focused on the lower river terraces, whilst the larger barrows were on slightly higher ground (Hey et al. 2011: 315–21). Around Raunds in the English Midlands, that relationship was reversed, but in each case the two zones were not far apart (J. Harding and Healy 2007: ch. 5). Close to Stonehenge a third pattern can be identified. Here the smallest barrows, which were associated with poorly furnished graves, were usually located on the lower ground and occurred in areas where there is evidence for the clearance of surface stones – presumably such regions were being tilled. The larger barrows, on the other hand, were located in prominent positions and on higher land. They were associated with a more complex series of graves and with a wider range of funeral gifts. Just as important, some of the monuments made greater use of turf, suggesting that they were built in areas of pasture (Peters 2000).

In other cases barrows were even closer to living areas. This can only be observed where the contents of the topsoil are recorded before a site is stripped to reveal subsoil features. This was what happened at Biddenham in the east Midlands (Luke 2016: fig. 3.1) and Over in the Fenland (C. Evans 2016: 85–93). At Mucking in the Thames Estuary it was possible to reconstruct similar patterns by considering the residual flintwork preserved in subsoil features of later date (C. Evans, Appleby, and Lucy 2015: 50–71). In every case concentrations of artefacts identified as settlement remains were found beside the mounds themselves.

At times barrows could be superimposed on settlement sites. This was particularly common in East Anglia, but it is found much more widely (A. Gibson 1982). Indeed, in a few cases, including the Brenig in North Wales (F. Lynch 1993: 158–61), mortuary monuments were built over the remains of older dwellings. That may have happened elsewhere, although the structural evidence is not always so convincing. On Dartmoor, it has been suggested that collapsed roundhouses were reused as mortuary cairns, but this idea needs to be checked by excavation (Butler 1997: 137).

Where barrows and settlement areas were further apart there might still be a connection between them. At Roughan Hill in the west of Ireland wedge tombs were constructed in between a number of enclosed settlements associated with Beaker pottery (Fig. 4.16; C. Jones 1998 and 2004). Again in north-east England the main areas with evidence of Early Bronze Age land use are overlooked by chains of barrows and cairns running across the higher ground. They enclose the valleys which were particularly suitable for settlement, and Spratt (1993) argued that they marked the outer limits of local territories.

Early Bronze Age Settlements and Houses

There are many reasons why domestic sites have been difficult to find. Excavation on the Scottish island of Arran showed that the sites of Beaker and

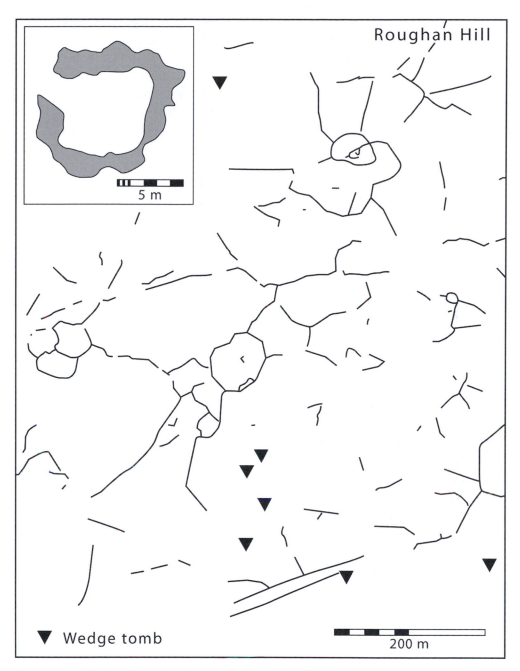

Figure 4.16 Field walls and enclosures at Roughan Hill in the west of Ireland, with an inset showing the plan of an excavated roundhouse. Information from C. Jones (1998 and 2004).

Early Bronze Age houses had been ploughed when they went out of use (J. Barber 1997). That is hardly surprising as they would have been exceptionally fertile. Another problem arises in field survey, for in upland areas the remains of dwellings resemble the specialised enclosures known as ring cairns which were built in increasing numbers during this phase. They played various roles as ceremonial sites, cremation cemeteries, and pyres, but on the ground they can be hard to distinguish from the remains of houses. In fact the link may have been intended, for there are indications that abandoned buildings were enclosed within a mantle of rubble so that they resembled monuments of this type (Bevan, Barnatt, and Edmonds 2017). Andy Jones (2008) has made the interesting observation that in south-west England roundhouses were constructed near to ring cairns but avoided the positions of mounds. Either the circular monuments were mistaken for the remains of older dwellings, or people associated the stone enclosures with the domestic domain rather than the dead.

A similar problem applies to many of the small cairns in the uplands, a number of which certainly date from this period. They seem to have accumulated around prominent boulders or outcrops which would have been difficult to move when the land was tilled. For that reason such features are interpreted as clearance cairns and have been taken as evidence of agricultural settlement. On the other hand, excavation has demonstrated that a number of them covered human burials or formal deposits of Early Bronze Age artefacts. Does this mean that they have been misunderstood? An interesting way of thinking about the problem is suggested by Robert Johnston (2000), who argues that the resemblance between mortuary monuments and field cairns was no accident, because the dead were integrated into the working of the land.

Timber structures illustrate a similar problem. Just as the distinctive settings inside henges look like enlarged versions of domestic dwellings, a number of graves were enclosed by circles of posts or stakes before barrows were built on the same sites. They raise similar problems to the ring cairns, for a few examples could be construed as the remains of dwellings, especially where such structures are associated with hearths or concentrations of artefacts (A. Gibson 1982). Perhaps these features were considered as the houses of the dead and their forms referred to those of domestic buildings. Again there is a significant overlap between all these categories. Nowhere is this more obvious than at West Whittlesey in the English Fenland, where a row of three circular structures was identified in excavation. Two of them were round barrows, whilst the third was an Early Bronze Age henge enclosing a ring of posts. 50 m away a settlement of the same date included the remains of a small roundhouse. In such cases the cross-reference between these different types must have been intentional (C. Evans and Knight 2000a).

As in the Beaker phase, some occupation sites survive because they are deeply buried. Well-preserved stone structures have been found among the coastal dunes in the Western Isles, for example on South Uist (Parker Pearson, Sharples, and Symonds 2004: 43–52). The sands are exceptionally fertile, and prehistoric ard marks are often recorded there. Although the evidence is limited, wooden roundhouses of Early Bronze Age date have also been found in increasing numbers. Entire settlements are rare and poorly dated, but there is enough evidence to shed a little light on the character of individual buildings. Like their Middle Bronze Age successors, they were generally circular rather than oval, but they were often constructed out of lighter materials, and their floor areas were generally smaller than those of the following period. It is not uncommon to find rings of comparatively insubstantial postholes enclosing areas that were as little as 4 m in diameter; more often the equivalent would be 5 or 6 m.

Fewer Early Bronze Age roundhouses were provided with porches than the dwellings of the succeeding phase, and the sites where this does occur in lowland Britain date from the end of this period, for example the settlement at West Row (Martin and Murphy 1988). At Stackpole Warren in South Wales a small roundhouse was entered by a ramp leading into a recessed interior (Benson, J. Evans, and G. Williams 1990): exactly the same technique was adopted during the Middle Bronze Age in south-west England.

The situation was rather different further to the north and especially in Scotland, where more substantial wooden buildings were established in upland areas (Pope 2015). Some have been identified because they were constructed on earthwork platforms. Again they resemble the structures of the Middle Bronze Age. Beaker pottery is not found on these sites, suggesting that more robust domestic buildings were a later development. There is little evidence that early dwellings were enclosed, but that may not apply to unexcavated sites like those described in the next section.

THE EXPANSION OF SETTLEMENT

The Settlement of Heathlands and Moorlands

The distribution of barrows, cairns, and other monuments suggests that the settled area expanded during this phase. The idea is supported by pollen analysis (Groves et al. 2012). The distribution of monuments is more extensive than that of their predecessors and includes large areas of lowland England which are presently covered by heathland. Among these areas were the New Forest and the Weald. Human activity extended into a wider range of environments, but it is often assumed that clearance and exploitation caused significant changes to the soils which became acidic and poorly drained. The finds from these regions support this sequence. Such areas rarely produce any Neolithic artefacts apart from arrowheads which may have been lost in hunting. Very few barrows contain Beaker pottery and most of the diagnostic material found there dates from the Early and Middle Bronze Ages (Bradley and Fraser 2010). Later prehistoric material is largely absent, although many areas of heathland were used on an occasional basis during the Middle Ages.

Similar trends have been identified by field survey in upland areas of Britain and Ireland. They include extensive tracts of moorland like Dartmoor, parts of the Peak District, the Pennines, and the North York Moors where barrows, cairns, and stone circles were built during the Early Bronze Age (Darvill 1986). The evidence from domestic sites has attracted less attention. That is not to deny that excavated settlements do date from this phase, but many others have been assigned to the Early Bronze Age on the unsatisfactory argument that climate change made the high ground uninhabitable during later periods (Burgess 1992). This idea is controversial (Tipping 2017), and at least some of the field evidence that had been confidently assigned to this phase dates from later periods.

The settlement evidence from the uplands often takes the same form. The stone-built houses which are visible on the surface were not necessarily the first to be built, and excavation has demonstrated that before the landscape was cleared and surface rock was exposed domestic buildings might have been of wood (Fleming 2008). Not many have been excavated, but they do seem to have been more substantial than the Beaker dwellings considered earlier. Unless such structures were replaced in stone they are difficult to find, although their positions can be located where their floors were levelled into sloping ground, leaving a distinctive earthwork. They can also be detected by empty patches within a wider distribution of boulders. A number of houses and cairns were linked by walls or banks of rubble which surrounded areas suitable for cultivation. Sometimes enclosures were tacked onto one another as increasingly large areas were occupied. They could incorporate clearance cairns, whilst others seem to have been scattered across the surrounding area. Irregular field systems of this kind are dated to the Early Bronze Age in the Scottish Highlands (McCullagh and Tipping 1998), and on the island of Arran (J. Barber 1997), but these projects could not investigate entire landscapes since many of the structures were buried under peat.

There is a problem in making observations of this kind. What is described is really a way of clearing areas with large amounts of surface stone. The result is a palimpsest of irregular field walls, enclosures, and patches of open ground with little obvious sign of order. These features are usually associated with clearance heaps of the kind considered earlier, but it can be difficult to locate house foundations without embarking on a programme of excavation. Those that are known are generally circular, but there is nothing to indicate their date. The only diagnostic elements are the non-domestic monuments – ring cairns, round barrows, and stone circles – that can be assigned to the Early Bronze Age, but there is no reason why they must be contemporary with these other elements. As on the lowland heaths, they record the construction of monuments to the dead but may not say much about the landscapes of the living.

In some cases the histories of settlements and specialised monuments did coincide. It was true in the research already described in the north and west of Scotland, but it was not the case with three other projects that set out to investigate the character of upland settlement during the earlier second millennium BC. At Gardom's Edge in the Peak District a complex landscape which had been assigned to this period actually dated from the Late Bronze Age: a time when some scholars had been confident that the local soils were too vulnerable to farm (Bevan, Barnatt, and Edmonds 2017). In south-west Ireland a project investigating the ancient landscape near the Bronze Age copper mine at Crumpane succeeded in discovering one of the rare field systems and domestic buildings of the Iron Age (O'Brien 2009). A similar project on Danby Rigg investigated the settlement pattern on the North York Moors (A. Harding et al. 1994). Like the work at Gardom's Edge, it dated a well-preserved ring cairn to the Early Bronze Age, but was unable to show whether it had been contemporary with the clearance heaps in the same area. That does not rule out an early phase of settlement, but the cairnfield itself appeared to be bounded by a substantial linear earthwork which produced radiocarbon dates in the Viking Age. It is difficult to interpret these results, but it is obvious that marginal areas were settled in much the same ways at several times in the past and that this process left similar traces behind. Early Bronze Age activity is documented by pollen analysis and by the presence of specialised monuments, but the fields and enclosures identified in field survey may date from other phases. These areas could have been occupied discontinuously and during different periods. In Wales, for example, it seems as if the highest settled land was occupied most intensively during the Bronze Age and the medieval phases (Browne and Hughes 2003). Only the presence of distinctive house plans – round versus rectangular – allowed archaeologists to tell them apart.

In the light of all these difficulties there may be only two regions in which the settlement of the uplands is clearly understood. The first is Dartmoor in south-west England (Fig. 4.17). Again the archaeology of the higher parts of the moor is confined to just two phases: the Bronze Age and the Middle Ages. In between those times settlement was confined to lower ground, although its margins must have been exploited on an occasional basis (Fleming 2008). Large tracts of moorland contained distinctive Early Bronze Age structures: stone circles, stone rows, ring cairns, round cairns, and cists (Butler 1997: chs. 3–5; P. Newman 2011: ch. 2). Sometimes their positions were reused in the layout of coaxial field systems around 1600 BC; in Chapter 5 these fields are discussed in relation to slightly later developments in lowland England. For the most part their distribution on Dartmoor complemented a network of more irregular

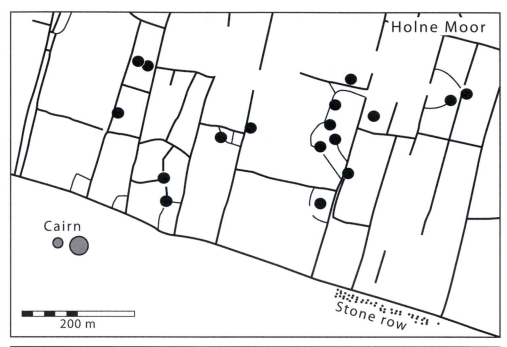

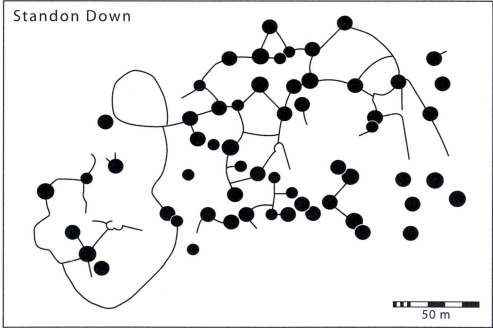

Figure 4.17 Contrasting landscapes on Dartmoor. (Upper) Coaxial fields and houses on Holne Moor and (lower) irregular field plots and houses on Standon Moor. Information from Fleming (2008).

enclosures associated with clearance cairns and roundhouses (some of them unusually small). In contrast to the rigidly rectilinear layout of the field systems, many of the enclosures were curvilinear and developed by piecemeal addition (P. Newman 2011: ch. 3). Occasionally irregular plots did abut parts of the new boundary system, but the fact that it happened so rarely suggests that the imposition of more regular land divisions across large areas of the moorland obliterated the features in their path. It happened towards the Middle Bronze Age but it is not clear how long the process took or how closely it was controlled (R. Johnston 2005).

A second project which shed new light on upland settlement took place in the Burren on the west coast of Ireland where large amounts of soil have eroded leaving an irregular network of field walls, enclosures, and house foundations exposed on the surface of the bedrock (C. Jones 1998 and 2004). What may seem a serious drawback was fundamental to the success of this project for the local limestone started to weather as soon as it was exposed to the elements. Only where it was protected beneath walls and other structures did it remain unaltered. In effect the archaeological remains were raised on plinths as the surrounding areas were lowered by natural processes. It meant that their heights above the bedrock provide some indication of their age. The process was aided by the recovery of pottery and radiocarbon samples from the protected surfaces. As a result it was possible to document a phase of settlement that included the creation of enclosures and irregular fields between 2400 and 1500 BC, although Jones emphasises that activity was not necessarily continuous. The study area at Roughan Hill included stone roundhouses and several wedge tombs. Analysis of the sediments carried by a local river offered an independent check on the rate at which the surface of the rock had been lowered. It agrees with the chronology established by archaeological fieldwork (C. Jones 2016).

Recent research in south-west England and the Burren helps to substantiate the models developed during projects in Scotland, but it remains to be seen whether the colonisation of areas which are currently heathland and moorland was a simple process with its emphasis on the Early Bronze Age. It may have commenced during that phase, but there is nothing to indicate that it happened simultaneously throughout the uplands. Nor is it obvious that these regions went out of use together. The conventional interpretations for their abandonment – increased rainfall, impeded drainage, the impact of increasingly acid soils – may not be acceptable in every case. As Chapter 1 observed, it is difficult to relate settlement patterns directly to changes in the natural environment, and examples like the settlement of Gardom's Edge suggest that archaeological orthodoxies may have to be reconsidered. Even if people faced difficulties in sustaining their way of life, not enough allowance is made for resilience and ingenuity.

Copper Mining in the Uplands

One case in which new research has happened is an important investigation of Bronze Age copper mining. Timberlake (2001) suggests that it was land use in the uplands that provided the context for early metal extraction in Wales and the west of Ireland. It was sometimes undertaken in landscapes that were being exploited for the first time. These sites were not obviously related to nearby settlements or monuments and may have been used on a seasonal basis by small numbers of people who brought the necessary equipment with them. The output of the mines was limited and for the most part their period of use was restricted to the Early Bronze Age. Like comparable sites in northern England, they seem to have operated between approximately 1800 and 1500 BC, after which they were abandoned. The one exception was at Great Orme Head in North Wales. It was the site of the largest group of mines in Britain or Ireland, and here activity continued (Timberlake 2016).

MONUMENTAL ARCHITECTURE IN THE NORTH AND WEST

Continuity of Culture?

The first chapter quoted two of the conclusions of Cyril Fox's book, *The Personality of Britain*. They are worth recalling now:

> New cultures of continental origin tend to be imposed. In the Highland [Zone], on the other hand, these tend to be absorbed.
>
> There is greater unity of culture in the Lowland Zone, but greater continuity of culture in the Highland Zone. (1932: 77–8)

Both statements apply to the period considered here. They are best illustrated by the kinds of monuments first established during the Neolithic period. With some notable exceptions, they retained their importance in Ireland and the west and north of Britain. It happened as their construction and use became less important towards the south and east. In some cases it seems to have lapsed altogether.

Certain biases result from the materials used to build these structures – stone was more often employed in highland areas – but the results of development-led excavations in southern and eastern England have been sufficiently extensive to show that wooden structures of similar kinds were comparatively rare. That applies to timber circles, post alignments, and palisaded enclosures as well as the circular earthworks identified as henges. Other kinds of building were peculiar to regions further to the north and west, and this was especially true of megalithic tombs.

The clearest contrast is between parts of lowland England in which Early Bronze Age cemeteries were created amidst the remains of Neolithic

Figure 4.18 Stone circle at Croftmoraig, central Scotland, where the structural sequence extended as late as the Middle Bronze Age. Photograph: Aaron Watson.

monuments, and other areas in which long-established styles of architecture still retained their importance. At sites like Stonehenge or Dorchester on Thames round barrows were built in places where signs of older structures could be recognised and acknowledged. In parts of Scotland, Wales, and Ireland, however, entirely new henges were built, and the same applies to stone circles, avenues of monoliths, and chambered tombs. With the possible exception of those tombs, the kinds of structure that retained their importance in the Chalcolithic and Early Bronze Age lack any equivalents in Continental Europe. Instead they conform to entirely insular traditions.

In highland areas there were many specialised monuments in the Beaker phase and, especially, in the Early Bronze Age (Fig. 4.18). Space does not permit the enumeration of all these separate types, and in any case they underwent constant modification. Like the round barrows considered earlier, they could change their outward appearance from one phase to the next, so that their surface remains provide little indication of how individual monuments developed over time (Bradley and Nimura 2016).

Several kinds of structure were important. Perhaps the most obvious examples are provided by chambered tombs, if only because they were originally assigned to the Neolithic period. As a result of recent fieldwork some distinctive kinds of passage grave have been dated to the Chalcolithic or Early Bronze Age. They have local distributions in south-west England (A. Jones and C. Thomas 2010), south-west Scotland (Cummings and C. Fowler 2007), and the inner Moray Firth (Bradley 2000a). An additional example is a

Balnuaran of Clava   Island

Loanhead of Daviot

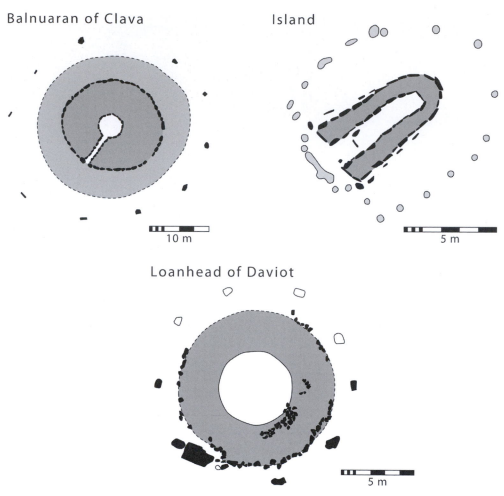

Figure 4.19 Passage grave at Balnuaran of Clava, northern Scotland, the recumbent stone circle at Loanhead of Daviot, north-east Scotland, and the wedge tomb at Island, south-west Ireland, which was surrounded by a later post circle. Information from Bradley (2000a and 2005a) and O'Kelly (1958).

small circular structure associated with Beaker pottery at Calanais which was built over the remains of an earlier wooden building (Ashmore 2016). These chambered tombs were entirely new constructions, but they were erected at a time when the remains of Neolithic monuments of similar form were reused for deposits of artefacts and human bone (Wilkin 2016).

The best-known regional group consists of the Clava Cairns of northern Scotland, which share the distinctive feature that they are enclosed by free-standing stone circles (Bradley 2000a). The monoliths are graded by height, so that the tallest are located in front of the entrance, on the south-west side of the monument. The chambered cairns are circular and supported by a kerb of boulders which follows the same convention (Fig. 4.19). Little is known about

Figure 4.20 Passage grave in the cemetery at Balnuaran of Clava, northern Scotland, with other monuments in the background. Photograph: Aaron Watson.

the primary burials associated with these structures, but at Corrimony there was evidence for a single inhumation. The two passage graves in the well-preserved cemetery at Balnuaran of Clava were orientated on the midwinter sunset (Bradley 2000a: 122–5).

Fieldwork at that site has added a few details. It is clear that the passage remained accessible for a very short time. It was partly blocked when a rubble platform was built to retain the material of the cairn. Its outer limit was marked by the ring of standing stones which was also a secondary development. Individual monoliths could be paired with the nearest components of the kerb according to their colours, textures, or mineral inclusions. The monoliths at the entrance of one of the cairns were red, and at sunset they absorbed the light. At the opposite end of the same cemetery the building stones were grey or white and contained inclusions of quartz that reflected the light of the rising sun (Fig. 4.20).

If Clava passage graves are orientated towards the south-west, the same applies to the last megalithic tombs in Ireland, the wedge tombs described on page 158. They seem to date from the same period as the monuments in northern Scotland, although they take a very different form (O'Brien 1999). They are found with Beaker ceramics and provide radiocarbon dates between 2400 and 2100 BC, but were reused for a considerable time afterwards (Brindley and Lanting 1992). The wedge tombs in the west of Ireland provided an alternative to the flat cemeteries in the east of the country. That is particularly striking as their focal point was like a massive cist; it seems possible that the cairn and passage were intended to monumentalise the deepest space inside these buildings. It happened in regions facing the Atlantic coast. Although wedge tombs have been compared with French allées couvertes (Schulting et al. 2008), it is not clear whether their chronologies overlapped, and they may have been a purely insular form. Perhaps they were the local equivalent of the Clava passage tombs, and one Irish site, Clogherny Meenerrigal, was enclosed by a stone circle (Bradley 2009b). Another was built entirely of wood and may be a little older than the others (O'Regan 2010). Again it was associated with cremation burials. In this case they date from the twenty-sixth to the twenty-third century BC.

There is another kind of Clava Cairn in the north of Scotland. Again these structures include a graded circle of monoliths with the tallest stone towards the south-west, but they enclose older ring cairns rather than passage graves. Like the chambered tombs in this tradition, they feature massive boulder kerbs, which can vary in height according to the same conventions as the standing stones. The ring cairns themselves were rubble enclosures and were originally open at the centre. Some may have been accessed through an entrance that was later blocked, and during a secondary phase the interior was filled with rubble to create a platform. These structures were contemporary with the chambered tombs, and at Balnuaran of Clava both kinds of monument occurred in the same cemetery (Bradley 2000a). Their original role is not so clear. Although they contained charcoal and deposits of cremated bone, radiocarbon dating suggests that they were secondary deposits, similar to those associated with the reuse of passage graves (Bradley and Nimura 2016: 122–4).

Another combination of ring cairn and stone circle is known in north-east Scotland and dates from the same period as the monuments considered so far. The one significant difference is that the outer ring of monoliths may have been provided with an 'entrance' that was closed by a massive block placed on the original ground surface. For that reason these structures are described as 'recumbent' stone circles (Bradley 2005). They share many features with the Clava Cairns. The ring of monoliths was built after the internal cairn, and in a sense its construction ended the use of the site. Again these places were associated with burnt deposits but they may not have been cremation pyres. The choice of raw materials according to their colours and textures suggests that a similar aesthetic connected these different kinds of architecture. Again it is important to emphasise that they lack any Continental counterparts. Instead they are closely related to insular traditions.

Later structures share some of the same attributes. Most ring cairns remained as freestanding structures and were used in similar ways to those enclosed by monoliths. The stone circles built after the Beaker phase were smaller than

Figure 4.21 Four poster on a reshaped natural mound at Lundin, central Scotland. Photograph: Aaron Watson.

their predecessors and were usually associated with burials (Bradley and Nimura 2016: ch. 7). Some examples were less accessible than before. They could be built in relatively remote locations and a few might almost have been hidden. It is obvious that they no longer commanded extensive views over the surrounding country, and for that reason they cannot be regarded as microcosms of a wider world.

Examples of these small structures abound. In eastern and central Scotland and north-east England, there are small rectangular stone settings ('four posters') which seem to include low cairns associated with cremation burials (Fig. 4.21; Burl 1988b and 2000: ch. 13). Local traditions can be identified in other areas, too. At a site like Beaghmore in the north of Ireland there are circular settings of small boulders laid out in complex geometrical patterns (Pilcher 1969). They include numerous concentric rings but also feature a series of straight alignments radiating out from a central cist. A few of the Irish examples are directly linked to stone rows.

Similar arguments apply to the earthwork enclosures of the Early Bronze Age. In the archaeological literature the henge is one of the most distinctive features of the insular Neolithic period, and one without any Continental counterparts. Chapter 3 made the case that, like the stone circles enclosing Clava Cairns, the construction of these earthworks brought the use of important monuments to an end. One implication of this argument is that what were essentially Neolithic sites might not have been bounded by an earthwork until the Chalcolithic period or even the Early Bronze Age. That sequence is supported by radiocarbon dating at North Mains (G. Barclay 1983), Dyffryn Lane (A. Gibson 2010b), and Broomend of Crichie (Bradley 2011). The case is most convincing where the monuments were conceived on a large scale. On the other hand, the situation was very different at a series of smaller earthworks of the same date. Some of them surrounded an empty area, while others enclosed quite modest settings of monoliths of the kind attributed to the earlier second millennium BC. Often they contained cremation burials, but it is clear that these monuments were only distantly related to the large structures discussed in Chapter 3. The bank and ditch did not present a conspicuous obstacle, and such low earthworks could hardly have screened the interior from view. Any entrances could be extremely narrow, and they were some-times blocked as the site went out of use. In Scotland this was accomplished by removing part of the causeway in between the ditch terminals. Alternatively, the gap might be closed by a pile of stones (Bradley 2011: chs. 5 and 6; Bradley and Nimura 2016: ch. 5). These miniature henges could share the southerly or south-westerly alignment of the stone circles of the same period. They were of approximately the same sizes as one another and in some cases were of similar proportions to individual roundhouses.

Anomalous Monuments

A variant is found at a small number of sites where the earthwork of a small henge is supplemented by a circular palisade or could even be rebuilt as a wooden enclosure. This is found at two important sites in north-west England: Street House (Vyner 1988) and Whitton Hill (Miket 1985), both of which were associated with cremated bones. They date from the Early Bronze Age and resemble other enigmatic monuments close to the North Sea coast. One was Seahenge where a continuous screen of posts enclosed the upturned bole of an oak tree (Brennand and Taylor 2003). Another example was found nearby and in each case it is not quite clear whether the timber settings originally revetted a barrow (D. Robertson 2016). Further to the east at Lockington there was a similar but larger palisaded enclosure which was replaced by a mound during a subsequent phase (Hughes 2000). In this case the site is famous for a hoard containing pottery and metal-work buried in its entrance. It included two gold arm rings, a bronze dagger, and parts of two Beakers whose position was indicated by a cup-marked boulder similar to those found at Street House. In the centre of the enclosure was an irregular hollow, and when it was built the enclosure may have surrounded a clump of trees. This early phase was not associated with any human remains.

It is easy to lose direction amidst so many local details, but many of them can be interpreted as manifestations of a series of simple ideas that were shared across the two islands. The stone circles of the Early Bronze Age were often graded in height towards the south or west, but, like the last henge monuments, they could be surprising small (Bradley and Nimura 2016: ch. 7). The same applied to the alignments of monoliths that led towards cairns of the same period in south-west England and the north of Scotland. They were often near Early Bronze Age barrows.

How were these monuments related to the mortuary rituals considered earlier? The relationship between such monuments and settlements changed from one region to another. Clava Cairns, for example, were built over, or near to, occupation sites, yet the stone circles of north-east Scotland, with which they had much in common, were in more conspicuous positions at the edge of the settled land (Bradley 2005: ch. 4). The stone settings at Beaghmore in the north of Ireland may even have been built amidst the remains of an older field system (Pilcher 1969). The distinctive stone rows of south-west England introduce another variation, for they seem to have run upslope from the areas with evidence of habitation (usually undated) towards Early Bronze Age mortuary monuments located on the higher ground (P. Newman 2011: 37–40).

The monuments were occasionally embellished with the pecked motifs known as cup marks, and many of them contain significant quantities of quartz which could be spread over an older monument when it went out of use (Bradley and Nimura 2016: 124). Often these sites provide evidence of burning in the form of pits filled with charcoal, but it need not have come from a pyre. Such associations connect a series of monuments of very different kinds which occur in widely separated areas: the recumbent stone circles of north-east Scotland, Clava Cairns, four-posters, wedge tombs, and small henges. These geographical links are reinforced by the movement of copper, tin, and, to some extent, pottery styles. Many of them emphasise south-westerly alignments and the direction of the setting sun (Bradley 2016).

These Chalcolithic and Early Bronze Age monuments do seem to bear out two of Cyril Fox's contentions in *The Personality of Britain*. Most of the insular structures with links to the Neolithic period are found in the north and west, although the palisaded enclosures along the east coast of Britain are an obvious exception. In most cases their distribution is in Fox's Highland Zone, although it also extends across the Irish Sea. It was there that traditional kinds of architecture were most closely integrated with the new ideas that appeared with the introduction of metals. At the same time, the kinds of structure that proved most resilient were precisely those which lacked any counterparts in Continental Europe. As Fox concluded at a time when less information was available, there was 'greater continuity of culture in the Highland Zone' (1932: 78).

'Nature' and 'Culture'

In Western thought nature and culture have been treated separately since the Enlightenment. This convention has already created problems in the Neolithic period. The same duality is found in studies of the Chalcolithic and the Early Bronze Age (Tilley 2004). Among the features with a geological origin are shafts and sink holes: dramatic openings in the earth that attracted offerings of artefacts as well as human burials. Similar material is found in caves during this period (Barnatt and Edmonds 2002; Dowd 2015; Leach 2015). In other cases natural boulders or larger outcrops were treated as if they were monuments and elaborated by enclosing them with a kerb (Fig. 4.22; Shepherd 2014). The same could have happened to mounds of glacial origin which were treated as if they were round barrows and used for burying the dead. These features have been recognised for a long time, but new work has widened the repertoire still further. In northern Ireland blocks of stone were raised above the surrounding area and supported on chocking stones to make a kind of sculpture (Burns and Nolan 2017). Otherwise large slabs of rock were propped at an angle to create an equally striking effect. Occasionally these structures were embellished with cup marks or more complex designs, but it is not clear when it happened.

The deposition of early metalwork emphasised the importance of such locations. Artefacts had been placed in rivers, lakes, and bogs since the Neolithic period, but after 2400 BC this practice extended to copper and bronze artefacts in Ireland (Needham 1988). By about 2000 BC, it extended to north-east Scotland and after that time it was adopted across an increasingly large area reaching into lowland England. At the same time deposits of early axes were associated with mounds, not all of which were of anthropogenic origin; few included any burials. Axes or other metal artefacts were deposited at older monuments, including the passage grave at Newgrange (O' Kelly 1982) and the henge of Mount Pleasant (Wainwright 1979). Most of the examples studied by Needham were in northern Britain, and the majority were in Scotland.

The Scottish sites have been considered by Cowie (2004) who points out that groups of early axes were sometimes placed at prominent locations in the landscape, and especially by natural mounds, outcrops, or other striking features of the terrain. Although one was just outside a Neolithic tomb, other places lacked any obvious monuments. The largest hoard, from Dail na Caraidh, was at the end of a glacial mound on a former river cliff (Barrett and Gourlay 1999). It was where a loch leading from the Irish Sea met the Great Glen which provided the easiest route across country to the region in which most metalwork was deposited. Dail na Caraidh itself featured both tools and weapons. The findspot commands a spectacular view south-eastwards into the mountains. From the findspot of the hoard the midwinter sun can be observed as it rises behind the Nevis range, which includes the highest mountain

Figure 4.22 A natural boulder enhanced by a setting of rubble above Stickle Tarn, Cumbria, north-west England. Photograph: Aaron Watson.

anywhere in Britain. Other Early Bronze Age hoards in the north command similar views of the sun at the solstices (Bradley, C. Green, and Watson 2018). Again this emphasises the difficulty of distinguishing between monuments that were built during this period and natural places which were selected to play a similar role.

THE END OF THE EARLY BRONZE AGE: A QUESTION OF SCALE?

A number of separate issues have been considered and need to be brought together now. They will be treated in greater detail in Chapter 5. Each concerns the distinctive developments of the Early Bronze Age and suggests that they were reaching their limits towards the middle of the second millennium BC.

This period between 2000 and 1500 BC is usually thought of in terms of its distinctive burials and the long-distance connections that they seem to illustrate, but in some ways both were changing by this time. It has been customary to treat Britain and Ireland as the periphery of Europe, but as long as local materials were being used that was quite untrue – bronze was produced in Britain at an unusually early date and Irish gold was exported. By 1500 BC, however, it appears that most of the British and Irish copper mines had gone out of use, although activity continued at Great Orme (Timberlake 2016). These developments have never been explained, but they form part of a more general development in the distribution of metalwork which saw quite rapid oscillations between the use of insular copper and a greater dependence on

Continental sources of supply. Those changes will be discussed in the next chapter, but they suggest that access to metal artefacts perhaps became more difficult.

There were also changes in the forms of barrow cemeteries. It has long been recognised that great concentrations of mounds were built near the monuments of the Neolithic period and that a few of the burials associated with them contain elaborate or exotic objects. What has not been so clear is that the great linear cemeteries in Wessex and the Thames Valley were a comparatively late development (Garwood 2007). A landscape which was already permeated with images from the past took on yet another layer of significance. It may be no accident that these formal arrangements of monuments were among the last to be built. The growing importance of cremation may be important too, for it required a greater consumption of human energy than inhumation burial. The barrow cemeteries built towards the end of the Early Bronze Age seem almost excessively elaborate, and the sheer complexity of references enshrined in these mounds and graves may no longer have had the intended effect. Perhaps they stopped being an adequate method of signalling social relationships. Those ideas might have been better expressed in a different medium. Chapter 5 documents that transformation.

There was another way in which the existing system approached its limits. Many monuments were built during the Late Neolithic and Early Bronze Age periods, but there is little to suggest that their construction depended on a major intensification of land use. Instead it seems possible that food production took place over an increasingly large area. That is indicated by the distribution of artefacts and monuments, and also by pollen analysis. The problem is that the expansion took in some regions that could not sustain a long period of settlement. Some of them were adversely affected by changes to the status of the soils, and others became increasingly waterlogged. Although there are many exceptions, parts of lowland Britain which were first colonised during the earlier second millennium BC were abandoned by the Iron Age (Bradley and Fraser 2010). The same was probably true in parts of the uplands, but, as this chapter has shown, the field evidence is difficult to use. If these suggestions have any merit, the consequence was much the same. A system which had been maintained by a process of continuous expansion was becoming vulnerable.

These were essentially local factors and were not directly linked to one another, but in each case matters had reached a crisis towards the middle of the second millennium BC. A development on an international scale had a still more serious impact.

In a recent paper Risch and Meller (2015) have drawn attention to the evidence for significant changes in the archaeological records of different parts of Europe during the sixteenth century BC. Their study covers an enormous area, extending from Denmark in the north to Egypt and the Mediterranean islands towards the south. It extends as far west as Portugal and to countries as far to the east as Turkey. These authors consider nearly twenty different regions and claim that significant changes occurred in no fewer than twelve of them. Those developments did not assume the same forms from one area to another, and their article distinguishes between three separate kinds of sequence. There were:

> Societies which exhibited a pronounced increase in production with unchanged rituals and symbolic forms of expression;
>
> [Those in which] significant economic and social crisis could lead to … collapse;
>
> [and] Societies which first appear around 1600–1500 BC and show hardly any contacts to earlier archaeological entities. (Risch and Meller 2015: 250)

It is hard to explain why changes were virtually synchronous among people who shared so little in common, but Risch and Meller identify one dramatic event that might have had far-reaching consequences. This was the eruption of Thera which happened at the beginning of the sixteenth century BC, although the exact date is disputed (S. Manning 2014). It may have led to some environmental changes, but away from the area directly affected by the catastrophe they lacked any lasting impact. Instead they 'touched the ideological realm' (Risch and Meller 2015: 239). An inexplicable natural event undermined the security of societies living in different parts of Europe, and they reacted in different ways.

In the case of Britain and Ireland, which were towards the outer edge of the Continent, the major impact could have been on the patterns of long-distance alliance on which the movement of artefacts and materials relied. It might have affected the sharing of ideas about the cosmos expressed through mortuary rituals. Another factor may have been equally relevant, as the British and Irish Early Bronze Ages were unusual for their emphasis on connections with the Neolithic past. The ideas and achievements of previous generations were celebrated even though an enormous expanse of time had elapsed, and this may have lent legitimacy to the societies that followed afterwards. Perhaps accounts of a distant disaster threatened the self-confidence of communities living in the offshore islands at just the time when they were becoming aware of local problems of their own. In common with communities in northern France and The Netherlands – two regions in which Risch and Meller (2015) recognise new developments – a volcanic eruption would be entirely outside the experience of the local inhabitants. For whatever reasons, both areas underwent a period of rapid change.

THE LAST DAYS OF STONEHENGE

In Britain this transformation is epitomised by the last use of Stonehenge: a monument whose earlier history encapsulated many of the trends considered in Chapter 3. It seems right to conclude this account by considering its latest manifestation (Fig. 4.23).

At the end of the Neolithic period Stonehenge assumed what was to be its definitive form: two settings of sarsen uprights which framed settings of smaller 'bluestones' introduced from Wales. The whole structure was ringed by a bank and ditch.

After that time there is evidence for episodes in which the details of the stone settings were rearranged (Pollard et al. 2017). These changes affected the placing of the smaller monoliths, but the basic layout of the monument remained the same, and an earthwork avenue linked it to the River Avon. By about 2000 BC any major developments were at an end. So, it seems, was the deposition of human remains inside the monument. After that time there were different developments at Stonehenge. Fragments of stone were removed from the settings of Welsh rock. Some may have been taken to other structures in the vicinity, and others could have been turned into portable objects. What is clear is that this distinctive material retained a special significance. At the same time drawings of axes and daggers were engraved on the sarsen monument. They were on the lower parts of the stones and appear in a range of different sizes. A recent study (Pollard et al. 2017) suggests that the objects are shown as if they are emerging from the ground. These drawings date from the end of the Early Bronze Age long after the monoliths had been set in place.

Another development was the digging of two concentric rings of pits around the perimeter of the stone circle. There is no evidence that these features were meant to hold stones, and they postdate all the other structures at Stonehenge. The inner circle has a date of 2030–1750 BC and the outer ring of 1640–1520 BC, but it is not certain that they were excavated at different times. Both circuits are misaligned towards the south-east where two stones in the sarsen monument seem to have been pushed over to create a kind of entrance. This may have been deliberate as they are on the axis of the midwinter sunrise.

It was while these developments were happening that the cemeteries around Stonehenge assumed their definitive form. It seems as if the positioning of these barrows defined two roughly concentric circuits with the monument in the centre. One linked a series of cemeteries about 1 km from the circle, while the second was 2.25 km away (A. Woodward and P. Woodward 1996). Neither followed an even curve, as the barrows were laid out in rows following the prevailing topography. Not all of them could be seen from the monument and it seems more likely that they were encountered by people travelling towards it. Seen from outside, they have more visual impact. The same applies to the mounds on the hills around Avebury (Watson 2001b).

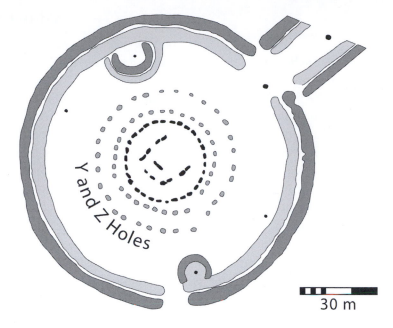

Y and Z Holes

30 m

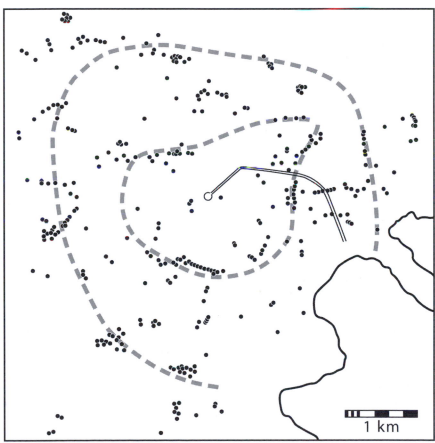

1 km

Figure 4.23 The circuits of Early Bronze Age round barrows in the area around Stonehenge with a detailed plan of that monument showing the rings of pits enclosing the megalithic monument. Information from Woodward and Woodward (1996) and Pollard et al. (2017).

In this way Stonehenge was contained within a new series of round barrows, and the monument itself was ringed by two circles of pits. It seems as if the significance of the Neolithic building was emphasised, and its boundaries were reinforced. At the same time its significance extended to the surrounding area in a way that had not been expressed so explicitly before. Even during the Middle Bronze Age the area around the monument was bounded by linear ditches associated with inhumation burials (D. Roberts et al. 2017). Might all these developments have been among the last efforts to assert the power of tradition during a time of crisis?

If so, they did not succeed. Other parts of the Stonehenge landscape were soon divided up by fields and ditches. Fewer artefacts were deposited around the monument, and the pits that were its latest feature filled with wind-blown silt as ground was cultivated in the vicinity. Houses were constructed on the sites of ancient constructions, and the history of the lowland landscape entered a new phase. It was a phase in which the distinctive elements discussed in this chapter had little role to play. Those new developments are considered in Chapter 5.

CHAPTER 5

PLOUGHSHARES INTO SWORDS

From the end of the Early Bronze Age major changes are apparent in several different spheres: in the organisation of settlements and land divisions, and in the treatment of the dead. Even the role of metalwork was changing. It is clear that these features were not evenly distributed across Britain and Ireland, but they did encapsulate a fundamental contrast. One was with the practices discussed in Chapter 4. The new developments cannot be dated accurately, but all these processes began towards the middle of the second millennium BC. During that time there was a continuous process of change, but it had its roots in the past. The Middle Bronze Age runs between about 1500 and 1100 BC, and the Late Bronze Age extends down to 800 BC. In some accounts these periods are treated together as the later Bronze Age (Bradley et al. 2016a: ch. 5). This term will be used where it applies to the entire period from the mid-second millennium BC, but the text refers to the Middle and Late Bronzes Ages respectively where it is concerned with specific developments.

CHARACTERISING A LATER BRONZE AGE

Settlement

None of the features that characterise the later Bronze Age in these islands was completely new. Rather, they grew out of those of the previous period. Each will be considered later, but it is important to trace their sources now.

Perhaps the most striking trend was a marked increase in the frequency of settlement sites. Both in Britain and Ireland they were widely distributed but generally contained more substantial structures than those of earlier periods; that was especially true in southern England. They were characterised by considerable stone or timber buildings (Fig. 5.3); they were sometimes enclosed by ditches, fences, or walls; and they were associated with significant collections of artefacts (Cooke, Brown, and Phillpotts 2008: ch. 4; Lewis et al. 2010: ch. 3). Moreover they could occur together with field systems or longer land

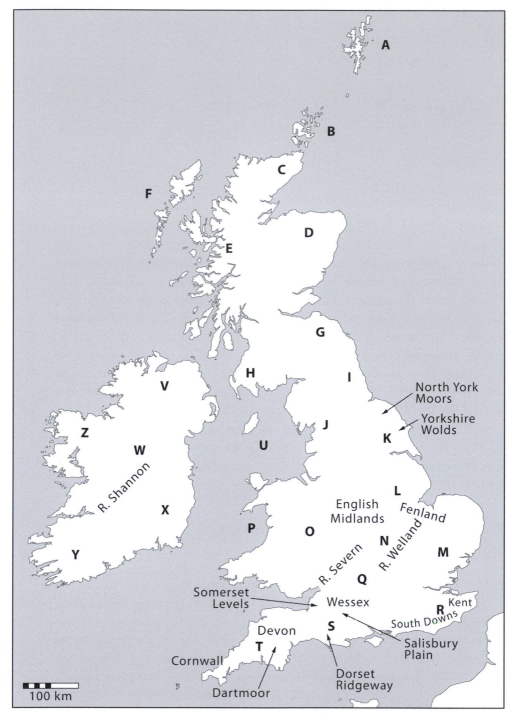

Figure 5.1 Places and regions mentioned in Chapter 5. For the purposes of this map Britain and Ireland have been divided into twenty-six areas and the individual sites are listed according to these divisions. A: Shetland; B: Orkney (Mine Howe); C: Northern Scotland; D: North-east and Central Scotland (Aberdeen Peripheral Road, Covesea, Kintore, Loanhead of Daviot, Tillycoultry, Tomnaverie); E: Western Scotland (Portree);

divisions. Such evidence was usually associated with the more productive soils, and settlements of later phases were often found nearby.

To a large extent their distribution contrasted with that of the sites discussed towards the end of Chapter 4. That is because Early Bronze Age examples were more ephemeral and left less trace behind, but it was also because the newer settlements were not so frequent in the marginal areas where remains of the previous phase are thought to survive. Those different observations may be linked, for the reorganisation of the lowland landscape that was so much a feature of the later Bronze Age may have been a response to deteriorating conditions in areas which could not sustain a lengthy occupation (Bradley and Fraser 2010). It is a popular view, but as Chapter 4 has shown, the reality could have been even more complex.

Figure Caption 5.1 *(Cont.)*

F: Outer Hebrides; G: Scotland on either side of the Firth of Forth (Duddingston Loch, Traprain Law); H: South-west Scotland (Drumcoltran); I: the English/Scottish borderland (Durham, Eildon Hill, Whitton Hill); J: North-west England; K: North-east England and the Peak District (Thwing); L: Eastern England between the Humber and the Fenland (Barleycroft, Bradley Fen, Flag Fen, Must Farm, Over, Washingborough); M: East Anglia; N: the English Midlands (Biddenham, Broom, Eye Kettleby); O: the English/Welsh borderland (Beeston Castle, Bredon, Huntsman's Quarry, the Breiddin, Worcester); P: North and West Wales (Great Orme); Q: the Thames Valley, Cotswolds, and South Midlands (Burghfield, Eton, Heathrow, Reading Business Park, Runnymede Bridge, Taplow, Wallingford, Wittenham Clumps); R: South-east England including the Thames Estuary and the South Downs (Belle Tout, Carshalton, Cliffs End Farm, Dover, Great Baddow, Greenlands, Harting Beacon, Itford Hill, Langdon Bay, Mucking, Peacehaven, Sheppey, Shinewater, South Hornchurch, Stane Street, Springfield Lyons, Syon Reach, Thanet, Thurnham, Vauxhall); S: Wessex (Bestwall Quarry, Down Farm, Portland, Rams Hill, Simons Ground, South Lodge Camp, Stoborough, Swanwick, Testwood, Twyford Down, Wilsford); T: South-west England and South Wales (Brean Down, Burgh Island, Callestick, Frocester, Greylake, Grimspound, Holne Moor, Llanmaes, Looe Island, Norton Fitzwarren, Salcombe, Sigwells, South Cadbury, Standon Down, St Michael's Mount, Mountbatten, Gwithian, Thurlestone); U: the Isle of Man (South Barrule); V: Northern Ireland (Ballybeen, Bishopsland, Corrstown, Cullyhanna, Downpatrick, Haughey's Fort, Killymoon, Lough Eskragh, Navan Fort, Whitepark Bay); W: from the Irish Midlands to the east coast (Balinderry, Dalkey Island, Lismullin, Lugg, Rathgall); X: South-east Ireland (Knockhouse Lower); Y: South-west Ireland (Derrycahoon, Drombeg); Z: the Irish west coast (Céide, Dun Aonghasa, Fermoyle, Lough Gara, Mooghaun, Rathtinaun).

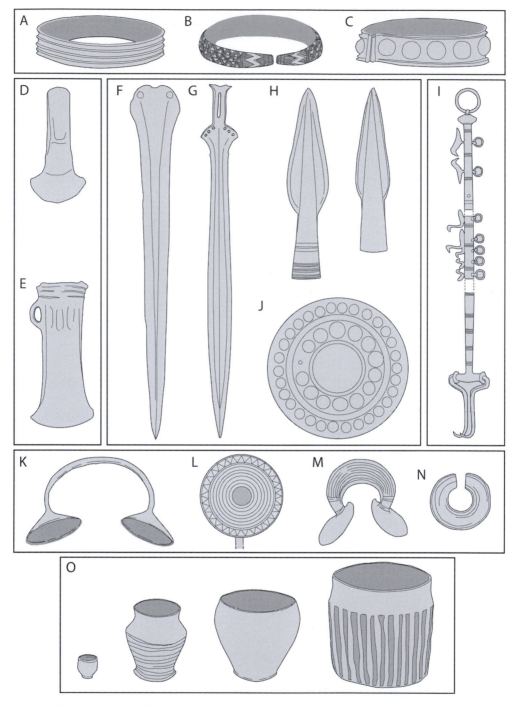

Figure 5.2 Artefact types mentioned in Chapter 5. A–C: decorated bronze bracelets; D and E: axeheads; F: rapier; G: sword; H: spearheads; I: flesh hook; J: shield; K–N: Irish gold ornaments; O: a Late Bronze Age ceramic 'set'.

Figure 5.3 The foundations of a stone roundhouse at Marrivale, Dartmoor. Photograph: Aaron Watson.

Despite such uncertainties, by the middle of the second millennium BC it is known that land was being used more intensively. This marks the start of a process which eventually extended to many parts of lowland Britain. From about 1500 BC there was a growing emphasis on the soils that retained their agricultural potential. The poorer land first settled during the Early Bronze Age was used less often, as occupation focused on the most productive areas. It was on the more fertile land that regular field systems were established, but in some regions, notably Dartmoor, there seems to have been an attempt to maintain activity in the uplands by creating an extensive system of boundaries (Fleming 2008). It is not clear how this process was organised. Nor is it clear whether it happened over a short period or was a piecemeal development, but pollen analysis suggests that the main period of upland land use was from about 1480 BC and lasted for four hundred years (Fyfe et al. 2008). Its scale and orderly layout cannot be denied, and in the end this development could have resulted in an equitable division of resources. By the Late Bronze Age the intensity of activity had diminished. In the same way, the remains of coaxial field systems are occasionally recognised in areas of heathland best known for their Early Bronze Age barrows (English 2013), but they may not have been used over a long period.

It would be wrong to treat enclosed landscapes as a completely new development. Although the field systems took little account of earlier prehistoric stone rows on Dartmoor, some of the existing cairns were integrated into the new layout (Fleming 2008; P. Newman 2011). In a few cases radiocarbon dating demonstrates that these changes began towards the end of the Early Bronze Age. They could have happened while traditional types of monuments were still in use. At present there is little to suggest developments on this scale in other parts of Britain and Ireland, but there seem to have been field systems of similar date in Cornwall, southern Wessex, Thanet, and East Anglia. Excavations at Bestwall Quarry near to the Channel coast have a special importance as the radiocarbon dates show that there fields were laid out on an impressive scale before the Early Bronze Age ended (Ladle and A. Woodward 2009: chs. 3–4). This is important as their chronology overlaps with that of an unusually monumental round barrow at Stoborough which is only 2 km away on the opposite bank of a river (Needham, Parfitt, and Varndell 2006: 103–4). It featured a massive log coffin and a burial associated with a shale cup. Perhaps land use was reorganised in coastal areas in parallel with developments on Dartmoor and the creation of the first regular field systems in lowland areas overlapped with the building of equally large mounds on the chalk (Fig. 5.4). A similar process was beginning at about the same time on the other side of the Channel and the southern North Sea. The first field systems in northern France contain similar pottery to southern England and can even be associated with circular houses (Bradley et al. 2016a: 169–70 and fig. 5.11).

For many years the remains of field systems had been recognised as earthworks on the chalk of southern England, and it was evident that the first of them must have been established during the Bronze Age. On the other hand, archaeologists were so sure that the majority were of Iron Age or Romano-British date that they became known as 'Celtic' fields to distinguish them from the 'English' fields attributed to the Anglo-Saxons (H. C. Bowen 1961). This term soon took on a life of its own, making it hard to accept that many of these land divisions predated the Celtic invasions described by Classical writers. Perhaps the best demonstration of the antiquity and extent of coaxial fields comes from the South Downs where the earthwork of Stane Street, the Roman road between Chichester and London, cut across a series of these boundaries.

The first studies of this evidence met with a problem. Regular systems of square or rectangular fields obviously developed during more than one period of prehistory. Recent research shows that they were widely distributed in lowland England and extended into areas in which earthworks do not survive. Here they are represented by ditches or occasionally by lines of posts. These were established at various times during the later Bronze Age, but most of them were of Middle Bronze Age origin (D. Yates 2007). The majority went out of use by about 800 BC and in some cases significantly before that time. The only coaxial fields that can definitely be attributed to the Iron Age belong to the later part of that period and remained important during the Roman

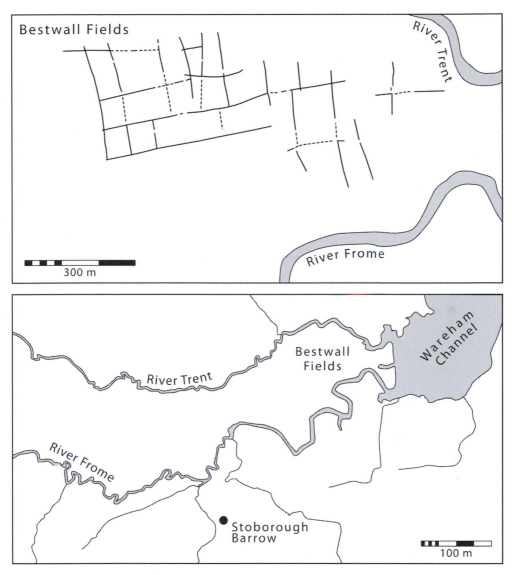

Figure 5.4 The Early Bronze Age coaxial field system at Bestwall Quarry, Wessex. The location map shows the position of the field system in relation to a complex barrow burial of similar date at Stoborough. Information from Ladle and Woodward (2009).

occupation. Some are in the same places as the Bronze Age systems, but others have a more extensive distribution (Bradley and Fulford 2008).

Were there similar developments in Ireland? Here the evidence presents problems. There was a similar increase in the evidence for houses at the beginning of the Middle Bronze Age. Some of the settlements were enclosed and were near to cremation cemeteries of the same date. As in Britain, deposits of metalwork and mounds of fire-cracked stones are found close to the Irish sites, but in this case there is little evidence of field systems. That is paradoxical since Céide on the west coast was long believed to preserve the oldest land boundaries in Europe. They were dated to an early stage of the Neolithic period contemporary with megalithic tombs. A new assessment of the evidence suggests another interpretation (Whitfield 2017). The coaxial fields buried below the peat were a later development and, like their English counterparts, could have been created in the Middle Bronze Age. The same possibility had been suggested for other walls buried beneath Irish bogs, but there is not enough evidence to suggest a wider pattern. Development-led excavations have identified what seem to be later Bronze Age land boundaries close to the east coast, and at Lismullin two features of this kind are assigned to the second millennium BC. One is associated with a date of 1500–1400 BC (O'Connell 2013: 50–1).

At the same time more marginal areas were increasingly used on a seasonal basis. On the English/Scottish border cereal cultivation was replaced by pastoralism (Tipping 2010a) – possibly transhumance – and elsewhere specialised forms of exploitation assumed a greater significance. Wooden paths or raised walkways were constructed across many areas of damp ground, including the Somerset Levels (B. Coles and J. Coles 1986) and parts of the East Anglian Fens (Hall and J. Coles 1994). A similar process happened along the banks of the Thames, where brushwood trackways, timber platforms, and even a metalled causeway were created to provide access to the rich grazing land beside the river (Sidell et al. 2002). A similar process is documented in the Shannon Estuary (A. O'Sullivan 1996) and also in South Wales where the remains of specialised wooden buildings have been recorded in the Severn Estuary (Bell 2013). In Britain the earliest bridges date from this phase (T. Allen 2002; Falkner 2004).

It would have been easier to move around the landscape than before, for the earliest convincing evidence of domesticated horses dates from the Middle Bronze Age (Bendrey 2012). They may have been used for riding or traction, and it can hardly be a coincidence that wooden wheels of similar date have been found during fieldwork. It seems as though wheeled transport was adopted in Britain and Ireland later than on the Continent.

Burial Rites

During the British later Bronze Age some burials were near settlements or even within them. This may well have applied to a number of the mounds built during the previous period, and, in Wessex, it certainly seems possible with the miniature round barrows found in low-lying positions which were associated with some of the poorest burials (Peters 2000). Normally they contained a cremation and a ceramic vessel, and few were associated with any metalwork.

Such monuments were sometimes in small groups and continued to attract burials during the later second millennium BC. What had formed only part of the earlier system now became the norm.

Cremation cemeteries were not a new development. They were already important in the uplands where they could be associated with ring cairns and small stone circles. In the lowlands a few examples were known in isolation and others were established outside the burial mounds of the same period. The novel development is that in most areas newly built barrows were significantly smaller, and eventually their construction lapsed (Cooper 2016a and b). Even then there were important variations within a single site. Simons Ground close to the coast of Wessex included no fewer than five separate groups of burials extending over a distance of 300 m, each of them associated with a small round barrow (White 1982). Something similar happened at Eye Kettleby in the east Midlands where four different groups of burials were dated between 1600 and 1440 BC (Finn 2011). Two were found with older barrows and a third was associated with a specially built enclosure.

It is usually assumed that cremation was the normal mortuary rite of the later Bronze Age, but this is only partly true. As more unaccompanied skeletons are dated by radiocarbon it has become apparent that inhumation was still practised at this time. The same applies to the circulation of unburnt human bones. One site which exemplifies this development is at Down Farm on the Wessex chalk where a Neolithic round barrow close to the Dorset Cursus was reused during this period (Barrett, Bradley, and M. Green 1991: 211–14). It was associated with three different ways of treating the dead. Just outside the earth-work was a cluster of urned and unurned cremations of the kind commonly found in this phase, but their distribution was complemented by a group of flexed inhumation burials which probably belonged to the same phase. The upper filling of the barrow ditch contained yet another set of human remains, but this time they consisted of disarticulated bones; they did not result from disturbance of these graves, and must have been a separate phenomenon. The distributions of all three deposits were mutually exclusive. Since this site was excavated, another burial of Middle Bronze Age date has been identified not far away. This was the most remarkable of all, for the bones seem to have been put there after the flesh had decayed and were pegged together to recreate the appearance of the cadaver (Bailey, M. Green, and M. Smith 2013). Other tightly crouched burials of the same date were those of mummified bodies, and in one case, at Cladh Hallan in the Hebrides, the preserved corpse was composed from the bones of more than one individual (Parker Pearson et al. 2005). Cremation was only one way of dealing with the dead during the later Bronze Age.

As these changes happened, metalwork was less often deposited in ceme-teries (Caswell and B. Roberts in press). Occasional metal items have been identified in the excavation of urnfields, but they were rather rare and were not always associated with one particular burial. They were usually small and fragmentary and could consist of a small personal item like a ring. This contrasts with the more elaborate graves of the previous period in which the dead might be accompanied by a wider range of weapons and ornaments. That is not because such types had gone out of use. Instead their contexts changed so that they are more likely to be discovered in isolation in the collections of metalwork known as hoards, or in rivers and watery environments.

There was a similar sequence in Ireland (Cooney 2017). Here the cemeteries of the later Bronze Age were located close to settlements of the same date. A new study suggests that they were usually within 100 m of one another (Ginn 2016). There is the same distinction between small mounds associated with human remains and the use of flat cemeteries in which some of the bones were in ceramic vessels. At times their positions could be marked by a setting of posts or a standing stone. The main contrast concerns the form taken by the earthwork monuments. They were generally 'ring barrows' with an external bank and a single entrance. Unlike their British counterparts, their currency extended from the Early Bronze Age into the Iron Age (McGarry 2009). Again none of these structures was associated with complex grave goods. Instead finds of later Bronze Age weapons are commonly found in rivers, lakes, and bogs.

This practice was not entirely new. Some of the last daggers produced during the Early Bronze Age in Britain are not only found in graves, they also occur in the Thames. The Irish and British evidence forms only part of a wider pattern. The deposition of metalwork in rivers was well established on the Continent, although it appeared in different manifestations at different times and places. For the most part it alternated with the deposition of similar artefacts in graves (Bradley 2017a: 152–4). The simplest explanation is that objects of the kinds that had once been buried with the dead were removed from the body in the course of the funeral and deployed in another context. This idea is considered on page 233.

Metalwork

Relations with the European mainland were important in another way. Chapter 4 ended by discussing how access to metal may have changed. After a period of stability in which south-west Ireland provided a major source of copper, there was more diversity, with mines in mainland Europe supplying some of the raw material (O'Brien 2015). More came from a series of sites in Ireland, Wales, and northern England. By 1600 BC, the exploitation of insular ores was reorganised, and most of those sources were no longer employed. The one exception was the large complex at Great Orme which was used most intensively between 1500 and 1300 BC (Timberlake 2016). Otherwise it seems as if the inhabitants of both islands depended on more distant sources. Metalwork was increasingly imported from the Continent; the one minor exception is the Irish trench mine at Derrycahoon with a date in the thirteenth century BC (O'Brien 2015: 135–7). This was only the last stage in a series of fluctuations in the supply of bronze, but it was certainly the most lasting. It was necessary for people to travel longer distances than before, and they may have done so increasingly often. Sewn-plank boats had been used from the Early Bronze Age (Van der Noort 2011), but the well-preserved vessel from Dover, which is dated to the following phase, shows how sophisticated this technology had become (P. Clark 2004). It is another feature that helps to establish the distinctiveness of the later Bronze Age.

How significant were these developments? For many years studies of this period were divided between groups of specialists, all with interests of their own. As a result they developed completely different interpretations from one another. At its simplest the contrast was between those researchers who postulated a social collapse around 1500 BC, and others who envisaged a much more radical transformation. The evidence of mortuary rites was critical. Considered in isolation, it suggested that two processes were taking place during the later second millennium BC. Older round barrows were being reused in Britain, while newly constructed mounds in both islands made fewer demands on human labour. During this period 'single' burials were less frequent and cemeteries were often organised around groups of cremations accompanied by ceramic vessels. The 'rich' graves that had been such a feature of the earlier period virtually disappeared (Caswell and B. Roberts 2018). It was easy to suggest that it reflected a wider change in which the differences of wealth and status expressed by the burial rite lost their importance. Rather than manifesting social distinctions, there was a new ethic of equality. Perhaps the power of a traditional elite had failed. Proponents of this view could draw attention to the limited range of variation among the excavated settlements, especially those of the Middle Bronze Age.

Bronze Age metalwork has often been studied for its own sake, as a self-contained field of research which had little contact with the results of field archaeology. That is not surprising, for, apart from the grave goods of the Early Bronze Age, little of this material came from excavated contexts. Even so, it is clear that bronze artefacts give a different impression of the transition. Such items were less often associated with the dead, but their overall frequency increased. It is simply that their contexts changed from an emphasis on round barrows to deposits in liminal locations. Although there are many exceptions, tools were generally deposited in hoards on dry land, ornaments might occur in terrestrial contexts or bogs, whilst weapons were most often deposited in rivers (Becker 2013; Bradley 2017a: 54–7). Certain types, notably dirks and rapiers, were the direct successors of those associated with Early Bronze Age

burials, but the shift of location meant that they were not always compared
with one another. In fact a greater amount of metalwork entered the archaeological record. That is inconsistent with the idea of a social collapse. The burials
and the portable artefacts supported very different interpretations.

In fact the significance of metalworking may have been changing at this
time. It has been all too easy to suppose that collections of bronze artefacts
were buried for practical reasons and that it was simply a matter of chance
that they were never recovered. Some collections, known as hoards, included
newly made objects which had yet to be finished; some contained worn or
broken objects that could have been melted down; whilst others incorporated
the residues of metalworking itself: casting jets, ingots, moulds, droplets, and
slag. The connection with metallurgy is clear, and the problem is to determine
whether the transformation of the metal should be viewed as a purely mech-
anical process. That is inconsistent with ethnographic accounts of the social
position of the smith (Budd and Taylor 1995), and certainly does not account
for some of the anomalies illustrated by the hoards themselves: the occasional
finds of human or animal bones in these deposits; the discovery of certain
of these collections in remote and inaccessible places; the representation of
broken objects, parts of which are missing; the reuniting of certain artefacts
after a period of use with the moulds in which they were made (Webley
and Adams 2016; Boutoille 2012). Equally important was the violence with
which some of these items had been fractured (Nebelsick 2000). Influenced
by New World ethnography, Helms (2012) suggests that the metal was seen
as an organic substance that grew beneath the ground. For all these reasons it
may be wise to suppose that the process of working it was attended by special
protocols. That was already suggested by the siting of Early Bronze Age hoards
like that from Dail na Caraidh, but these elements assumed even greater significance after that time.

Other deposits of later Bronze Age metalwork come from the sites of older
monuments. For example, a Middle Bronze Age axe was found at, or near, the
recumbent stone circle at Tomnaverie in north-east Scotland and there was a
Late Bronze Age hoard next to a site of the same kind at Tillycoultry. A third
example, Loanhead of Daviot, provides evidence of metal production (Bradley
and Nimura 2016: 124).

THE MIDDLE BRONZE AGE, 1500–1100 BC

Fields, Houses, and Enclosures

There are good reasons for beginning with the English evidence. The first
is to make the point that the establishment of the larger field systems took a
considerable effort. It is easy to be misled by the evidence of burial mounds
which were smaller during this phase, for the amount of labour invested in

the division of the land was probably equivalent to that devoted to monument building during earlier periods (Cooper 2016a and b). It would be wrong to suppose that workforces could no longer be mobilised for large-scale projects – it is the nature of those tasks that had changed. Entire landscapes might be organised around a series of parallel boundaries. Some of the dominant axes travelled a considerable distance, and, as if to echo older concerns, a few were orientated on the solstices (McOmish, D. Field, and G. Brown 2002). That is particularly revealing where they cut across the grain of the local topography, with the result that certain plots were left in shadow. Another connection with established practice was the way that some of the field boundaries ran up to older mounds, cairns, or even the remains of houses. It is commonly supposed that the barrows provided landmarks on which to align them, but a number of them could not be seen from far away, suggesting that it was the associations of such monuments that were more significant (Cooper 2016b). If the creation of land divisions facilitated new kinds of land use, it is clear that the process was ritualised.

That connection with mounds and cairns is particularly plausible since the first field systems seem to have been established whilst large round barrows were still being built. That was obviously the case on Dartmoor where the landscape was reorganised during the Early Bronze Age (Fleming 2008), but it may apply to the information from other areas, including Wessex. It seems quite possible that these elements were linked with one another and that the first stages in the enclosure of the landscape were overseen by the people commemorated in these graves. If so, the process continued after mortuary practices had changed.

One reason for suggesting that these developments played a part in the political process is that the newly created field systems were poorly integrated with the settlements; it is difficult to think of them as a unified design (Fig. 5.5). Although the rectilinear field systems may have grown over a significant period, the houses and enclosures found within them did not conform to the overall layout. Rather, they were scattered at irregular intervals across their area, and the evidence of excavation suggests that they were sometimes a secondary development. That is fascinating, for it raises the possibility that the earliest dwellings in these places may have been ephemeral structures of the kind already identified in the Early Bronze Age. Another possibility, first raised by D. Field (2001), is that these changes were implemented from settlements which lay outside the areas with coaxial fields. The land divisions were clearly of special significance, for at Gwithian in Cornwall the field boundaries incorporated cremated bones (Nowakowski et al. 2007: 29), and at Twyford Down on the chalk of Wessex one was marked by a line of pits, some of them containing human remains (Walker and Farwell 2000: 21). There were other cases in which the orientation of a field system must have been established by burying people or animals before those boundaries were established. A good example of this practice

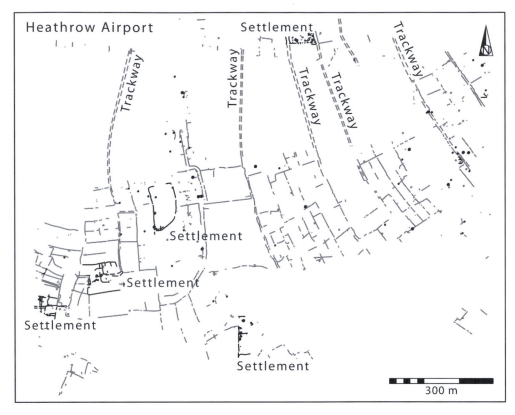

Figure 5.5 Part of the coaxial field system and associated settlement sites at Heathrow, Thames Valley. Information from Lewis et al. (2010).

was at Peacehaven on the Channel coast where an elongated pit containing Early Bronze Age faunal remains established the alignment of a large coaxial field system (Hart 2015). Such sequences need more investigation, for there are even cases in which the enclosed settlements associated with field systems may have been created at a time when these landscapes were already going out of use. That was first observed on the Wessex chalkland (Barrett, Bradley, and M. Green 1991: 181–3), but now the same development has been shown by excavation in East Anglia (Mortimer and Phillips 2012).

There was also a mismatch between the extent of the larger enclosed landscapes and the small size of the first settlements that have been identified within them (Fig. 5.6). In some cases the houses formed a dispersed pattern, with different buildings inside individual plots or attached to their boundaries. In other instances, a single field was occupied by a settlement, but even here the number of houses was limited. Indeed, the dwellings of the Middle Bronze Age seem to have shifted their locations, giving the illusion of a larger unit than was actually the case (Brück 1999). For instance, the well-known 'village' at Itford Hill in southern England was nothing of the kind. It was a

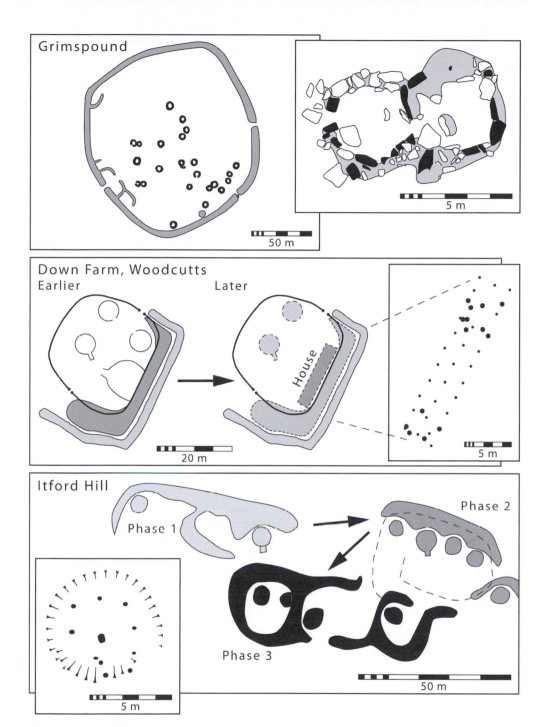

Figure 5.6 Middle Bronze Age settlements and buildings. Grimspound, south-west England, illustrates a large domestic enclosure; the inset shows two conjoined houses on the site. Down Farm, Wessex, is shown in two successive phases, during the later of which a long house was constructed; this is shown as a detail. The open settlement at Itford Hill, south-east England, has been described as a village, but it seems to have been a smaller group of dwellings, which were relocated on two occasions. An inset illustrates one of the post-built houses. Information from Butler (1991), Barrett, Bradley, and Green (1991), and Ellison (1978).

small cluster of houses defined by an embanked enclosure which changed its position on three separate occasions (Ellison 1978). What was new was that the sites of the older buildings were not removed by the plough.

In lowland Britain the domestic structures were usually roundhouses. There are few signs of specialised facilities such as stables or byres, and the only ancillary structures may have been small granaries or storehouses. This suggests that the circular buildings played a variety of roles, and it is true that they could occur in pairs, one of them a more substantial structure than the other. It often included a series of storage pits beneath its eaves, whilst its neighbour may have been associated with craft production, particularly weaving. There might be several of these modules within a single settlement. Whether or not individual sites were enclosed, the domestic dwellings seem to have been accompanied by a variety of other features. Often the area around them was defined by a fence, a low earthwork, or a hedge. Not all these enclosures were complete and L–shaped compounds have been observed in lowland England. Perhaps they were integrated into land divisions that have since disappeared. The same applies to small D–shaped compounds. There were also oval and circular post settings, not all of which contained any buildings.

If these structures appear to be a new development, the same applies to other features that suggest that people were living in the same place for a significant period of time. That would certainly apply to ponds and waterholes, which seem to have developed during the Middle Bronze Age. The same argument would apply to wells. The shallower examples might be lined by a hollowed-out tree trunk, as happened at Frocester in the south-west (Price 2000: 179–80), but much deeper examples are dated to this period at Wilsford Shaft (Ashbee, Bell, and Proudfoot 1989), and to the Late Bronze Age at Belle Tout on the Channel coast (Mike Allen pers. comm.). The example at Belle Tout was provided with regular footholds cut into the wall of the shaft. Such features provided a dependable water supply and this development would have allowed people to occupy locations that could not be settled before. The significance of this development can hardly be overstated, and in recent years the excavation of these features has found evidence of later Bronze Age offerings including human and animal skulls, and metalworking debris. A waterhole at Thurnham in south-east England included a bronze dagger (Booth et al. 2011: 228–9). An early find at Swanwick was interpreted as a 'ritual shaft' (Fox 1930). In the light of comparable discoveries it can be identified as a Middle Bronze Age well, 8 m deep, associated with what was probably a log ladder. In this case its upper filling contained a remarkable number of loom weights. A metalwork hoard was found nearby.

The evidence for sustained occupation contrasts with that from individual dwellings, which may have been abandoned every generation (Brück 1999). Those dated to the Middle Bronze Age tended to be replaced in a different position, and, when it happened, the site of the older building might be marked by an animal burial, a deposit of pottery, human bones, or perhaps a metal artefact. Sometimes the remains of earlier houses were covered over (Nowakowski 2001), and in south-west England the hollows left by their floors were carefully refilled. At Callestick, the outline of an abandoned house was marked by pieces of quartz (A. Jones 1999), and at South Lodge Camp in Wessex the site of a similar building was commemorated by a low mound (Barrett, Bradley, and M. Green 1991: 183). At Bestwall Quarry in the same region an abandoned house was formally closed by a heap of burnt stone. A bronze bracelet was deposited just outside the building, and there was another in the middle of its floor (Ladle and A. Woodward 2009: 69–72). Such practices were not peculiar to England. In the Outer Hebrides the successive house floors at Cladh Hallan were associated with groups of metal artefacts and the burials of mummified corpses (Parker Pearson et al. 2005). In Orkney domestic buildings were characterised by deposits of stone ard shares (Downes and Lamb 2000).

It was not uncommon for several groups of dwellings to occur within the same field system, and that also applied to the insubstantial enclosures connected with some of the settlements. The evidence is not easy to interpret. On the one hand, the regular replacement of houses meant that certain of the sites may have been used in succession over a relatively short period of time; the intervals between these occupations could have been too short to measure by radiocarbon dating. On the other hand, the small scale of these different units was occasionally at odds with the extent of the surrounding fields, suggesting that a single block of land was worked by several communities. That makes it still more difficult to decide how the field systems were established, but there is another problem, too. There is nothing to show how many individual plots were in use simultaneously, and in theory large parts of landscape may have lain fallow at any one time.

Irish settlements of the same date have been studied by Ginn (2016). They follow similar trends to their British counterparts, but with the crucial difference that large coaxial field systems must have been rare, assuming they existed in the first place. Another problem is that virtually all the evidence comes from sites that have been levelled by cultivation, so that their remains are represented by subsoil features. Again the occupation sites of the Middle Bronze Age were associated with a restricted range of artefacts, and in neither country do these settlements provide much indication of a social hierarchy. Irish roundhouses were more substantial than their predecessors, but there is little indication of rebuilding or repairs to these structures. Most of them formed part of an open settlement, but 35 per cent of the occupation sites had been enclosed, usually by a palisade or a shallow ditch. Only here are there any signs of social divisions, as Ginn (2016) has shown that these enclosures were associated with better quality land than the other sites. A typical example

Knockhouse Lower   Cullyhanna

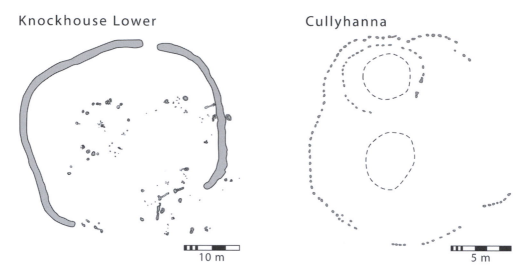

10 m   5 m

Figure 5.7 The excavated settlements at Cullyhanna, northern Ireland, and Knockhouse Lower, south-east Ireland. At Knockhouse only subsoil features remained, but at Cullyhanna waterlogged posts survived. Information from Hodges (1958) and Richardson and Johnson (2007).

comes from Cullyhanna where a fenced compound was associated with two roundhouses. Unusually, their remains survived because they were preserved in peat (Fig. 5.7). The site has been misunderstood as its unusual setting suggested that it was a 'hunting lodge'. There is no longer any reason to accept this interpretation as its plan is similar to that of dryland sites. To add to the confusion, it was originally assigned to the Early Bronze Age, but dendrochronology provides a date of 1526 BC (Hodges 1958; Ó Néil, Plunkett, and Whitehouse 2007: 47). Similar but less complete enclosures have been identified more recently. Another anomaly is the excavated settlement at Corrstown on the north coast of Ireland where excavation revealed an extraordinary complex of forty roundhouses (Ginn and Rathbone 2012). It was remarkable for its size, but in other respects it resembles other open settlements in the country.

There is evidence for cereal cultivation in Britain and Ireland, with barley as the main crop, and Stevens and Fuller (2012) have suggested that arable farming resumed after it had been abandoned during the Neolithic period. This is an exaggeration, but it is true that carbonised grain is found more frequently from this time, and there is greater evidence of cereal pollen in Britain and Ireland. Its importance is reinforced by the discovery of corn-drying kilns in the excavation of Irish settlements. Unfortunately, it is only possible to find direct evidence of cultivation where fields survive as earthworks or where they have been deeply buried. A good example of the latter process is at Gwithian in south-west England where large areas of plough marks were preserved beneath blown sand, together with a series of field boundaries and evidence of spade cultivation (Nowakowski et al. 2007: 30). On the other hand, many of the field systems recently identified in the river valleys of lowland England may have been for raising livestock. They included paired ditches which can be interpreted as droveways communicating between different parts of the landscape; such features were normally integrated with ponds and waterholes, and the environmental evidence recovered from those features suggests that they were located in pasture. These landscapes were best suited to cattle, but the only direct evidence is provided by occasional finds of animal bones.

In fact the evidence is likely to introduce certain biases. By their very nature waterholes will be associated with areas of pasture rather than cultivated land. Most excavated settlements produce carbonised grain, and there is little to suggest that it had been brought there after it was processed. Moreover, some of the chalkland settlements in southern England show a stronger emphasis on sheep than other animals. This was a largely new feature. It may have been connected with the discovery of artefacts associated with textile production, principally spindle whorls and loom weights. On the other hand, recently excavated field ditches of this date at Over in the Fenland were associated with unusual quantities of grain (Chris Evans pers. comm.).

There is also a possibility that larger settlements existed at the same time, although the clearest indication of this comes from Dartmoor where the dating evidence is meagre (Fleming 2008; P. Newman 2011). The edges of the high ground were divided into a series of separate territories by the continuous boundaries known as reaves. They may have originated as fences, but today they can be recognised as low walls. They are in more sheltered areas and those with the most productive soils. The larger settlements were usually found beyond their limits, but it is not clear how this observation should be interpreted. As Chapter 4 suggested, they may represent the surviving fraction of what was once a wider distribution of houses and irregular enclosures established during the Early Bronze Age. If so, then further examples may have been removed when more formal field systems were established.

A few enclosures were built on such a large scale that they might have been higher-status settlements. At present, they seem to be commonest in western Britain and were defined by an unusually substantial perimeter. At places like Grimspound on Dartmoor, this was a massive stone wall (P. Newman 2011). At Norton Fitzwarren a hoard of Middle Bronze Age ornaments and tools was found on the edge of what might have been a ditched enclosure overlain by a later hillfort (P. Ellis 1989). Similar structures have been identified in the Cotswolds (Darvill 2011: 160–1) and at two sites on the Cheshire ridge (Garner 2016: chs. 9 and 12). There was another at Durham in north-east England (Brogan and Hodgson 2011), and a hoard of rapiers was buried in the defences of a hillfort at Drumcoltran in south-west Scotland (F. Coles 1892: 106). On the Wessex chalk significantly smaller enclosures were bounded by a ditch. They stood out from the slighter compounds associated with the remaining settlements of this date. They were by no means common, and for a long time these enclosures were thought to have been used for livestock. Re-excavation of one of the type sites, South Lodge Camp, has shown that the postholes of wooden houses were missed by the original excavator, General Pitt Rivers (Barrett, Bradley, and M. Green 1991: 156–61). Its main distinguishing feature was the enclosure ditch which was excavated 2 m into the bedrock. This earth-work was approximately square and conformed to the layout of an existing group of fields. A comparable sequence was identified on a nearby site at Down Farm, Woodcutts, where the final phase of activity was marked by the demolition of two roundhouses and their replacement by a massive rect-angular building with parallels in the Low Countries (Barrett, Bradley, and M. Green 1991: 198–9). This is one of a small group of rectilinear structures recognised during recent years. A very similar long house has been iden-tified at Barleycroft in the Fenland (C. Evans and Knight 1996). Again it seems to have replaced a pair of roundhouses. It was associated with another enclosure and with a coaxial field system (Fig. 5.8).

One of the most remarkable results of recent fieldwork has been to show that the distribution of enclosed landscapes was virtually confined to the south and east of Britain (Fig. 5.9). Coaxial field systems were ubiquitous on the chalk and the river gravels, extending in a broad swathe along the North Sea coastline from Norfolk (Gilmour et al. 2014) to the north as far as Kent to the south (D. Yates 2007). They were uncommon over large parts of the Midlands but probably extended along the English Channel as far west as Devon or Cornwall. Beyond that restricted area, settlements may have taken a similar form, but do not seem to have been associated with many ditched fields. It may be that these landscapes were characterised by more ephemeral bound-aries, but it seems as if the density of settlements was lower. Some were small groups of roundhouses and others were associated with earthwork enclosures. Although longer boundary earthworks are known in these areas, few have been dated to this early phase.

Such contrasts extend to northern England, Wales, and Scotland, but they may prove to be more apparent than real. One reason is that there have been fewer development-led excavations there. That is important as small open settlements are most likely to be found in large stripped areas and will rarely be discovered by more modest evaluations. That is amply demonstrated by work at Kintore in north-east Scotland where a continuous sequence of roundhouses, extending from the Early Bronze Age to the Iron Age, has been identified (Cook and Dunbar 2008). Again Middle and Late Bronze Age houses were found in unexpected numbers before the construction of the Aberdeen Peripheral Road (Dingwall in press). Although the evidence is limited, their architecture had more in common with those of the Early Bronze Age than their counterparts in the south.

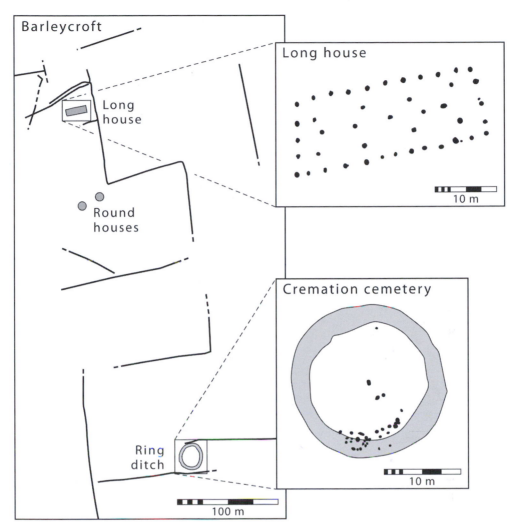

Figure 5.8 Plan of part of a coaxial field system at Barleycroft, eastern England, showing the positions of two roundhouses, a long house, and a cremation cemetery. Plan courtesy of Chris Evans, Cambridge Archaeological Unit.

Artefact Production

There is only limited evidence of artefact production on these sites. A few settlements in Britain and Ireland produce clay moulds for metalworking, but there is nothing to suggest that there were restrictions on where particular objects were made, and tools, weapons, and ornaments may have been produced in similar places, but not necessarily by the same people (Ó Faoláin 2004). Textile production was equally important, but its extent is difficult to document as the artefacts usually described as loom weights may also have been used as hearth furniture, and in the Late Bronze Age even in the production of

Figure 5.9 The distribution of Middle and/or Late Bronze Age coaxial field systems. Information from Yates (2007) with additions.

ceramics (Best and A. Woodward 2012). It can hardly be a coincidence that they are found together in quantity in some regions but do not occur often in others. For example, entire groups of settlements, like those on the Sussex chalk or their counterparts in the Middle Thames, provide large numbers of these finds, whilst there are areas, like the downland of southern Wessex, in which they are comparatively unusual. It is clear that certain settlements had a more specialised economy. The significance of textile production may be illustrated by the practice of decorating these artefacts in the same style as Middle Bronze Age Globular Urns (K. Ritchie et al. 2008: fig. 8). It was unusual, but in one case a complete set of decorated 'loom weights' was buried in an isolated pit (A. Chapman 2012). Salt production was another largely new development on the coast. It is first evidenced at Brean Down during the Early Bronze Age (Bell 1990: 165–73), but from that time onwards finds of the distinctive pottery containers in which concentrated brine was processed are commonly found on the coast. It happened so widely in the Fenland that it may have been a speciality of that region (Daniel 2009: 74–82).

A novel development in Ireland was the production of gold ornaments, including discs, neck rings, and torcs, during the thirteenth and twelfth centuries BC (G. Eogan 1994b). They were surely made from native metal and formed part of a more extensive tradition which was represented along the Atlantic coast from Portugal to north-west France. The products of the Irish industry are also found in Britain, with distinct concentrations in Wales, the Severn Estuary, and southern England, and close connections still existed between northern Ireland and north-east Scotland. A few of these artefacts have been found in graves, but most were deposited in hoards and often in bogs (Becker 2013). It is not clear how their production was related to the settlement sites of this period, but their chronology may overlap with the first development of fortified enclosures in Ireland which is discussed later in this chapter.

Mortuary Rituals

The mortuary rituals of the Middle Bronze Age pose many problems. The British evidence is abundant (Fig. 5.10). From the Yorkshire Wolds to the English Channel coast, cremation cemeteries are easy to identify because they are associated with readily recognised styles of pottery. The same is true in the south-west, but beyond these areas the ceramic evidence is so unsatisfactory that at different times the same kinds of vessels have been attributed to every phase from the Neolithic period to the Iron Age.

It was not until 1972 that it was possible to link a Middle Bronze Age settlement with its cemetery. A group of cremations associated with a small round barrow was discovered close to the excavated site at Itford Hill in Sussex. The connection between them was confirmed when it was realised that a sherd associated with one of the houses fitted a broken vessel associated with the burials (Holden 1972). Subsequent fieldwork has shown that other cemeteries of this kind were associated with settlements, and there were burials or smaller deposits of cremated bone among the dwellings themselves. In these cases the main groups of cremations were located behind the living area but within about 200 metres (Bradley 1981). New research suggests that this was more common on the chalk of southern England than it was elsewhere, and it can no longer be claimed as a general pattern (Caswell and B. Roberts 2018). In some cases the cemeteries were located at pivotal positions within the local landscape. Thus groups of cremation deposits could be placed in field corners or at the entrances of droveways or the junctions between them (Cooper 2016b).

The links between settlements and cemeteries extended to other features. At one time it was thought that the pottery associated with Early Bronze Age burials was different from that employed in daily life, but it was certainly not

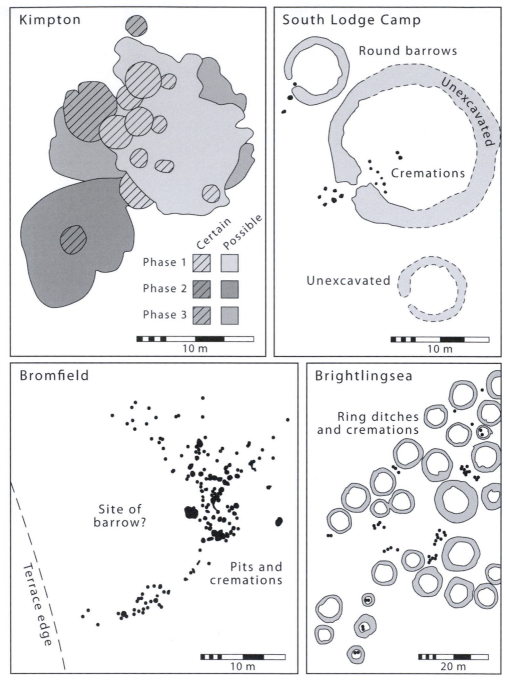

Figure 5.10 Middle Bronze Age cemeteries. At Kimpton, Wessex, cremation burials were associated with a sequence of flint platforms. At South Lodge Camp, Wessex, they were found with small round barrows, each with an entrance on one side. At Bromfield close to the English/Welsh border urned and unurned cremations were arranged in an arc forming a sector of an enclosure about 25 m in diameter, and at Brightlingsea in the Thames Estuary they were associated with a dense distribution of small ring ditches. Information from Dacre and Ellison (1981), Barrett, Bradley, and Green (1991), Stanford (1982), and N. Brown (2000).

true during this phase as the ceramics associated with cremation cemeteries are indistinguishable in type, fabric, and decoration from those used in the houses. In the same way, the occasional metal items found with cremation cemeteries were of the same types as the artefacts deposited in settlements, often when individual structures were built or went out of use. There were even cases in which the layout of an individual cemetery reflected that of the domestic buildings. In lowland England newly constructed barrows were about the same size as the houses of the same period, and sometimes both kinds of structure had an entrance to the south or south-east. It was often on this side of the mound that the main group of burials was concentrated. In such cases it seems as if the settlement and its cemetery were mirror images of one another (Bradley 1998a: 150–8; Bradley and Fraser 2010). The distribution of cremations could be divided into a series of separate clusters, but little was done to distinguish one burial from another. These deposits did not exclude any section of the population; the cremations included men, women, and children. There is little sign of the complex spatial organisation that typifies the cemeteries of the Early Bronze Age. Rather, it seems as if social distinctions were being suppressed.

There were a few striking exceptions. At Eye Kettleby in the east Midlands the remains of adults were treated separately from those of the young (Finn 2011). The use of oak was restricted to the pyres of older members of the community, and their ashes were more likely to be buried in urns. By contrast, the remains of the young were probably under-represented. Again at Kimpton in Wessex the successive clusters of cremation burials resembled the sequence of dwellings within a settlement site (Dacre and Ellison 1981). They occupied flint platforms that built up gradually over time. Similarly, at a number of places in the Thames Estuary the burials were associated with groups of small ring ditches very similar to those of the same date in the Low Countries (N. Brown 2000; C. Clarke and Lavender 2008). The same applies to cemeteries in Ireland, but in every case the associated pottery was in a distinctive local style. Yet another arrangement has been identified at Bromfield in the west Midlands where the burials described an enormous arc, rather like one section of a circular enclosure. Perhaps the cemetery formed around a barrow which has since disappeared (Stanford 1982).

Until recently, it would have been difficult to discuss the northern and western British equivalents of these practices. The situation has improved considerably as a result of new excavations. The direct dating of cremated bone from older projects has made a special contribution. This evidence is difficult to evaluate, but there have been three crucial developments. The first has been a campaign of dating human remains from reliable contexts. This has produced unexpected evidence that during the Middle and Late Bronze Ages a whole variety of Scottish monuments were reused, often as cemeteries or pyres. The original monuments had been built between the Late Neolithic and the Early

Bronze Age and included stone circles, henges, and ring cairns (Bradley and Nimura 2016: ch. 8). A similar development has been identified at some of the henge monuments of north-east England, which appear to have been revisited at about this time. It happened at two monuments at Whitton Hill in the Milfield Basin in north-east England which were reused as cremation cemeteries between 1400 and 1020 BC (C. Fowler 2013: table 4.1); the original use of one of these monuments had taken place much earlier. Similarly, at Bredon in the Severn Valley a henge was modified by erecting a palisade which was probably associated with more cremation burials (Lewis and Mullin 2016). This time they dated between about 1550 and 1250 BC. In Wales standing stones were erected on the sites of earlier houses and associated with settings of pebbles and deposits of burnt human bone (Benson, J. Evans, and G. Williams 1990).

The second result is equally challenging, for it has shown that the rather nondescript pottery associated with these developments ('flat-rimmed ware') had a finite currency (Sheridan 2003b). It was not used for as long as once supposed, and in most areas it was made between about 1600 and 800 BC. That is important because it suggests that still more monuments were being reused as cemeteries during this phase. It also raises the possibility that structures which had been assigned to earlier periods were actually built during the later Bronze Age. In the north, traditional forms of public monument retained their importance for longer than had been thought.

Lastly, there could have been a close connection between the sequences in Scotland and Ireland. There was a striking resemblance between the smallest Scottish 'henges' and a series of Irish earthworks known as 'ring barrows' (Bradley 2009b). These were not really mounds but circular enclosures defined by an external bank and a wide internal ditch. Sometimes there is evidence for an eastern entrance that seems to have been blocked. The British monuments, which are mainly in the north of Scotland, had very similar features, and were first built at the end of the Early Bronze Age (Bradley 2011: chs. 5 and 6). In Ireland, the situation is slightly more encouraging, and it is clear that these sites were among the principal mortuary monuments of the later Bronze Age and, indeed, the Iron Age (McGarry 2009). Until about 1300 BC they were associated with burials containing grave goods similar to those of the Early Bronze Age, but after that time barrows and other monuments rarely contained more than a token collection of bones. As in Britain, the treatment of the dead seems to have changed, but in Scotland earthworks of this kind were used or reused until the Late Bronze Age. A typical example was associated with the important site of Mine Howe on the Mainland of Orkney (Card et al. 2005). A variant was a ring ditch almost 20 m in diameter at Portree in the Inner Hebrides. Unlike the other sites, it lacked an obvious entrance, but it was built between about 1250 and 1000 BC and was close to two roundhouses of the same date (Suddaby 2013).

The Treatment of Metalwork

During the same period some of the types of artefacts which had previously been placed in graves were deposited in other locations. In the Middle Bronze Age ornaments were often buried in hoards, either in dry ground or in bogs. Detailed analysis of the associated artefacts suggests that they were sets of personal equipment (B. Roberts 2007). Different items were worn to different extents, raising the possibility that they had been accumulated during the course of people's lives and may even have been deposited when they died (R. Taylor 1993). Something similar happened with the bronze weapons of this period. Many of the daggers are found in Wessex barrows, but their direct successors were usually deposited in water. The Thames has produced the largest number of examples (York 2002), but in Ireland there was another concentration of these finds in the Shannon (Bourke 2001).

It must be more than a coincidence that as elaborate artefacts disappear from the funerary record, they occur with increasing frequency in other contexts. The connection between these deposits is especially obvious in the case of daggers, rapiers, and dirks. The dagger had been one of the main artefacts associated with Early Bronze Age burials, and it is generally agreed that it provided the prototype for these other weapons. The two groups of finds had mutually exclusive distributions. Those associated with barrows were mostly from Wessex, but the river finds were from the Thames. Very few dirks and rapiers were associated with human burials, but the number associated with water increased sharply (Bradley 1998b: fig. 20). The rate of consumption changed as barrow building became less important.

Taken in isolation, the cemeteries provide a misleading impression of Middle Bronze Age society. Overt distinctions may have been suppressed in the mortuary rite (although nothing is known about the rituals taking place around the pyre), and it seems as if the dead were denied the conspicuous memorials that had been provided for earlier generations. In Britain the mounds were smaller, and some sites lacked them entirely. Similarly, in Ireland many burials were in flat cemeteries with few, if any, grave goods. One possibility is that only part of the population was buried, whilst the people who had access to elaborate metalwork were commemorated at a different location and in a different way (Bradley 2017a: ch. 8). Another possibility is that the finery traditionally associated with the dead was removed from contact with their bodies and deposited somewhere else. If so, then it may have been the structure of the mortuary rites that altered, rather than the structure of society. There is another complication. These fine objects may not have been the possessions of the dead, but the material equipment associated with the performance of particular roles in the community. They could have been discarded once those roles had been accomplished and not necessarily on the death of the office-holder. In that case their deposition was intended to protect the special significance of these artefacts and not to commemorate the dead (Bradley 2017a: 148–9).

It is difficult to decide between these various models, but one point is quite clear. In southern Britain and probably much more widely, the embellishment of barrow cemeteries had reached its limit by the end of the Early Bronze Age. As Chapter 4 suggested, one way of considering the problem is to suggest that these earthworks were no longer such an effective way of communicating relationships with the dead. New ways of expressing these ideas developed.

But is there any direct evidence that the river metalwork was associated with the dead? It is not enough to say that its immediate predecessors had been found in graves, for cemeteries were still being created during the Middle Bronze Age. There are two arguments that might support this hypothesis. The first concerns the treatment of the corpse. Although cremation was certainly the principal rite, there is an increasing amount of evidence for inhumation burials during this period, and also for smaller deposits of human remains. Because they are seldom associated with diagnostic artefacts they are rarely dated. In recent years it has become clear that unburnt bones, mainly skulls, are found in rivers or in other watery locations, usually in the same locations as the weapons. This raises many problems – the skulls may have been separated from the other parts of the body as a result of taphonomic processes; both weapons and human remains may have been brought together by the action of the river – but it happened too often to be entirely coincidental. That is particularly true of the skulls from the River Thames where a detailed study of their condition does not support these objections (Schulting and Bradley 2014). There are radiocarbon dates for a number of skulls from the Thames and its tributaries, and it is clear that nearly all of them were deposited there between the middle of the Bronze Age and the end of the pre-Roman Iron Age. Although this may be evidence for some kind of 'river burial', the presence of injuries suggests that it was not a normal way of disposing of the dead. Again this could have developed out of an existing practice, as Early Bronze Age skeletons were associated with artefacts from wet deposits in the Fenland (Healy and Housley 1992).

The second point is rather more tentative, but recent analysis of the weapons from British and Irish rivers has shown that they had obviously been used in combat over a significant period before they were deposited (York 2002). These objects had not been made as votive offerings, and they were only discarded at the end of a lengthy history. That might mirror the lives of those who had used them.

THE LATE BRONZE AGE, 1100–800 BC

Although this chapter treats the Middle and Late Bronze Ages together, there were important developments from the twelfth century BC. Most grew directly out of existing processes of change. There are signs of climatic deterioration at this time (Bevan et al. 2017), but there is no need to postulate a major crisis.

The Treatment of Metalwork

The practice of depositing metalwork in rivers continued unabated. It may even have intensified, although in England its geographical focus changed from the Fenland to the Thames. There was more continuity in the use of other British and Irish rivers. In some respects the deposition of weaponry underwent a subtle modification. Throughout the later Bronze Age it is clear that these artefacts had been used in combat and that some of them had been repaired or resharpened long before they were taken out of circulation. At the same time, a detailed study of the metalwork from the Thames itself shows that they were normally disabled before they were committed to the water. The frequency of deliberately damaged items increased steadily through time, whilst the proportion of artefacts showing signs of use remained at a constant level (York 2002). It took considerable effort to damage the finest swords and spears. Some of these weapons were burnt, and it seems possible that they had been present on a pyre. They include examples from Duddingston Loch in Edinburgh which were associated with human bones (Callender 1922). As in the Middle Bronze Age, Late Bronze Age swords and spearheads have also been found in rivers together with unburnt skulls. It is difficult to interpret their relationship to one another, but it is unlikely to be coincidental (Schulting and Bradley 2014).

The deposition of weaponry may have involved a greater spectacle than before. One reason for suggesting this is the amount of damage inflicted on many of the weapons. Another is that there is an increasing number of sites where such deposits seem to be directly associated with timber structures in rivers and similar settings. Some were conceived on a massive scale, and where they have been excavated in recent years they were associated not only with finds of metalwork but also with ceramic vessels, human remains, and animal bones. They were laid down with a certain formality. Thus entire pots could be placed beside upright timbers (Bell 2013); human and animal remains might have different distributions from one another (Pryor 2001); and the faunal remains could have an unusual composition, with an emphasis on horses and dogs that has no counterpart in the settlement sites of the same period (Bradley 2017a: ch. 4).

Structures in the Wetlands

The wooden structures are difficult to explain. Some of them were considerable undertakings. A causeway at Flag Fen in eastern England linked a platform built in open water to two areas of settled land. Bones were deposited on one side of this alignment, and items of metalwork on the other (Pryor 2001).

Although this was an unusually elaborate construction, a similar structure has been identified at Must Farm not far away (Knight, Harris, and Appleby 2016), and there are signs of similar features elsewhere in southern and eastern England. They might have provided a stage for public ceremonies, but it is likely that they played a practical role as well, connecting the mainland to islands that were permanently occupied. Middle and Late Bronze Age finds are associated with the remains of bridges, jetties, or causeways at a number of places in England (they belong to both phases as such structures were sometimes long-lived). They include Testwood in southern Wessex, Shinewater in south-east England, Greylake in the Somerset Levels, and two sites along the River Thames, one at Vauxhall, and the other at Eton Rowing Lake where several of these structures have been identified (Brunning 2013: 146–50). Not all these sites are associated with weapons. They do occur in most instances, but at Eton the river contained pottery and human bones, and Greylake was associated with a broken axehead and more human remains. Chris Evans (2002) has suggested that similar deposits were made at other places where people travelled across water, and it certainly seems as if major deposits of metalwork were associated with the routes leading to the Isle of Ely. There are also cases in which deposits of weapons have been found with the remains of log boats (D. Gibson, Knight, and Murrell 2012). Some of the richest collections of metalwork come from the River Shannon in Ireland, where they are often associated with fords (Bourke 2001). The very act of crossing the water might have been conceived as a rite of passage.

The platform at Flag Fen has features in common with the recently excavated 'pile dwelling' at Must Farm (Fig. 5.11). It overlays another post alignment which predated the settlement by about three hundred years and had been built over a minor channel of the River Nene. It was enclosed by a palisade (D. Gibson et al. 2016; Knight, Harris, and Appleby 2016). Only part of the original settlement is preserved, but it is thought that it had originally been oval in plan and might have contained as many as ten roundhouses. Occupation was brief as the surviving part of the site was destroyed before work had been completed on erecting one of these structures. The buildings collapsed into the waterlogged silts, preserving their remains in exceptional detail. It is likely that the settlement had been attacked and the buildings were set on fire.

The surviving houses were very similar to one another, and there were no obvious differences in their construction methods, sizes, or contents. What was remarkable was the degree of preservation which meant that the Must Farm pile dwelling included the remains of plant foods, meat joints, ceramic and wooden containers, and a variety of textiles. Although it was built in a waterlogged environment there was little evidence of fishing, and most of the bones were those of farm animals.

Several features of the site have wider implications. The exceptional richness of the excavated material provides some indication of the kinds of artefacts that

Figure 5.11 The Late Bronze Age settlement at Must Farm, eastern England, under excavation showing the positions of circular houses destroyed by fire. Photograph by courtesy of Mark Knight and the Cambridge Archaeological Unit.

do not survive on dry land sites. They also show that Late Bronze Age metal-work was abundant, including tools and weapons of kinds that might normally be discovered on their own (Knight, Harris, and Appleby 2016). This raises two possibilities. Perhaps similar material would usually be recycled, leaving little trace behind. Alternatively, some of the items abandoned in the burning buildings would normally be deposited in hoards or rivers. Because the contents of the settlement were left behind when it was set on fire, it could not have happened here. One clue comes from the excavation of a nearby river channel which contained a number of bronze weapons and unburnt human bones. In this case the sediments also preserved a series of boats which had been deliber-ately sunk when they went out of use (D. Gibson, Knight, and Murrell 2012).

It is not clear whether the Must Farm settlement was typical of the settlements of the Late Bronze Age, but in Britain there is evidence for the occupation of small islands during this period. Two examples have been excavated in recent years, at Runnymede Bridge and Wallingford, both in the Thames (Needham 1991 and 1992; Needham and Spence 1997; Cromarty et al. 2005). In each case its perimeter seems to have been delimited by vertical piles driven into the river bed. At Runnymede the site was located at a confluence between the Thames and one of its tributaries and formed only part of a larger complex; there could have been an enclosed settlement nearby. Both islands were in a river that has produced many finds of weapons, but there is no direct association between them, and those from Wallingford seem to be earlier in date than the finds from the excavation.

Little is known about the structures on these sites, although it is interesting that at Runnymede they seem to have included rectangular buildings quite different from the roundhouses found with the enclosure on dry land (Needham 1992). There were midden deposits at both sites. Runnymede Bridge also provided evidence of metalworking. It would be impossible to raise many animals on the islands themselves, so the large quantity of faunal remains may be evidence of feasting. A possible link with river finds is the burial of a human skull. Another island in the Thames was at Syon Reach (Corcoran, Nicholls, and Cowie 2012). In this case nothing is known of any structures, but the site is exceptional because of the number and quality of artefacts found in the river. Again human bones come from the same contexts.

Another comparison is with the artificial islands known as crannogs, although there is no evidence that structures of this kind were built in Britain before the Iron Age (Fig. 5.12). On the other hand, a recent study of the Irish evidence suggests a different situation. Fredengren (2002) has undertaken a survey of the evidence from Lough Gara in the west of the country and has compared her results with those of older fieldwork. At three of the sites structural timbers were dated by radiocarbon. In each case the results fall between 930 and 800 BC and clearly relate to activity towards the end of the Bronze Age. That is consistent with the results of earlier excavations on this kind of monument.

Such crannogs may have played many different roles, and the same must surely apply to the wooden platforms built in areas of blanket bog. Their characteristics overlap, and a number of prehistoric crannogs may actually have been built around natural islands. They were generally composed of brushwood and large quantities of stones, and despite the good conditions of preservation the structural evidence from these sites can be surprisingly meagre. It is often assumed that they included the sites of houses like those from the Middle Ages, but the main evidence is that of hearths. In some cases they would have been under water for part of the year and cannot have been inhabited continuously

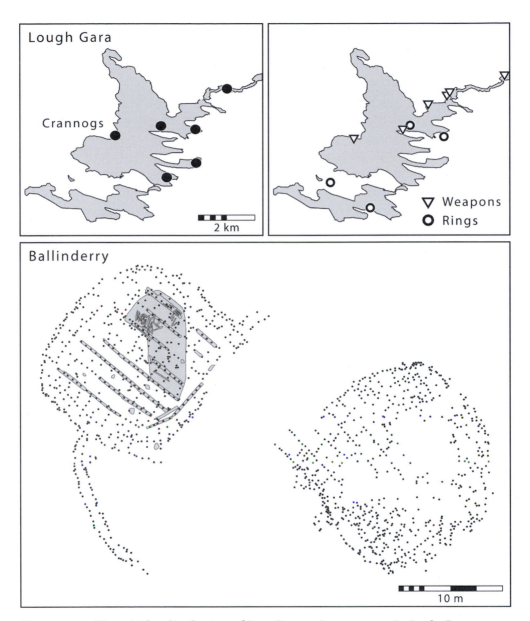

Figure 5.12 (Upper) The distribution of Late Bronze Age crannogs in Loch Gara in the west of Ireland and the findspots of weapons and rings from watery contexts. (Lower) Two timber structures, perhaps connected by a path, at Ballinderry, Irish midlands. Information from Fredengren (2002) and Newman (1997b).

(Fredengren 2002). The two timber platforms at Ballinderry were more substantial undertakings. One had a foundation of parallel beams, but again the nature of their superstructure is not clear (C. Newman 1997b). They seem to have been connected to one another by a path. Something similar has been found at Killymoon, where a platform associated with a small gold hoard is linked to an earthwork enclosure on dry land (Hurl 1995). There seems to have been a comparable site at Moynagh Lough (J. Bradley 2004).

These structures are dominated by burnt stone and animal bones, perhaps suggesting that, among other activities, they were used for cooking and consuming food; there was even a flesh hook among the finds from Ballinderry. Other associations of the crannogs are more distinctive and perhaps compare with the British finds mentioned earlier. Some of them are associated with items of fine metalwork of kinds which are rarely, if ever, found in settlements on dry land. This need not reflect the unusual preservation of the sites, for the artefacts include formal deposits. At Rathtinaun, for instance, a number of them had been deposited together just beyond the limits of the platform. They were inside a wooden box and included bronze rings, amber beads, a pair of tweezers, a pin, and boars' tusks (Raftery 1994: 32–5). This is particularly interesting as other Bronze Age crannogs have produced finds of rings, as well as swords. These sites also contain the moulds for making weapons.

Unlike the pile dwelling at Must Farm, crannogs were located in open water, and it seems clear that they provided a focus for further deposits. They were of two main kinds. There were a considerable number of bronze weapons, especially swords (Fredengren 2002). That is hardly surprising since these kinds of artefacts were apparently being made on sites like Rathtinaun (Raftery 1994: 32–5) and Lough Eskragh (B. Williams 1978). Human skulls also occurred (Fredengren 2002). Their discovery is especially significant as their presence does not raise the taphonomic problems that affect the finds from fast-flowing rivers. Most of them came from the still waters of lakes, and were found in the same areas as the artificial islands.

Weapons and Fortifications

Although weapons seem to have been discarded according to specific conventions, it would be wrong to suppose that their main function was as votive offerings. Again there is evidence that they had been used in combat. That is most apparent from the damage that they had sustained in the course of their histories (York 2002). There are also a number of instances in which human remains show signs of fatal or healed wounds. Another indication of the importance of conflict is the evidence of fortifications. It needs to be treated rather cautiously for the terminology used by archaeologists can be very misleading. Near to some of the English weapon finds are circular earthworks described as 'ringforts' or 'ringworks' (Needham and Ambers 1994). These sites were first investigated because they looked like earlier prehistoric henges. Others have been discovered in the course of developer-funded fieldwork or have been recognised through retrospective analysis of already excavated sites.

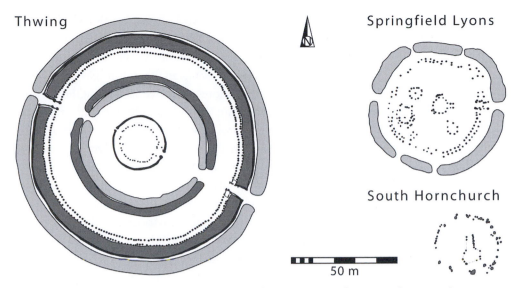

Figure 5.13 Plans of Late Bronze Age ringworks in Britain. Information from Manby, King, and Vyner (2003), Brown and Medlycott (2013), Guttmann and Last (2000), and Evans, Appleby, and Lucy (2015).

The features that first attracted attention were the circular layout of these monuments, the presence of one or two main entrances (although a few members of this group actually had interrupted ditches), and hints that at their centre there was a circular timber building (Fig. 5.13). Most examples fall in the centuries between 1000 and 800 BC (Needham and Ambers 1994), but at least two sites may be significantly earlier than that: the inner enclosure at Thwing which dates from the Middle Bronze Age and resembles an older henge (Manby, King, and Vyner 2003: 70–8), and a palisaded enclosure 27 m in diameter of similar age at Worcester (Griffin et al. 2002).

Later work has modified these clear distinctions. Not all the enclosures are precisely circular, nor was there necessarily one main building inside them. Some of these sites had internal ramparts with a vertical timber face reinforced by upright posts, yet the earliest enclosure at Thwing had an external bank like a Late Neolithic monument. Even so, several members of this group were remarkably similar to one another. Rams Hill on the northern margin of the Wessex chalk had a timbered rampart of the same kind as another example at Taplow in the Middle Thames (Bradley and Ellison 1975; T. Allen, Hayden, and Lamdin-Whymark 2009). It also had a distinctive entrance structure that it shares with Thwing on the Yorkshire Wolds. Similarly, the earthwork monument at South Hornchurch is the same size and shape as two wooden enclosures on the same site (Guttmann and Last 2000). Another example was at Huntsman's Quarry in the Severn Valley in western England, some way outside the usual distribution of these monuments (R. Jackson 2015).

In fact one result of the expansion of fieldwork in the last few years is that the number of ringworks has increased and their distribution has extended from the North Sea coastline inland at least as far as Wessex and possibly Cornwall (A. Jones, Gossip, and Quinnell 2015: 203–25). Similarly, it is clear that their earthworks formed part of a more extensive landscape. For a long time it has been accepted that Bronze Age ringworks provided an important focus for public events, including the provision of offerings. Excavation outside one such monument at Carshalton shows that these activities may have extended into the surrounding area (Proctor 2002). Here there were a number of unusual deposits and a small semi-circular enclosure associated with a horse skull. Fieldwork outside similar enclosures has identified roundhouses and traces of rectangular buildings (A. Manning and C. Moore 2003).

It is possible to interpret the ringworks in more than one way. They may have been elite residences, cut off by earthworks from the surrounding area and possibly protected from attack. Like Irish crannogs, these sites can be associated with weapon production. Both the entrances to the enclosure at Springfield Lyons contained clay moulds for making swords (N. Brown and Medlycott 2013). Another possibility is that they were public buildings and employed in a similar fashion to the henges with which they had been confused. The principal buildings could be protected by a screen like those at Durrington Walls and Stonehenge in the Neolithic period, and it seems possible that feasts had taken place there (Bishop and Boyer 2014; Boyer et al. 2014). The ditch at Thwing contained a large deposit of animal bones (Mounteney 1981), and South Rings at Mucking was associated with a considerable amount of fine pottery suitable for serving food and drink (C. Evans, Appleby, and Lucy 2015: 185–8). A number of sites in south-east England produced perforated clay slabs which were probably used in cooking. Their overall distribution is like that of weapon deposits (Champion 2014).

The local setting of these earthworks is revealing. Their positions could have made a direct reference to the past. One example on the island of Sheppey was placed in between the remains of two causewayed enclosures (M. Allen, Lewis, and C. Ellis 2008), and the Late Bronze Age ringwork at Springfield Lyons was built next to a similar monument of Middle Neolithic date (N. Brown and Medlycott 2013). Deposits of metalwork can also be found close by, like the striking concentration of dry land hoards around the enclosure at Springfield and its neighbour at Great Baddow (N. Brown and Medlycott 2013: fig. 5.2), or the weapons recovered from the Thames near the ringforts at Taplow and Wittenham Clumps (T. Allen, Hayden, and Lamdin-Whymark 2009; T. Allen et al. 2010).

Yates (2007) has argued that most ringworks occur in regions with coaxial land divisions. It is true that from the twelfth century BC the lowland landscape assumed a uniform character, but its typical features had developed well before that time. They included fields and droveways and some of these features were going out of use by the time the enclosures were built.

Settlements and Land Divisions

The settlements themselves were becoming more diverse. They were no longer restricted to small groups of houses and could extend over a considerable area. In England most of these sites were entirely open, but the dwellings within them were frequently superimposed. They were associated with a similar range of ancillary structures – granaries, storehouses, pits, ponds, and occasional rectangular buildings – but they may have been occupied more intensively or over longer periods of time. Many were new creations in the Late Bronze Age, and produce finds of carbonised grain (Brossler, Early, and C. Allen 2004; Lewis et al. 2010).

In Ireland Ginn (2016) has identified some striking features of the Late Bronze Age settlements. The occupied area increased to take in greater areas of wetland. The associated artefacts contrast with those of the Middle Bronze Age, and the domestic assemblage included more metalwork. It was found at the sites with access to the most productive land. As in the previous period, there were cremation burials in the vicinity. The number of separate sites known from excavation was a little lower than before, but the houses themselves were bigger and seem to have remained in use for longer periods of time. Now they might have been occupied over more than one generation. During the Late Bronze Age settlements were commonly associated with raised storage structures like those in England. Moulds for working metal may have been confined to fewer settlements than before, but they were mainly a feature of two kinds of site that were a largely new development: hillforts and crannogs.

So far very few fields have been found in Ireland. In Britain a significant number of those established during the Middle Bronze Age had gone out of use by this time (D. Yates 2007). On the Wessex chalk they were supplemented, and more often slighted, by long linear earthworks which defined the limits of a series of territories (Fig. 5.14). They usually extended from the rivers onto the higher ground, but in other cases they followed the upper limits of fertile valleys in a similar manner to the land boundaries on Dartmoor during an earlier period. Their interpretation has always been controversial, although it seems to be agreed that most of these developments began during the Late Bronze Age (Bradley, Entwistle, and Raymond 1994; McOmish, D. Field, and G. Brown 2002). Such earthworks were once described as 'ranch boundaries' on the assumption that cattle raising became more important at this time, but other researchers have suggested that there may have been a greater emphasis on sheep, an interpretation supported by the faunal remains from the local settlements (McOmish 1996). Another possibility is that land holding

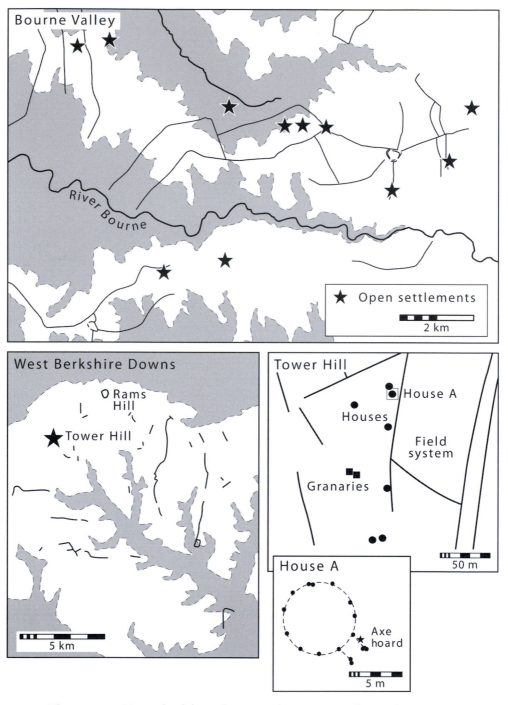

Figure 5.14 Linear land boundaries in the Bourne Valley and on the Berkshire Downs, Wessex, showing the position of the ringwork on Rams Hill and a series of open settlements. Insets show the distribution of houses and granaries within one of these settlements at Tower Hill and the Plan of House A which was associated with a hoard of metalwork. Information from Bradley, Entwistle, and Raymond (1993) and Miles (2003).

was reorganised around a series of enclosed 'estates', each of which contained a variety of different resources, extending from grazing land on the flood plains, through arable land on the valley sides, to summer pasture on the high downland. Fieldwork on Salisbury Plain suggests that each of these territories included the position of at least one large open settlement (Bradley, Entwistle, and Raymond 1994).

Something similar happened on the Yorkshire Wolds (Fenton-Thomas 2003). In this case less is known about the location of Late Bronze Age settlements, and field systems of this period have not been identified. On the other hand, one of the points where several of these territories converged was the defended enclosure at Thwing. It occupied a prominent hilltop, but the main role of the ditched boundaries may have been to define a series of territories in the valleys. A vital element was water, and some of the linear ditches could have been intended to control access to springs (Fenton-Thomas 2003). Something similar may have happened in lowland areas of Britain where similar systems of ditched boundaries and pit alignments became established, but they have been difficult to date. It is likely that this development extended over a larger area than the distribution of field systems. At the same time long linear boundaries cut off bends in major rivers, for example Biddenham Loop in the English Midlands (Luke 2016).

There is no reason to suppose that the open settlements associated with land boundaries were any different from those discovered with the field systems that still remained in use in southern England. The expansion of development-led excavations has helped to put these sites in context. It is clear that they contain a number of specialised deposits which recall those of the Neolithic period. They include offerings of pottery, grain, and animal remains which were connected with houses, pits, ponds, the entrances of enclosures and buildings, and even the foundations of granaries (Brudenell and Cooper 2008). They were not a completely new development, but their frequency was increasing. The deposits found in ponds and wells are especially revealing for they emphasise the special importance of these places (D. Yates 2007: 136). Less is known about the open settlements in other parts of Britain and Ireland, although their sites are gradually being discovered in excavation. In areas without diagnostic ceramics the structures of these two periods can only be told apart by radiocarbon dating.

Cemeteries, Hoards, and Burnt Mounds

It is commonly supposed that Late Bronze Age settlements in lowland England did not have cemeteries like those of their Middle Bronze Age predecessors (Fig. 5.15). In Ireland that was not the case, and they have been identified in increasing numbers during developer-funded projects. Here ring barrows remained important and were associated with cremation burials (McGarry

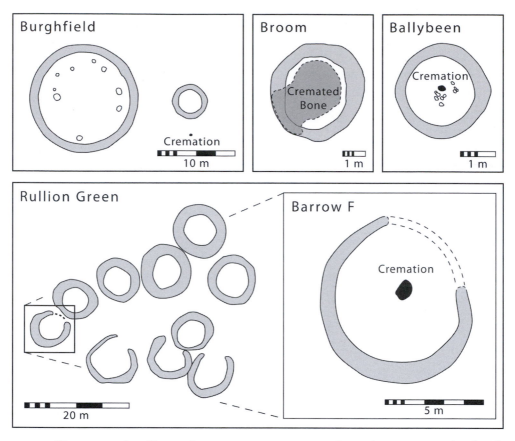

Figure 5.15 Late Bronze Age mortuary monuments. Cremations were associated with the excavated ring ditches at Burghfield (Kennet Valley), Broom (English Midlands), Ballybeen (northern Ireland), and Rullion Green (southern Scotland). The monument at Broom was associated with the remains of bronze cauldrons. Information from Bradley at al. (1980), Palmer (1999), Mallory (1984), and Watkins (1985).

2009). Even in southern England a few small ring ditches have been identified on the edges of living areas or field systems. Most were associated with a single cremation, and at Broom in the English Midlands an unusual burial found with one of these monuments was accompanied by the remains of several cauldrons (Palmer 1999: 36–56). These miniature round barrows had not been recognised until recently, and their distribution has still to be worked out. Another practice that has been identified for the first time is the deposition of small quantities of cremated human bone within the settlement itself (Brück 1995; Brudenell and Cooper 2008). It began in the Middle Bronze Age, and this phenomenon has now been traced across a wide area from Kent to the Severn Valley. It is also recognised in Ireland (Becker 2014). Detailed analysis of the contents of these features suggests that they were no more than token deposits of material taken from a pyre. That implies that the burning of human bodies may have been more common than archaeologists have supposed and that most of the remains were not preserved. Often they were incorporated in middens and did not receive any special treatment (Brudenell and Cooper 2008). Other practices continued unchanged from the Middle Bronze Age. The most important was the deposition of artefacts and animal bones in waterholes. On rare occasions it extended to the placing of human skulls in these locations (D. Yates 2007).

Other features are associated with settlement sites, but until recently they had been treated in isolation. There were the deposits of bronze metalwork known as hoards, but there were also distinctive mounds of burnt stone. As mentioned earlier, these hoards have been associated with the activities of smiths. Statistical analysis of the fragments supports the idea that they contained random accumulations of scrap (Wiseman 2018), but it seems doubtful whether they were simply stores of raw material. It is more likely that they represented the deliberate offering of part of the stock of metal which had been processed there (Bradley 2017a: 138–41). There were also small hoards of ornaments or weapons which may have been connected with particular individuals. Although some sites could have been genuinely isolated, others were clearly on the edge of settlements and have been found by open area excavation during recent years. Perhaps the clearest example of this is at Bradley Fen in eastern England (Fig. 5.16). Here a series of single finds of spearheads had been placed along the boundary between a long established field system and the edge of the wetland. Outside the enclosed area there was a hoard (D. Gibson and Knight 2006).

Similar evidence comes from field survey in southern England which has investigated the findspots of other collections of metalwork. They were originally studied for their associated artefacts, but the new work has established that they had often been deposited by springs, streams, and confluences (D. Yates and Bradley 2010a). Other finds from dry land come from the junctions of different kinds of subsoil which would have acted as aquifers before the water table was lowered during the historical period.

It is usual to contrast these dry land finds of metalwork from those in lakes, bogs, and rivers, and at one time this analysis distinguished between 'ritual' and 'non-ritual' hoards (Bradley 1998b). This procedure was justified by arguing that material buried on land could have been retrieved. It had been stored or hidden, but for some reason it was never recovered. Objects placed in water, on the other hand, would be difficult or impossible to retrieve. For that reason they were interpreted as offerings. If so many of the dry land deposits were buried close to rivers and springs, the contrast loses its force. Perhaps the nature of the water itself was the determining factor (D. Yates and Bradley 2010b; Becker 2013). Where it behaved in unexpected ways – by emerging from the ground, or where eddies developed at confluences – it took on an animated quality that had to be acknowledged. In fact there were very different kinds of water. In the English Fenland complete weapons were associated with fast-flowing

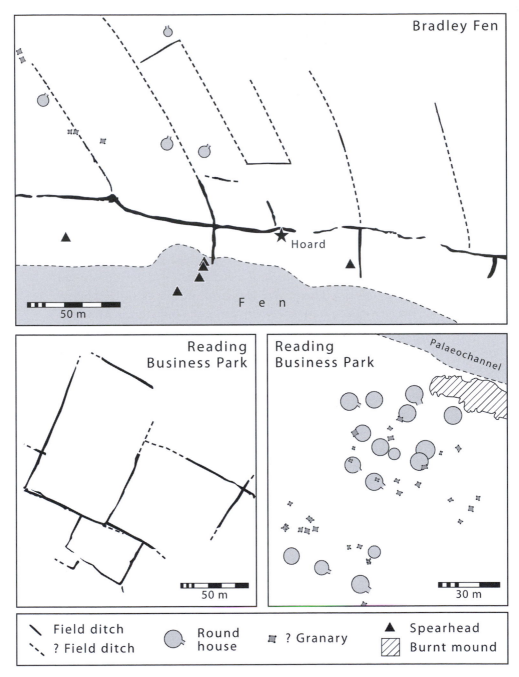

Figure 5.16 (Upper) Coaxial fields, houses, and possible granaries at Bradley Fen, eastern England, showing the findspots of individual spearheads and a metalwork hoard. (Lower) Successive phases in the development of the settlement at Reading Business Park where the structures overlie part of an earlier field system. Information from Gibson and Knight (2006) and Brossler, Early, and Allen (2004).

currents, and ornaments with the still water of bays and pools (D. Yates and Bradley 2010b). Similarly, the distribution of metalwork in the Thames focuses on the tidal head where freshwater and saltwater meet (Jon Cotton pers. comm.). Sometimes such relationships can be especially striking. In southern England hoards have been identified beside mineral springs which were used as spas during the nineteenth century. They have also been recognised where the water changes colour (D. Yates and Bradley 2010a). Other features have to be considered. The hoard that gave its name to the Bishopsland phase of the Irish Bronze Age was located by a dramatic series of waterfalls (Delaney 2016), and in Scotland a sword was found in a river by someone panning for gold (Cowie 2008); it was the source of another precious and mysterious metal. Of course such examples are purely anecdotal, but they are a reminder of the elements that can be overlooked in stricter analyses of this material.

A few hoards were outside settlement sites dating from this period and others were associated with hilltops. Below the open site at South Cadbury in south-west England there was a remarkable deposit of a shield (J. Coles et al. 1999). The nearby enclosure at Sigwells produced evidence of bronze working together with a human jaw and cranial fragment, again suggesting that metal production took place at special locations (Tabor 2007). The same considerations apply to a number of caves. They often produce unusual assemblages of artefacts, including metalwork (Dowd 2015). At Covesea in northern Scotland they are found with Late Bronze Age human skulls (Armit et al. 2011; Armit and Büster in press).

Some collections of metalwork were close to distinctive features which are described as burnt mounds (fulachta fiadh in Ireland). They have a lengthy history, for the oldest belong to the Neolithic period and others are associated with Beaker pottery, although radiocarbon dating suggests that many examples formed during the later Bronze Age. Iron Age examples are rare or non-existent (Ripper and Beamish 2012, 197–200). As their English name suggests, they are simply mounds of fire-cracked stones, although excavated examples are usually associated with a trough and sometimes with a small building. They are particularly common in Ireland, Scotland, and Wales. There are several peaks in the dates of Irish examples – 1800 BC, 1500 BC, and 900 BC – and their chronological distribution matches the cumulative evidence from Irish settlements and enclosures (Ginn 2016). It also corresponds with the main phases of later Bronze Age burial. In the Northern Isles burnt mounds are associated with stone buildings. They are normally found beside freshwater streams and seem to result from a specific technology in which heated stones were employed to boil large amounts of water. It is less clear why it was done and there may have been more than one reason for this practice in these islands (A. Hawkes 2014). One possibility is that the sites were used to cook joints of meat, yet it is often claimed that few animal bones are preserved at these locations. That does not apply to new projects in Ireland in which small fragments have been found by sieving (Tourunen 2007). Enough is known to reject the old idea that they were used by hunting parties, as the faunal remains are those of domesticates. In the west of Ireland one example was reconstructed after an interval. The excavator concluded that the earlier structure, which dates from the fourteenth or thirteenth century BC, had been used for boiling meat. Between 900 and 800 BC it was replaced by a hearth or oven in which the meat could be roasted (O'Brien 2012).

Another interpretation is that the objective was to create large amounts of steam, so that they may have been used like North American sweat lodges (A. Hawkes 2014). Again there is no clear evidence of this, although the small size of the structures associated with them might support the idea. They have few artefact associations, but they suggest that these sites may have played a part in specialised activities. They include pieces of fine metalwork, the moulds for making them, and occasional human remains. One example at Drombeg in southwest Ireland was only 50 m from a stone circle of the same date (Fahy 1959 and 1960). That does not mean that the burnt mounds themselves were used for bronze working or played a part in mortuary ritual. Rather, it suggests that they were in places where such activities took place. They may not have been accessible to everyone, and perhaps that is why they are often outside the settlements.

A related structure has been investigated at Washingborough on the bank of the River Witham in eastern England (C. Allen 2009). It was close to the findspots of a series of bronze weapons and dates between 1100 and 800 BC. Here a wooden tank was identified, together with a timber platform and a deposit of pebbles which had obviously been heated. Unusually, these features were associated with a variety of artefacts and other finds, including a large quantity of pottery, crucibles and moulds for metalworking, a wooden bowl, and objects made out of amber, shale, bone, and antler. There were also human long bones and skulls. The excavators concluded that the site had been used in feasting; the residues preserved inside the ceramics came from a kind of meat stew. At Washingborough the separate elements identified by fieldwork in other areas were directly associated with one another. They included the use of a trough to heat water, metalworking, and the treatment of the dead.

Hillforts, Ringworks, and Occupation Sites

Few of the Irish settlements were directly associated with burnt mounds, although they can be found nearby. Sometimes they were clearly separated from one another, as some of the recently excavated settlements had been enclosed by a circular fence or earthwork (Ginn 2016). The smallest were insubstantial structures which contained a single roundhouse, but they form a continuum which extends to some of the most impressive monuments created during this period. Again a comparison with Britain is appropriate, for some of these sites resemble those on the opposite shore of the Irish Sea, on Anglesey, and in north-west Wales (K. Waddington 2013). The larger Irish enclosures resemble English ringworks. A number of famous settlements in Ireland may belong to this tradition, and again they take the form of circular ditched or walled enclosures with a central house. Perhaps the best known of these are from Lough Gur where the features associated with 'Class II' pottery have been shown to date to the Late Bronze Age and not to the Neolithic, as was thought by the original excavator (Cleary 2003). Specialised activities must have taken place there. One of the enclosures provided evidence of metal-working; another included a series of human burials, whilst the water of the lake beside the occupied area contained a number of weapons.

At the opposite end of the continuum are four sites which are equally well known: Navan Fort, Downpatrick, Lugg, and Rathgall. They shared the same basic characteristic. They were circular enclosures which probably had a roundhouse or other structure in the centre, but in each case they possess some exceptional features. The enclosure at Navan Fort was rebuilt throughout the pre-Roman Iron Age, and eventually the site was identified as the capital of Ulster (Waterman 1997). The hilltop at Downpatrick, which was enclosed by a rampart and ditch, was the findspot of three important hoards of gold ornaments (Proudfoot 1955). Another enclosed site at Lugg contained a series of roundhouses but also had a large mound inside it (Kilbride-Jones 1950). Before its date became apparent, the excavator interpreted Lugg as a henge monument, and even now its original role is uncertain. Rathgall is even more spectacular and combined evidence of craft production with the commemoration of the dead (Raftery 2004), but here it has been difficult to date the earthworks themselves.

The similarity between the Irish enclosures and the English ringworks is not surprising, for both these groups of monuments occur in areas with important deposits of swords and spears (Fig. 5.17). They were studied by Margaret Ehrenberg (1989), who made the interesting point that the contents of these two 'weapon zones' included the same kinds of artefacts. On that basis she suggested a close relationship between Late Bronze Age communities in the two islands. Not only were they associated with similar earthworks and deposits of metalwork, there may have been other links between these areas. The gold ring with a cremation pyre at Rathgall resembles one from a ring-work (North Ring) at Mucking in the Thames Estuary (Bond 1988). Other sites may be relevant to the argument. The contents of Irish crannogs are very similar to those of the occupied islands and timber platforms used during this period, and so are the deposits found in rivers and lakes.

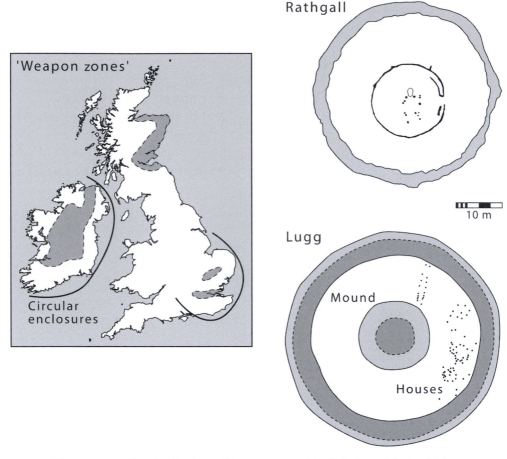

Figure 5.17 The distribution of 'weapon zones' in Britain and Ireland. The contour delimits the areas with the main concentrations of circular enclosures, and these are illustrated by two monuments towards the east coast of Ireland: Rathgall and Lugg. Information from Ehrenberg (1989), Raftery (1994), Kilbride-Jones (1950), and Roche and Eogan (2008).

In recent years a distinct group of hillforts with spaced ramparts has been identified in Ireland, one of the best dated of which is Haughey's Fort in the north which was used around 1100 BC (Fig. 5.18). A new project has examined more hilltop sites with either two or three concentric earthworks (O'Brien and O'Driscoll 2017). Some of these enclosures were apparently empty, but those at Dun Aonghasa (Cotter 2012) and Mooghaun (Grogan 2005) did contain groups of roundhouses. Haughey's Fort included a circular timber structure 30 m in diameter which included pits containing bronze and gold artefacts (Mallory and Baban 2014). Two other features are especially striking. These enclosures were very extensive compared with their counterparts on domestic sites, and in most cases their defences consumed considerable amounts of

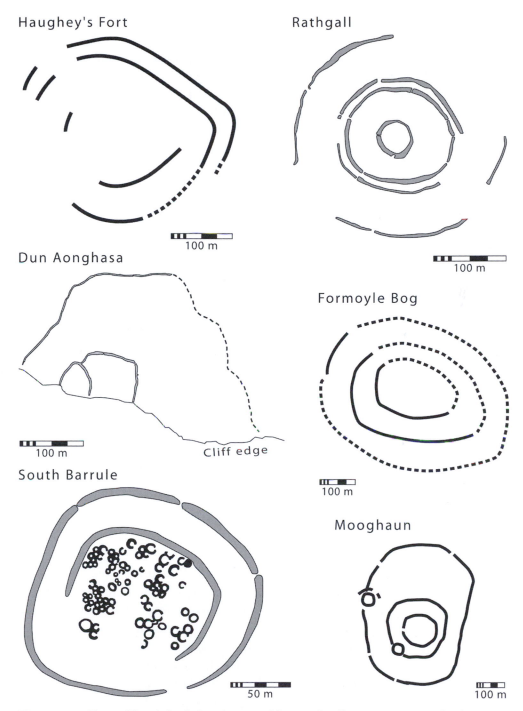

Figure 5.18 Plans of five defended enclosures with spaced walls or ramparts in Ireland, compared with that of South Barrule on the Isle of Man. Information from Raftery (1994), Grogan (1996), Cotter (2012), O'Brien and O'Driscoll (2017), and Gelling (1972).

timber. At the same time they had sometimes been destroyed by fire (O'Brien and O'Driscoll 2017). It cannot have happened by accident as there are cases in which more than one circuit was ignited. Only once was a site rebuilt afterwards. The distribution of these monuments may not be limited to Ireland. Another candidate, this time with two spaced ramparts, is South Barrule on the Isle of Man. The associated pottery could be of Late Bronze Age date, and the hillfort contained a series of circular houses (Gelling 1972).

Activity on these sites involved some of the same elements as Irish crannogs and English ringworks. Dun Aonghasa was associated with weapon production on an unusually large scale (Cotter 2012), and an artificial pool outside Haughey's Fort was used for the deposition of sword moulds and human skull fragments (Lynn 1977); there is a similar assemblage from a natural pool at Greenlands not far from the Thames Estuary (Timby et al. 2007: 44). Rathgall contained a still more exceptional assemblage, including pieces of metalwork, many mould fragments, evidence of shale working, and glass beads imported from the Continent (Raftery 2004).

It is too soon to say when the occupation of Irish hillforts began, but it was clearly under way during the Middle Bronze Age and continued on an increasing scale in the Late Bronze Age. It is known that the Irish Iron Age was aceramic. The pottery that used to be attributed to that period is older than it seemed. It means that any site dated by such material may be earlier than was once supposed (Raftery 1995). It appears that the creation of some of these monuments followed a peak in the deposition of swords between 1300 and 1100 BC and is not matched by similar finds from wet places. This evidence cannot be ignored as Ireland had the highest density of these weapons in Bronze Age Europe. The large-scale burning identified at recently excavated hillforts is surely an indication of warfare,.

Gold Working and Earthwork Monuments

The making and use of weapons did not take place in isolation. There was a second phase of gold working in Ireland during the tenth century BC, following a hiatus of between one and two hundred years (G. Eogan 1994b). The scale of production had certainly increased, and so did the amount of gold employed in making individual objects and the extent to which the finished artefacts were deposited in bogs and similar locations (Becker 2013). Again these objects had a wider currency, and certain types have a distribution extending well beyond Ireland itself. Some share features in common with artefacts in the Iberian Peninsula, and others suggest links with Scandinavia. There are indications that two regional styles existed within the island itself. One was in the north-east and was closely linked to Britain and the Nordic culture area; the other was around the River Shannon and seems to have had connections with Spain and

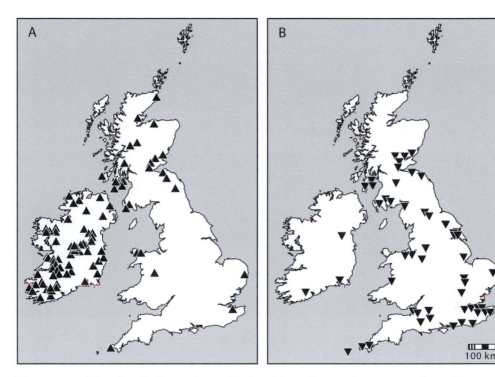

Figure 5.19 The distributions of two kinds of Late Bronze Age pennanular gold bracelet. A: the distribution of the 'Irish type'; it emphasises the links between Ireland and northern Scotland. B: the distribution of the 'British type'; it emphasises the remaining part of Britain. Information from Eogan (1994).

Portugal (Fig. 5.19). Rather more is known about the social context of this second period of gold working. Although there is little evidence of where they were made, pieces of gold and small personal ornaments are associated with a number of the monuments discussed in this section: crannogs, ringworks, and hillforts. Most of the large collections of goldwork come from bogs, but the largest of all was apparently associated with a burnt mound below the hillfort of Mooghaun (Condit 1996).

The nature of these artefacts is not the only indication of regional developments at this time. In south-west Ireland the Late Bronze Age is characterised by a distinctive range of ceremonial monuments, including small stone circles, ring barrows, and burials beneath conspicuous boulders (O'Brien 1992 and 2004b). In the past they were misunderstood as some of them bore a superficial resemblance to structures in Britain. The short stone rows were compared with those in south-west England, although similar structures occur in other areas, most obviously the north of Ireland. Because they feature a recumbent stone, the stone circles were also related to British prototypes (Burl 2000: ch. 14), but it is clear that the resemblance is superficial as those

Figure 5.20 Stone circle at Drombeg, south-west Ireland. Photograph: Aaron Watson.

architectural traditions were separated by a thousand years (Fig. 5.20). By contrast, the earthwork enclosures associated with some of the Irish monument complexes might have overlapped with the history of similar monuments in northern Britain, but in this case they shared such a long history in both islands that it is a moot point whether such similarities were significant (Bradley 2011). It is ironic that the recumbent stone circles of north-east Scotland are treated as an expression of local identity, but their supposed equivalents in Ireland have been attributed to outside influence.

Other comparisons raise problems, but it is clear that hilltop enclosures originated in Britain during the Late Bronze Age, most probably a short time after the earliest examples in Ireland. A series of other hills were associated with metal hoards or large settlements. The difficulty is in establishing whether the structural evidence is of the same date as the defences. Among the most obvious candidates are two sites in southern Scotland – Eildon Hill North (Owen 1992), and Traprain Law (Armit et al. 2005) – which included artefacts and buildings dating from this period. The same is true of a number of sites in Wales and north-west England where the defences were associated with radiocarbon dates or bronze artefacts. The best-dated examples are probably Beeston Castle (P. Ellis 1993) and the Breiddin (Musson 1991). Again each provided evidence of domestic occupation, as well as food storage, craft production, and the working of metals, but in no case was it absolutely clear that these locations were permanently occupied. In the south there are other signs that large hilltop enclosures were established in the Late Bronze Age, but they can be difficult to date because of a plateau in the radiocarbon calibration curve. One clue to their wider relationships is provided by the early hillfort at Harting Beacon on the South Downs (Bedwin 1979). In its gateway was a pair of gold rings which can be compared with those from Rathgall and a Late Bronze Age ringwork at Mucking. Again they were associated with a human skull. Unlike their Irish counterparts, the first British hillforts extended into the Iron Age and for that reason they are considered in more detail in Chapter 6.

OCEAN CROSSINGS

Earlier chapters considered a series of coastal locations interpreted as maritime havens. Their main periods of use were between the Mesolithic period and the Early Bronze Age (Bradley et al. 2016b). In their later manifestation they could be associated with cairns or urned cremations, but before that time they provided at least some evidence of metal production. They were occupied during a period in which the importance of boats was occasionally symbolised in the burial rite (Bradley 2018). Sites of this kind would have offered sheltered conditions for craft travelling along the coast or occasionally making longer journeys.

Maritime technology seems to have changed with the adoption of sewn-plank vessels, and it may be no coincidence that they came into use at about the time when most insular copper mines were abandoned (Timberlake 2016). From then on a greater amount of metalwork had to be introduced from the Continent, either as finished products or as raw material for recycling. That may have encouraged the use of larger or more robust vessels, and it is obvious that by the middle of the Bronze Age long-distance voyages connected the inhabitants of both islands with communities on the European mainland. It accounts for the growing similarities between portable artefacts, field systems, settlements, and mortuary rituals on either side of the water (Bradley et al. 2016a: ch. 6). The movement of metalwork has attracted most attention, but the evidence from settlement excavations suggests that hides and textiles may also have been exchanged.

The extent of these connections is remarkable. They were especially important along the western margin of the Continent where the strength of these links has encouraged researchers to write of an 'Atlantic Bronze Age' (Ruiz-Gálvez Priego 1998; Cunliffe 2001a). This approach has both strengths and weaknesses.

The first point to make is that long-distance contacts along the Atlantic coastline had existed for a long time. They apply to the aptly named Maritime Beakers, and during the Early Bronze Age there were connections between these islands, Brittany, and north-west Spain, so why were the developments of the later Bronze Age distinctive? The quantity and quality of the metalwork transported along the Atlantic seaways are altogether remarkable, but difficulties arise once these objects are studied in more detail. Some were truly exotic, but others were made in regional styles, distinguished by minor differences of form, technology, and chronology. In the circumstances a different approach is needed. What kinds of metalwork were represented, and how were they used and deposited? These questions apply to the archaeology of the second millennium BC, but are especially relevant to the Late Bronze Age.

The artefacts included some personal ornaments, but most of them were weapons and feasting equipment: swords, spears, cauldrons, spits, and flesh hooks (Needham and Bowman 2005). Their presence evoked a distinctive lifestyle and it can be no accident that some of these types were associated with crannogs, ringworks, and hillforts. In some cases they could even have been made there. A second question poses a more pressing problem. Did similar conventions influence the ways in which they were used and deposited? The weapons are particularly informative as careful observation shows that many had been used and some had been repaired. That evidence was not confined to those found in Britain. Moreover they were often broken and deposited in watery environments: a practice that extended from Ireland to Portugal (C. Gibson 2013). Irrespective of minor differences in their forms and manufacture, their histories were much the same. It follows that similar ideas were favoured by people along the western margin of Europe. So great were these similarities that they may have adopted the related languages that contemporary linguists classify as Celtic (Koch 2013; Cunliffe 2018: ch. 4).

The distribution of complex artefacts has another dimension, as more becomes known about the vessels on which they were carried and the composition of the cargoes. Of even greater importance, there is some information on where these artefacts were unloaded and exchanged. Parts of sewn-plank boats come from several Middle and Late Bronze Age sites, but only at Dover did most of a seagoing vessel survive (P. Clark 2004). It is dated between 1575 and 1520 BC: a period when Continental metalwork was introduced to Britain on an increasing scale. Not far away a collection of artefacts recovered by divers from Langdon Bay was probably from the site of a wreck (Needham, Parham, and Frieman 2013). Another has been found at Salcombe in southwest England. No trace of a vessel survived on the seabed. Both collections date from the thirteenth century BC, although there may have been a second, later deposit at Salcombe (Wang et al. 2016). Middle and Late Bronze Age metalwork has been recovered from the sea in other places (Needham, Parham, and Frieman 2013). Its distribution extends from Wales and Cornwall as far as the Thames Estuary and the majority of the diagnostic material is dated between 1400 and 1125 BC.

The limited evidence provided by material recovered from the sea can be augmented by the artefacts found on dry land. Some of them were in hoards or were associated with evidence of metalworking. Most of the evidence comes from southern England, although in Ireland there are important finds from the beach of Whitepark Bay in northern Ireland (Ó Faoláin 2004: 176–7), Dalkey Island in Dublin Bay (Ó Faoláin 2004: 64 and 151), and from the Late Bronze Age hillfort of Dun Aonghasa in the Aran Islands (Cotter 2012, vol. 2: 228–57). Susan Pearce (1983) has studied the metalwork of south-west England, which provided an important source of tin (cf. Knight, Ormrod, and Pearce 2015). In the Middle Bronze Age there were numerous finds along the coast, but only one is noteworthy: a palstave mould from Burgh Island. This location may have been significant as it commanded the approach to Bantham Sands which played a role in long-distance trade during the first millennium AD (Griffith and Wilkes 2006).

Later finds were also associated with offshore islands, although they were rarely documented in any detail (Pearce 1983; Knight, Ormrod, and Pearce 2015). They include Looe Island on the Channel coast, and St Michael's Mount. An important site at Mountbatten in Plymouth Harbour was probably an island in the Late Bronze Age (Cunliffe 1988), and another prolific source of metal finds was at Portland, which was joined to the mainland by a shingle bar. More finds came from Thurlestone beach and from the estuaries of two important rivers, the Tamar and the Fal. Such finds were widely distributed but one observation stands out: almost all of them were on the Channel coast rather than the opposite side of the south-western peninsula (Pearce 1983). Their distribution is important in another way. Although there was little patterning in the first part of the Late Bronze Age, towards its close it focused on a few pivotal areas (Fig. 5.21). In the south-west they included St Michael's Mount, Salcombe, Mountbatten, and Portland (Pearce 1983: figs. 5.13 and 6.23). Further to the east the most important locations were Dover and the Isle of Thanet (Needham, Parham, and Frieman 2013).

It is not a new idea that beaches and offshore islands were the ideal places at which to exchange with strangers. They can be considered as neutral locations where special conventions could apply. Some were readily accessible, for example Mountbatten or Dalkey Island, but others were much more remote. The clearest example is Dun Aonghasa where the fortification was on top of a massive cliff on an island exposed to the full force of Atlantic storms (Cotter 2012). Here weapons were made in some quantity, but elsewhere the evidence is more restricted. Mountbatten was obviously inhabited and excavation found evidence of a Late Bronze Age midden (Cunliffe 1988). Something similar has been observed at St Michael's Mount where Late Bronze Age metalwork was also discovered in some quantity (Fig. 5.22). In common with Mountbatten, an ingot has been found here (Herring 2000). This site is especially striking

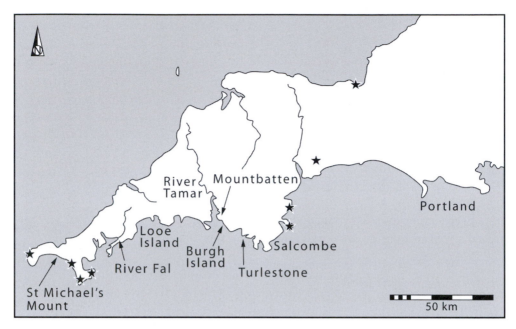

Figure 5.21 The distribution of later Bronze Age metalwork found at coastal locations in south-west England. The stars indicate discoveries of ingots. Information from Pearce (1983) and Knight, Ormrod, and Pearce (2015).

Figure 5.22 St Michael's Mount off the coast of south-west England. Photograph: Aaron Watson.

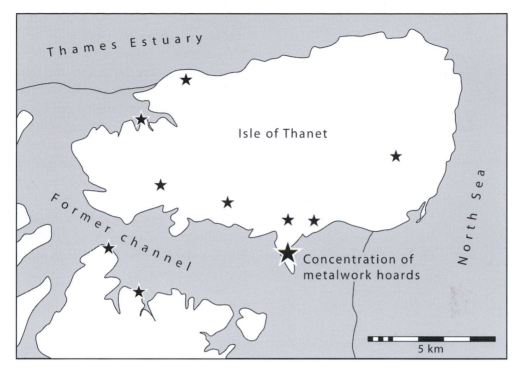

Figure 5.23 The siting of the Isle of Thanet and the findspots of Late Bronze Age metalwork hoards. The main concentration was close to Cliffs End Farm. Information from McKinley et al. (2014).

since it can only be accessed at low tide. Nearly all these places play a special role in accounts of trade during the pre-Roman Iron Age, and two of them are among the candidates for the island where Pytheas records that tin was obtained from the inhabitants of south-west England (Cunliffe 2001b).

The production of weapons is evidenced at some of the ringworks, crannogs, and hillforts of the Late Bronze Age, but the evidence is difficult to interpret. There is new information from Cliffs End Farm on the former island of Thanet (McKinley et al. 2014: 18–52). It was the meeting point of the Channel and the North Sea and commanded a passage through to the Thames Estuary. It featured a sheltered spit of land like those associated with maritime havens during earlier periods. This was an important place because it was associated with rich prehistoric middens, and a remarkable series of metalwork hoards composed of both bronze and gold (Fig. 5.23; McKinley et al. 2014; Andrews et al. 2015: fig. 3.21). The site already contained a group of earlier prehistoric round barrows when it was chosen for reuse during the Late Bronze Age.

These mounds were enveloped by a sequence of earthwork enclosures, only one of which could be excavated in its entirety. It was a little less than 30 m in diameter and similar in form to the Late Bronze Age ringworks which exist in some numbers in the same region, although there was no evidence that it contained any buildings. The site also included a remarkable series of inhumation burials plus a single cremation. A minimum of twenty-four individuals were associated with the Late Bronze Age phase; others dated from the Iron Age. Isotopic analysis of their bones led to the remarkable conclusion that some of the people buried had lived in distant areas and must have come there by sea. One group seems to have had links with Scandinavia and another with the Iberian Peninsula. There was no direct evidence for metal production from the excavated area (although it is indicated by the contents of nearby hoards), but the site was associated with the beam for a balance, a lead weight, and no fewer than sixteen copper ingots (McKinley et al. 2014: 179–82). It suggests that this remarkable complex had been used by people from overseas and that it was one of the places where commodities changed hands. The site at Cliffs End Farm provides some indication of what may be found at other coastal locations. Perhaps the movement of valuables was being monitored more closely than before.

SUMMARY

Recent years have seen a considerable increase in the amount of later Bronze Age material available for study. It has also become more diverse. The final section of this chapter reflects on the significance of this evidence and provides a possible interpretation.

The first question to ask is whether the change from the Early to the Middle Bronze Age represented a social collapse. There is no reason to take this view. It is true that there were certain tensions towards the middle of the second millennium BC – fluctuations in the supply of metals, changes of burial customs, the settlement of increasingly marginal land – but it is better to think in terms of transformation rather than catastrophe. Around this time there were important changes in many parts of Continental Europe, and it was not a specifically insular development. There is nothing to indicate that social distinctions had disappeared; rather, they were expressed in different ways, and the emphasis on mortuary monuments gradually became less important. Now the consumption of wealth focused not on the grave but on different locations such as rivers and lakes. The reduced significance of mortuary monuments might suggest a society that placed less weight on genealogy.

There is a direct relationship between these Middle Bronze Age practices and an important change of political geography, for now the main deposits of portable wealth were to be found in different areas. In Britain, they were most evident in those parts of lowland England where the landscape was transformed by the creation of coaxial field systems, although this evidence cannot be treated in isolation. Similar settlements are found in regions where these boundaries do not appear, and there are other areas with major collections of artefacts made of bronze and gold. What is important is that the regions over which land holding was reorganised are precisely those with the closest connections to Continental Europe, for it soon became the source of the metalwork used during this period (Bradley et al. 2016a: ch. 5). Perhaps it was the intensification of food production that made these changes possible, and one wonders whether hides and textiles were among the commodities exchanged for supplies of metal or finished artefacts. Grain was important too, and that is why the chapter has the title 'Ploughshares into Swords'. Of course it is possible that long-distance exchange was managed by a social elite, but the only evidence for its existence is provided by the bronzes, for there are few, if any, signs of specialised or high-status settlements at this time.

In Ireland, however, events took a different course. Again the inhabitants seem to have been dependent on foreign sources of bronze, but they had their own supplies of gold, and during the thirteenth and twelfth centuries BC they deployed them to spectacular effect, producing a series of personal ornaments of the highest quality. Some of the gold was exchanged with communities on the Continent, whilst the products that remained in the country were commonly deposited in bogs. Environmental evidence suggests that the land was used more intensively than before, but this process does not seem to have involved the creation of extensive field systems or territorial boundaries. The earliest hillforts date from this time and lack close counterparts in Britain. It may be that relations with the European mainland took a different form, and the most likely points of contact would have been along the Atlantic coastline and perhaps in Scandinavia.

It was during the Late Bronze Age that the settlement pattern became more diverse, and this was when a series of largely new kinds of field monuments first emerged in both islands: fortifications such as ringworks and hillforts; wooden platforms, bridges, and crannogs in the wetlands. Despite the formal differences between these sites, they had much in common. Some were associated with metal production, especially the making of weapons, and they were also connected with feasting. They included large quantities of animal bones, fine pottery (where it was available), the residues of craft production, occasional items of gold, bronze metalwork, and human skulls. The strongest connections may have been between the British and Irish 'weapon zones' identified by Ehrenberg (1989). It seems likely that they were associated with a restricted section of society and that members of that select group formed alliances with one another. Some connected people in the two islands, and others linked them to groups in Continental Europe. The close connection between production and exchange is illustrated by the Late Bronze Age ringworks in eastern England. Almost all of them were in areas with field systems and large open settlements, and it can be no coincidence that the very same areas contain the largest number of weapon deposits, including material that had been imported across the Channel. A different system might have prevailed in Ireland, where land boundaries of similar extent have not been discovered, but here there must have been a similar relationship between status and the conspicuous consumption of wealth. In this case it included the fine goldwork produced towards the end of this period.

Those changes did not extend into every region, and it is important to remember that the settlement pattern in northern Britain shows much more continuity than it does in the south. Here there was a more gradual increase in the number and density of settlements and also in the evidence of personal wealth. This may provide the background to the appearance of the first hillforts or hilltop settlements, although the dating evidence is not satisfactory. At the same time, it is clear that traditional forms of public monument had not gone out of use in the way that was once supposed. A variety of stone and earthwork enclosures may still have been constructed during the Late Bronze Age and represent the very last stage in a sequence that had started in the Neolithic period (Bradley 2011). The same is true in Ireland, where it is clear that local kinds of ringworks, hillforts, and stone circles were all used at this time.

In many ways this interpretation is rather like conventional accounts of the Early Bronze Age. It presupposes that developments in these islands were largely dependent on outside sources of raw material and artefacts. That was not the case when south-west Ireland had been an important source of copper and Britain first developed bronze, but during the period considered here this model is much more plausible. Metal analysis has shown that an increasing proportion of the artefacts that circulated during the later Bronze Age made use of ores whose ultimate source was in the copper mines of the Alps. Most of the metal had been recycled many times, but it is clear that much of it had been imported across the Channel.

That surely provides a context for the shipwrecks with cargoes of metalwork dating to the thirteenth century BC. It could also account for some specialised sites along the southern English coast. Ireland participated in a network which extended along the Atlantic to the West Mediterranean, and again there is evidence for metalworking by the sea and on an offshore island. It may be no accident that in southern Britain some of the very same locations were associated with long-distance trade during the late pre-Roman Iron Age.

During the Bronze Age similar relationships seem to have been sustained for nearly seven hundred years, and there can be no doubt that the Middle and Late Bronze Ages represent a period of growing prosperity, even if it was sometimes characterised by conflict and competition. Only two elements were vulnerable. One was the changing climate during the first millennium BC. The other was the flow of metal which was no longer under local control. This was one of the features on which social relationships were based and, if it came under pressure, the situation was liable to change. That is exactly what happened towards 800 BC, and over a comparatively short period of time the system seems to have collapsed. The reasons for this are complex and need to be treated in detail, but not only did these changes undermine the developments described throughout this chapter, they led to the emergence of a very different kind of society.

Both that crisis and its resolution are studied in Chapter 6.

CHAPTER 6

THE ENDING OF PREHISTORY

FOREGROUND AND BACKGROUND

There have been two approaches to the archaeology of the Iron Age, and as a result the term means different things to different people. One treats it as a self-contained entity, giving way to the Roman occupation of Britain. It can even emphasise a certain continuity between those phases. A good example is Cunliffe's *Iron Age Communities in Britain*, now in its fourth edition (2005). The other approach envisages a much longer sequence of change and interprets the distinctive features of the Iron Age as the outcome of processes which started late in the second millennium BC. It is illustrated by Kristiansen's account of *Europe before History* (1998). Following his lead, this chapter begins with the closing years of what is still called the 'Bronze Age'. It ends as these islands came into contact with the peoples of the Classical world, since Millett (1992) and Creighton (2000 and 2006) have shown that in England the Late Iron Age is better studied in relation to the Roman period.

The earliest use of iron was not a sudden event. In fact it was probably precipitated by a shortage of metals of any kind. Indeed, it may be that the period around 800 BC is characterised by a reduced supply of bronze rather than the adoption of an unfamiliar technology (Needham 2007). Such developments are not well understood. Some of the Alpine copper mines ceased operation, and new ones took their place, but the situation did not change significantly (O'Brien 2015: ch. 10). In southern Europe iron was easier to obtain, and this may have reduced the demand for bronze, but in North-west Europe these developments had more serious consequences. The metal supply came under pressure, and attempts were made to recycle the material that remained in circulation. Those difficulties began about 1100 BC and became especially severe during the ninth century.

Such developments did not take place in isolation, for the late eighth century BC saw the establishment of a Phoenician trading network extending as far west as the Iberian Peninsula, where it exploited established contacts along the

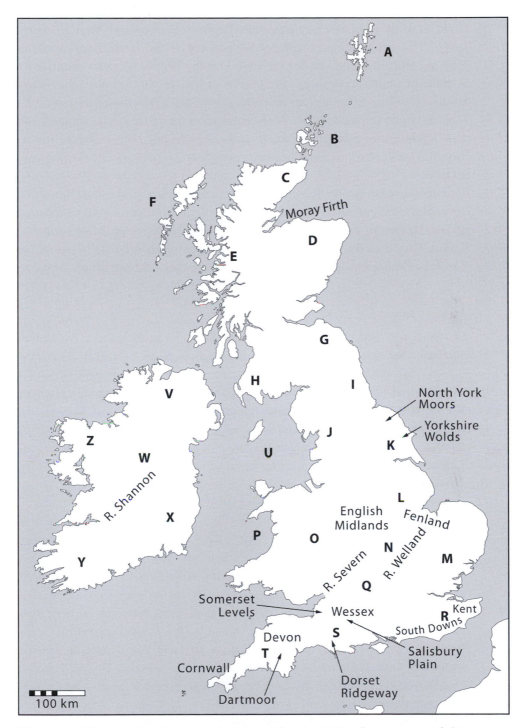

Figure 6.1 Places and regions mentioned in Chapter 6. For the purposes of this map Britain and Ireland have been divided into twenty-six areas and the individual sites are listed according to these divisions. A: Shetland (Clickhimin, Old Scatness); B: Orkney (Howe, Mine Howe); C: Northern Scotland (Kilphedir, Loch Borralie);

coast in order to obtain raw material (Campos Carrasco and Alvar Ezquerra 2013). This axis assumed a greater importance as the circulation of metals became more difficult. The last metalwork of the Bronze Age was obtained by a different route from most of the objects of that period and placed a greater emphasis on the Atlantic (Cunliffe 2001a: 275–89). This change of geographical alignment proved to be short-lived, for soon the process was curtailed, and the deposition of artefacts in hoards and rivers declined. The clearest indication that established practices had been abandoned is provided by the working of iron.

These developments affected both Britain and Ireland and can be illustrated in several different ways. There is evidence that bronze was being distributed in standard forms so that some of the latest axeheads were probably treated as ingots. They contained so much lead that they could hardly have been used as tools, and in north-west France, where many of them had been made, it seems

Figure Caption 6.1 (*Cont.*)

D: North-east and Central Scotland (Blair Drummond, Deskford); E: Western Scotland (Dun Troddan); F: Outer Hebrides (Cnip); G: Eastern and Central Scotland on either side of the Firth of Forth (Broxmouth, Inverkeilor, Newbridge); H: South-west Scotland (Over Rig); I: the English/Scottish borderland (Glenachan, Hayhope Knowe, West Brandon); J: North-west England (Meols); K: North-east England and the Peak District (Dalton Parlours, Devil's Hill, Fin Cop, Garton Slack, North Ferriby, Pocklington, Rudston, Staple Howe, Sutton Common, Thwing, West Heslerton); L: Eastern England between the Humber and the Fenland (Fengate, Ferrybridge, Fiskerton, Over, War Ditches); M: East Anglia (Snettisham, West Harling); N: the English Midlands (Crick, Glenfield, Weekley, Whitchurch); O: the English/Welsh borderland (Collfryn, Meole Brace, the Breiddin); P: North and West Wales (Castell Henllys, Dan Y Coed, Moel Y Gaer, Walesland Rath, Woodside); Q: the Thames Valley, Cotswolds, and South Midlands (Aylesbury, Bancroft, Crickley Hill, Devil's Quoits, Gravelly Guy, Runneymede Bridge, Wallingford, Wittenham Clumps, Woodeaton); R: South-east England including the Thames Estuary and the South Downs (Mucking, Springfield Lyons, Thanet); S: Wessex (All Cannings Cross, Balksbury, Barbury, Bury Hill, Chiseldon, Cleavel Point, Danebury, 'Duropolis', East Chisenbury, Fyfield Down, Green Island, Hambledon Hill, Hengistbury Head, High Post, Hod Hill, Langton Maltravers, Little Woodbury, Longbridge Deverill, Marlborough Downs, Potterne, Quarley Hill, Rams Hill, Sidbury, Vale of Pewsey, Winklebury); T: South-west England and South Wales (Bathampton Down, Bredon Hill, South Cadbury, Glastonbury, Ham Hill, Harlyn Bay, Llanmaes, Meare, Merthyr Mawr, Mountbatten, Trevelgue Head); U: the Isle of Man; V: Northern Ireland (Haughey's Fort, Kiltierney, Navan Fort); W: from the Irish Midlands to the east coast (Lambay Island, Knockaulin, Knowth, Lismullin, Loughcrew, Newgrange); X: South-east Ireland; Y: South-west Ireland; Z: the Irish west coast.

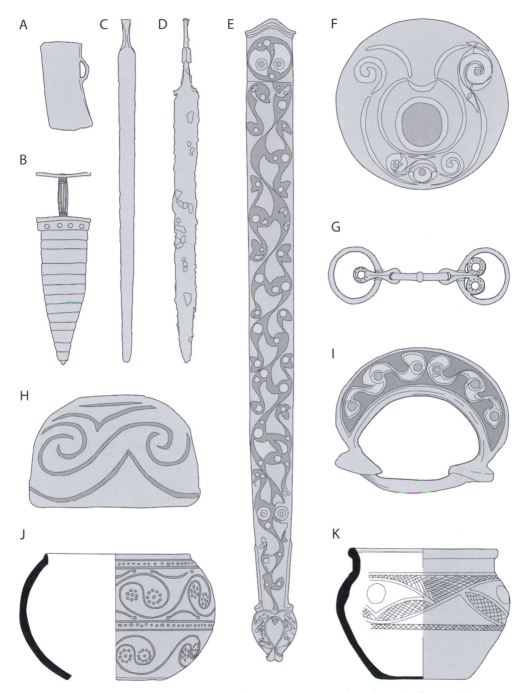

Figure 6.2 Artefact types mentioned in Chapter 6. A: iron socketed axe; B: dagger; C and D: iron swords; E: decorated sword scabbards; F: decorated bronze disc; G: horse harness; H: decorated rotary quern; I: decorated terret; J and K: pottery with La Tène decoration.

as if they conformed to standard weights (Briard 1965). Discarded artefacts were increasingly recycled. This is most obvious from metal analysis, but it may also be reflected by the large number of 'scrap hoards' that were deposited in Britain during the ninth century BC. They include fragments of many different kinds of objects, including tools, ornaments, and weapons, and some contained traces of slag. Burgess (1979) suggested that people were dumping surplus artefacts; by withdrawing so much material from circulation they might have forced its value to rise. The reasoning behind this hypothesis is anachronistic for it suggests a degree of coordination which would be possible only in the modern economy – in many ways the best comparison is with the operation of the stock exchange. It is equally unsatisfactory to suppose that supplies of bronze were concealed during a political crisis, for the main evidence of such a crisis is provided by the hoards themselves. Perhaps they were really offerings associated with the transformation of the raw material. That is certainly consistent with accounts of metalworking in traditional societies (Budd and Taylor 1995; Helms 2012).

One clue is provided by changes in the circulation of bronze artefacts which emphasised the importance of the Atlantic seaways, and a growing number of metal items were exchanged or copied along the western rim of Europe, from Scotland and Ireland in the north, to Spain and Portugal in the south. Some of these connections even extended into the Mediterranean (Cunliffe 2001a: ch. 7). Such links had always been important, especially in prehistoric Ireland, but now they seem to have assumed a greater prominence than before, and ultimately this network reached across southern and eastern England into Northern Europe. The latest bronze hoards reflected the new alignment. Such evidence suggests that the inhabitants of these islands were drawing on different sources of supply, but any relief was short-lived. Towards the end of the Bronze Age there are indications that people started to experiment with iron production, using ores that could probably be discovered locally; only the techniques of working them were foreign. It is not clear quite when this process began, or how far iron was intended to take the place of bronze. Writing in 2000, Lawson catalogued at least thirty sites in Britain where iron slag had been found in contexts dating from the ninth century BC (Lawson 2000). At the same time, the new technology could be used to make composite tools in combination with bronze or could even be employed to produce traditional forms of artefact in a different material. This was certainly the case with socketed axes (W. Manning and Saunders 1972).

The deposition of metalwork became an important issue as bronze was supplemented, and to some extent replaced, by iron. The latest bronze hoards date from the Llyn Fawr industrial phase which ran from approximately 800 to 600 BC, and the quantity of river metalwork decreased sharply at that time (O'Connor 2007). It happened throughout Britain and Ireland, but it can hardly suggest a shortage of both kinds of metal since exactly the same pattern is found in Continental Europe, where iron weapons were commonly deposited in graves. In terms of the Three Age Model, the last axe hoards in southern England and the west of France are Iron Age rather than Bronze Age; it seems to have been important that votive deposits should contain foreign material. That might apply to the styles of the objects themselves, but it also reflects the metal from which they were made. It may have happened as a response to diminishing supplies, but, if so, it was a ritual that failed (Koutrafouri and Sanders 2013). Copper and tin did not occur in many of the areas with these artefacts, and this may have provided one source of their power. In that case locally produced iron would not have been an acceptable substitute. Although prehistorians treat bronze and iron as if they were equivalent to one another, people in the past may have categorised them in a different way. One of the strangest discoveries of recent years illustrates this point. It is a collection of 373 bronze socketed axes from Langton Maltravers in southern England. They were brittle and poorly finished, yet they seem to have been made individually, and some were deliberately coloured to imitate the appearance of iron (B. Roberts et al. 2015).

FROM POSSESSION TO DISPOSSESSION

Access to foreign metal had been of fundamental importance in later Bronze Age society, so that these changes would have had drastic consequences. The crucial point was made by Gordon Childe more than seventy years ago (1942: 82–3). The production of bronze artefacts involved a combination of copper, tin, and sometimes lead, all of which had restricted distributions. One problem lay in bringing these materials together, and another concerned the circulation of the finished products (Earle et al. 2015). Some of the densest concentrations of Late Bronze Age metalwork were in areas that lacked any sources of their own. They included southern and eastern England. There are other regions where metalwork could have been produced locally but seems to have been imported. Among them are Ireland, Scotland, and Wales. Because high-quality artefacts were being introduced from distant areas, it would have been possible to control their circulation, and the same applies to the raw material from which they were made. Access to such objects could have been restricted in two ways. It involved a process of long-distance travel by sea which might have been in the hands of specialist traders, or of a restricted group who controlled their activities (Earle et al. 2015). The skills needed to make the finest objects were not generally available, and again the work of smiths may have come under political control. Some of it was so demanding that they must have depended on a patron for support; that need not apply to the production of simpler objects (Kuijpers 2018). At the same time, it would be necessary to accumulate suitable commodities with which to participate in exchange. It could have featured the movement of textiles, hides, and agricultural produce. For Childe, the long-distance movement of bronze involved the creation of alliances and was a source of power.

Iron, on the other hand, was widely available and could have been worked in many parts of these islands. Unless the process took place on a large scale – and that is not evidenced before the production of 'currency bars' in the third century BC (Hingley 2005) – it would be difficult to control. Thus the virtual collapse of the long-distance circulation of bronze might have undermined the influence of an elite, but the first adoption of ironworking would not have offered an equivalent power base. For Childe, Iron Age society became more 'democratic'. It is possible to quarrel with the idea that the adoption of iron improved the quality of life, but there is certainly some evidence of social change.

It takes two forms. There are the new developments that happened during the period of transition, and there are signs that older practices were abandoned. Both occurred simultaneously between about 800 and 600 BC, but it will make the argument clearer if they are treated separately.

This account starts with the new developments. One of the most dramatic discoveries of recent years is the identification of a series of large middens in southern Britain whose chronology appears to span the later Bronze Age and the period of transition. Ironically, the first of them to be investigated, All Cannings Cross in Wessex, was once treated as the type site for the Early Iron Age (Cunnington 1923). That was not because of the structural evidence from the excavation, which was meagre, but because of an extraordinary abundance of artefacts. The same applies to the sites recognised more recently, whose distribution extends from East Anglia to South Wales (Needham and Spence 1997; Sharples 2010, 52–3 and 87–8). They attract attention for several reasons. It is unusual to find such enormous accumulations of cultural material, for in normal circumstances these deposits would have been removed from settlements and spread on cultivated land. Instead the material was allowed to build up into considerable mounds. It happened at Potterne on the chalk of southern England (Lawson 2000) and on another site, East Chisenbury, which was identified as a standing earthwork (McOmish 1996) (Fig. 6.3). Similar deposits have been recognised at some of the Bronze Age sites discussed in Chapter 4, including the occupied islands at Wallingford (Cromarty et al. 2005) and Runnymede Bridge (Needham and Spence 1997), the coastal site at Mountbatten (Cunliffe 1988), and the extraordinary group of hoards, monuments, and burials on the coast of Thanet (McKinley et al. 2014: 18–52).

The middens have an unusual composition. The sediments at Potterne include a considerable quantity of cattle dung, but there are also significant amounts of bronze metalwork. The upper levels contain a little iron slag

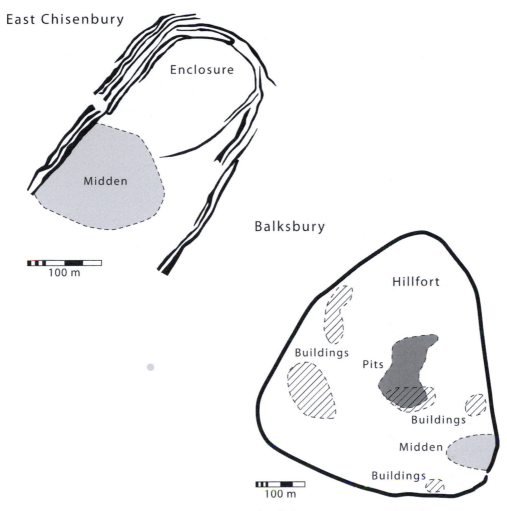

Figure 6.3 The middens at East Chisenbury and Balksbury, Wessex. East Chisenbury is associated with an earthwork enclosure, and the site at Balksbury with a defended settlement. Information from McOmish, Field, and Brown (2002) and Ellis and Rawlings (2001).

(Lawson 2000). There is an abundance of fine pottery and animal bones, and some unburnt human bone. There is similar information from East Chisenbury where the dominant animals were sheep (McOmish 1996; Valdez–Tullett 2017). The sheer abundance of bones suggests that feasts were taking place, and this is particularly likely at Runnymede Bridge where the midden was located on an island. It has produced another large assemblage, but here there is evidence that some of the faunal remains were carefully organised within the filling of the midden (Needham 1992). At Llanmaes in South Wales, where the metalwork included fragments of bronze cauldrons, large quantities of pork were consumed. Pigs accounted for over 70 per cent of the animals; most bones came from their right forequarter (Madgwick and Mulville 2015). Isotopic analysis shows that some of them had been brought from distant areas, and it is obvious that their consumption was carefully controlled. There are indications of craft production from most of the midden sites, including bronze working, the working of antler, spinning, and the production of textiles. Detailed study of the ceramics from Potterne suggests that the people who used that site had a wide range of contacts with other places (Lawson 2000: 166). The same is true of the metalwork from Runnymede (Needham 1991). A striking feature of the middens at Whitchurch and Woodeaton is the presence of miniature copies of familiar kinds of bronze artefact (K. Waddington and Sharples 2011; D. Harding 1987). They are best interpreted as votives, like their counterparts in the Mediterranean.

Not all these sites show much evidence of structures contemporary with the accumulation of middens. There is considerable uncertainty, for pits and postholes are difficult to recognise within the dark soil of these deposits; the same problem affects research in the late levels of Roman towns in England (Courty, Goldberg, and Macphail 1989: ch. 15). It is true that a range of timber buildings was identified at Runnymede Bridge and Whitchurch and that the middens at Potterne and Llanmaes overlay occupation sites. Even so, the only structural evidence found within some of these accumulations consists of small patches of cobbling, hearths, and the remains of ovens. It may be that in their final form some of these places were not settlements at all. They could have been the sites of assemblies or even fairs like those of the first millennium AD (Pantos and Semple 2003). Given the unusual character of the excavated evidence, the same ideas provide a plausible explanation of the prehistoric middens. It would certainly apply to their distribution in the Vale of Pewsey which follows the natural division between two parts of the Wessex chalk: the Marlborough Downs to the north and Salisbury Plain to the south. Perhaps these places were located in a liminal area (Tubb 2011). Alternatively they were the bases from which the higher ground was grazed on a seasonal basis (Valdez-Tullett 2017).

Occasionally the middens can be associated with other features. The example at East Chisenbury overlay one side of an earthwork enclosure (McOmish, D. Field, and G. Brown 2002). A similar deposit at Wittenham Clumps in the Upper Thames was just outside a hillfort notable for its deposits of human remains (T. Allen et al. 2010), and one has been identified 500 m outside another early hillfort on Bathampton Down (R. Thomas, Oswin, and L. Brown 2012). At Balksbury on the chalk of Wessex the midden, which included large amounts of cattle dung, was within a defended enclosure (C. Ellis and Rawlings 2001). Again there was possible evidence of feasting.

Balksbury is one of a group of earthwork enclosures which were built in southern England during this period. They are closely related to the Late Bronze Age hillforts discussed in Chapter 4, but some of them may be later in date and are usually assigned to an Earliest Iron Age that extends from about 800 to 600 BC. They shared certain features in common. They were of considerable extent and occupied prominent hills. They were enclosed by surprisingly slight earthworks, and excavations inside them suggest that they were not intensively occupied. They provide evidence for a limited number of dwellings, but the main structures were small square buildings usually interpreted as raised granaries or storehouses. They do not produce many artefacts. In the absence of more detailed information, it has been suggested that these places were used intermittently and perhaps on a seasonal basis. In that respect they share features in common with the midden sites.

In each case the evidence suggests that certain locations served as focal points for a wider population. Indeed, they could have played a part in public events at which feasting was particularly important. In the early first millennium BC there was probably an added element, for they seem to have been where people congregated for the purpose of production and exchange. The great accumulations of manure might not mean that large numbers of livestock were collected for slaughter; surely there were also gatherings at which animals changed hands. Similarly, there is evidence that artefacts were being made, including metalwork. In the past it had taken place at more secluded locations, including Irish crannogs, Welsh hillforts, and some of the English ringworks, where it might have been easier to exercise control over its circulation. The new sites may have been where people transacted public business, but if so, it was a novel development. Perhaps the community was assuming greater authority than before.

If these were unfamiliar elements, other features of the landscape seem to have gone out of use. One characteristic of the Late Bronze Age landscape was the presence of fortified ringworks. In most cases activity ended during the Bronze Age/Iron Age transition, and the same applies to the building of Irish crannogs. That may be significant as they have similar contents and both may have possessed a special status. Just as the deposition of fine metalwork in water seems to have diminished, these locations lost their significance, and the same is true of most of the platforms and islands discussed in Chapter 4. It is a trend that applies to other sites in the English landscape, for the coaxial field systems which were such a feature of the later Bronze Age were largely abandoned during this phase, if not before (Bradley and D. Yates 2007). The significance of the change will be considered in due course; what matters is that some of the associated settlements were deserted or moved to new positions.

HOUSES AND ENCLOSURES

There are other signs of dislocation in the settlement pattern. Two features are particularly important.

The first is a gradual shift in the distribution of prehistoric activity. During the Late Bronze Age there was an extraordinary density of occupation sites along rivers discharging into the North Sea. That is where many of the field systems were created and it accounts for the siting of most of the ringworks. Perhaps more important, it is in this area that the principal deposits of fine metalwork occur: there are weapons and ornaments in the Fenland, and more artefacts are found in the Thames. The previous chapter suggested that these features were directly related to one another: communities associated with the ringworks and perhaps other settlements controlled the flow of metalwork and engaged in long-distance exchange. They were able to do so because of the surplus provided by stock and crop cultivation, and it even seems possible that these people were commemorated in death by the objects deposited in water.

During the Early Iron Age the distribution of weapon deposits contracted until it was practically confined to the Middle Thames (Jope 1961), and in some regions settlement sites can be difficult to find. There is less evidence of occupation in the areas that had played a prominent role before, and instead there are more signs of activity in other regions. In the south, they include the Midlands, the upper reaches of the Thames, and the south-western peninsula. In the north, there was a similar increase in settlement sites, especially in the uplands on either side of the modern border between Scotland and England. It may also have happened in Wales, although the evidence is more limited, but in Ireland, Iron Age domestic sites of any kind proved difficult to find before the expansion of development-led excavation (Corlett and Potterton 2012).

Regional Developments

On one level the new settlements took distinctly regional forms, just as the ceramics of this period can be divided into a series of mutually exclusive style zones (Cunliffe 2005: ch. 5). To some extent these contrasts may also be deceptive as Chapter 4 showed that Late Bronze Age settlements are not easy to identify without large-scale excavation. It is because many were open sites. That is especially true outside the distribution of field systems. Iron Age settlements, on the other hand, were sometimes enclosed by a palisade or more often by a bank and ditch. That was certainly the case in England, Scotland, and Wales.

Roger Thomas (1997) has offered an interesting discussion of this phenomenon. The process of enclosure began at about the same time as the decline in the supply of bronze entering these islands from the Continent. The new sites were usually associated with agricultural production, and there is every reason to suppose that Iron Age activity had a greater impact on the landscape than that of the previous period. Excavations at these enclosures support this interpretation. They provide evidence for stock raising and cereal growing on a substantial scale and include a whole range of agricultural facilities within their area, in particular raised granaries or storehouses, and silos for keeping grain over the winter. Such sites can produce large collections of carbonised cereals, and faunal remains almost entirely of domesticates. Thomas suggests that with the decline in the circulation of prestigious metalwork people were placing more emphasis on food production. His discussion is paralleled by Valdez–Tullet (2017) who emphasises the social importance of stock raising.

The landscape was divided according to simple conventions, but in this case it was occupied by a number of communities who seem to have emphasised the differences between them by monumentalising the limits of their settlements (Sharples 2010: ch. 3). To an increasing extent they also imbued those boundaries with a special significance by the deposition of human bones and other items (Hill 1995). This is a special feature of the enclosure ditch and the area around the entrance. Few of the enclosures could be defended against attack. Thomas (1997) suggests that the inhabitants of these places were increasingly self-sufficient. Once founded, many settlements were occupied and rebuilt over a considerable period of time.

Dwelling Places

The forms of the enclosures have attracted less attention than their chronology, and yet they support a similar interpretation. The dominant feature of the Late Bronze Age ringworks had been large roundhouses like those at Mucking, Springfield Lyons, and Thwing (Sharples 2010: 212–15). They were generally located within a circular enclosure whose defences could be built on an extravagant scale. Such buildings were generally aligned on the gateway, but could be separated from it by a screen. Like the henge monuments of the Neolithic period, the entire structure gives the impression of one enormous house, and this is even more obvious at a transitional site like West Harling in East Anglia, where the earthwork perimeter abutted the outer edge of an unusually large circular building (Fig. 6.4; J. G. D. Clark and Fell 1953).

Houses of similar size occur quite widely between 600 and 400 BC, but after that time they are comparatively rare (Sharples 2010). Two examples are particularly interesting. One was at Bancroft in the east Midlands. It was associated with a perforated clay slab of a kind associated with large-scale food preparation (Champion 2014), and a quern was buried in the centre of its floor. When the surrounding area was occupied by domestic buildings, its position was respected. There may have been some awareness of its special significance for the site was eventually used as a Roman mausoleum and a shrine (R. Williams and Zeepfat 1994). The other site is Longbridge Deverill Cow Down in Wessex where a group of enormous roundhouses has been excavated (S. Hawkes and C. Hawkes 2012). Each of them contained a remarkable

West Harling
Eastern enclosure   Western enclosure

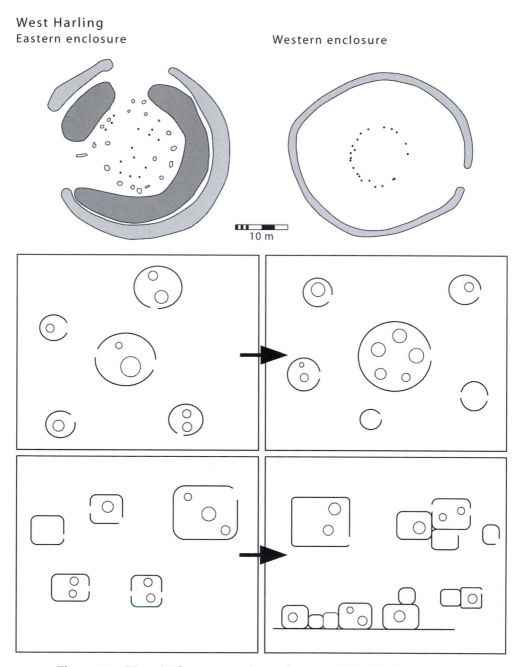

Figure 6.4 (Upper) The two circular enclosures at West Harling, East Anglia, and their associated roundhouses. Information from Clark and Fell (1953). (Lower) Model suggesting the evolution over time of landscapes with circular and rectangular enclosures respectively.

assemblage of fine pottery which seems to have been deposited there before the buildings were set alight. The excavators suggested that this might have happened on the death of one of the occupants; all these structures were raised and destroyed in sequence.

Such buildings were by no means the standard form of dwelling. Like the Late Bronze Age buildings they resemble in many respects, these were the largest examples in a wide range of timber structures. Their associations changed, too. Ringworks with their timbered ramparts were no longer built during the Early Iron Age, but large circular buildings could still be the dominant feature inside the new earthwork enclosures and even occurred on open sites. Others were inside some of the early hillforts.

What is less often considered is the importance of the circular or sub-circular ground plan. This was not confined to the major houses but extended to the earthwork perimeter as well (Bradley 2012). Again it was a format that applied to several different classes of monument: to enclosures and even to the organisation of hillforts. It was by no means ubiquitous, but at its simplest it had two elements. The perimeter was curvilinear and was frequently breached by an entrance to the east or south (Hill 1996). In both respects it resembled the plan of a roundhouse. There could be some elaborations of this format. A second entrance might be provided on the opposite side of the circuit, but even this feature is shared with a number of timber buildings in northern Britain. It is often argued that such buildings have their doorways towards the south or east to allow the morning light to illuminate the interior (Pope 2007), but the relationship between these houses and the position of the sun may have a cosmological significance as well, for such a practical argument can hardly explain why the same principle should extend to the gateway leading into the settlement (Bradley 2012).

Not all the enclosures adopted this layout, nor was every settlement defined by a ditch or palisade, but circular enclosures are far too common to have developed fortuitously. Others were roughly square or rectangular, but these variations usually follow regional lines. Thus circular enclosures are common in the archaeology of Wessex, south-west England, and the Scottish borders; rectilinear compounds are more often found in the east Midlands, the coastal plain of north-east England, and the Welsh Marches. These distinctions may have been influenced by the pattern of settlement. Like roundhouses, circular enclosures were usually set apart from one another, but rectilinear enclosures could easily be joined together. It often happened on the river gravels of midland England. Although many of them maintained their isolation, sometimes they occurred in groups together with linear land boundaries.

If there were practical advantages to a rectangular ground plan, why did so many communities in Britain choose to build circular enclosures? Was it to evoke connections with domestic architecture? One reason why the house may have been such an important symbol during the Early Iron Age was that it stood for the integrity and independence of different groups of people (R. Thomas 1997). Perhaps that was less important in those regions where other kinds of enclosure were built. There is also some evidence that in the east Midlands rectilinear enclosures were preferred in intensively farmed lowland areas, while curvilinear plans were favoured on higher land in the same region (J. Thomas 2010). There were important changes over time, and it is clear that square or rectangular circuits became more popular during the Late Iron Age, although roundhouses themselves remained in use until well into the Roman period (A. Smith et al. 2016).

It is difficult to discuss the Irish evidence as it has only recently come to light (Corlett and Potterton 2012), but in most parts of Britain it is clear that large domestic buildings were gradually replaced by smaller circular structures (Sharples 2010: ch. 4). They are a particular feature of the Middle Iron Age, which ran from about 400 to 150 BC. For the most part they followed the same conventions as the earlier houses, but it seems as if there were few significant differences of size between individual dwellings. Indeed, they present such a uniform appearance that it seems as if any overt distinctions between them were suppressed. Like the buildings of the Late Bronze Age and Early Iron Age, they were normally replaced in exactly the same positions. Where it did not happen, successive structures overlapped, implying a set of conventions that were respected over the generations. Important thresholds could be marked by offerings of artefacts, animal bones, or even human remains. This is clearly indicated at Crick where deposits of this kind were associated with the entrances and backs of the dwellings; occasionally their contents varied between the left- and right-hand sides of the buildings (Hughes et al. 2015). Within such settlements there seems to have been an emphasis on the continuity of the domestic group. At the same time, certain of the enclosures were reconstructed on an increasing scale. It is possible that the social distinctions signified by domestic buildings now applied to the settlement as a whole. Perhaps the main differences of status were between the inhabitants of different sites and were expressed by the size and elaboration of the earthworks that enclosed them.

THE ORGANISATION OF THE LAND

Settlements and Boundaries

Iron Age farming has always provided a major topic for research. Food remains are well preserved and many settlements have seen large-scale excavation. Surviving earthworks in England, Scotland, and Wales have all been the subject of field survey. The resulting interpretations were tested by a series of experiments. They were concerned not only with the practicalities of constructing Iron Age buildings but with raising livestock and cultivating crops. The Butser Ancient Farm on the chalk of southern England was claimed as a working model of the prehistoric landscape (P. Reynolds 1979).

For this reason it might seem easy to characterise Iron Age agriculture, and exactly this assumption lay behind a series of important excavations at Fyfield and Overton Downs on the Wessex chalk. The findings of that work show how far knowledge of the subject has changed. When the project was devised in the 1960s, it seemed important to investigate a series of Iron Age settlements, land boundaries and 'Celtic' fields which were located not far from a major hillfort. When the report on this project was published, those elements proved to be less closely related than originally supposed (P. J. Fowler 2000). The fields which seemed to unite the different features actually dated from the Bronze Age and, like many others, they went out of use in the Early Iron Age. One of the settlements was integrated into these boundaries, but by the time it was established few of the plots were being used. Instead domestic buildings were fitted into the surviving earthworks. Although it was accompanied by a patch of arable land, the area may have been used as pasture. The project did not investigate the hillfort, Barbury Castle, but comparison with similar sites in the same region suggests that it would have included the remains of houses, granaries, and storage pits; this is indicated by its earthworks and by geophysical survey (Bowden 2005). Such monuments were linked with the process of crop production, but may not have been linked with the use of regular field systems. How, then, was Iron Age agriculture organised?

Yates (2007) has shown that coaxial fields were established in lowland England by 1500 BC. Chapter 4 argued that they were first created towards the end of the Early Bronze Age and that the same form of land organisation was adopted widely on the chalk and river gravels of lowland England during the later part of that period. Not all the systems initiated during the Early and Middle Bronze Ages remained in use for long, but new ones were probably established in the Late Bronze Age. Except in the Upper Thames, these systems went out of use during, or soon after, the transition to the Early Iron Age (Bradley and D. Yates 2007). Many of the associated settlements were abandoned and others spread across their boundaries. Long-established hedges might have survived as features in the landscape, but a second group of coaxial field systems was not created until the Middle to Late Iron Age when it covered a larger area of Britain (Bradley and Fulford 2008). That process continued into the Roman period and is not considered here. Not only were a number of relict field systems reused at that time, many new ones were created. There is no sign of a similar development in Ireland.

Those changes should not have seemed so troubling, for some of the best recorded prehistoric landscapes are without surviving fields of any kind, even though there is evidence that animals were raised and crops were grown. Perhaps the most obvious example is provided by the Yorkshire Wolds. The problem needs to be approached in another way. Environmental evidence shows that, unlike the situation in Ireland where pollen analysis identifies a period of reduced activity (Plunkett 2007), the British landscape in the south and east was largely open and was being exploited on a large scale. There are signs of soil erosion caused by cultivation and over-grazing, and carbonised cereals are virtually ubiquitous on excavated sites (Cunliffe 2005: ch. 16). So are the remains of domesticated livestock. Many settlements in southern England contain grain storage pits which can preserve traces of their original contents. Where they do not occur there may be the foundations of timber granaries. The problem is not whether Iron Age people engaged in intensive mixed farming, it is how that activity was carried out on the ground. If Celtic fields went out of use, what does this imply for the nature of Iron Age society? If older land divisions were no longer important, how was farming organised? That discussion must take in other elements: settlements, boundary ditches, and hillforts.

Chapter 5 discussed the origin of the linear earthworks which divided up large tracts of the later prehistoric landscape. Many were poorly dated, but, with a few exceptions, they seem to have originated during the early first millennium BC, and in central southern England they cut across groups of coaxial fields in a way that must have put them out of use (McOmish, D. Field, and G. Brown 2002). Unlike the coaxial fields, these boundaries remained important during the Iron Age. Indeed, more of them were constructed at that time, and they occur across a greater area, including the Midlands, north-east England, and the Welsh borderland. The simple banks and ditches that seem to characterise the earliest examples were increasingly supplemented by other kinds of feature, including multiple dykes and pit alignments.

Such changes happened in many areas, but they have been studied in particular detail on Salisbury Plain. During the Late Bronze Age a series of long linear earthworks cut obliquely across the existing plots, meaning that some of them would have been abandoned. Like those field boundaries, the ditches could be orientated on ancient mounds. The new land divisions extended from the river valleys onto the high chalk plateaus and defined a series of elongated blocks of land, not unlike the parishes of the early medieval period (Bradley, Entwistle, and Raymond 1994; McOmish, D. Field, and G. Brown 2002). Each territory contained at least one open settlement, and beyond the limits of this system there were burnt mounds, sources of workable flint, and the findspot of an important metal hoard. During the Early and Middle Iron Ages some of the earthworks were rebuilt, often on several occasions, and deposits of human bone and animal skulls were placed within them; similar material was associated with the boundaries of settlements. Certain earthworks were extended while others were levelled. Curvilinear and recti-linear enclosures were built within these land blocks, and some of the points

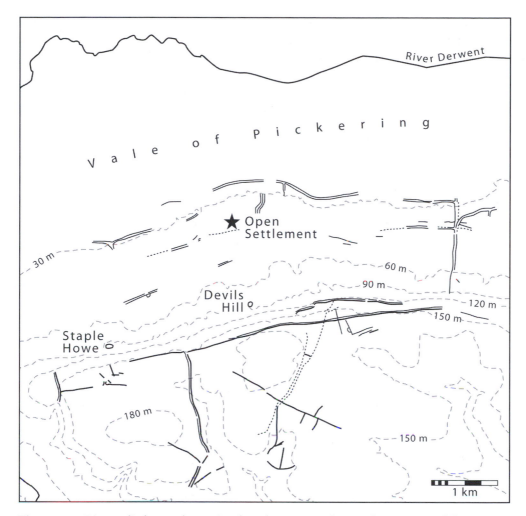

Figure 6.5 Linear ditches and associated settlement on the northern scarp of the Yorkshire Wolds, north-east England. They are associated with two hilltop enclosures, Staple Howe and Devil's Hill, and with a large open settlement on the lower ground. Information from Powelsland (1988).

at which separate territories converged became the sites of hillforts. It was not until such monuments had gone out of use in the Late Iron Age that field systems were re-established on Salisbury Plain.

A comparable process happened on the Yorkshire Wolds, where some of the boundaries were defined by lines of pits rather than ditches (Stoertz 1997; Fenton-Thomas 2003). Excavation at West Heslerton has shown that the land divisions long recognised on the chalk hills extended down into the Vale of Pickering to their north (Fig. 6.5). At least two of these territories were dominated by palisaded enclosures situated on prominent summits, whilst a large open settlement with roundhouses and raised granaries was identified on the lower ground (Powelsland 1988). Another unenclosed settlement has been investigated in the valley known as Garton / Wetwang Slack (Brewster 1984; Dent 1982). It contained a similar range of structures distributed on one side of a prominent earthwork boundary which was maintained throughout the Iron Age. It is doubly important because a major cemetery developed there.

In Yorkshire and to some extent in Wessex, these linear earthworks coexisted with pit alignments, and there are even cases in which a discontinuous boundary was replaced by a more substantial feature. In Lincolnshire and Yorkshire there was also a predilection for constructing several earthworks side by side. Such features are difficult to date as linear ditches might be recut many times. Pit alignments, on the other hand, could have had a more restricted currency and are easy to identify on air photographs (Boutwood 1998; Roberts 2005). Their distribution extends across large areas of the English river gravels, into the Welsh borderland to the west and northwards into Scotland. It is unfortunate that so few of these boundaries produce any artefacts, but what little dating evidence is available suggests that the earliest were built around the Bronze Age/Iron Age transition, and the latest were probably constructed in the Middle Iron Age (Fig. 6.6). Still more massive dyke systems developed towards the end of this period and are poorly understood. All these features are occasionally associated with human and animal burials and with deposits of querns and other artefacts.

These land divisions seem to have been employed in the same ways across a considerable area of Britain. Like recently investigated earthworks in eastern England (Ladd and Mortimer 2017), they defined large blocks of land. Often the boundaries ran parallel to one another and at right angles to a river. Although their layout may have changed over time, the effect was to include a mixture of different resources extending from the floodplain to the higher ground (Bradley, Entwistle, and Raymond 1994). A number of these units show evidence of subdivision, but normally they are of similar extent to the land of an average modern farm. There are few signs of field systems within these enclosures, and what excavated evidence exists suggests that they either predate these boundaries or were created after those features had gone out of use. It does not seem likely that these elements were contemporary with one another.

At the same time the large areas of land defined by these divisions might include the positions of one or more settlements, which varied in their layouts and histories (J. Thomas 2010). Some were established beside the boundaries and could have been contemporary with them; others were some distance away, but were situated within one of the land blocks they defined. It was unusual for any settlement to extend across such boundaries, and, when this happened, it was often because that feature had already gone out of use. The settlements themselves might be open or enclosed, and in some cases they

Figure 6.6 A pit alignment at the Cotswold Community Park in the Upper Thames Valley. Photograph courtesy of Gill Hey and Oxford Archaeology.

oscillated between these forms more than once in the course of their histories. Several settlements could be established within a single land unit or
were located along its limits. Sometimes their use was short-lived, so that one
occupation site replaced another, but just as often they coexisted. It is clear that
the boundaries usually show a greater stability than the rather fluid pattern of
occupation inside them, and it is unlikely that these ditched territories had a
single role. Rather, they seem to be associated with a mixed farming regime in
which cultivation and the raising of livestock were both important. Nearly all
the excavated settlements include large collections of faunal remains and are
associated with carbonised cereals, raised granaries, and storage pits.

The main difference between the later Bronze Age and Iron Age systems is
that now there seem to have been fewer fixed boundaries within the separate
land units; Celtic fields had virtually disappeared, although the sharp edges
to the distribution of storage pits on sites in the Thames Valley suggest that
more ephemeral boundaries did exist (Lambrick and T. Allen 2004; Lambrick
and Robinson 2009). They could have been established on a temporary basis,
but have left no trace behind. It is sometimes suggested that the landscape
was broken up by hedges, but even these would have been bedded in a low
earthwork if they were to flourish. At the same time, arable land needed to be
protected from predators and the movement of livestock had to be controlled.
Maybe this was achieved using a series of temporary divisions that could be
changed on a regular basis.

A possible model is provided by Caesar's account of the early Germans
(*De Bello Gallico* IV, 1; VI, 22). Decisions were made at a communal level and
leaders were elected to serve on a temporary basis. Access to land was allocated
every year, so that differences of wealth and power were reduced to a minimum. The distribution of agricultural produce may have been administered
in the same way. This method had certain advantages, for it would be difficult
to accumulate and control a surplus in the way that seems to have happened
at other times. This is simply an analogy, but it is similar to the excavators'
reconstruction of the Iron Age landscape around Gravelly Guy in the Thames
Valley (Lambrick and T. Allen 2004). It would account for the surprising rarity
of Early and Middle Iron Age field systems and it may provide a reason why
the houses within the settlements developed such a uniform character. If the
later Bronze Age had seen the development of social distinctions, this phase
illustrates their decline.

Earlier Hillforts

It may also provide the background to the development of early hillforts in
Britain (it is unlikely such monuments were used during the same period in
Ireland). They are widely distributed across the south and west. Cunliffe dates

them to the period between about 600 and 400 BC (2005: ch. 15), and in some respects they follow a similar trend to the enclosures considered in the previous section (Fig. 6.7). Some of the oldest examples, such as Crickley Hill, Balksbury, or Winklebury, contained unusually large roundhouses rather like those associated with Late Bronze Age ringworks, but the later buildings were smaller and of roughly uniform size (Sharples 2010: 215–20). If the first of these structures could be used to express social distinctions, those differences had either disappeared or were no longer emphasised. A second link concerns the 'defences' of these sites. They were built on a variety of different scales, and the more impressive examples often included ramparts that were reinforced with timber in the manner of an older site like Springfield Lyons, Rams Hill, or Thwing (Cunliffe 2005: 349–53). The less monumental examples were perhaps no different from other ditched enclosures. They have been identified as hillforts by their positions in the landscape, but, like the roundhouses of the Early Iron Age, such earthworks really form a continuum. That is not to deny that some of these places could have been attacked. A recently excavated site is the aptly named War Ditches in East Anglia. It was abandoned in the fifth or early fourth century BC before construction was complete, and human bodies and disarticulated bones were found in its ditch (Pickstone and Mortimer 2012). The same happened at Fin Cop in the Peak District where the remains of women and children were also associated with the defences. This episode occurred between 355 and 300 BC (C. Waddington 2012). Hillforts in western and northern Britain were sometimes destroyed by fire. They include Crickley Hill on the Cotswolds where the defences are associated with slingstones, a feature which is usually associated with a later phase of the Iron Age (Dixon 1994: 105 and 115–16).

Although Cunliffe distinguishes between 'early' and 'developed' hillforts, this is not based on major differences in their forms and associations but on their chronology and distribution. The earlier hillforts were widely distributed; developed hillforts will be considered in due course. The first examples provide only limited evidence for the activities taking place inside them. Their ramparts often had a vertical outer face, supported by a stone wall or a setting of timbers, and these sites often had two opposing entrances. Inside the enclosures there were houses and storage structures.

How were these places related to exploitation of the wider landscape? Their construction and maintenance must have drawn on corporate labour (Sharples 2010), and it has always been tempting to think of them as the power bases of local leaders, but it is difficult to find much evidence for that idea. In southern England a few of the sites, like Sidbury and Quarley Hill, were established at the meeting points of territories defined by linear ditches (Bradley, Entwistle, and Raymond 1994), and in eastern England the land associated with them was indicated by linear earthworks (Ladd and Mortimer 2017). For the most

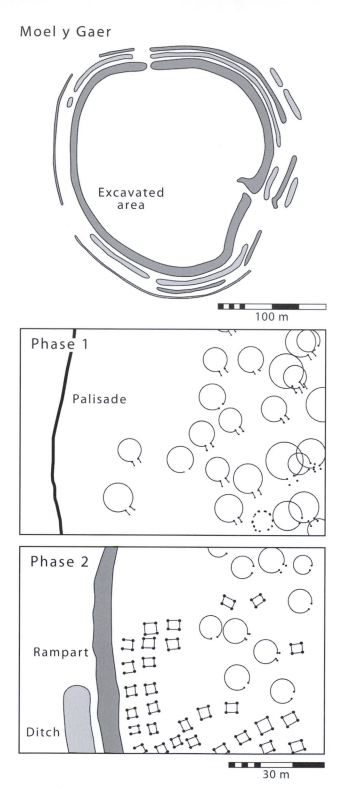

Moel y Gaer

Excavated
area

100 m

Phase 1

Palisade

Phase 2

Rampart

Ditch

30 m

Figure 6.7 Plan of the excavated area of the hill fort of Moel Y Gaer, North Wales, showing the dense distribution of roundhouses and possible storehouses associated with successive phases of activity. Information from Guilbert (1981).

part the artefacts from these places have a similar character to those at other settlements (Hill 1996). Perhaps these hillforts represented a more public expression of the same concerns as those sites. The main difference between these two categories is that in the hillforts certain activities were performed in a more ostentatious manner. Thus the defences might be constructed on an altogether larger scale than the domestic enclosures and were maintained more often (Sharples 2010), yet there seems to have been as much emphasis on their appearance as there was on military architecture. It is not easy to see how they would have provided much defence against attack, although this question has been reopened through studies of the effectiveness of sling warfare (R. Robertson 2016). Hillforts in both the categories recognised by Cunliffe include an exceptional number of raised storehouses, which were probably used to hold grain. These buildings were often the most conspicuous features of these sites, and in several areas, including the Wessex chalk and the Welsh Marches, they could be laid out in rows or organised on a grid. It may have been as important to display the harvested crop as it was to protect it.

A number contain specialised structures which have been interpreted as shrines, but their chronology varies from site to site, and they are not confined to the defended sites, as was once supposed. At Danebury they were used throughout the occupation (Cunliffe 1995: 24–5 and 28), yet at Cadbury Castle a similar building was not constructed until the use of the hilltop was largely over (Barrett, A. Woodward, and Freeman 2000: 172–3). Before then, the same area had been used for the production and deposition of bronze metalwork and for a series of animal burials. Even these specialised buildings have parallels on other kinds of site.

The animal burials at Cadbury recall the wide range of offerings associated with Iron Age settlements, although much of the evidence comes from a small number of regions: Kent, central southern England, the south Midlands, East Anglia, north-east England, the Hebrides, and Orkney; they are largely absent from Ireland. Their main association seems to be with food production and the agricultural cycle, although they extend from the burial of selected artefacts to the treatment of dead people (M. Williams 2003). Such deposits are found in different contexts, but are especially common in hillforts, where such monuments were built. Some were associated with the perimeters of these sites, and others with earthwork enclosures, land boundaries, and the limits of open settlements. They were directly linked with the storage of food, so they are found in grain silos in southern Britain and in the underground cellars known as souterrains in Orkney. The human remains reveal some striking patterns. In certain cases there were important differences between these groups, so that in the hillfort at Danebury the remains of adults were kept separate from those of the very young who were associated with the houses (Cunliffe and Poole 1991: ch. 8). In the open settlement at Glastonbury adult skulls were distributed along the edge of the settled area, and the remains of children were found in the platforms on which people lived (J. Coles and Minnitt 1995: 17–24). It seems possible that skulls and other body parts had been removed from older burials (Sharples 2010: 268–72).

What distinguishes the sites known as hillforts from the other earthwork enclosures of the same period? Apart from their size and the labour devoted to their construction, there seem to be three important features (Hill 1996). These monuments include a greater density of storage facilities than most (but not all) the other sites. That applies not only to the raised granaries mentioned earlier but also to the evidence of pits, which may have become more frequent over time. Given the comparatively limited number of houses inside many excavated hillforts, it seems unlikely that so much food was produced by the occupants. At the same time, there is more evidence for ritual practices in hillforts than there is in most settlements of the same period. They focused on the process of crop production, and the main focus was the storage pit, which may have been selected because of its links with the cycle of death and regeneration associated with the harvesting and keeping of grain (M. Williams 2003).

Lastly, not all these sites need have been continuously occupied. The idea is suggested by the insects preserved by a pond within the Breiddin on the Welsh border, for despite the presence of houses and granaries within the defences, the use of the site had little impact on the local environment (Buckland et al. 2001). A similar argument applies to the 'marsh fort' at Sutton Common in north-east England which contained no fewer than 150 structures interpreted as raised granaries. Excavation did not identify any dwellings and the artefact assemblage from the project was unusually small. Pollen analysis could not show that the site was inhabited (Van de Noort, Chapman, and Collis 2007). The same interpretation is suggested by storage pits inside the Wessex hillfort of Winklebury that seem to have been left open over the winter, trapping a number of wild animals which must have been living there (K. Smith 1977). Another possibility that needs to be considered in future work is that occupation extended outside the defences. That seems to be indicated in a few cases (French 2004; T. Allen et al. 2010).

The relationship between hillforts and ordinary settlements remains quite problematical. The defended sites can contain less substantial domestic buildings, and yet they may have a higher density of storehouses and pits. A few of them included shrines, whilst the proportion of special deposits exceeds that at other sites. Large numbers of people obviously made use of these places, but it is not clear that they settled there on a permanent basis. In many ways they were public monuments which reflected the concerns of people during this period and emphasised them on an impressive scale. Indeed, the very form of some of these hillforts still seems to echo the basic principle of the round-house. They could adopt a roughly circular ground plan with an entrance that faced the rising sun. Such places may have been conceived as the 'houses' of an entire community who could have used them in much the same way as early medieval assembly sites in Ireland which were spaced at similar intervals to the larger British hillforts (Gleeson 2015). Perhaps they were where communal business was transacted and important decisions were made. Again Caesar's description of the early Germans could be relevant to the argument. Such an arrangement would not have been unprecedented for it is also the interpretation suggested for the middens which are such a striking feature of the Bronze Age/Iron Age transition. It may have been through periodic meetings in such places that land and its products were distributed among the population. That did not require a stable social hierarchy.

The very term 'hillfort' is probably a misnomer. At times they may have served as fortifications, as places where resources were protected from attack — there is evidence of occasional massacres which were once attributed to the Romans — but even then the use of these places may have been ritualised. Moore has observed that the deposits of human remains and weapons found in the entrance of a hillfort at Bredon Hill were organised as a kind of display: the bodies had been dismembered and the heads were deposited separately from the limbs (T. Moore 2006; 118–20). Something similar happened at South Cadbury (S. Jones and Randal 2010) and at a rectilinear enclosure within the enormous monument at Ham Hill in south-west England (Brittain, Sharples, and C. Evans 2014). Its ditch was associated with partially articulated bodies which had possibly been exposed before they were buried. They were accompanied by animal bones. Human skulls, three of them with evidence of wounds, were placed in the defences themselves. But such hillforts were not just fortifications; they were also production sites and even a kind of theatre at which public events took place and the concerns of a farming people were played out in ritual and ceremonial. That may not have changed until the end of their period of use.

One of the most important practices was feasting. It was associated with the middens considered earlier in this chapter, but its character may have changed during later phases. By the fifth or fourth centuries BC it was documented by other kinds of evidence: by massive accumulations of animal remains deposited on the ground surface or in disused storage pits, and by the renewed importance of cauldrons for cooking great quantities of food. This could have happened in the course of assemblies and communal business. Sharples has argued that feasting also supported the workforces building and maintaining monuments (2010: 116–24). That is entirely plausible as hillforts and other enclosures were modified surprisingly often. To quote one well-documented example, the entrance to the Welsh hillfort of Castell Henllys went through five phases of construction and reconstruction in only forty years (Mytum 2013: ch. 3).

Sharples's case is supported by the evidence from two sites in southern England. At High Post in Wessex the remains of a 'communal feast' were preserved beneath the bank of a newly built enclosure. They included twenty-five cattle, six sheep, a pig, and a horse and must have been deposited when the earthwork was constructed, otherwise they would not have survived (A. Powell 2011). The same might apply to a deposit found at the hillfort at Aylesbury which was composed of a mass of animal bones associated with the disarticulated remains of a woman and four children (Farley and G. Jones 2012). This deposit contained at least twenty-one sheep, and again it may have been deposited when the structure was being built. Both assemblages formed at about the same time and in similar circumstances. Other deposits come from the interior of hillforts, enclosures, and open settlements. Again large quantities of meat bones were buried together, although some of the carcasses were intact and cannot have been consumed. It is more difficult to interpret the collections of carbonised grain found in similar contexts, because it is seldom clear how they had been burnt and why they entered the ground.

Deposits like these were not restricted to defended sites. A recent development is the discovery of two large hoards of iron cauldrons, one from Glenfield in the Midlands (J. Thomas 2018), and the other from an unenclosed settlement at Chiseldon in Wessex (Baldwin and Joy 2017). The Chiseldon hoard contained seventeen cauldrons and two cattle skulls and dated to the fourth or third century BC. The authors of the definitive account of this discovery conclude that the intact cauldrons in this collection could have supplied enough food for a gathering of 600 people.

Similar events may have taken place at other settlements. In spite of their marginal locations, the wetland settlements of Glastonbury and Meare in south-west England are associated with an extraordinary abundance of artefacts (J. Coles 1987; J. Coles and Minnitt 1995). The authors of the most recent account of these two sites suggest that they acted like medieval fairs, as seasonal meeting places where goods were made and exchanged and where social transactions took place. That seems even more likely in the light of new evidence that these 'lake villages' were readily accessible at the head of a channel leading to the sea (Aalbersberg and T. Brown 2011). The same interpretation might apply to other areas that were occupied on a discontinuous basis or where large numbers of people gathered for only part of the year, for example the high-quality grazing land at Crick in the east Midlands (Hughes et al. 2015), or some of the Iron Age settlements of the Fenland (C. Evans and Hodder 2006). A further possibility is that older monuments were brought back into use by the wider community. One candidate is the henge monument of the Devil's Quoits in the Upper Thames Valley (Fig. 6.8). Lambrick and Allen have suggested that it was surrounded by a large area of pasture shared by the occupants of different settlements (2004). Another example might be

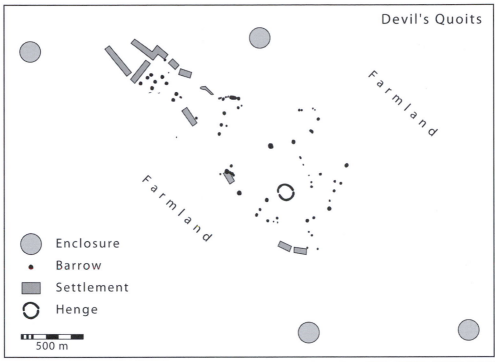

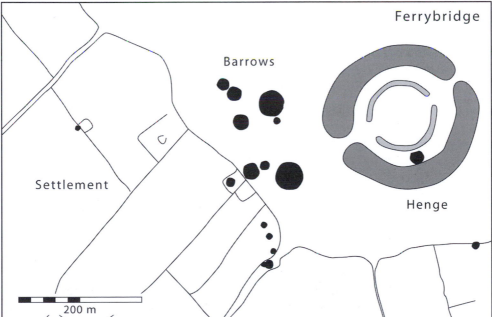

Figure 6.8 (Upper) The henge monument of Devil's Quoits, upper Thames Valley, and the areas occupied by enclosures and open settlement in the Iron Age. (Lower) A similar monument at Ferrybridge, north-east England, compared with the distribution of Iron Age enclosures, and land boundaries outside it. Information from Lambrick and Allen (2004) and Roberts (2005).

the Ferrybridge henge in north-east England. In this case the area outside the Neolithic monument was enclosed by a series of pit alignments associated with human burials, and a scabbard was deposited inside the ancient enclosure. In the surrounding area there was probably a small shrine (Roberts 2005). The activities that took place at the most famous hillforts may have happened in other places, too.

VARIATIONS ON AN ORIGINAL THEME

The West and North

If these features represent the main currents in the archaeology of the Iron Age, in some parts of Britain and Ireland they were expressed in very different ways. Until recently little was known about Irish settlements of the late first millennium BC, and hillforts had apparently gone out of use there. The best chance way of finding the 'missing' sites is by dating the ore roasting pits and grain drying kilns identified in fieldwork. A few do date from this period; the 'royal sites' which assumed a growing importance during the first century BC are considered separately. Otherwise it is clear that post-built roundhouses similar to those of the Bronze Age remained important in the pre-Roman Iron Age, but they are so rare that other settlements may have contained more ephemeral structures which have left no trace behind. Recently published excavations suggest that there were few buildings on any one site, and there is little to show that these places were enclosed (Corlett and Potterton 2012). There was possibly a reduction in the cultivated area or in the intensity with which the land was exploited. That is certainly suggested by pollen analysis (Plunkett 2007).

The field evidence from western Britain is very different. It possesses a distinctive character which is not a unique feature of insular prehistory, for there are similar sites in a number of regions along the Atlantic seaboard of Europe, including Finistère, Galicia, and northern Portugal (Cunliffe 2001a: 336–52). In each case the settlement pattern was dominated by a dense distribution of small fortified enclosures. These were often circular constructions, but along the coast they could be supplemented by a distribution of promontory forts. Those in Brittany are compared with examples in south-west England.

There were other links between the regions along the western limit of the Continent. In the Iberian Peninsula the circular enclosures or castros were normally associated with roundhouses – it was only during the Roman period that they were replaced by rectangular buildings – and, where more impressive defences were built, they could be supplemented by a chevaux de frise: a setting of upright stones so called because it was thought to impede attackers on horseback. Their distribution is revealing for, like that of circular dwellings, it focuses on Britain, Ireland, and Iberia. Examples are found on sites in north and west Wales, in eastern and south-west Scotland, and along the west coast of Ireland (Harbison 1972). Their overall chronology is uncertain, and individual examples could be earlier or later than the period considered here, but the chevaux de frise at Castell Henllys in south-west Wales is dated to 400–370 BC (Mytum 2013: ch. 5).

Several distinctive features characterise the earthwork enclosures of western Britain, including those on the Isle of Man. Most are fairly small, but individual examples can be massively defended (Fig. 6.9). In south-west Wales the entrance is sometimes emphasised by monumental outworks. They contain a relatively small number of circular houses as well as raised storage structures, but their relationship to one another is not consistent from site to site. At Walesland Rath the putative granaries lined the inner edge of the rampart, and the houses were located in the middle of the enclosure (Wainwrght 1971); at Woodside they were to the right of the gateway, and the dwellings were towards the rear of the enclosure; whilst at Dan Y Coed the positions of both groups of buildings overlapped (G. Williams and Mytum 1998). Another way of providing secure storage was by constructing a kind of cellar. In Cornwall, it took the form of a stone-lined trench, roofed by a series of lintels, and in this case it could be associated with an individual house (Christie 1978; Herring et al. 2016: ch. 7). These features are called souterrains and also occur in Brittany (Cunliffe 2001a: 248–9). There is no obvious difference between the structures found on these sites and those inside the larger enclosures described as hillforts. Although there are some signs of open settlements during the Early and Middle Iron Ages, enclosures are densely distributed across the landscape and may have been largely self-sufficient.

Apart from differences of size – most of the enclosures are quite small – the main distinctions between them concern the scale of the surrounding earthworks. In west Wales and south-west England many conformed to a precisely circular ground plan, as if to echo the same principle as the roundhouse. It was a tradition that was to last into the post-Roman period, when it had its counterpart among early ring forts in Ireland. The latter normally contain circular buildings. The early medieval Irish laws show that it was the scale of the perimeter earthwork that was the main way of displaying status. It was carefully controlled, so that the number of concentric earthworks enclosing a settlement site might have been related to the social position of its occupants (N. Edwards 1990: 33). Perhaps a similar model would explain the evidence from western Britain in the pre-Roman period.

There were other regions with a dense distribution of small circular enclosures. They include the uplands of northern England and southern Scotland, where the field evidence can be exceptionally well preserved (Fig. 6.10). The pattern extends further up the North Sea coast (Sherlock 2012). It is clear that it goes back to the beginning of the Iron Age and that on either

Woodside

Dan Y Coed

Collfryn

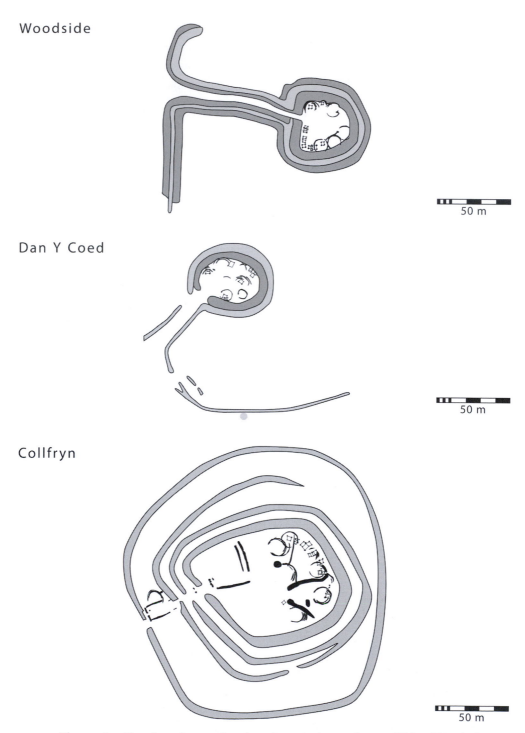

50 m

50 m

50 m

Figure 6.9 Two Iron Age enclosed settlements in south-west Wales (Woodside and Dan Y Coed), and a more elaborate enclosure in North Wales (Collfryn) showing the distributions of roundhouses and square storehouse or granaries. Information from Williams and Mytum (1998) and Britnell (1989).

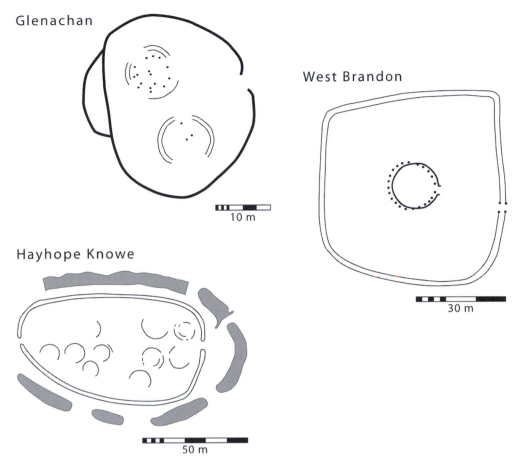

Glenachan

West Brandon

Hayhope Knowe

10 m

30 m

50 m

Figure 6.10 Plans of three enclosed settlements with roundhouses in the English/Scottish borderland. Glenachan is bounded by a single palisade, and there were paired palisades at West Brandon and Hayhope Knowe. There was also an earthwork enclosure on the latter site. Information from D. Harding (2017).

side of the English/Scottish border individual sites might be rebuilt on an increasingly impressive scale, so that an enclosure could be defined first by a palisade, and then by a low earthwork; certain sites were eventually defended by a rampart and ditch or by a substantial wall (D. Harding 2017: ch. 3). The main feature inside these enclosures was the roundhouse. These structures occurred in varying numbers, from a single example to a dense distribution of buildings, but some of them were as large as any dwellings occupied during this period. Individual settlements can be associated with plots of cultivated land which seem to have been worked by hand (Topping 1989), but in this case there is no sign of specialised storage structures. The upland enclosures have counterparts on lowland soils, for instance the excavated hillfort at Broxmouth (Armit and McKenzie 2013), but they are difficult to interpret as few artefacts or food remains survive. The results of development-led excavation show that open sites also existed there. In central and north-east Scotland houses within these settlements were often associated with souterrains (Dunwell and Ralston 2008; D. Harding 2017). There is also evidence of iron working, especially on the Moray Firth (Hatherley and R. Murray in press). Both elements are largely absent from the hillforts of the same period, suggesting that these places were used in a different way.

It is hard to say whether the upland enclosures which have dominated the discussion were inhabited all year. Many were in exposed positions and might have been inhospitable or inaccessible in winter. Moreover, the houses rarely show much sign of maintenance or repair, suggesting that they had not been occupied for long (Halliday 1999). The same problems affect the largest hillforts in highland Britain. They are strongly defended, they were built in dominant positions, and they enclose the sites of many circular buildings, but it is difficult to see how they could have been inhabited continuously. They might have been used during the summer months when conditions were more favourable, but in any case the sheer density of internal buildings is not consistent with the character of the local environment which would not have been capable of supporting a large population. Again it is tempting to suggest that these were aggregation sites, used on an occasional basis and possibly in the course of transhumance. A number of these monuments adopted a curvilinear ground plan.

The tendency to build self-contained enclosures reached its apogee in northern Scotland, the Hebrides, Orkney, and Shetland where some of the strongest patterning has been obscured by disagreements about terminology and chronology (D. Harding 2017: ch. 5). Again the circular archetype was very important and extended from individual dwellings to monumental walled enclosures (Fig. 6.11). All these features were conceived on an impressive scale. They vary from crannogs built in open water to small walled compounds, and from relatively insubstantial dwellings to massive domestic buildings, the most impressive of which – the brochs or 'Atlantic round houses' of the Scottish mainland, the Western and Northern Isles – resemble towers (Romankiewicz 2011). Some of these structures are isolated but densely distributed and were surely designed to impress, whilst others can be found inside defended enclosures which contain a variety of other buildings. Many were along the coast where there were also promontory forts.

Here is another case in which large roundhouses may have been an important settlement form from an early stage of the Iron Age. Armit (2003b) argued that structures ancestral to brochs were built as early as 600 BC and that during the Iron Age stone buildings in Atlantic Scotland became increasingly complex. Excavations at Old Scatness in the Shetland Islands provide evidence that the first brochs were in the north, rather than the west as was once supposed. Here an ambitious dating programme showed that a well-preserved

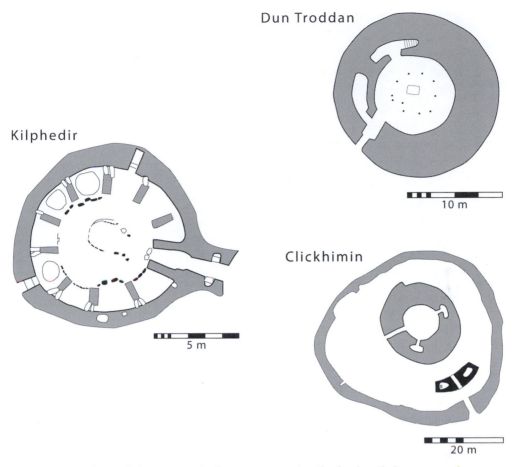

Figure 6.11 Plans of three stone-built monuments in Shetland and the west and north of Scotland. Dun Troddan is an Atlantic roundhouse or 'broch' and a comparable building is recorded inside the walled enclosure at Clickhimin. The structure at Kilphedir is a wheelhouse. Information from D. Harding (2017).

example was constructed between 390 and 200 BC and was enclosed by a circular ditch (Dockrill et al. 2015). These structures are characterised by such features as internal staircases and guard cells. They had more than one storey, and it is obvious that they were roofed (Romankiewicz 2011). They have been interpreted as defended high-status dwellings, but Atlantic roundhouses occur so widely that this could be misleading (Fig. 6.12).

Some of the structural principles that characterise brochs extend to other forms of defensive architecture: to the circular walled enclosures known as duns and even to the monumental gateways of a number of promontory forts in Shetland (D. Harding 2017: 188–92). Another key element is the way in which domestic structures were organised. In some brochs there seems to have been a communal space with a hearth in the centre of the

Figure 6.12 Atlantic roundhouse and enclosing earthworks at Gurness, Orkney. Photograph: Aaron Watson.

building. It was ringed by a range of compartments which were divided from one another by partitions projecting from the interior wall (Romankiewicz 2011). In Shetland and the Hebrides, this principle was expressed on a smaller scale by the buildings known as 'wheelhouses'. Sometimes they were built after the broch themselves, but at Old Scatness they formed part of a larger settlement that extended between the central structure and the earthwork perimeter (Dockrill et al. 2015). Here they were built while the broch remained in use. Another example at Cnip in the Hebrides was of the same age – the second or first century BC – although similar buildings were occupied beyond the period considered in this chapter (Armit 2006). There are important contrasts between these different kinds of structures. Wheelhouses were sometimes recessed into the ground, whereas brochs were conspicuous monuments, and on certain sites the domestic accommodation was probably at first-floor level. Wheelhouses were occasionally associated with souterrains, but the connection between storage structures and individual dwellings was entirely different from the more centralised system illustrated by hillforts in southern England. Both kinds of structure were associated with deposits of artefacts and animal bones similar to those in other parts of Iron Age Britain, and Kate Waddington (2014) has shown how their distribution within the Orcadian structure at Howe was similar to that inside timber roundhouses in the south.

The Midlands and the East Coast

In many ways the Scottish sites combine two of the elements discussed so far, the enclosure and the roundhouse, and sometimes they fused them together in a single structure. A very different tradition remains to be defined. If the Atlantic roundhouses are conspicuous features of the northern landscape, the settlements of eastern and midland England have left little trace behind, and most are known from air photography or from development-led excavations. Others have been identified from scatters of surface finds identified by metal detectors.

In his study of Iron Age Britain Cunliffe suggests that the region between the Thames and the Humber was dominated by 'villages and open settlements' (Fig. 6.13; Cunliffe 2005: fig. 4.3). That pattern extended further to the north and westward as far as the zone of hillforts that follows the modern border between England and Wales, but the division is not clear-cut, for earthwork enclosures are common in both the Midlands and the Thames Estuary, and some hillforts occur in both areas. Moreover, open settlements are among the largest occupation sites in the Yorkshire Wolds and neighbouring areas (Fenton-Thomas 2009 and 2011; F. Brown et al. 2007). Such regional divisions only describe broad tendencies in the evidence, but there are similar distinctions in the settlement pattern of the Roman period (A. Smith et al. 2016).

There is considerable variation. At the heart of this zone are eastern England, the Midlands, and parts of north-east England. Enclosed sites are not particularly common here. Although some standing earthworks have been identified as hillforts, it is uncertain whether all of them were used intensively (J. Davies et al. 1991). Instead, occupation sites extend over considerable areas, sometimes changing their centre of gravity over time (C. Evans, Appleby, and Lucy 2015: ch. 4; Lewis et al. 2010: 223–75; Roberts 2005: 53–125). They had few fixed boundaries, although individual houses or small groups of houses might have been located in compounds within a more extensive living area (Fig. 6.14; Hill 1999; J. Thomas 2010; K. Powell, Smith, and Laws 2010; Lambrick and Robinson 2009). These houses were interspersed with granaries and storage pits, but they could also occupy distinct zones within the occupied area, much as they did within hillforts. In some cases rectilinear compounds were built onto one another as the settled area increased in size, a process that would have been difficult to achieve in a landscape of circular enclosures. These settlements contain larger and more varied artefact assemblages than their predecessors.

It is not clear how many of the structures were contemporary with one another, making it difficult to decide whether these sites should be described as villages. Hill (1999) suggests an interesting comparison between these places and the 'wandering settlements' of the same date in Northern Europe, where houses and other structures were abandoned and replaced after a limited period

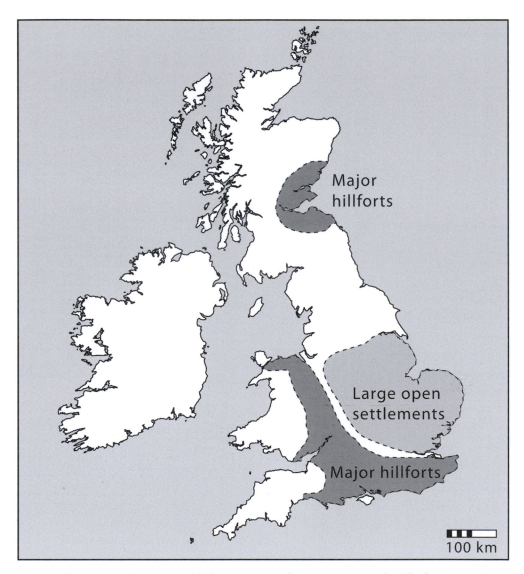

Figure 6.13 Regions with large open settlements compared with those containing major hillforts. Information from Cunliffe (2005).

of use. Their positions shifted, but over a restricted area so that the dwellings occupied during successive phases had mutually exclusive distributions. In eastern and midland England that process could easily have generated the large areas of buildings, pits, and ditches that now survive. Another possibility is that certain of the settlements resulted from the amalgamation of smaller units as larger numbers of people elected to live together in one place and to give up such independence as they had once possessed. The relationships between their separate elements may be expressed by the ways in which compounds and individual dwellings were joined on to one another over time.

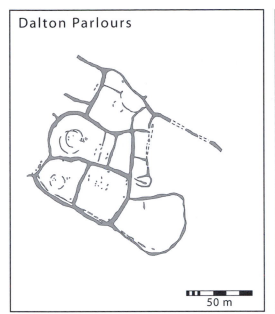
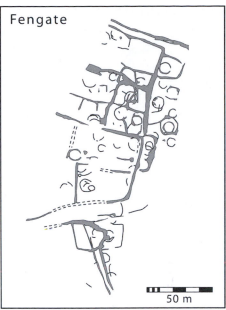

Figure 6.14 Conjoined enclosures at the open settlements of Dalton Parlours, north-east England, and Fengate, eastern England. Information from Wrathmell and Richardson (1990) and Pryor (1984).

If the occupation sites served large communities in this way, it could explain why there was less need to coordinate activities through the use of hillforts. That is why some of the large open settlements in midland England have been characterised as 'hillforts without the hills' (J. Thomas 2010: 22). One reason for making this comparison is that both of them include small square structures that are usually interpreted as shrines. Such buildings have long been recognised as an important characteristic of hillforts, but new excavation has shown that they occur even more often in the open settlements of the Thames Valley, the Midlands, and eastern England (Lyons 2011).

The most extensively investigated of these settlements was at Crick where the number of houses increased sharply from about 450 BC and continued to grow until the middle of the second century BC (Hughes et al. 2015). This 'aggregated settlement' was composed of a series of separate clusters of roundhouses and enclosures that developed around a low-lying area which was probably used as summer pasture (Fig. 6.15). Its outer limit was defined by a linear earthwork. Small enclosures or other compounds were constructed increasingly often, but there is little sign of an orderly layout. The excavators favour the view that some of the structures were used seasonally. There was little evidence of craft production, and the only specialised structure at Crick was a small shrine. Even so, it can hardly be a coincidence that the settlement increased in size and complexity in parallel with the developed hillforts

Hambledon Hill

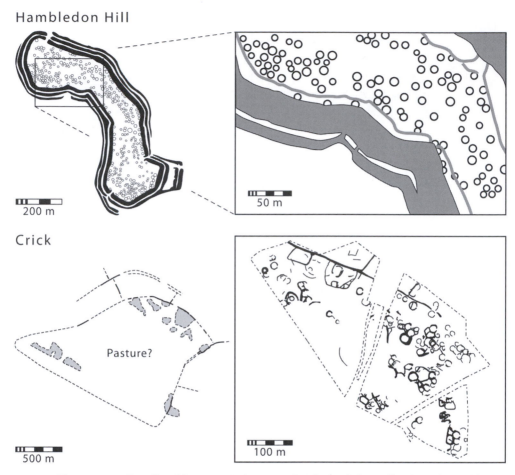

Crick

Pasture?

Figure 6.15 Details of the occupied areas at Crick, English Midlands, and Hambledon Hill, Wessex, showing the high density of circular buildings. Information from Hughes et al. (2015), Sharples (2014), and Stewart and Russell (2017).

in other parts of Britain. Indeed the number of buildings in some of the defended sites was similar to that at Crick (and other settlements which have been investigated on a smaller scale). It is even more striking that when the intensity of activity at Crick diminished during the second century BC some of the largest defended sites also went out of use. Apart from the obvious point that these open settlements were never fortified, the main contrast is between the orderly layout observed at some – but not all – of the hillforts, and the more fluid organisation of space in these 'villages' (J. Thomas 2010). Even that statement would not apply to a few open settlements in south-east England and the upper Thames which include rows or grids of raised storehouses like those at the defended sites (Booth et al. 2011; Hayden et al. 2017: ch. 5).

In some respects this account has followed a conventional sequence, starting with the larger enclosures and hillforts, and then turning to smaller sites in the north and west before finally considering the open settlements of eastern and midland England. That reflects the extent of current knowledge, where certain regions have been intensively excavated at the expense of others, but it may not reflect the actual situation in prehistory. For all the labour invested in their construction, hillforts could have been a rather peripheral phenomenon, on the margin of a more prosperous and perhaps more expansive system with its emphasis on the English Midlands and the North Sea coast. Perhaps it would be better to think in even broader geographical terms, so that the large open settlements of those areas could be the local equivalents of sites in Northern Europe, whilst the enclosed sites in the south might be compared with their counterparts in the north of France (Bradley 2016: 265–85). The tradition of building small but monumental compounds along the west coast of Britain may be part of a still wider phenomenon extending southwards into Atlantic Europe (Cunliffe 2001a: fig. 8.16). That mental adjustment provides a corrective to accounts of this period which are conceived on too small a scale.

THE PATTERN OF CHANGE

Later Hillforts

The character of the largest hillforts seems to have changed in parallel with the growth of open settlements, but for the most part these sites are found in different areas: villages in the Midlands and eastern England, and the largest defended sites in a zone extending from the south coast through the Welsh Marches (Cunliffe 2005: fig. 4.3). With notable exceptions, there were fewer of these monuments to the east, and those in the west of Britain were usually smaller and assumed local forms. Only after the largest hillforts went of use were large open settlements distributed across a wider area. In Dorset, for instance, the large open settlement known as Duropolis was established after the local hillforts had been abandoned (Russell and Cheetham 2016).

Just as the villages showed a gradual evolution between about 450 and 150 BC, the character of some of the best-known defensive sites changed, but again this does not appear to have been a sudden event. Cunliffe's distinction between 'early' and 'developed' hillforts identifies some contrasts in their morphology but is also influenced by changes in the way in which individual examples were used (Cunliffe 2005: ch. 15).

The most obvious feature is that their number decreased at the same time as particular sites were rebuilt on a larger scale (Fig. 6.16). This applies to a number of separate elements. In some cases, for instance Maiden Castle or the Iron Age phase of Hambledon Hill, the enclosed area increased, and the defences took in a larger area of ground. As a result the circular layout of the original enclosure was lost. At the same time the number of entrances might be reduced, restricting access to the interior (Cunliffe 2005: 378–96). The

Figure 6.16 The developed hillfort on Herefordshire Beacon. Photograph: Aaron Watson.

defensive circuit could also be rebuilt on a more impressive scale. The banks might be higher and the ditches wider and deeper, and less use was made of timber revetments that would have required constant maintenance. Most of the earlier hillforts had been defined by a single defensive circuit. Now their earthworks could be replicated so that they had wider perimeters. Thus Maiden Castle was defined by three concentric ramparts and the neighbouring sites of Hod Hill and Hambledon Hill by two. Their number could be augmented by the construction of outworks to protect the entrance which became more elaborate over time. It is a moot point how far these changes resulted from increased fears of attack, but a few of these sites include large collections of slingstones (R. Robertson 2016).

Significant changes happened inside these monuments. In several cases there is evidence that many more people lived there, and it seems possible that some of the settlements in the vicinity went out of use. This seems particularly likely in the case of Danebury and Maiden Castle, but the excavated evidence from these hillforts is complemented by earthwork and geophysical surveys at other sites which have identified the positions of a large number of houses (D. Stewart and Russell 2017). It seems as if some of Cunliffe's developed hillforts assumed new roles towards the end of their history (O. Davis 2013). Sharples (2014) argues that in their later phases these places were effectively 'hill towns'. That development ran in parallel with the growth of open settlements in other parts of England, and in each case the largest examples contained a similar number of buildings. A defended site like that at Hod Hill where numerous structures are documented had more in common with an unenclosed settlement than is often supposed. At the same time storage pits assumed a greater importance than raised granaries. Now it was more important to conceal the harvested grain than it was to put it on display.

A number of developed hillforts contain a distinctive artefact assemblage. Sheet bronze artefacts were being made at Danebury and Maiden Castle during their later phases, and the same happened at Cadbury Castle (Northover 1984). This is only one of a series of new associations. Swords are also found at these places (Stead 2006). From the third century BC, so are iron currency bars (Hingley 2005). Another clue to the changing role of the last hillforts has been suggested by Creighton, who draws attention to the increasing importance of the horse, both as a symbol of power displayed on the first pre-Conquest coins and for its use in warfare (2000). Horse bones were particularly common at the Hampshire hillfort of Bury Hill which included the remains of a burnt chariot (Garrow and Gosden 2012: 280–7). They also occur in a number of specialised deposits on open sites in eastern England. Perhaps the roles of important places were changing.

Early hillforts were widely distributed, but their successors were fewer and more strongly fortified. They were also more evenly distributed, and in regions like the South Downs, the Wessex chalk, the Cotswolds, and the Welsh Marches they do appear to have dominated specific areas of land. Places that originated as ritual centres and assembly sites developed into defended settlements. It is hard to resist the argument that the status of their occupants changed and that social distinctions were forming where they had been under-emphasised or suppressed before. Iron Age society was becoming more violent and more competitive.

Royal Centres in Ireland

If the history of British hillforts was influenced by two important factors – control over agriculture and its products, and the growing importance of armed conflict – events in Ireland took a different course, and here a mythical past was more important. Hillforts had gone out of use by the end of the Bronze Age, and direct evidence of cereal and livestock farming is very limited indeed (Corlett and Potterton 2012). Burials still took place at small monuments of a kind that had been built since the Early Bronze Age, but the artefacts deposited with the dead do not suggest any significant differences of status or wealth; the commonest grave goods were glass beads. By the end of the first century BC, however, a series of remarkable monuments, described as royal capitals in the literature of the Middle Ages, had been established, and the landscapes around them were transformed. What accounts for this development?

One point is generally agreed. The royal centres of Iron Age Ireland owed little or nothing to developments in Continental Europe. They were an almost defiantly local phenomenon with no close counterparts even in the neighbouring island. The Irish sites include massive timber buildings which were greatly enlarged versions of insular prototypes (Bradley 2013b). At the same time they incorporated the remains of more ancient monuments, and their outward forms even emulated those constructions. In some cases older enclosures of some importance were reused. That was the case at Navan Fort (Waterman 1997). On other sites early mounds or stone settings took on a new significance. That was certainly the case at Tara where a Neolithic passage grave provided the focus for a new series of monuments (C. Newman 1997a). That seems doubly significant as it had already been reused as one of the largest Early Bronze Age cemeteries in Ireland (M. O'Sullivan 2005). At Knockaulin a structure associated with Carrowkeel Ware was situated in the centre of the Iron Age complex (S. Johnston and Wailes 2007). In the second or first century BC decorated bone plaques were deposited inside two of the Neolithic monuments at Loughcrew (Vejby 2016), and another megalithic monument at Kiltierney was ringed by low mounds and brought back into commission as a cemetery (Raftery 1994: 192–3). It even seems possible that small stone chambers were constructed at that time and decorated with a peculiarly local version of La Tène art (Shee Twohig 1981: 235–7; Vejby 2016).

This was not a sudden development, although the largest monuments – those at Navan Fort and on the Hill of Tara – were constructed during the first century BC. There were precedents for the creation of specialised monuments at an earlier stage. The clearest example is a circular enclosure at Lismullin on the edge of the Tara landscape (Fig. 6.17; A. O'Connell 2013). It conforms to the same organisation of space as the earthworks constructed on the hilltop, but it was conceived on a modest scale and used in the fourth and third centuries BC. The same is true of the earlier enclosures and buildings at Navan (Waterman 1997). They were created in what were already special places, some of which evoked links with the distant past. Navan Fort overlooks a lake containing a remarkable collection of metalwork (Raftery 1994: 184), but the earthwork was within sight of a Bronze Age hillfort which had been associated with another pool with votive deposits (Lynn 1977). Similarly, a decorated stone introduced to the site at Lismullin seems to have been taken from a Neolithic tomb (A. O'Connell 2013: 36–9), and the same may have happened at Haughey's Fort (Mallory 1995: 81). Later Iron Age burials clustered around the principal passage grave at Knowth (G. Eogan and Roche 1997), and in the Roman period votive deposits were placed in front of the entrance of Newgrange which may have been modified at this time (Ó Néil 2013). If the growth of Irish royal centres owed little to outside influence, it seems to have been impelled by a concern with the insular past. These places provide

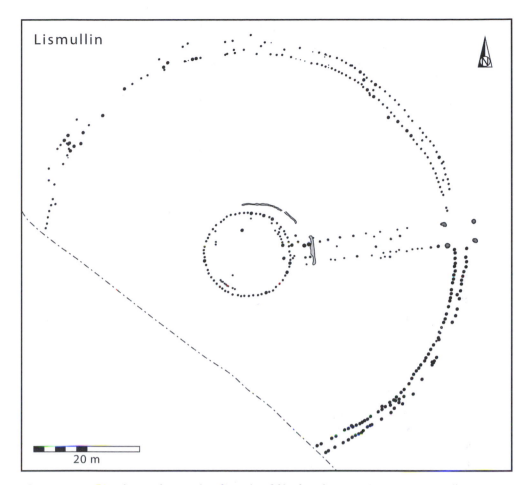

Figure 6.17 Circular enclosure dated to the fifth–fourth centuries BC at Lismullin close to the Hill of Tara, Ireland. Information from O'Connell (2013).

evidence of feasting, craft production, and the deposition of human and animal remains. They may have been the sites of assemblies not unlike those associated with Neolithic monuments, and the bones found at Navan Fort show that animals were taken there from many parts of Ireland (Madgwick et al. 2017). Again relations with the past and the supernatural may have been as important as more direct expressions of political authority.

Only one of these sites is documented in any detail (Fig. 6.18). Navan Fort in northern Ireland is best known as the legendary capital of the kingdom of Ulster and the home of the gods of the underworld, but the archaeological sequence has much to add to what is known about its legendary associations. It was originally one of the Late Bronze Age ringworks discussed in Chapter 5, but, unlike the other examples, it remained in use throughout the pre-Roman Iron Age. During that period the monument consisted of a circular earthwork

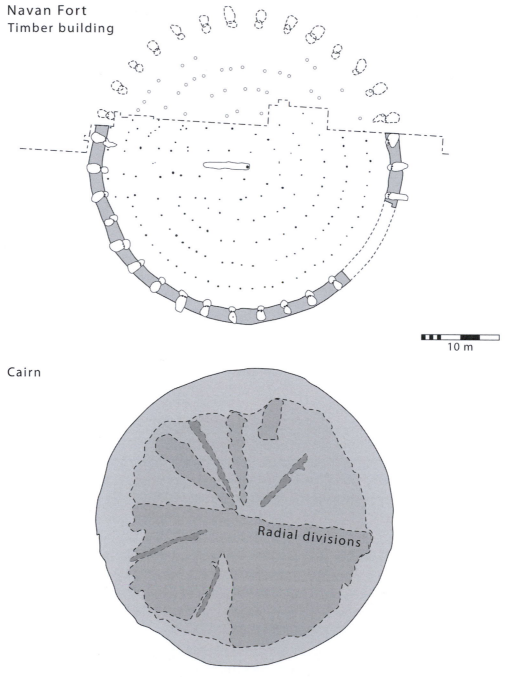

Figure 6.18 The great timber structure at Navan Fort, northern Ireland, and the cairn that was built after its destruction by fire. Information from Waterman (1997).

enclosure with a sequence of wooden buildings in the centre. It was not until the beginning of the first century BC that the scale of the monument increased significantly, and it may be no accident that during the later pre-Roman Iron Age there is unusual evidence for long-distance contacts along the Atlantic coastline (Waterman 1997). Excavation of the monument between 1961 and 1971 brought to light the skull of a Barbary ape, which must have been introduced to the site from its natural habitat in Gibraltar or North Africa. Its authenticity is confirmed by radiocarbon dating. At the same time the landscape to the south of Navan Fort was subdivided by linear earthworks, part of a system that seems to be contemporary with the royal centres in the north of the island. A timber road was built at Corlea during this phase (Raftery 1996), and the entire hill at Navan was enclosed by an earthwork which resembled a Neolithic henge. Its Iron Age date was established by excavation (Mallory 2000).

At the centre of this enclosure there was what may have been the largest roundhouse ever constructed, a massive building 37 m in diameter with a gigantic post at its centre. According to dendrochronology the timber was felled in 95 or 94 BC. Unlike a domestic structure, it was entered from the west, the position of the setting sun (Waterman 1997). It is possible that it was roofed, but there was no sign of a hearth, nor were any domestic artefacts found there. No sooner had it been constructed than the interior was packed with rubble and the outer wall was set on fire. Then, once it had collapsed, it was buried beneath an enormous mound. Warner (2000) is surely right when he suggests that the site was regarded as an entrance to the underworld and that this building was the dwelling place of supernatural beings. The purely archaeological evidence is extraordinary, and this monument surely took the symbol of the circular building to its limits. This development traces a very different trajectory from the history of hillforts on the neighbouring island.

AN END OF ISOLATION

The Early and Middle Iron Ages are sometimes characterised as periods of comparative isolation, and it is true that they provide less evidence than the later Bronze Age for the movement of valuable artefacts between these islands and the Continent. This may be deceptive. In 1964 Roy Hodson wrote an influential article emphasising the individual character of the lowland English Iron Age. It was typified by a distinctive type of personal ornament and by two widely distributed features which seemed to be peculiar to this region: bone or antler weaving combs and the occupation of roundhouses. More recent work, much of it necessitated by commercial development between The Netherlands and Brittany, has weakened this assertion. Objects that once appeared to be exclusively British types have been identified on both sides of the water, and new fieldwork in northern France has identified some circular buildings (Cunliffe 2015; Webley 2015).

Hodson also commented on the absence of formal cemeteries in Britain until the middle of this period. He described it as a 'negative type fossil' (Hodson 1964: 105) and placed it the heart of an insular 'Woodbury Culture', named after Little Woodbury, one of the first Iron Age settlements to be excavated on a large scale. The choice of name was unfortunate as a small inhumation cemetery has since been discovered only 200 m from that site (A. Powell 2015). Others have been identified in the same region and can also be found in northern Britain. It is true that Early Iron Age cemeteries are still very rare, but it is becoming clear that even on the Continent they were only one way of treating the dead. The distinctive deposits found in grain storage pits are not peculiar to Britain and are common from the north of Germany to the west of France (Bradley et al. 2016a: fig. 6.20). Similarly, the distribution of the bog bodies which are so famous in Scandinavia and the Low Countries extends to Britain and Ireland (E. Kelly 2006). They may be related to the deposits of human remains, mainly skulls, in rivers like the Thames. That practice was considered in Chapter 5 but extended continuously from the Middle Bronze Age to the end of the pre-Roman Iron Age (Schulting and Bradley 2014). Something similar has been identified by excavation at Over in the Fenland where disarticulated human bones were associated with a platform on the edge of a river and were found together with the remains of birds, animals, and a collection of brooches (C. Evans 2013).

More obvious links were formed between these regions from the fourth century BC and possibly before. The principal sources of information are these: the development of specialised sites on the coast; increasing evidence of craft production in the hinterland; the appearance of more formal cemeteries; the adoption of 'Celtic art'; and the first use of coins.

Trading Places

There were specialised sites on the coast during several periods of prehistory. They provided sheltered harbours where commodities could change hands. These places were associated with the making of special artefacts, and unusual numbers of non-local objects have been found there. During the early fourth century BC one was the offshore island of Ictis. Pytheas records that it was where tin was obtained by traders from overseas, but 'Ictis' may have been a generic name for this kind of location (Griffith and Wilkes 2006). Similar places are widely distributed (Cunliffe 2001a: 402–7). One was Mountbatten in Plymouth Harbour, and others included Merthyr Mawr in South Wales, Meols in north-west England, and North Ferriby on the Humber Estuary. The same could apply to Harlyn Bay in Cornwall and Lambay Island off the

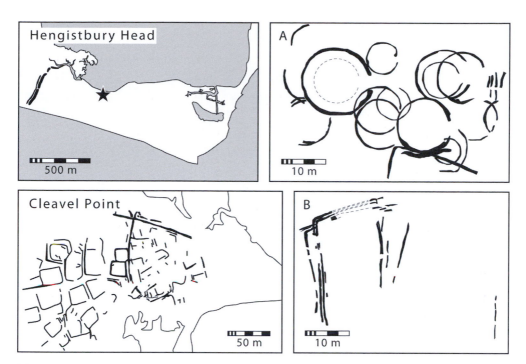

Figure 6.19 Two Iron Age coastal settlements in southern England. A and B show successive phases in the occupation of the excavated area at Hengistbury Head. The second phase is compared with an outline plan of a Late Iron Age and Roman site at Cleavel Point nearby. Information from Cunliffe (1987) and Sunter and Woodward (1987).

east coast of Ireland where Iron Age cemeteries have been identified (Cunliffe 2001a: 345 and 417). Most of these places had played a similar role during earlier periods.

The best known of these sites was Hengistbury Head: a defended promontory protecting a sheltered harbour and an important river leading into Wessex (Figs. 6.19 and 6.20; Cunliffe 1987). It was one of a series of coastal settlements engaged in overseas trade at the Bronze Age/Iron Age transition. During this phase the excavated part of the site was dominated by an unusually large roundhouse, comparable to those further inland. Hengistbury Head became even more important during the period in which southern Britain again engaged in regular contact with the mainland, and at this stage it seems to have acted as both a seaport and a production site. From 100 BC, if not before, it enjoyed a wide range of contacts extending from northern and western France to south-west England, and it was through this site that metals were exported to the Continent and a variety of exotic commodities, including wine, were introduced. Only a small part of the site has been investigated, but it seems to have been most important during the earlier first century BC. Not far away at

Figure 6.20 View of Christchurch Harbour from Hengistbury Head with the main area of the Iron Age settlement beside the water's edge. Photograph: Richard Bradley.

Green Island in Poole Harbour massive piers or jetties were built during the second century BC (Markey, Wilkes, and Darvill 2002; Wilkes 2007).

Craft Production

Not surprisingly, the resurgence of long-distance trade depended on craft production in the hinterland, and it was about this time that ironworking assumed a new significance. That applied to important places by the sea – Hengistbury Head was an important source of ore, and a series of settlements in Scotland also engaged in metalworking (Hunter 2015). It is possible that the new development ran in parallel with increased salt production which is evidenced along the shoreline from north-east England to Cornwall; there were other production sites at brine springs in the Midlands (Kinory 2012). Decorated pottery was distributed from a series of specialised workshops (Cunliffe 2005: ch. 5), and the same applies to the querns needed to process grain (Peacock 2013: 135–41). None of these processes should be described as an 'industry' in the terms that are familiar today. Some of the ceramic vessels carried similar motifs to fine metalwork, and intact or broken querns were often deposited in hoards or built into the fabric of houses (Watts 2014). From the third century BC iron was formed into standard units some of which were modelled on the forms of swords; they were often deposited at the boundaries of settlements and hillforts (Hingley 2005).

The production of iron may have involved similar protocols to Bronze Age metalworking. There are several clues. At Garton Slack in north-east England the tools used for working iron were buried together in a deposit of burnt grain (Giles 2007), and in Orkney the unusual ceremonial site of Mine Howe was associated with evidence of smithing as well as feasting and the treatment of the dead (Card et al. 2005). Here a natural mound was enclosed by a ditch, with a deep shaft at its centre. In the Irish midlands iron was smelted in a series of secluded locations, but finished artefacts were made in public on prominent hilltops (Dolan 2016). Similarly, the impressive promontory fort on Trevelgue Head in south-west England was not only associated with ironworking, it included an enormous roundhouse. Something of its significance is indicated by its use during the Roman period when the site became an 'open cere-monial centre' (Nowakowsi and Quinnell 2011). By that time it included an unusual ceramic assemblage best suited to large-scale food consumption, and a large collection of coins whose composition recalls the offerings at rural shrines. Yet another indication of the special role of craft production is the use of caves for working iron. They might have been kept apart from settlements to avoid the risk of accident, but a recent commentator has pointed out that those in the Mendips were hidden and difficult to reach (Bryant 2011). The transformation of the raw material might have taken place in secret.

Inhumation Cemeteries

In his discussion of this period Hodson (1964) commented on the striking similarity between the Iron Age burials of the Yorkshire Wolds and those in Champagne, the Ardennes, and the Middle Rhine. They stood out from the insular character of the British Iron Age and probably originated during the fourth century BC, but they may have gone out of use during the first century when settlements expanded over some of the graves.

These burials have been attributed to a unitary 'Arras Culture', but in some respects they are surprisingly diverse. The best known are a small series of vehicle burials, which have occasional counterparts elsewhere in eastern and southern Britain (Stead 1991; Giles 2012). They were deposited over a comparatively short period around 200 BC. They resemble their Continental counterparts in many ways, but the details of the funeral rite are subtly different and so are the associated artefacts. The vehicles were usually dismantled, and the bodies were laid out in the crouched position that characterises the British Iron Age. Even the associated artefacts are insular versions of European prototypes.

The same applies to barrow cemeteries in north-east England (Dent 1982; Stead 1991). They include concentrations of square mounds, defined by shallow ditches which allow these distinctive monuments to be recognised as crop marks. They developed over a long period of time but probably increased in number during the late third and second centuries BC. Occasional examples are associated with wooden shrines or mortuary houses similar to those in other parts of England. Many of the burials were laid out according to the specifically British tradition of flexed inhumation and accompanied by a selection of personal ornaments which were insular versions of Continental forms. It is possible that their distribution has been underestimated, as similar structures have been identified by air photography extending in smaller numbers down the North Sea into East Anglia (Whimster 1981). Similar monuments also follow the east coast of Scotland, but are normally dated to the later first millennium AD. In most cases this must be correct, but one example at Inverkeilor included an inhumation with a Roman Iron Age pin (D. Murray and Ralston 1997). A square cairn with a similar association at Loch Borralie was associated with a burial dated between 40 BC and AD 210 (MacGregor 2004). By contrast, an exceptionally early chariot burial has been excavated at Newbridge on the outskirts of Edinburgh and dates from the fifth century BC (Carter, Hunter, and A. Smith 2010).

There is a subgroup of Arras Culture graves which differs from the norm. They contained extended inhumation burials accompanied by weapons and are a particular feature of the Makeshift cemetery at Rudston (Stead 1991). They seem to be a late development within this local tradition and are probably related to a series of isolated 'warrior burials' found in other parts of these islands (Collis 1973). There are not many, but their distribution extends across lowland England with a distinct concentration in Wessex. Outlying examples of burials with swords are recorded from central Scotland, North Wales, and the east coast of Ireland. Weapons were also found in the entrance of a ditched enclosure at Meole Brace in the Welsh Marches where a scabbard was deposited in one ditch terminal and a sword or dagger in the other one (Bain and J. Evans 2011). These discoveries are important because they suggest that the symbolism of conflict and warfare was becoming increasingly significant (Fig. 6.21; Hunter 2005). On the Yorkshire Wolds the same ethos is illustrated by a series of small chalk sculptures which depict warriors carrying swords (Giles 2017). Like the changing character of southern and western British hillforts, this evidence suggests that the 'egalitarian' ethos of the earlier Iron Age had broken down.

The most extensively excavated barrow cemeteries are at Pocklington in Yorkshire (Ware 2017), and at Garton Slack where the burials were placed by a linear earthwork on a site with earlier prehistoric round barrows (Brewster 1981; Dent 1982). Here the cemetery developed alongside a large open settlement which contained the usual mixture of roundhouses, raised granaries, and storage pits. What is especially interesting is that there are few signs of social distinctions within the living area, even though the cemetery contained some exceptionally rich burials. There are certain anomalies – a few of the houses

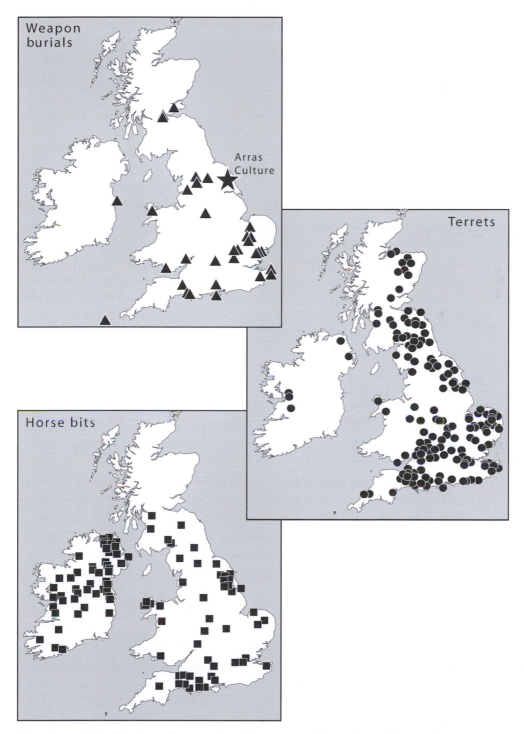

Figure 6.21 Distributions of weapon burials, terrets, and horse bits in the British and Irish Iron Ages. Information from Jope (2000) and Hunter (2005).

departed from the usual easterly alignment; some of the buildings contained deposits of animal bone like those in southern England – but it would be impossible to postulate major differences of status from the structures in the settlement (Parker Pearson 1999). Moreover, it is surely significant that the one region of Britain to possess a tradition of weapon graves does not seem to have included any hillforts of the same date. Even though the skeletal evidence from the cemeteries shows that certain individuals had engaged in combat (Dent 1993), there is nothing that might be interpreted as military architecture. Perhaps the power of local communities depended on the large-scale production of iron in the Humber Estuary to the south of the Wolds (Halkon 2011). They could have controlled access to this valuable material and may have managed its export to other regions.

The evidence from the Yorkshire Wolds is quite anomalous, and nowhere more so than in the combination of square barrows of Continental inspiration with roundhouses of an insular kind. It is hard to understand their relationship. To add to the confusion, there are cases in which square mounds were built over the positions of circular dwellings and others where these two types respected one another, suggesting that circular houses of the living were replaced by rectilinear monuments' to the dead (Figs. 6.22 and 6.23; Brewster 1981). Both halves of the same complex seem to have maintained their distinctive character over time. Perhaps this is most obvious from the concentration of infant burials associated with houses at Garton Slack. Similar deposits are widespread in Iron Age Britain, and yet the burials of adults were carried out with greater formality in the cemetery beside the living area (Parker Pearson 1999).

Although the burials of the Arras Culture are different from their Continental counterparts, there was obviously a close relationship between them: so much so that it is perfectly possible that the Yorkshire Wolds were settled from overseas. This cannot be proved. Like Champagne, they are an area of chalk, meaning that so far isotopic analyses of human bone have not been able to distinguish between immigrants and people who were brought up locally (Jay et al. 2013).

Celtic Art

The distinctive artefacts associated with some of the graves pose a more general problem, for they clearly form part of a wider network that extended across large parts of Europe. It took its name from the famous Swiss site of La Tène (Jope 2000). The forms of the British artefacts were clearly inspired by those on the mainland, but there is little to suggest that they were imports. Rather, they were made according to specifically local techniques and often show regional distinctions of their own.

The quality of these objects is exceptional as they include small personal items such as brooches and pins as well as swords with decorated hilts and

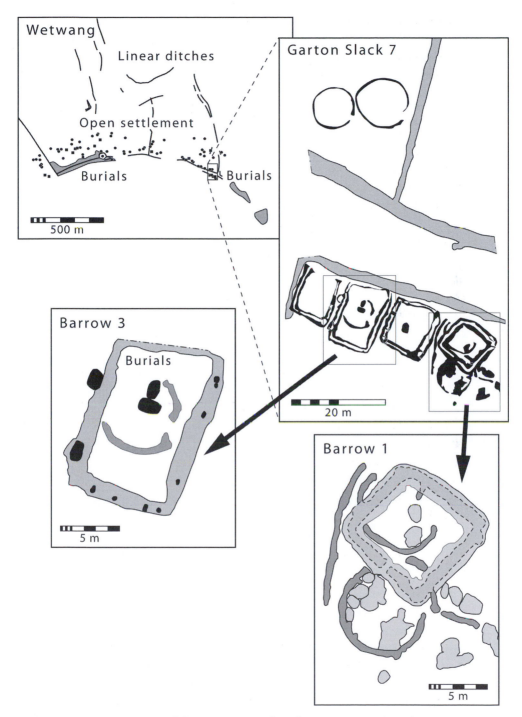

Figure 6.22 Outline plan of the cemetery and settlement at Garton and Wetwang Slacks, north-east England, showing the close relationship between roundhouses and square barrows. Information from Dent (1982), Brewster (1981), and Giles (2012).

Figure 6.23 An Iron Age vehicle burial under excavation at Ferrybridge, north-east England. Photograph courtesy of Oxford Archaeology.

scabbards, spearheads, cauldrons, and horse harnesses. They must have been produced by specialists and surely provide evidence for the importance of new patrons whose concerns included riding, feasting, and warfare. Much of this material may have been used to communicate the special status of particular people or ceremonies, but in the end it was placed in graves and votive deposits.

Fine metalwork was produced in Britain and Ireland with increasing frequency from the fourth century BC and some of the most distinctive items including torcs and horse gear were among the first to be made (Garrow and Gosden 2012). The artefacts associated with weapon burials generally date between the fourth and second centuries BC, but some types were longer lived than others. For many years such objects were dated according to stylistic criteria, but the new research has been based on radiocarbon dating (Garrow et al. 2009). It has had the welcome result that insular La Tène art is known to be contemporary with its Continental counterparts, even though it lasted longer in these islands.

Until comparatively recently fine metalwork had not played a major role in studies of the British Iron Age. Instead it was investigated by methods that combined archaeology with the history of art. Apart from those in graves, these objects lack an obvious context for they can be found in rivers rather than dry land. This evidence occurs in most parts of Britain and Ireland, but perhaps the best-documented group comes from Fiskerton in the Witham Valley in eastern England, where a timber causeway was associated with a large number of tools and weapons dating from this period (N. Field and Parker Pearson 2003). Fine metalwork also comes from a series of hoards. At Snettisham in eastern England gold and silver ornaments were deposited at a dry land sanctuary (Stead 2014) – one of a series with views towards the Wash (Hutcheson 2004) – while in Scotland there are smaller sites that have been interpreted in the same terms. One was the findspot of the Deskford carnyx – a kind of trumpet (Hunter 2001). Another was a circular structure associated with four gold torcs which was built within a wet area at Blair Drummond (Hunter 2010). An earthwork reminiscent of a henge – perhaps a reused Neolithic monument – was established in a similar environment at Pict's Knowe in the south-west, but in this case it contained wooden figurines (J. S. Thomas 2007b; Crone 2007). The ditch of another enclosure at Over Rig in the same region contained a wooden sword, a wooden platter or skillet, and a model boat. These distinctive sites are discussed by Mercer (2018: ch. 16).

The La Tène style of 'Celtic art' extended into other spheres and is represented by decorated pottery in several areas of Britain, including parts of East Anglia and the east Midlands, but it is not found in the same area as the Arras Culture burials where the ceramics were plain. It is unclear whether decorated vessels played a specialised role, but they were particularly common in an enclosure at Weekley which seems to have been attached to a larger settlement with a different pottery assemblage. This enclosure was associated with a roundhouse, with finds of three iron spears and with evidence of metalworking. Again it could have been a sanctuary (D. Jackson and Dix 1987). A small selection of other artefacts, often personal ornaments, have been identified in excavation, but many more are known as chance finds. Their distribution is very striking indeed. The most elaborate metalwork, which is often described as parade armour, is mainly associated with the rivers discharging into the North Sea. The principal concentrations of surface finds echo this pattern and seem to be in the zone of large open sites in eastern England. Although there are numerous exceptions, the best provenanced artefacts often come from sites of that kind, although few examples have been investigated. From about 300 BC they include objects made of gold, whose use had lapsed since the Bronze Age. It seems increasingly likely that the largest settlements in this area provided the power base of new leaders.

If these observations apply to the British finds, they are even more relevant to Ireland. Because pottery went out of use around 800 BC, settlements have been difficult to identify. Instead attention has focused on other kinds of artefact. This approach poses problems. Again most of the metalwork comes from votive deposits in rivers, bogs, and lakes, and a smaller amount is found in hoards (Raftery 1984). It is associated with burials, but only a few graves contain brooches or other ornaments in the La Tène style. Querns, on the other hand, are domestic artefacts, but even these could take on a special character. Again some were placed in bogs, whilst others were decorated with the same designs as the finest artefacts, a style that extends to a series of decorated standing stones (Raftery 1994: 123). A particularly striking discovery came from a waterlogged site at Ballynaclogh in the west of the country (Maginess, O'Dowd, and Tierney 2014). It was by a spring that had been used intermittently since the Neolithic period. Here excavation recorded a series of deposits including part of a rotary quern, but there were also the bones of wild and domesticated animals which had been slaughtered on the site, a white quartz pebble, a decorated wooden bowl, and the head of a dog with a carved stick in its mouth. They were placed there at different times, but this collection provides some indication of the kinds of evidence that rarely survives.

The Irish evidence presents two special problems. There are very few finds of metalwork between the end of the Irish Bronze Age and the adoption of new styles inspired by developments on the Continent. Either fine artefacts were no longer being made, or the tradition of depositing them had lapsed. The latter seems more likely for it is a trend that can be recognised across much of North-west Europe. A second difficulty is that when the circulation of fine metalwork resumed – or rather its use as offerings – these finds were confined to only part of Ireland and almost entirely absent from the south (Raftery 1984). The same applies to the distribution of rotary querns which should date from the same period; in fact they are absent over an even larger area. How can such anomalies be explained? Perhaps the best solution is to focus on these supposedly mundane artefacts. They were obviously used for processing grain and seem to have replaced less efficient saddle querns, but the reasons for this change are seldom considered. Did it happen because they were more effective, or was it because the new technology allowed the preparation of greater amounts of food? In that case they could have played a social role. Maybe they were used in contexts that required large-scale consumption, and that may be why a few of them were decorated. Indeed their distribution may overlap with that of La Tène metalwork because both were associated with the activities of a restricted social group. In the south, life may have continued as before. Here there could have been less incentive for acts of conspicuous consumption, and a simpler way of treating cereals continued unchanged. Just as the use of decorated metalwork in Britain overlapped with developments in the pattern of settlement, in Ireland it was used in the period when the royal centres were established.

The Earliest Coins

The redating of La Tène art in Britain not only shows that it originated at the same time there and on the Continent, it also suggests that the supply of lavishly embellished artefacts was reduced at an earlier date than was originally supposed. This is important since the new chronology means that fine metalwork was less often made (or deposited) when coins entered the country. They can be considered as another kind of Iron Age 'art' but are usually studied separately (Haselgrove 1987; Nick 2018).

The first coins date to the mid-second century BC when their distribution centred on the Thames Estuary, although it extended into Kent and East Anglia. By 70 BC their numbers had increased, and in the middle of the first century BC they are also found along the south coast of England. The first coins were of gold, and because of their high value it is likely that they were employed in social transactions along with other valuables (Haselgrove 1987). That may be why their distribution complements that of torcs. It is likely that their roles included the formation and maintenance of alliances, diplomatic gifts, and offerings at temples and sanctuaries. The early issues have been described as 'Gallo-Belgic', but the term is confusing. The origins of these issues were indeed in Gaul, but the adjective 'Belgic' refers to a group of settlers from Continental Europe – the Belgae – whose presence was documented by Caesar. They are difficult to recognise from purely archaeological evidence.

A few coins from Brittany may have entered southern England through Hengistbury Head, and some potin coins (made from an alloy of bronze) appeared about 90 BC. The number of coins in circulation increased sharply at the time of Caesar's invasion of Gaul, and it seems likely that by this time high-value coins were used to pay mercenaries who had taken part in the conflict (Wigg-Wolf 2018). Like the complex metalwork of this period, some were deposited in hoards and never recovered. Although the earliest Iron Age coins have restricted distributions, they provide yet another indication of the closeness of links between southern England and mainland Europe.

SUMMARY

It is difficult to sum up such a wide range of evidence, particularly when it comes from so many sources: the use of hillforts in some areas; the evidence of burials in others; the discovery of open settlements with a distinctive range of surface finds; the growth of Irish royal sites; and the fine metalwork found in rivers and hoards. Even so, they all lead to a similar conclusion.

This discussion began by considering the impact of a diminishing supply of bronze from overseas. Access to this material had been one source of power, and food production may well have been reorganised so that local leaders could participate in exchange. As those connections fell away, their authority was threatened and, with it, their ability to form long-distance alliances. There followed a period in which social differences were less apparent, and the community itself may have played an important role. The house became a dominant symbol, and its characteristic layout may have influenced the organisation of enclosures and fortifications. Control over agricultural land and its products seems to have been of central importance. That is why grain storage pits were suitable places for burials.

That egalitarian ethos was not to last, and from about the fourth century BC in parts of Britain there was a greater emphasis on certain individuals, expressed through the development of new burial rites and particularly the importance of warfare. They were closely related to practice in Continental Europe, and that link was emphasised even more strongly by the adoption of a new suite of fine metalwork of foreign inspiration. Although these special artefacts had different associations, a similar process affected much of Britain as well as the northern half of Ireland. The circulation of these objects suggests some new concerns: the display of personal wealth and adornment, feasting, horse riding and the use of wheeled vehicles, and, above all, the importance of armed conflict. The latter is surely expressed by the later burials of the Arras Culture and perhaps by the changing character of major hillforts, and yet it was around the open settlements of the North Sea coastline and the royal centres of Ireland that much of the new wealth was concentrated. Eastern England enjoyed ready access to the sea and easy communications with Continental Europe. In that respect the new system had something in common with the political geography of the Late Bronze Age.

Between the fourth and second centuries BC both Britain and Ireland became more closely integrated with the European mainland than had been the case for many years, and it is no accident that it was in this period that Pytheas made the famous voyage described in Chapter 1. It seems clear that by then these islands already played a part in long-distance trade. It is sometimes claimed that it was the northward expansion of Roman power that provided the catalyst for changes in the insular sequence, but the chronological developments considered here suggest that it merely accelerated processes that were already under way. British society was very different when Julius Caesar first invaded lowland England in 55 BC, and between his second expedition and the Claudian conquest nearly a century later a more profound economic and political transformation occurred. These processes tend to overshadow the more subtle developments that have been considered here, but it is to see events through the eyes of Classical writers to believe that the influence of Rome was the only important factor. As Chapter 1 has demonstrated, these authors knew little about the societies they were describing, and could not understand the geography of the countries where those people lived.

That is not to underestimate the importance of contacts with the outside world, but it deserves a book in itself, and so do the intricate political relationships that developed between different areas before and after the Conquest of AD 43. Fortunately, such work is already available and rightly advances the view that the archaeology of the Late Iron Age is best studied in relation to a much longer process of interaction with the Mediterranean which did not end with the withdrawal of the Roman army from Britain. There was considerable variation during this period, and it took too many guises for it to be considered here. Over four thousand years the archaeological sequence had assumed very different forms, but now for the first time people living in lowland Britain experienced the full impact of complex societies on the Continent. Caesar's expeditions illustrate the point. He justified his invasion by claiming that British warriors had fought against him in Gaul – there could be no clearer statement that cross–Channel relations were important. The offshore islands whose existence bewildered so many writers were no longer inconceivable places on the outermost edge of the world. As they became better known, they were losing their mystery.

BIBLIOGRAPHY

Aalbersberg, G. and Brown, T. (2011). The environment and context of the Glastonbury lake village: A reassessment. *Journal of Wetland Archaeology* 10, 136–51.

Aalen, F., Whelan, K. and Stout, M. (1997). *Atlas of the Irish Rural Landscape*. Cork: Cork University Press.

Allen, C. (2009). *Exchange and Ritual at the Riverside: Late Bronze Age Life in the Lower Witham Valley at Washingborough, Lincolnshire*. Lincoln: Pre-construct Archaeology.

Allen, M. (2005). Beaker settlement and environment on the chalk Downs of southern England. *Proceedings of the Prehistoric Society* 71, 219–45.

Allen, M., Chan, B., Cleal, R., French, C., Marshall, P., Pollard, J., Pullen, R., Richards, C., Ruggles, C., Robinson, D., Rylatt, J., Thomas, J., Welham, K. and Parker Pearson, M. (2016). Stonehenge's Avenue and 'Bluestonehenge'. *Antiquity* 90, 991–1008.

Allen, M. and Gardiner, J. (2009). If you go down to the woods today: A re-evaluation of the chalkland postglacial woodland. Implications for prehistoric communities. In M. Allen, N. Sharples and T. O'Connor (eds.), *Land and People*. Oxford: Prehistoric Society Research Paper 2, pp. 49–66.

Allen, M., Lewis, M. and Ellis, C. (2008). Neolithic causewayed enclosures and later prehistoric farming: Imposition and the role of predecessors at Kingsborough, Isle of Sheppey, Kent. *Proceedings of the Prehistoric Society* 74, 235–322.

Allen, T. (2002). Eton College rowing course at Dorney. *Current Archaeology* 181, 20–5.

Allen, T., Barclay, A., Cromarty, A. M., Anderson-Whymark, H., Parker, A., Robinson, M. and Jones, G. (2013). *Opening the Wood, Making the Land: The Archaeology of a Middle Thames Landscape*. Oxford: Oxford Archaeology.

Allen, T., Cramp, K., Lamdin-Whymark, H. and Webley, L. (2010). *Castle Hill and its Landscape: Archaeological investigations at the Wittenhams, Oxfordshire*. Oxford: Oxford Archaeology.

Allen, T., Hayden, C. and Lamdin-Whymark, H. (2009). *From Bronze Age Enclosure to Anglo-Saxon Settlement: Archaeological Excavations at Taplow Hillfort, Buckinghamshire*. Oxford: Oxford Archaeology.

Anderson-Whymark, H. and Thomas, J. S. eds. (2012). *Regional Perspectives on Neolithic Pit Deposition*. Oxford: Oxbow.

Andrews, P., Booth, P., Fitzpatrick, A. and Welsh, K. (2015). *Digging at the Gateway*. Oxford / Salisbury: Oxford Archaeology / Wessex Archaeology.

Aranyosi, E. F. (1999). Wasteful advertising and variation reduction: Darwinian models for the significance of non-utilitarian architecture. *Journal of Anthropological Archaeology* 18, 356–75.

Ard, V. and Darvill, T. (2015). Revisiting old friends: The production, distribution and use of Peterborough Ware in Britain. *Oxford Journal of Archaeology* 34, 1–31.

Armit, I. (2003a). The Drowners: Permanence and transience in the Hebridean Neolithic. In I. Armit, E. Murphy, E. Nelis and D. Simpson (eds.), *Neolithic Settlement in Ireland and Western Britain*. Oxford: Oxbow, pp. 93–100.

Armit, I. (2003b). *Towers in the North: The Brochs of Scotland*. Stroud: Tempus.

Armit, I. (2006). *Anatomy of an Iron Age Roundhouse: The Cnip Wheelhouse Excavations, Lewis*. Edinburgh: Society of Antiquaries of Scotland.

Armit, I. and Büster, L. (in press). *Darkness Visible: Later Prehistoric Ritual and Identity at the Sculptor's Cave, North-East Scotland*. Edinburgh: Society of Antiquaries of Scotland.

Armit, I., Dunwell, A., Hunter, F. and Nelis, E. (2005). Traprain Law: Archaeology from the ashes. *Past* 49, 1–4.

Armit, I. and McKenzie, J. (2013). *An Inherited Place: Broxmouth Hillfort and the South-East Scottish Iron Age*. Edinburgh: Society of Antiquaries of Scotland.

Armit, I., Schulting, R., Knüsel, C. J. and Shepherd, I. A. G. (2011). Death, decapitation and display? The Bronze and Iron Age human remains from the Sculptor's Cave, Covesea, north-east Scotland. *Proceedings of the Prehistoric Society* 77, 251–78.

Ashbee, P., Bell, M. and Proudfoot, E. (1989). *Wilsford Shaft: Excavations 1960–2*. London: Historic Buildings and Monuments Commission.

Ashmore, P. (2016). *Calanais: Survey and Excavation 1979–88*. Edinburgh: Historic Environment Scotland.

Atkinson, R. (1956). *Stonehenge*. Harmondsworth: Penguin.

Baczkowski, J. (2014). Learning by experience: The flint mines of southern England and their Continental origins. *Oxford Journal of Archaeology* 33, 135–53.

Baczkowski, J. and Holgate, R. (2017). Breaking chalk: The archaeological investigation of Early Neolithic flint mines at Long Down and Harrow Hill, West Sussex, 1984–86. *Sussex Archaeological Collections* 155, 1–29.

Bailey, L., Green, M. and Smith, M. (2013). Keeping the family together: Canada Farm's Bronze Age burials. *Current Archaeology* 279, 20–6.

Bain, K. and Evans, J. (2011). A Late Iron Age and Early Roman enclosure at Meole Brace, Shrewsbury, Shropshire. *Shropshire Archaeology and History* 86, 121–51.

Baldwin, A. and Joy, J. (2017). *A Celtic Feast: The Iron Age Cauldrons from Chiseldon, Wiltshire*. London: British Museum.

Ballin, T. B. (2009). *Archaeological Pitchstone in Northern Britain: Characterisation and Interpretation of an Important Pitchstone Source*. Oxford: Archaeopress.

Ballin, T. B. (2011). *Overhowden and Airhouse, Scottish Borders: Characterisation and Interpretation of Two Spectacular Lithic Assemblages from Sites near to the Overhowden Henge*. Oxford: British Archaeological Reports.

Ballin, T. B. (2016). Rising waters and processes of diversification and unification in material culture. *Journal of Quaternary Science* 32, 329–39.

Ballin-Smith, B. (1994). *Howe: Four Millennia of Orkney Prehistory*. Edinburgh: Society of Antiquaries of Scotland.

Ballin-Smith, B. (2014). *Between Tomb and Cist*. Kirkwall: The Orcadian.

Ballin-Smith, B. (2018). *Life on the Edge: The Neolithic and Bronze Age of Iain Crawford's Udal, North Uist*. Oxford: Archaeopress.

Bamford, H. (1985). *Briar Hill: Excavation 1974–1978*. Northampton: Northampton Development Corporation.

Barber, A. and Hart, J. (2015). *South Wales Gas Pipeline Project Site 503*. Cirencester: Cotswold Archaeology.

Barber, J. (1997). *The Archaeological Investigation of a Prehistoric Landscape: Excavations on Arran 1978–81*. Edinburgh: Scottish Trust for Archaeological for Research.

Barber, M., Field, D. and Topping, P. (1999). *The Neolithic Flint Mines of England*. London: English Heritage.

Barclay, A. and Bayliss, A. (1999). Cursus monuments and the radiocarbon problem. In A. Barclay and J. Harding (eds.), *Pathways and*

Ceremonies: The Cursus Monuments of Britain and Ireland. Oxford: Oxbow, pp. 11–29.

Barclay, A., Gray, M. and Lambrick, G. (1995). *Excavations at the Devil's Quoits, Oxfordshire*. Oxford: Oxford Archaeological Unit.

Barclay, A. and Halpin, C. (1999). *Excavations at Barrow Hills, Radley, Oxfordshire. Vol. 1: The Neolithic and Bronze Age Monument Complex*. Oxford: Oxford Archaeological Unit.

Barclay, G. (1983). Sites of the third millennium BC to the first millennium AD at North Mains, Strathallan, Perthshire. *Proceedings of the Society of Antiquaries of Scotland* 113, 122–281.

Barclay, G. (2001). 'Metropolitan' and 'parochial / core' and 'periphery': A historiography of the Neolithic of Scotland. *Proceedings of the Prehistoric Society* 35, 1–18.

Barclay, G., Brophy, K. and MacGregor, G. (2002). Claish, Stirling: An early Neolithic structure in its context. *Proceedings of the Society of Antiquaries of Scotland* 132, 65–137.

Barclay, G. and Maxwell, G. (1998). *The Cleaven Dyke and Littleour*. Edinburgh: Society of Antiquaries of Scotland.

Barclay, G. and Russell-White, C. (1993). Excavations in the ceremonial complex of the fourth to second millennium BC at Balfarg, Glenrothes, Fife. *Proceedings of the Society of Antiquaries of Scotland* 123, 43–210.

Barnatt, J. and Edmonds, M. (2002). Places apart? Caves and monuments in Neolithic and Earlier Bronze Age Britain. *Cambridge Archaeological Journal* 12, 113–29.

Barnatt, J. and Edmonds, M. (2014). Walking the furrows: A lithic transect across the Peak. *Derbyshire Archaeological Journal* 134, 1–77.

Barrett, J. (1994). *Fragments from Antiquity*. Oxford: Blackwell.

Barrett, J., Bradley, R. and Green, M. (1991). *Landscape, Monuments and Society: The Prehistory of Cranborne Chase*. Cambridge: Cambridge University Press.

Barrett, J. and Fewster, K. (1998). Stonehenge: *Is* the medium the message? *Antiquity* 72, 847–52.

Barrett, J. and Gourlay, R. (1999). An early metal assemblage from Dail na Caraidh, Inverness-shire and its context. *Proceedings of the Society of Antiquaries of Scotland* 129, 161–87.

Barrett, J., Woodward, A. and Freeman, P. (2000). *Cadbury Castle, Somerset: The Later Prehistoric and Early Historic Archaeology*. London: English Heritage.

Batchelor, R., Branch, N., Allison, E., Austin, P., Bishop, B., Elias, S., Green, C. and Young, D. (2014). The timing and causes of the Neolithic elm decline: New evidence from the Lower Thames Valley. *Environmental Archaeology* 19, 263–90.

Bayliss, A. (2015). Quality in Bayesian chronological models in archaeology. *World Archaeology* 47, 677–700.

Bayliss, A., Cartwright, C., Cook, G., Griffiths, S., Madwick, R., Marshall, P. and Reimer, P. (2017a). Rings of fire and Grooved Ware settlement at West Kennet, Wiltshire. In P. Bickle, V. Cummings, D. Hofmann and J. Pollard (eds.), *The Neolithic of Europe*. Oxford: Oxbow, pp. 249–77.

Bayliss, A., Marshall, P., Richards, C. and Whittle, A. (2017b). Islands of history: The Late Neolithic timescape of Orkney. *Antiquity* 91, 1171–89.

Bayliss, A. and Whittle, A. eds. (2007). Histories of the dead: Building chronologies for five southern British long barrows. *Cambridge Archaeological Journal* 17.1 (supplement).

Becker, K. (2013). Transforming identities – new approaches to Bronze Age deposition in Ireland. *Proceedings of the Prehistoric Society* 79, 225–63.

Becker, K. (2014). Token explanations: Rathgall and the interpretation of cremation deposits in later prehistoric Ireland. *Archaeology Ireland* 28, 13–5.

Bedwin, O. (1979). The excavations at Harting Beacon, West Sussex. *Sussex Archaeological Collections* 117, 21–35.

Bell, M. (1990). *Brean Down: Excavations 1983–1987*. London: English Heritage.

Bell, M. (2013). *The Bronze Age in the Severn Estuary*. York: Council for British Archaeology.

Bell, M. and Walker, M. (2004). *Late Quaternary Environmental Change*, 2nd edition. London: Edward Arnold.

Bendrey, R. (2012). From wild horses to domesticated horses – a European perspective. *World Archaeology* 44, 135–57.

Bennett, P., Clarke, P., Hicks, A., Rady, A. and Riddler, I. (2008). *At the Great Crossroads*. Canterbury: Canterbury Archaeological Trust.

Benson, D., Evans, J. and Williams, G. (1990). Excavations at Stackpole Warren, Dyfed. *Proceedings of the Prehistoric Society* 56, 179–245.

Benson, D. and Whittle, A. eds. (2007). *Building Memories: The Neolithic Cotswold Long Barrow at Ascott-under-Wychwood, Oxfordshire*. Oxford: Oxbow.

Bergh, S. (1995). *Landscape of the Monuments*. Stockholm: Riksantiqvarieämbetet.

Bergh, S. (2015). Where worlds meet: Two Irish mountain-top villages. *Il Capitale Culturale: Studies on the Value of Cultural Heritage* 12, 21–44.

Bergh, S. and Hensey, R. (2013). Unpicking the chronology of Carrowmore. *Oxford Journal of Archaeology* 32, 343–66.

Besse, M. and Desideri, J. (2005). La diversidad Campaniforme: Hábitats, sepulturas y céramicas. In M. Rojo-Guerra, R. Garrido-Pena and I. García-Martíinez de Lagrán (eds.), *El Campaniforme en la Península Ibérica y su contexto Europeo*. Valladolid: Universidad de Valladolid, pp. 61–105.

Best, J. and Woodward, A. (2012). Late Bronze Age pottery production: Evidence from a 12th–11th century BC settlement at Tinney's Lane, Sherborne, Dorset. *Proceedings of the Prehistoric Society* 78, 207–57.

Bevan, A., Colledge, S., Fuller, D., Fyfe, R., Shennan, S. and Stevens, C. (2017). Holocene fluctuations in human population demonstrate repeated links to food production and climate. *Proceedings of the National Academy of Sciences*. doi: 10.1073/pnas.1709190114.

Bevan, B., Barnatt, J. and Edmonds, M. (2017). *An Upland Biography: Landscape and Prehistory on Gardom's Edge, Derbyshire*. Oxford: Windgather.

Bishop, B. and Boyer, P. (2014). A Late Bronze Age enclosed settlement at the Oliver Close Estate, Leyton. *Transactions of the London and Middlesex Archaeological Society* 65, 51–102.

Bishop, R. (2013). Did Late Neolithic farming fail or flourish? A Scottish perspective on the evidence for Late Neolithic arable cultivation in the British Isles. *World Archaeology* 47, 34–55.

Blair, J. (2018). *Building Anglo-Saxon England*. Princeton: Princeton University Press.

Boast, R. (1995). Fine pots, pure pots, Beaker pots. In I. Kinnes and G. Varndell (eds.), *Unbaked Urns of Rudely Shape*. Oxford: Oxbow, pp. 69–80.

Bogaard, A., Fraser, R., Heaton, T. H. E., Wallace, M., Vaiglova, P., Charles, M., Jones, G., Evershed, R. P., Styring, A. K., Andersen, N. H., Arbogast, R.-M., Bartosiewicz, L., Gardeisen, A., Kanstrup, M., Maier, U., Marinova, E., Ninov, L., Schäfer, M. and Stephan, E. (2013). Crop manuring and intensive land management by Europe's first farmers. *Proceedings of the National Academy of Sciences* 110, 12589–94.

Bogaard, A. and Jones, G. (2007). Neolithic farming in Britain and central Europe: Contrast or continuity? In A. Whittle and V. Cummings (eds.), *Going Over: The Mesolithic–Neolithic Transition in North-West Europe*. London: British Academy, pp. 357–75.

Bond, D. (1988). *Excavations at North Ring, Mucking*. Norwich: East Anglian Archaeology 43.

Bonsall, C., Macklin, M., Anderson, E. and Payton, R. (2002). Climate change and the adoption of agriculture in north-west Europe. *European Journal of Archaeology* 5(1), 9–23.

Booth, P., Champion, T., Foreman, S., Garwood, P., Glass, H., Munby, J. and Reynolds, A. (2011). *On Track: The Archaeology of High Speed 1 Section 1 in Kent*. Oxford Wessex Archaeology Monograph 4, Oxford: Oxford Archaeology.

Boulter, S. (2012). *Circles and Cemeteries: Excavations at Flixton*. Norwich: East Anglian Archaeology 147.

Bourke, L. (2001). *Crossing the Rubicon: Bronze Age Metalwork from Irish Rivers*. Galway: Department of Archaeology, National University of Ireland, Galway.

Boutoille, L. (2012). The copper smith and the caster: Initial thoughts on Irish stone casting mould hoards. *Ulster Journal of Archaeology* 71, 5–15.

Boutwood, Y. (1998). Prehistoric land boundaries in Lincolnshire and its fringes. In R. Bewley (ed.), *Lincolnshire's Archaeology from the Air*. Lincoln: Society for Lincolnshire Archaeology and History, pp. 29–46.

Bowden, M. (2005). The middle Iron Age on the Marlborough Downs. In G. Brown, D. Field and D. McOmish (eds.), *The Avebury Landscape: Aspects of the Field Archaeology of the Marlborough Downs*. Oxford: Oxbow, pp. 156–63.

Bowen, E. G. (1972). *Britain and the Western Seaways*. London: Thames and Hudson.

Bowen, H. C. (1961). *Ancient Fields*. Wakefield: S. R. Publishers.

Boyer, P., Keith-Lucas, F., Bishop, B., Jarrett, C. and Rayner, L. (2014). Bronze Age and Early Saxon activity at Dagenham Highway. *Transactions of the London and Middlesex Archaeological Society* 65, 103–48.

Brace, S., Diekmann, Y., Booth, T. J., Faltyskova, Z., Rohland, N., Mallick, S., Ferry, M., Michel, M., Oppenheimer, J., Broomandkhoshbacht, N., Stewardson, K., Walsh, S., Kayser, M., Schulting, R., Craig, O., Sheridan, A., Parker Pearson, M., Stringer, C., Reich, D., Thomas, M. G. and Barnes, I. (2018). Population replacement in early Neolithic Britain. doi: 10.1101/267443.

Bradley, J. (2004). Moynagh Lough, Co. Meath, in the Late Bronze Age. In H. Roche, E. Grogan, J. Bradley, J. Coles and B. Raftery (eds.), *From Megaliths to Metals*. Oxford: Oxbow, pp. 91–8.

Bradley, R. (1975). Maumbury Rings, Dorchester: The excavations of 1908–13. *Archaeologia* 105, 1–97.

Bradley, R. (1981). 'Various styles of urn': Cemeteries and settlement in southern England, 1400–1000 BC. In R. Chapman, I. Kinnes and K. Randsborg (eds.), *The Archaeology of Death*. Cambridge: Cambridge University Press, pp. 93–104.

Bradley, R. (1983). The bank barrows and related monuments of Dorset in the light of recent fieldwork. *Proceedings of the Dorset Natural History and Archaeological Society* 105, 15–20.

Bradley, R. (1987). Flint technology and the character of Neolithic settlement. In A. Brown and M. Edmonds (eds.), *Lithic Analysis and Later British Prehistory*. Oxford: British Archaeological Reports, pp. 181–5.

Bradley, R. (1992). The excavation of an oval barrow beside the Abingdon causewayed enclosure, Oxfordshire. *Proceedings of the Prehistoric Society* 58, 127–42.

Bradley, R. (1997). *Rock Art and the Prehistory of Atlantic Europe*. London: Routledge.

Bradley, R. (1998a). *The Significance of Monuments*. London: Routledge.

Bradley, R. (1998b). *The Passage of Arms*, 2nd edition. Oxford: Oxbow.

Bradley, R. (2000a). *The Good Stones*. Edinburgh: Society of Antiquaries of Scotland.

Bradley, R. (2000b). *An Archaeology of Natural Places*. London: Routledge.

Bradley, R. (2005a). *The Moon and the Bonfire*. Edinburgh: Society of Antiquaries of Scotland.

Bradley, R. (2009a). *Image and Audience: Rethinking Prehistoric Art*. Oxford: Oxford University Press.

Bradley, R. (2009b). Missing links and false equations: Architecture and ideas in Bronze Age Scotland and Ireland. In G. Cooney, K. Becker, J. Coles, M. Ryan and S. Sievers (eds.), *Relics of Old Decency: Archaeological Studies of Later Prehistory*. Dublin: Wordwell, pp. 221–32.

Bradley, R. (2011). *Stages and Screens: An Investigation of Four Henge Monuments in Northern and North-Eastern Scotland*. Edinburgh: Society of Antiquaries of Scotland.

Bradley, R. (2012). *The Idea of Order: The Circular Archetype in Prehistoric Europe*. Oxford: Oxford University Press.

Bradley, R. (2013a). Houses of Commons, Houses of Lords: Domestic dwellings and monumental architecture in prehistoric Europe. *Proceedings of the Prehistoric Society* 79, 1–17.

Bradley, R. (2013b). Enclosures, mounds and great houses. In M. O' Sullivan, C. Scarre and M. Doyle (eds.), *Tara from the Past to the Future*. Dublin: Wordwell, pp. 249–55.

Bradley, R. (2014). Where the land ends: Isolation and identity on the western edge of prehistoric Europe. *Complutum* 25(1), 129–37.

Bradley, R. (2016). The dark side of the sky: The orientations of earlier prehistoric monuments in Ireland and Britain. In M. Dowd and R. Hensey (eds.), *The Archaeology of Darkness*. Oxford: Oxbow, pp. 51–61.

Bradley, R. (2017a). *A Geography of Offerings: Deposits of Valuables in the Landscapes of Ancient Europe*. Oxford: Oxbow.

Bradley, R. (2017b). The beach as source and destination. In R. Shaffrey (ed.), *Written in Stone*. St Andrews: Highfield Press, pp. 215–28.

Bradley, R. (2018). Early Bronze Age boat graves in the British Isles. *Analecta Praehistorica Leidensia* 49, 29–34.

Bradley, R. and Chambers, R. (1988). A new study of the cursus complex at Dorchester on Thames. *Oxford Journal of Archaeology* 7, 271–89.

Bradley, R. and Edmonds, M. (1993). *Interpreting the Axe Trade: Production and Exchange in Neolithic Britain*. Cambridge: Cambridge University Press.

Bradley, R. and Ellison, A. (1975). *Rams Hill: A Bronze Age Defended Enclosure and its Landscape*. Oxford: British Archaeological Reports.

Bradley, R., Entwistle, R. and Raymond, F. (1994). *Prehistoric Land Divisions on Salisbury Plain*. London: English Heritage.

Bradley, R. and Fraser, E. (2010). Bronze Age barrows on the heathlands of southern England: construction, forms and interpretations. *Oxford Journal of Archaeology* 29(1), 15–33.

Bradley, R. and Fulford, M. (2008). The chronology of co-axial field systems. In P. Rainbird (ed.), *Monuments in the Landscape*. Stroud: Tempus, pp. 114–22.

Bradley, R., Green, C. and Watson, A. (2018). The placing of Early Bronze Age metalwork deposits: New evidence from Scotland. *Oxford Journal of Archaeology* 37, 137–45.

Bradley, R., Haselgrove, C., Vander Linden, M. and Webley, L. (2016a). *The Later Prehistory of North-West Europe: The Evidence of Development-Led Fieldwork*. Oxford: Oxford University Press.

Bradley, R., Lobb, S., Richards, J. and Robinson, M. (1980). Two Late Bronze Age settlements on the Kennet gravels. *Proceedings of the Prehistoric Society* 46, 217–95.

Bradley, R. and Nimura, C. eds. (2016). *The Use and Reuse of Stone Circles*. Oxford: Oxbow.

Bradley, R., Phillips, T., Richards, C. and Webb, M. (2001). Decorating the houses of the dead: Incised motifs in Orkney chambered tombs. *Cambridge Archaeological Journal* 11, 45–67.

Bradley, R., Rogers, A., Sturt, F. and Watson, A. (2016b). Maritime havens in earlier prehistoric Britain. *Proceedings of the Prehistoric Society* 82, 125–59.

Bradley, R. and Smith, A. (2007). Questions of context: A Greek cup from the River Thames. In C. Gosden, H. Hamerow, P. de Jersey and G. Lock (eds.), *Communities and Connections: Essays in Honour of Barry Cunliffe*. Oxford: Oxford University Press, pp. 30–42.

Bradley, R. and Watson, A. (in press). Langdale and the Neolithic of the north. In E. Hey and P. Frodsham (eds.), *The Neolithic of Northern England*. Oxford: Oxbow.

Bradley, R. and Yates, D. (2007). After Celtic fields: The social organisation of Iron Age agriculture. In C. Haselgrove and R. Pope (eds.), *The Earlier Iron Age in Britain and the Near Continent*. Oxford: Oxbow, pp. 94–102.

Brandt, G., Haak, W., Adler, C. J., Roth, C., Szécsényi-Nagy, A., Karimia, S., Möller-Rieker, S., Meller, H., Ganslmeier, R., Friederich, S., Dresely, V., Nicklisch, N., Pickrell, J. K., Sirocko, F., Reich, D., Cooper, A., Alt, K. W. and Consortium, T. G. (2013). Ancient DNA reveals key stages in the formation of central European mitochondrial genetic diversity. *Science* 342, 257–61.

Bray, P. J. and Pollard, A. M. (2012). A new interpretive approach to the chemistry of copper-alloy objects: Source, recycling and technology. *Antiquity* 86, 853–67.

Brennand, M. and Taylor, M. (2003). The survey and excavation of a Bronze Age timber circle at Holme-next-the Sea, Norfolk, 1998–9. *Proceedings of the Prehistoric Society* 69, 1–84.

Brewster, T. (1981). *The Excavation of Garton and Wetwang Slacks*. London: Royal Commission on the Historical Monuments of England (published in microfiche).

Brewster, T. (1984). *The Excavation of Whitegrounds Barrow, Burythorpe*. Wintringham: East Riding Archaeological Research Committee.

Briard, J. (1965). *Les dépôts bretons du l'âge du bronze Atlantique*. Rennes: Laboratoire d'anthropologie préhistorique de la Faculté des Sciences de Rennes.

Brindley, A. (1999). Irish Grooved Ware. In R. Cleal and A. MacSween (eds.), *Grooved Ware in Britain and Ireland*. Oxford: Oxbow, pp. 23–35.

Brindley, A. (2007). *The Dating of Food Vessel Urns in Ireland*. Galway: Department of Archaeology, National University of Ireland, Galway.

Brindley, A. and Lanting, J. (1990). Radiocarbon dates for Neolithic single burials. *Journal of Irish Archaeology* 5, 1–7.

Brindley, A. and Lanting, J. (1992). Radiocarbon dates from wedge tombs. *Journal of Irish Archaeology* 6, 19–26.

Britnell, B. (1989). The Collfryn hill-slope enclosure, Llansantffrid, Deuddwr, Powys: Excavations 1980–82. *Proceedings of the Prehistoric Society* 55, 89–134.

Britnell, B. and Savory, H. (1984). *Gwernvale and Penywyrlod*. Cardiff: Cambrian Archaeological Association.

Brittain, M., Sharples, N. and Evans, C. (2014). *Excavations at Ham Hill, Stoke-sub-Hamdon 2013*. Cambridge: Cambridge Archaeological Unit.

Brogan, G. and Hodgson, N. (2011). A Bronze Age site at Mountjoy, Durham City. *Archaeologia Aeliana* 40, 41–84.

Broodbank, C. (2013). *The Making of the Middle Sea*. London: Thames and Hudson.

Brophy, K. (2007). From big house to cult house: Early Neolithic timber halls in Scotland. *Proceedings of the Prehistoric Society* 73, 75–96.

Brophy, K. (2016). *Reading between the Lines: The Neolithic Cursus Monuments of Scotland*. Abingdon: Routledge.

Brophy, K. and Barclay, G. (2004). A rectilinear timber structure and post-ring at Carsie Mains, Meikleour, Perthshire. *Tayside and Fife Archaeological Journal* 10, 1–22.

Brossler, A., Early, R. and Allen, C. (2004). *Green Park, Phase 2 Excavations, 1995*. Oxford: Oxford Archaeology.

Brown, F., Howard-Davies, C., Brennand, M., Boyle, A., Evans, T., O'Connor, S., Spence, A., Heawood, R. and Lupton, A. (2007). *The Archaeology of the A1 (M)*. Lancaster: Lancaster Imprint.

Brown, N. (2000). *The Archaeology of Ardleigh, Essex*. Norwich: East Anglian Archaeology 90.

Brown, N. and Medlycott, M. (2013). *The Neolithic and Bronze Age Enclosures at Springfield Lyons, Essex: Excavations 1981–91*. Norwich: East Anglian Archaeology 149.

Brown, T. (1997). Clearances and clearings: Deforestation in Mesolithic / Neolithic Britain. *Oxford Journal of Archaeology* 16, 133–46.

Browne, D. and Hughes, S. eds. (2003). *The Archaeology of the Welsh Uplands*. Aberystwyth: Royal Commission on the Ancient and Historical Monuments of Wales.

Brück, J. (1995). A place for the dead: The role of human remains in late Bronze Age Britain. *Proceedings of the Prehistoric Society* 61, 245–77.

Brück, J. (1999). Houses, life cycles and deposition on Middle Bronze Age settlements in Southern England. *Proceedings of the Prehistoric Society* 65, 145–66.

Brück, J. (2004). Material metaphors: The relational construction of identity in Early Bronze Age burials in Ireland and Britain. *Journal of Social Archaeology* 4, 307–33.

Brudenell, M. and Cooper, A. (2008). Postmiddenism: Depositional histories on later Bronze Age settlements at Broom, Bedfordshire. *Oxford Journal of Archaeology* 27, 15–36.

Brunning, R. (2013). *Somerset's Peatland Archaeology*. Oxford: Oxbow.

Bryant, A. (2011). Iron Age cave use on Mendip: A re-evaluation. In J. Lewis (ed.), *The Archaeology of Mendip*. Oxford: Oxbow, pp. 139–57.

Buckland, P., Parker Pearson, M., Wigley, A. and Girling, M. (2001). Is there anybody out there? A reconsideration of the environmental evidence from the Breiddin hillfort, Powys. *Antiquaries Journal* 81, 51–76.

Buckley, D., Hedges, J. and Brown, N. (2001). Excavations at the Neolithic cursus, Springfield, Essex, 1979–85. *Proceedings of the Prehistoric Society* 67, 101–62.

Buckley, R. and George, S. (2003). Archaeology in Leicestershire and Rutland 2002. *Transactions of the Leicestershire Antiquarian and Historical Society* 77, 125–56.

Budd, P. and Taylor, T. (1995). The faerie smith meets the bronze industry: Magic versus science in the interpretation of prehistoric metal making. *World Archaeology* 27, 133–43.

Burgess, C. (1979). A find from Boyton, Suffolk, and the end of the Bronze Age in Britain and Ireland. In C. Burgess and D. Coombs (eds.), *Bronze Age Hoards: Some Finds Old and New*. Oxford: British Archaeological Reports, pp. 269–82.

Burgess, C. (1992). Discontinuity and dislocation in later prehistoric settlements from Atlantic Europe. In C. Mordant and A. Richard (eds.), *L'habitat et l'occupation du sol à l'Age du Bronze en Europe*. Paris: Editions du Comité des Travaux historiques et scientifiques, pp. 21–40.

Burgess, C. (2001). Note to the Phoenix Press edition. In C. Burgess (ed.), *The Age of Stonehenge*, 2nd edition. London: Phoenix Press, pp. 13–14.

Burl, A. (1988a). Coves: Structural enigmas of the Neolithic. *Wiltshire Archaeological Magazine* 82, 1–18.

Burl, A. (1988b). *Four-Posters: Bronze Age Stone Circles of Western Europe*. Oxford: British Archaeological Reports.

Burl, A. (1994). Long Meg and her Daughters, Little Salkeld. *Transactions of the Cumberland and Westmorland Antiquarian and Archaeological Society* 94, 1–11.

Burl, A. (2000). *The Stone Circles of Britain, Ireland and Brittany*. New Haven, CT: Yale University Press.

Burns, G. and Nolan, J. (2017). *Burren-Marlbank: A Prehistoric Monumental Landscape*. Privately published.

Burrow, S. (1997). *The Neolithic Culture of the Isle of Man: A Study of the Sites and Pottery*. Oxford: British Archaeological Reports.

Burrow, S. (2010a). The formative henge: Speculations drawn from the circular tradition of Wales and adjacent countries. In J. Leary, T. Darvill and D. Field (eds.), *Round Mounds and Monumentality in the British Neolithic and Beyond*. Oxford: Oxbow, pp. 182–96.

Burrow, S. (2010b). Bryn Celli Ddu passage tomb, Anglesey: Alignment, construction, date and ritual. *Proceedings of the Prehistoric Society* 76, 249–70.

Bush, M. (1988). Early Mesolithic disturbance: A force on the landscape. *Journal of Archaeological Science* 15, 45.

Buteaux, S. and Chapman, H. (2009). *Where Rivers Meet*. York: Council for British Archaeology.

Butler, J. (1997). *Dartmoor Atlas of Antiquities*, Vol. 5. Exeter: Devon Books.

Cahill, M. and Sikora, M. eds. (2011). *Breaking Ground, Finding Graves*. Dublin: National Museum of Ireland.

Cahill, M. and Sikora, M. (2014). More evidence from Bronze Age body-piercing. *Archaeology Ireland* 28(2), 30–1.

Callaghan, R. and Scarre, C. (2009). Simulating the western seaways. *Oxford Journal of Archaeology* 28, 357–72.

Callender, J. (1922). Three hoards recently added to the national collection, with notes on the hoard from Duddingston Loch. *Proceedings of the Society of Antiquaries of Scotland* 56, 351–65.

Campbell, E. (2001). Were the Scots Irish? *Antiquity* 75, 285–92.

Campos Carrasco, J. M. and Alvar Ezquerra, J. (2013). *Tarteso: El emporio del metal*. Córdoba: Editorial Almuzara.

Card, N. (2018). The Ness of Brodgar. *Current Archaeology* 335, 20–8.

Card, N., Downes, J., Gibson, J., Murray, D., Sharman, P. and Whalley, T. (2005). *Mine Howe: Fieldwork and Excavation 2000–2005*. Kirkwall: Friends of the Orkney Archaeological Trust.

Card, N., Mainland, I., Timpany, S., Towers, R., Batt, C., Bronk Ramsey, C., Dunbar, E., Reimer, P., Bayliss, A., Marshall, P. and Whittle, A. (2017). To cut a long story short: Formal chronological modelling for the Late Neolithic site of Ness of Brodgar,

Orkney. *European Journal of Archaeology* 21(2), 217–63.

Carew, T., Bishop, B., Meddens, F. and Ridgeway, V. (2006). *Unlocking the Landscape: Archaeological Excavations at Ashford Prison, Middlesex.* London: Pre-Construct Archaeology.

Carlin, N. (2017). Getting into the groove: Exploring the relationship between Grooved Ware and developed passage tombs in Ireland c. 3000–2700 cal BC. *Proceedings of the Prehistoric Society* 83, 155–88.

Carlin, N. and Brück, J. (2012). Searching for the Chalcolithic: Continuity and change in the Irish Final Neolithic/Early Bronze Age. In M. Allen, A. Sheridan and D. McOmish (eds.), *Is There a British Chalcolithic: People, Place and Polity in the Later Third Millennium.* Oxford: Prehistoric Society Research Paper 4, pp. 193–210.

Carlin, N. and Cooney, G. (2017). Transforming our understanding of Neolithic and Chalcolithic society (4000–2200 BC) in Ireland. In M. Stanley (ed.), *Stories of Ireland's Past.* Dublin: National Roads Authority, pp. 23–56.

Carsten, J. and Hugh-Jones, S. (1995). Introduction. In J. Carsten and S. Hugh-Jones (eds.), *About the House: Levi-Strauss and Beyond.* Cambridge: Cambridge University Press, pp. 1–46.

Carter, S., Hunter, F. and Smith, A. (2010). A 5th century BC chariot burial from Newbridge, Edinburgh. *Proceedings of the Prehistoric Society* 76, 31–74.

Carver, M. (2005). *Sutton Hoo: A Seventh-Century Princely Burial Ground and its Context.* London: British Museum Press.

Case, H. (1966). Were the Beaker-people the first metallurgists in Ireland? *Palaeohistoria* 12, 140–77.

Cassidy, L., Mariano, R., Murphy, E., Teasdale, M., Mallory, J. and Hartwell, B. (2016). Neolithic and Bronze Age migration to Ireland and establishment of the insular genome. *Proceedings of the National Academy of Sciences* 113, 368–73.

Caswell, E. and Roberts, B. (2018). Reassessing community cemeteries: Cremation burials in Britain during the Middle Bronze Age (*c.* 1600–1150 BC). *Proceedings of the Prehistoric Society* 84, 329–57.

Chaffrey, G. and Brook, E. (2012). Domesticity in the Neolithic: Excavations at Kingsmead Quarry, Horton, Berkshire. In H. Anderson-Whymark and J. Thomas (eds.), *Regional Perspectives on Neolithic Pit Deposition.* Oxford: Oxbow, pp. 200–15.

Champion, T. (1982). The myth of Iron Age invasions in Ireland. In B. Scott (ed.), *Studies on Early Ireland: Essays in Honour of M. V. Duignan.* Belfast: Association of Young Irish Archaeologists, pp. 39–44.

Champion, T. (2004). Exotic materials in the Early Bronze Age of south eastern Britain. In H. Roche, E. Grogan, J. Bradley, J. Coles and B. Raftery (eds.), *From Megaliths to Metals.* Oxford: Oxbow, pp. 51–5.

Champion, T. (2014). Food technology and culture in the Late Bronze Age of southern Britain: Perforated clay plates of the Lower Thames Valley. *Proceedings of the Prehistoric Society* 80, 279–98.

Chapman, A. (2007). A Bronze Age barrow cemetery and later boundaries, pit alignments and enclosures at Gayhurst Quarry, Newport Pagnell, Buckinghamshire. *Records of Buckinghamshire* 47(2), 83–211.

Chapman, A. (2012). A group of Bronze Age decorated loomweights from Magna Park, Milton Keynes. *Records of Buckinghamshire* 52, 25–32.

Charman, D. (2010). Centennial climate variability in the British Isles during the mid–late Holocene. *Quaternary Sciences Reviews* 29, 1539–54.

Childe, V. G. (1940). *Prehistoric Communities of the British Isles.* London: Chambers.

Childe, V. G. (1942). *What Happened in History.* London: Penguin.

Christie, P. (1978). The excavation of an Iron Age souterrain and settlement at Carn Euny, Sancreed, Cornwall. *Proceedings of the Prehistoric Society* 44, 309–433.

Clare, T. (1978). Recent work on the Shap 'avenue'. *Transactions of the Cumberland and Westmorland Antiquarian and Archaeological Society* 78, 5–15.

Clark, J. G. D. and Fell, C. (1953). The Early Iron Age site at Micklemoor Hill, West Harling, Norfolk, and its pottery. *Proceedings of the Prehistoric Society* 19, 1–40.

Clark, J. G. D., Higgs, E. and Longworth, I. (1960). Excavations at the Neolithic site of Hurst Fen, Mildenhall. *Proceedings of the Prehistoric Society* 26, 202–45.

Clark, J. G. D. (1966). The invasion hypothesis in British archaeology. *Antiquity* 40, 172–89.

Clark, P. ed. (2004). *The Dover Bronze Age Boat.* Swindon: English Heritage.

Clarke, C. and Lavender, N. (2008). *An Early Neolithic Ring Ditch and Middle Bronze Age Cemetery: Excavation and Survey at Brightlingsea, Essex.* Norfolk: East Anglian Archaeology 126.

Clarke, D. L. (1970). *Beaker Pottery of Great Britain and Ireland.* Cambridge: Cambridge University Press.

Cleal, R., Walker, K. and Montague, R. (1995). *Stonehenge in its Landscape: Twentieth Century Excavations.* London: English Heritage.

Cleary, R. (2003). Enclosed Late Bronze Age habitation-site and boundary wall at Lough Gur, Co. Limerick. *Proceedings of the Royal Irish Academy* 103C, 97–189.

Cleary, R. (2015). Excavation at Grange Stone Circle B, Lough Gur, Co Limerick, and a review of the dating. *Journal of Irish Archaeology* 24, 51–77.

Cleary, R. and Kelleher, H. (2011). *Archaeological Excavations at Tullahedy, County Tipperary.* Cork: The Collins Press.

Coles, B. and Coles, J. (1986). *Sweet Track to Glastonbury.* London: Thames and Hudson.

Coles, F. (1892). The motes, forts and doons in the east and west divisions of the Stewartry of Kirkudbright. *Proceedings of the Society of Antiquaries of Scotland* 27, 92–182.

Coles, J. (1987). *Meare Village East.* Exeter: Somerset Levels Project.

Coles, J., Leach, P., Minnitt, S., Tabor, R. and Wilson, A. (1999). A Later Bronze Age shield from South Cadbury, Somerset, England. *Antiquity* 73, 33–48.

Coles, J. and Minnitt, S. (1995). *'Industrious and Fairly Civilized': The Glastonbury Lake Village.* Taunton: Somerset County Museum Service.

Coles, S., Ford, S. and Taylor, A. (2008). An early Neolithic grave and occupation and early Bronze Age hearth on the Thames foreshore at Yabsley Street, Blackwall, London. *Proceedings of the Prehistoric Society* 74, 215–33.

Collard, M., Edinborough, K., Shennan, S. and Thomas, M. G. (2010). Radiocarbon evidence indicates that migrants introduced farming to Britain. *Journal of Archaeological Science* 37, 866–70.

Collis, J. (1973). Burials with weapons in Iron Age Britain. *Germania* 51, 121–33.

Condit, T. (1996). Gold and fulachta fiadh – The Mooghaun find, 1854. *Archaeology Ireland* 10, 20–3.

Conneller, C. (2004). Becoming deer: Corporeal transformations at Star Carr. *Archaeological Dialogues* 11, 37–56.

Conolly, J. ed. (2017). *Costly Signalling. World Archaeology* 49(4).

Cook, M. and Dunbar, L. (2008). *Rituals, Romans and Roundhouses: Excavations at Kintore, Aberdeenshire.* Edinburgh: Scottish Trust for Archaeological Research.

Cook, M., Ellis, C. and Sheridan, A. (2010). Excavations at Upper Largie quarry, Argyll and Bute, Scotland: New light on the prehistoric ritual landscape of the Kilmartin Glen. *Proceedings of the Prehistoric Society* 76, 165–212.

Cooke, N., Brown, F. and Phillpotts, C. (2008). *From Hunter Gatherers to Huntsmen: A History of the Stansted Landscape.* Oxford / Salisbury: Framework Archaeology.

Coombs, D. (1976). Callis Wold round barrow, Humberside. *Antiquity* 50, 130–31.

Cooney, G. (2000). *Landscapes of Neolithic Ireland.* London: Routledge.

Cooney, G. (2006). Newgrange – a view from the platform. *Antiquity* 80, 697–710.

Cooney, G. (2014). The role of cremation in mortuary practices in the Irish Neolithic. In I. Kuijt, S. Quinn and G. Cooney (eds.), *The Archaeology of Cremation in Cultural Context.* Tucson, AZ: University of Arizona Press, pp. 189–206.

Cooney, G. (2017). Pathways for the dead in Middle and Late Bronze Age Ireland. In J. Cerezo-Román, A. Wessmann and H. Williams (eds.), *Cremation and the Archaeology of Death.* Oxford: Oxford University Press, pp. 117–29.

Cooper, A. (2016a). 'Held in place': Round barrows in the later Bronze Age of lowland Britain. *Proceedings of the Prehistoric Society* 82, 291–322.

Cooper, A. (2016b). Other types of meaning: Relationship between round barrows and landscape from 1500 BC–AD 1086. *Cambridge Archaeological Journal* 26, 665–96.

Coppock, T. (1976a). *An Agricultural Atlas of England and Wales*. London: Faber and Faber.

Coppock, T. (1976b). *An Agricultural Atlas of Scotland*. Edinburgh: John Donald.

Corcoran, J., Nicholls, M. and Cowie, R. (2012). The geoarchaeology of past River Thames channels at Syon Park, Brentford. *Transactions of the London and Middlesex Archaeological Society* 63, 1–18.

Corlett, C. (2014). Some cursus monuments in South Leinster. *Archaeology Ireland* 28, 20–5.

Corlett, C. and Potterton, M. eds. (2012). *Life and Death in Iron Age Ireland in the Light of Recent Archaeological Excavations*. Dublin: Wordwell.

Cotter, C. (2012). *The Western Stone Forts Project: Excavations at Dun Aonghasa and Dun Eoghanachta*. Dublin: Wordwell.

Courty, M., Goldberg, P. and Macphail, R. (1989). *Soils and Micromorphology in Archaeology*. Cambridge: Cambridge University Press.

Cowie, T. (2004). Special places for special axes? Early Bronze Age metalwork from Scotland in its landscape setting. In I. Shepherd and G. Barclay (eds.), *Scotland in Ancient Europe*. Edinburgh: Society of Antiquaries of Scotland, pp. 247–61.

Cowie, T. (2008). Mennock Water, near Wanlockhead. *Discovery and Excavation in Scotland* 9, 54.

Cowie, T. and Shepherd, I. (2003). The Bronze Age. In K. Edwards and I. Ralston (eds.), *Scotland after the Ice Age*. Edinburgh: Edinburgh University Press, pp. 151–68.

Craig, O., Shilito, L. M., Albarella, U., Vuiner-Daniels, S., Chan, B., Cleal, R., Ixer, R., Jay, M., Marshall, P., Simmons, E., Wright, E. and Parker Pearson, M. (2015). Feeding Stonehenge: Cuisine and consumption at the Late Neolithic site of Durrington Walls. *Antiquity* 89, 1096–109.

Cramp, L., Jones, J., Sheridan, A., Smyth, J., Whelton, H. and Mulville, J. (2014). Immediate replacement of fishing with dairying by the first farmers of the northeast Atlantic archipelago. *Proceedings of the Royal Society B* 281, 1–8.

Creighton, J. (2000). *Coins and Power in late Iron Age Britain*. Cambridge: Cambridge University Press.

Creighton, J. (2006). *Britannia: The Creation of a Roman Province*. Abingdon: Routledge.

Cromarty, A. M., Barclay, A., Lambrick, G. and Robinson, M. (2005). *Late Bronze Age Ritual and Habitation on a Thames Eyot at Whitecross Farm, Wallingford*. Oxford: Oxford Archaeology.

Crone, A. (1993). Excavation and survey of sub-peat features of Neolithic, Bronze Age and Iron Age date at Bharpa Carnish, North Uist, Scotland. *Proceedings of the Prehistoric Society* 59, 361–82.

Crone, A. (2007). God-dollies? An assemblage of peg-like objects from the Pict's Knowe. In C. Green (compiler), *Archaeology from the Wetlands: Recent Perspectives*. Edinburgh: Society of Antiquaries of Scotland, pp. 339–42.

Cummings, V. (2017). *The Neolithic of Britain and Ireland*. Abingdon: Routledge.

Cummings, V. and Fowler, C. (2007). *From Cairn to Cemetery: An Archaeological Investigation of the Chambered Cairns and Early Bronze Age Mortuary Deposits at Cairnderry and Bargrennan White Cairn, South-West Scotland*. Oxford: Archaeopress.

Cummings, V. and Richards, C. (2014). How to build a dolmen: Exploring Neolithic construction at Garn Turne. *Current Archaeology* 286, 32–5.

Cummings, V. and Richards, C. (2016). A monumental task: Building the dolmens of Britain and Ireland. In L. Laporte and C. Scarre (eds.), *The Megalithic Architectures of Europe*. Oxford: Oxbow, pp. 49–58.

Cummings, V. and Whittle, A. (2004). *Places of Special Virtue: Megaliths in the Neolithic Landscape of Wales*. Oxford: Oxbow.

Cunliffe, B. (1987). *Hengistbury Head, Dorset*, Vol. 1. Oxford: Oxford University Committee for Archaeology.

Cunliffe, B. (1988). *Mount Batten, Plymouth: A Prehistoric and Roman Port*. Oxford: Oxford University Committee for Archaeology.

Cunliffe, B. (1995). *Danebury*, Vol. 6. London: Council for British Archaeology.

Cunliffe, B. (2001a). *Facing the Ocean: The Atlantic and Its Peoples 8000 BC–AD 1500*. Oxford: Oxford University Press.

Cunliffe, B. (2001b). *The Extraordinary Voyage of Pytheas the Greek*. London: Allen Lane.

Cunliffe, B. (2005). *Iron Age Communities in Britain*, 4th edition. Abingdon: Routledge.

Cunliffe, B. (2013). *Britain Begins*. Oxford: Oxford University Press.

Cunliffe, B. (2015). Facing the Northern Ocean: The British Late Bronze and Iron Ages in their continental perspective. In F. Hunter and I. Ralston (eds.), *Scotland in Later Prehistoric Europe*. Edinburgh: Society of Antiquaries of Scotland, pp. 5–17.

Cunliffe, B. (2017). *On the Ocean: The Mediterranean and the Atlantic from Prehistory to AD 1500*. Oxford: Oxford University Press.

Cunliffe, B. (2018). *The Ancient Celts*, 2nd edition. Oxford: Oxford University Press.

Cunliffe, B. and Poole, C. (1991). *Danebury: An Iron Age Hillfort in Hampshire*, Vol. 4. London: Council for British Archaeology.

Cunnington, M. (1923). *Early Iron Age Inhabited Site at All Cannings Cross Farm, Wiltshire*. Devizes: George Simpson.

Dacre, M. and Ellison, A. (1981). A Bronze Age urn cemetery at Kimpton, Hampshire. *Proceedings of the Prehistoric Society* 47, 147–203.

Dalland, M. (1999). Sand Fiold: The excavation of an exceptional cist in Orkney. *Proceedings of the Prehistoric Society* 65, 373–413.

Danaher, E. ed. (2007). *Monumental Beginnings: The Archaeology of the N4 Sligo Inner Relief Road*. Dublin: National Roads Authority.

Daniel, P. (2009). *Archaeological Excavations at Pode Hole Quarry*. Oxford: British Archaeological Reports.

Dark, P. and Gent, H. (2001). Pest and diseases of prehistoric crops: A yield 'honeymoon' for early grain crops in Europe? *Oxford Journal of Archaeology* 20, 59–78.

Darvill, T. (1986). *The Archaeology of the Uplands*. London: Council for British Archaeology.

Darvill, T. (1996). Neolithic buildings in England, Wales and the Isle of Man. In T. Darvill and J. Thomas (eds.), *Neolithic Houses in Northwest Europe and Beyond*. Oxford: Oxbow, pp. 77–111.

Darvill, T. (2004). *Long Barrows of the Cotswolds and Surrounding Areas*. Stroud: Tempus.

Darvill, T. (2010). *Prehistoric Britain*, 2nd edition. Abingdon: Routledge.

Darvill, T. (2011). *Prehistoric Gloucestershire*, 2nd edition. Stroud: Amberley.

Darvill, T. (2016). Houses of the Holy: Architecture and meaning in the structure of Stonehenge, Wiltshire, UK. *Time and Mind* 9, 89–121.

Darvill, T., Marshall, P., Parker Pearson, M. and Wainwright, G. (2012). Stonehenge remodelled. *Antiquity* 86, 1021–40.

David, A. (2007). *Palaeolithic and Mesolithic Settlement in Wales with Special Reference to Dyfed*. Oxford: British Archaeological Reports.

David, A., Cole, M., Horsley, T., Linford, N., Linford, P. and Martin, L. (2004). A rival to Stonehenge? Geophysical survey at Stanton Drew, England. *Antiquity* 78, 341–58.

Davidson, J. and Henshall, A. (1989). *The Chambered Cairns of Orkney*. Edinburgh: Edinburgh University Press.

Davies, J., Gregory, T., Lawson, A., Pickett, R. and Rogerson, A. (1991). *The Hillforts of Norfolk*. Norwich: East Anglian Archaeology 54.

Davies, M. (1946). The diffusion and distribution pattern of the megalithic monuments of the Irish Sea and North Channel coastlands. *Antiquaries Journal* 26, 38–60.

Davis, O. (2013). Re-interpreting the Danebury assemblage: Houses, households and communities. *Proceedings of the Prehistoric Society* 79, 353–75.

De Valera, R. (1960). The court tombs of Ireland. *Proceedings of the Royal Irish Academy* 60C, 9–140.

Debert, J. (2016). When artefacts can't speak: Towards a new understanding of British Early Neolithic timber structures. In J. Debert, M. Larsson and J. Thomas (eds.), *In Dialogue: Tradition and Interaction in the Mesolithic–Neolithic Transition*. Oxford: British Archaeological Reports, pp. 19–26.

Delaney, S. (2016). Bishopsland – settlement above the Golden Falls. *Archaeology Ireland* 30, 16–20.

Dent, J. (1982). Cemeteries and settlement patterns of the Iron Age on the Yorkshire Wolds. *Proceedings of the Prehistoric Society* 48, 437–57.

Dent, J. (1993). Weapons, wounds and war in the Iron Age. *Archaeological Journal* 140, 437–57.

Dingwall, K. ed. (in press). *'The Land was Forever': 15,000 years in North-East Scotland*. Oxford: Oxbow.

Dixon, P. (1994). *Crickley Hill: The Hillfort Defences*. Nottingham: Nottingham University Department of Archaeology.

Dockrill, S., Bond, J., Turner, V., Brown, L., Bashford, D., Cussans, J. and Nicholson, R. (2015). *Excavations at Old Scatness, Shetland*, Vol. 2. Lerwick: Shetland Heritage Publications.

Dolan, B. (2016). Making iron in the Irish midlands: The social and symbolic role of Iron Age ironworkers. *Journal of Irish Archaeology* 25, 31–48.

Dowd, M. (2015). *The Archaeology of Caves in Ireland*. Oxford: Oxbow.

Downes, J. and Lamb, R. (2000). *Prehistoric Houses at Sunburgh in Shetland*. Oxford: Oxbow.

Drisse, M. (2017). Polissoirs: Social memory in the Avebury landscape. In R. Shaffrey (ed.), *Written in Stone*. St Andrews: Highfield Press, pp. 275–302.

Dronfield, J. (1995). Subjective vision and the sources of Irish megalithic art. *Antiquity* 69, 539–49.

Duffy, P. (2007). Excavations at Dunure Road, Ayrshire: A Bronze Age cist cemetery and standing stone. *Proceedings of the Society of Antiquaries of Scotland* 137, 69–116.

Dunwell, A. and Ralston, I. (2008). *Archaeology and Early History of Angus*. Stroud: Tempus.

Durden, T. (1995). The production of specialised flintwork in the later Neolithic: A case study from the Yorkshire Wolds. *Proceedings of the Prehistoric Society* 61, 409–32.

Earle, T. (1991). Property rights and the evolution of chiefdoms. In T. Earle (ed.), *Chiefdoms: Power, Economy and Ideology*. Cambridge: Cambridge University Press, pp. 71–99.

Earle, T., Ling, J., Uhnér, C., Stos-Gales, Z. and Melheim, L. (2015). The political economy and metal trade in Bronze Age Europe: Understanding regional variability in terms of comparative advantage and articulations. *European Journal of Archaeology* 18, 633–57.

Edwards, K. (1998). Detection of human impact on the natural environment. In J. Bayley (ed.), *Science in Archaeology: An Agenda for the Future*. London: English Heritage, pp. 69–88.

Edwards, N. (1990). *The Archaeology of Early Medieval Ireland*. London: Routledge.

Ehrenberg, M. (1989). The interpretation of regional variability in British and Irish metalwork. In H.-Å. Nordström and A. Knape (eds.), *Bronze Age Studies*. Stockholm: Statens Historiska Museum, pp. 77–88.

Ellis, C. (2004). *A Prehistoric Ritual Complex at Eynesbury, Cambridgeshire*. Norwich: East Anglian Archaeology Occasional Paper 17.

Ellis, C. and Rawlings, M. (2001). Excavations at Balksbury Camp, Andover, 1995–97. *Proceedings of the Hampshire Field Club and Archaeological Society* 56, 21–94.

Ellis, P. (1989). Norton Fitzwarren hillfort: A report on the excavations by Nancy and Philip Langmaid between 1968 and 1974. *Proceedings of the Somerset Archaeological and Natural History Society* 133, 1–74.

Ellis, P. ed. (1993). *Beeston Castle, Cheshire*. London: English Heritage.

Ellison, A. (1978). The Bronze Age of Sussex. In P. Drewett (ed.), *Archaeology in Sussex to AD 1500*. London: Council for British Archaeology, pp. 30–7.

English, J. (2013). *Pattern and Progress: Field Systems of the Second and First Millennia BC in Southern Britain*. Oxford: British Archaeological Reports.

Eogan, G. (1986). *Knowth and the Passage Tombs of Ireland*. London: Thames and Hudson.

Eogan, G. (1994a). *Excavations at Knowth, 1*. Dublin: Royal Irish Academy.

Eogan, G. (1994b). *The Accomplished Art: Gold and Gold-Working in Britain and Ireland during the Bronze Age*. Oxford: Oxbow.

Eogan, G. (1997). Overlays and underlays: Aspects of megalithic art succession at Brugh na

Bóinne, Ireland. In J. M. Bello Diéguez (ed.), *III Coloquio internacional de arte megalítico: Actas.* Corunna: Brigantium 10, pp. 217–34.

Eogan, G. (2009). Dowth passage tomb: Notes on possible structural sequence. *Riocht na Midhe* 20, 1–4.

Eogan, G. and Cleary, K. (2017). *The Passage Tomb Archaeology of the Great Mound at Knowth.* Dublin: Royal Irish Academy.

Eogan, G. and Roche, H. (1997). *Excavations at Knowth, 2.* Dublin: Royal Irish Academy.

Eogan, J. (2004). The construction of funerary mounds in the Irish Early Bronze Age: A review of the evidence. In H. Roche, E. Grogan, J. Bradley, J. Coles and B. Raftery (eds.), *From Megaliths to Metals.* Oxford: Oxbow, pp. 56–60.

Eriksen, P. (2008). The great mound of Newgrange: An Irish multi-period mound spanning the megalithic tomb period to the early Bronze Age. *Acta Archaeologica* 79, 250–73.

Evans, C. (2002). Metalwork and the 'cold clay-lands': Pre-Iron Age occupation on the Isle of Ely. In T. Lane and J. Coles (eds.), *Through Wet and Dry.* Sleaford: Heritage Trust of Lincolnshire, pp. 33–53.

Evans, C. (2013). Delivering bodies unto waters: A Late Bronze Age midden settlement and Iron Age ritual complex in the Fens. *Antiquaries Journal* 93, 55–79.

Evans, C. (2016). *Twice-crossed River: Prehistoric and Palaeoenvironmental Investigations at Barleycroft Farm / Over, Cambridgeshire.* Cambridge: McDonald Institute for Archaeological Research.

Evans, C., Appleby, G. and Lucy, S. (2015). *Lives in land – Mucking Excavations by Margaret and Tom Jones 1965–78: Prehistory, Context and Summary.* Cambridge: Cambridge Archaeological Unit.

Evans, C. and Hodder, I. (2005). *The Haddenham Project. Vol. 1: A Woodland Archaeology.* Cambridge: McDonald Institute for Archaeological Research.

Evans, C. and Hodder, I. (2006). *The Haddenham Project. Vol. 2: Marshland Communities and Cultural Landscapes from the Bronze Age to the Present Day.* Cambridge: McDonald Institute for Archaeological Research.

Evans, C. and Knight, M. (1996). An Ouse-side longhouse – Barleycroft Farm, Cambridgeshire. *Past* 23, 1–2.

Evans, C. and Knight, M. (2000a). Henge to house – Post-circles in a Neolithic and Bronze Age landscape at King's Dyke West, Whittlesey, Cambridgeshire. *Past* 34, 3–4.

Evans, C. and Knight, M. (2000b). A Fenland delta: Later prehistoric land-use in the lower Ouse reaches. In M. Dawson (ed.), *Prehistoric, Roman and Post-Roman Landscapes of the Great Ouse Valley.* York: Council for British Archaeology, pp. 89–106.

Evans, C., Pollard, J. and Knight, M. (1999). Life in woods: Tree-throws, 'settlement' and forest cognition. *Oxford Journal of Archaeology* 18, 241–54.

Evans, E. E. (1953). *Lyles Hill: A Late Neolithic Site in County Antrim.* Belfast: HMSO.

Evans, E. E. (1973). *The Personality of Ireland.* Cambridge: Cambridge University Press.

Fahy, E. (1959). A hut and cooking-place at Drombeg, Co. Cork. *Journal of the Cork Historical and Archaeological Society* 65, 1–17.

Fahy, E. (1960). A recumbent stone circle at Drombeg, Co. Cork. *Journal of the Cork Historical and Archaeological Society* 64, 1–27.

Falkner, N. (2004). Testwood Bridge. *Current Archaeology* 190, 428–9.

Farley, M. and Jones, G. (2012). *Iron Age Ritual: A Hillfort and Evidence for a Minster at Aylesbury, Buckinghamshire.* Oxford: Oxbow.

Fell, C. and Davis, R. V. (1988). The petrological identifications of stone implements from Cumbria. In T. Clough and W. Cummins (eds.), *Stone Axe Studies*, Vol. 2. London: Council for British Archaeology, pp. 71–7.

Fenton-Thomas, C. (2003). *Late Prehistoric and Early Historic Landscapes on the Yorkshire Chalk.* Oxford: British Archaeological Reports.

Fenton-Thomas, C. (2009). *A Place by the Sea.* York: On-Site Archaeology.

Fenton-Thomas, C. (2011). *Where Sky and Yorkshire and Water Meet: The Story of the*

Melton Landscape from Prehistory to the Present. York: On-Site Archaeology Monograph 2.

Fenwick, J. (2017). A reappraisal of the archaeological remains in the vicinity of the great passage tomb and manorial village at Dowth, Brú na Bóinne, Co. Meath. *Journal of Irish Archaeology* 26, 143–66.

Field, D. (2001). Place and memory in Bronze Age Wessex. In J. Brück (ed.), *Bronze Age Landscapes: Tradition and Transformation.* Oxford: Oxbow, pp. 157–65.

Field, N. and Parker Pearson, M. (2003). *Fiskerton: An Iron Age Timber Causeway with Iron Age and Roman Votive Offerings.* Oxford: Oxbow.

Finn, N. (2011). *Bronze Age Ceremonial Enclosures and Cremation Cemetery at Eye Kettleby, Leicestershire.* Leicester: University of Leicester Archaeological Services.

Fischer, A. (2002). Food for feasting? In A. Fischer and K. Kristiansen (eds.), *The Neolithisation of Denmark.* Sheffield: J. R. Collis, pp. 343–93.

Fitzgerald, M. (2006). Archaeological discoveries on the N2 Finglas – Ashbourne road scheme. *Seanda* 1, 40–3.

Fitzpatrick, A. (1989). The submission of the Orkney islands to Claudius: New evidence? *Scottish Archaeological Review* 6, 24–33.

Fitzpatrick, A. (2005). A sacred circle on Boscombe Down. *Current Archaeology* 195, 106–7.

Fitzpatrick, A. (2011). *The Amesbury Archer and the Boscombe Bowmen.* Salisbury: Wessex Archaeology.

Fleming, A. (2008). *The Dartmoor Reaves: Investigating Prehistoric Land Divisions*, 2nd edition. Oxford: Windgather.

Fowler, C. (2004). *The Archaeology of Personhood: An Anthropological Approach.* Abingdon: Routledge.

Fowler, C. (2013). *The Emergent Past.* Oxford: Oxford University Press.

Fowler, P. J. (2000). *Landscape Plotted and Pieced.* London: Society of Antiquaries.

Fox, C. (1932). *The Personality of Britain: Its Influence on Inhabitant and Invader in Prehistoric and Early Historic Times.* Cardiff: National Museum of Wales.

Fox, C. F. (1930). The Bronze Age pit at Swanwick, Hants: Further finds. *Antiquaries Journal* 10, 30–3.

Fredengren, C. (2002). *Crannogs.* Bray: Wordwell.

French, C. (2004). Evaluation, survey and excavation at Wandlebury ringwork. *Proceedings of the Cambridgeshire Antiquarian Society* 93, 15–66.

French, C., Lewis, H., Allen, M., Green, M., Scaife, R. and Gardiner, J. (2007). *Prehistoric Landscape Development and Human Impact in the Upper Allen Valley, Cranborne Chase, Dorset.* Cambridge: McDonald Institute for Archaeological Research.

French, C. and Pryor, F. (2005). *Archaeology and Environment of the Etton Landscape.* Norwich: East Anglian Archaeology 109.

Frieman, C. (2012). Going to pieces at the funeral: Completeness and complexity in early Bronze Age 'jet necklace' assemblages. *Journal of Social Archaeology* 12, 334–55.

Fyfe, R., Brück, J., Lewis, H., Johnston, R. and Wickstead, H. (2008). Historical context and chronology of Bronze Age land enclosure on Dartmoor, UK. *Journal of Archaeological Science* 35, 2250–61.

Fyfe, R., Twiddle, C., Sugita, S., Gaillard, M.-J., Barratt, P., Caseldine, C., Dodson, J., Edwards, K., Farrell, M., Froyd, C., Grant, M., Huckerby, E., Innes, J., Shaw, H. and Waller, M. (2013). The Holocene vegetation cover of Britain and Ireland: Overcoming problems of scale and discovering patterns of openness. *Quaternary Science Reviews* 73, 132–48.

Gaffney, V., Thomson, K. and Fitch, S. (2007). *Mapping Doggerland: The Mesolithic Landscapes of the Southern North Sea.* Oxford: Archaeopress.

Gardiner, J. (1987). Excavations at Crouch Hill 1921, 1969. In B. Cunliffe (ed.), *Hengistbury Head, Dorset*, Vol. 1. Oxford: Oxford University Committee for Archaeology, pp. 40–7.

Gardiner, J. (1989). Flint procurement and Neolithic axe production on the South Downs: A reassessment. *Oxford Journal of Archaeology* 9, 119–40.

Gardiner, J. (2008). On the production of discoidal knives and changing patterns of specialist flint production on the South Downs, England. *Analecta Praehistorica Leidensia* 40, 235–46.

Garner, D. (2016). *Hillforts of the Cheshire Ridge.* Oxford: Archaeopress.

Garrow, D. (2007). Placing pits: Landscape, occupation and depositional practice during the Neolithic in East Anglia. *Proceedings of the Prehistoric Society* 73, 1–24.

Garrow, D., Beadsmoore, E. and Knight, M. (2005). Pit clusters and the temporality of occupation: An earlier Neolithic site at Kilverstone, Thetford, Norfolk. *Proceedings of the Prehistoric Society* 71, 139–57.

Garrow, D. and Gosden, C. (2012). *Technologies of Enchantment? Exploring Celtic Art 400 BC to AD 100.* Oxford: Oxford University Press.

Garrow, D., Gosden, C., Hill, J. D. and Bronk Ramsey, C. (2009). Dating Celtic art: A major radiocarbon dating programme of Iron Age and early Roman metalwork in Britain. *Archaeological Journal* 166, 79–123.

Garrow, D., Meadows, J., Evans, C. and Tabor, J. (2014). Dating the dead: A high-resolution radiocarbon chronology of burial within an Early Bronze Age barrow cemetery at Over, Cambridgeshire. *Proceedings of the Prehistoric Society* 80, 207–36.

Garrow, D. and Sturt, F. (2017). *Neolithic Stepping Stones: Excavation and Survey within the Western Seaways of Britain, 2008–2014.* Oxford: Oxbow.

Garton, D. (2017). Prior to peat: Assessing the hiatus between Mesolithic activity and peat inception on the South Pennine Moors. *Archaeological Journal* 174, 281–334.

Garwood, P. (1999). Grooved Ware in Southern Britain: Chronology and implications. In R. Cleal and A. MacSween (eds.), *Grooved Ware in Britain and Ireland.* Oxford: Oxbow, pp. 143–76.

Garwood, P. (2003). Round barrows and funerary traditions in Late Neolithic and Bronze Sussex. In D. Rudling (ed.) *The Archaeology of Sussex to AD 2000.* Great Dunham: Heritage Marketing and Publications, pp. 47–68.

Garwood, P. (2007). Before the hills in order stood: Chronology, time and history in the interpretation of Early Bronze Age round barrows. In J. Last (ed.), *Beyond the Grave: New Perspectives on Barrows.* Oxford: Oxbow, pp. 30–52.

Gelling, P. (1972). The hill fort on South Barrule and its position in the Manx Iron Age. In C. Burgess and F. Lynch (eds.), *Prehistoric Man in Wales and the West.* Bath: Adams and Dart, pp. 285–92.

Germany, M. (2007). *Neolithic and Bronze Age Monuments and Middle Iron Age Settlement at Lodge Farm, St Osyith, Essex.* Norwich: East Anglian Archaeology 117.

Gibson, A. (1982). *Beaker Domestic Sites.* Oxford: British Archaeological Reports.

Gibson, A. (1999). *The Walton Basin Project: Excavation and Survey in the Prehistoric Landscape.* York: Council for British Archaeology.

Gibson, A. (2005). *Stonehenge and Timber Circles.* Stroud: Tempus.

Gibson, A. (2010a). Dating Balbirnie: Recent radiocarbon dates from the stone circle at Balbirnie, Fife, and a review of its place in the Balfarg / Balbirnie site sequence. *Proceedings of the Society of Antiquaries of Scotland* 140, 51–77.

Gibson, A. (2010b). Excavation and survey at Dyffryn Lane henge complex, Powys, and a reconsideration of the dating of henges. *Proceedings of the Prehistoric Society* 76, 213–48.

Gibson, A. (2016). Who were these people? In K. Brophy, G. MacGregor and I. Ralston (eds.), *The Neolithic of Mainland Scotland.* Edinburgh: Edinburgh University Press, pp. 57–73.

Gibson, A. (2017). Excavation of a Neolithic house at Yarnbury, near Grassington, North Yorkshire. *Proceedings of the Prehistoric Society* 83, 189–212.

Gibson, A. (2018). Llandegia A – sanctuary or settlement? *Archaeologia Cambrensis* 67, 95–108.

Gibson, A. and Bayliss, A. (2009). Recent research at Duggleby Howe, North Yorkshire. *Archaeological Journal* 166, 39–78.

Gibson, A. and Bayliss, A. (2010). Recent work on the round barrows of the upper Great Wolds Valley, Yorkshire. In J. Leary, T. Darvill and D. Field (eds.), *Round Barrows and Monumentality in the British Neolithic and Beyond.* Oxford: Oxbow, pp. 72–107.

Gibson, A. and McCormick, A. (1985). Archaeology at Grendon Quarry. *Northamptonshire Archaeology* 125, 292–67.

Gibson, C. (2013). Beakers into bronze: Tracing connections between Western Iberia and the British Isles, 2500 BC–800 BC. In J. Koch and B. Cunliffe (eds.), *Celtic from the West 2.* Oxford: Oxbow, pp. 71–99.

Gibson, C. (2016). Closed for business or cultural changes? Tracing the reuse and final blocking of megalithic tombs during the Beaker period. In J. Koch and B. Cunliffe (eds.), *Celtic from the West 3.* Oxford: Oxbow, pp. 83–110.

Gibson, D. and Knight, M. (2006). *Bradley Fen Excavations, Whittlesey, Cambridgeshire: An Assessment Report.* Cambridge: Cambridge Archaeological Unit.

Gibson, D., Knight, M., Davenport, S. and Wakefield, C. (2016). The Must Farm inferno. *Current Archaeology* 312, 12–18.

Gibson, D., Knight, M. and Murrell, K. (2012). Waterworld: Must Farm's Bronze Age boats. *Current Archaeology* 263, 12–9.

Giles, M. (2007). Making metals and forging relations: Ironworking in the British Iron Age. *Oxford Journal of Archaeology* 26, 395–413.

Giles, M. (2012). *A Forged Glamour: Landscape, Identity and Material Culture in the Iron Age.* Oxford: Windgather Press.

Giles, M. (2017). The beauty of the chalk warrior. *European Journal of Archaeology* 20, 59–64.

Gillings, M., Pollard, J., Wheatley, D. and Peterson, R. (2008). *Landscape of the Megaliths: Excavation and Fieldwork on the Avebury Monuments, 1997–2003.* Oxford: Oxbow.

Gilmour, N., Horlock, S., Mortimer, R. and Tremlett, S. (2014). Middle Bronze Age enclosures in the Norfolk Broads. *Proceedings of the Prehistoric Society* 80, 141–57.

Ginn, V. (2016). *Mapping Society: Settlement Studies in Later Bronze Age Ireland.* Oxford: Archaeopress.

Ginn, V. and Rathbone, S. (2012). *Corrstown: A Coastal Community. Excavations of a Bronze Age Village in Northern Ireland.* Oxford: Oxbow.

Girling, M. and Greig, J. (1985). A first fossil record for Scolytus scolytus (F.) (Elm Bark beetle): Its occurrence in elm decline deposits from London and its implications for the Neolithic elm decline. *Journal of Archaeological Science* 12, 347–51.

Gleeson, P. (2015). Kingdoms, communities and Óenach: Irish assembly practices in their Northwest European context. *Journal of the North Atlantic* 8, 33–51.

Green, H. S. (1974). Early Bronze Age burial, territory and population in Milton Keynes, Buckinghamshire, and the Great Ouse Valley. *Archaeological Journal* 131, 75–139.

Green, M. (2000). *A Landscape Revealed: 10,000 years on a Chalkland Farm.* Stroud: Tempus.

Greenwell, W. (1877). *British Barrows.* Oxford: Clarendon Press.

Griffin, S., Dalwood, H., Hurst, D. and Pearson, E. (2002). Excavations at the Perdiswell Park and Ride, Droitwich Road, Worcester. *Transactions of the Worcestershire Archaeological Society* 18, 1–24.

Griffith, F. and Wilkes, E. (2006). The land named from the sea? Coastal archaeology and place-names of Bigbury Bay, Devon. *Archaeological Journal* 163, 67–91.

Griffiths, S. (2014). Points in time: The Mesolithic–Neolithic transition and the chronology of late rod microliths in Britain. *Oxford Journal of Archaeology* 33, 221–43.

Grogan, E. (2005). *The North Munster Project,* Vol. 1. Dublin: Wordwell.

Groves, J. A., Waller, M. P., Grant, M. J. and Schofield, J. E. (2012). Long-term development of a cultural landscape: The origins and dynamics of lowland heathland in southern England. *Vegetation History and Archaeobotany* 21, 453–70.

Guerra-Doce, E. (2006). Exploring the significance of Beaker pottery through residue analyses. *Oxford Journal of Archaeology* 25, 247–59.

Guilbert, G. (1981). Hill-fort functions and populations: A sceptical view. In G. Guilbert (ed.), *Hill-Fort Studies.* Leicester: Leicester University Press, pp. 104–21.

Guttmann, E. (2005). Midden cultivation in prehistoric Britain: Arable crops in gardens. *World Archaeology* 37, 224–39.

Guttmann, E. and Last, J. (2000). A Late Bronze Age landscape at South Hornchurch, Essex. *Proceedings of the Prehistoric Society* 66, 319–59.

Haak, W., Lazaridis, I., Patterson, N., Rohland, N., Mallick, S., Llamas, B., Brandt, G.,

Nordenfelt, S., Harney, E., Stewardson, K., Fu, Q., Mittnik, A., Bánffy, E., Economou, C., Francken, M., Friederich, S., Garrido Pena, R., Hallgren, F., Khartanovich, V., Khokhlov, A., Kunst, M., Kuznetsov, P., Meller, H., Mochalov, O., Moiseyev, V., Nicklisch, N., Pichler, S. L., Risch, R., Rojo Guerra, M. A., Roth, C., Szécsényi-Nagy, A., Wahl, J., Meyer, M., Krause, J., Brown, D., Anthony, D., Cooper, A., Alt, K. W. and Reich, D. (2015). Massive migration from the steppe was a source for Indo-European languages in Europe. *Nature* 522, 207–11.

Haggarty, A. (1991). Machrie Moor, Arran: Recent excavations of two stone circles. *Proceedings of the Society of Antiquaries of Scotland* 58, 51–94.

Hale, D., Platell, A. and Millard, C. A. (2009). A Late Neolithic palisaded enclosure at Marne Barracks, Catterick, North Yorkshire. *Proceedings of the Prehistoric Society* 75, 265–304.

Halkon, P. (2011). Iron, landscape and power in Iron Age East Yorkshire. *Archaeological Journal* 168, 133–65.

Hall, D. and Coles, J. (1994). *Fenland Survey: An Essay in Landscape and Persistence*. London: English Heritage.

Halliday, S. (1999). Hut circle settlements in the Scottish landscape. *Northern Archaeology* 18, 49–65.

Hansen, S. (2016). 'Arm und Reich' in der Bronzezeit Europas. In H. Meller, H. Hahn, R. Jung and R. Risch (eds.), *Arm und Reich – Zur Resourceenverteilung in prähistorischen Gesellschaften*. Halle: Landesmuseum for Vorgeschichte, pp. 197–218.

Harbison, P. (1972). Wooden and stone chevaux-de-frise in Central and Western Europe. *Proceedings of the Prehistoric Society* 37, 195–225.

Harding, A., Ostoja-Zagorski, J., Healey, E., Turner, J. and Alexander, M. (1994). Prehistoric and Early Medieval activity on Danby Rigg, North Yorkshire. *Archaeological Journal* 151, 16–97.

Harding, D. (1987). *Excavations in Oxfordshire, 1964–66*. Edinburgh: Edinburgh University Department of Archaeology.

Harding, D. (2017). *The Iron Age in Northern Britain*, 2nd edition. London: Routledge.

Harding, J. (1996). Reconsidering the Neolithic round barrows of eastern Yorkshire. *Northern Archaeology* 14, 67–78.

Harding, J. (2003). *Henge Monuments of the British Isles*. Stroud: Tempus.

Harding, J. (2013). *Cult, Religion and Pilgrimage: Archaeological Investigations at the Neolithic and Bronze Age Monument Complex of Thornborough, North Yorkshire*. York: Council for British Archaeology.

Harding, J. and Healy, F. (2007). *The Raunds Area Project: A Neolithic and Bronze Age Landscape in Northamptonshire*. Swindon: English Heritage.

Hart, D. (2015). *Around the Ancient Track: Archaeological Excavations at Peacehaven, East Sussex*. London: Spoilheap Publications.

Hartwell, B. (1998). The Ballynahatty complex. In A. Gibson and D. Simpson (eds.), *Prehistoric Ritual and Religion*. Stroud: Sutton, pp. 32–44.

Haselgrove, C. (1987). *Iron Age Coinage in Southern England: The Archaeological Context*. Oxford: British Archaeological Reports.

Hatherley, C. and Murray, R. (in press). *Culduthel: An Iron Age Craft Centre in North-East Scotland*. Edinburgh: Society of Antiquaries of Scotland.

Haughton, C. and Powelsland, D. (1999). *West Heslerton: The Anglian Cemetery*, Vol. 1. Yedingham: Landscape Research Centre.

Havard, T., Darvill, T. and Alexander, M. (2017). A Bronze Age round barrow cemetery, pit alignments, Iron Age burials, Iron Age copper working and later activity at Four Crosses, Llandysilo, Powys. *Archaeological Journal* 174, 1–67.

Hawkes, A. (2014). Fulachta Fiadh and Bronze Age cooking in Ireland: Reappraising the evidence. *Proceedings of the Royal Irish Academy* 115C, 47–77.

Hawkes, S. and Hawkes, C. (2012). *Longbridge Deverill Cow Down*. Oxford: Oxford University School of Archaeology.

Hayden, C., Early, R., Biddulph, E. and Anderson-Whymark, H. (2017). *Horcott Quarry, Fairford, and Arkell's Land, Kempsford: Prehistoric, Roman and Anglo-Saxon Settlement and Burial in the Upper Thames Valley in Gloucestershire*. Oxford: Oxford Archaeology.

Healy, F. (1987). Prediction or prejudice? The relationship between field survey and excavation. In A. Brown and M. Edmonds (eds.), *Lithic Analysis and Later British Prehistory*. Oxford: British Archaeological Reports, pp. 9–18.

Healy, F. (1988). *The Anglo-Saxon Cemetery at Spong Hill, North Elmham: Occupation during the Seventh to Second Millennia BC*. Norwich: East Anglian Archaeology 39.

Healy, F. (2012). Chronology corpses, ceramics, copper and lithics. In M. Allen, J. Gardiner and A. Sheridan (eds.), *Is There a British Chalcolithic?* Oxford: Prehistoric Society Research Paper 4, pp. 144–63.

Healy, F. and Housley, R. (1992). Nancy was not alone: Human skeletons of the Early Bronze Age from the Norfolk peat fen. *Antiquity* 66, 948–55.

Hedges, J. and Buckley, D. (1978). The excavation of a Neolithic causewayed enclosure at Orsett, Essex, 1975. *Proceedings of the Prehistoric Society* 44, 219–308.

Helms, M. (1998). *Ulysses' Sail: An Ethnographic Odyssey of Power, Knowledge and Geographical Distance*. Princeton, NJ: Princeton University Press.

Helms, M. (2004). Tangible materialities and cosmological others in the development of sedentism. In E. DeMarrais, C. Gosden and C. Renfrew (eds.), *Rethinking Materiality*. Cambridge: McDonald Institute for Archaeological Research, pp. 117–27.

Helms, M. (2012). Nourishing a structured world with living metal in the Bronze Age. *World Art* 2, 105–18.

Hensey, R. (2015). *First Light: The Origins of Newgrange*. Oxford: Oxbow.

Hensey, R. and Shee Twohig, E. (2017). Facing the cairn at Newgrange, Co. Meath. *Journal of Irish Archaeology* 26, 57–76.

Henshall, A. and Ritchie, J. N. G. (1995). *The Chambered Cairns of Sutherland*. Edinburgh: Edinburgh University Press.

Herring, P. (2000). *St Michael's Mount, Cornwall*. Truro: Cornwall County Council.

Herring, P., Johnson, N., Nowakowsi, J., Sharpe, A. and Young, A. (2016). *Archaeology and Landscape at the Land's End: The West Penwith Surveys 1980–2010*. Truro: Cornwall Archaeological Unit.

Hey, G., Dennis, C. and Robinson, M. (2016). *Yarnton: Neolithic and Bronze Age Settlement and Landscape*. Oxford: Oxford Archaeology.

Hey, G., Garwood, P., Robinson, M., Barclay, A. and Bradley, P. (2011). *The Thames though Time: Early Prehistory to 1500 BC, part 2: Mesolithic to Early Bronze Age*. Oxford: Oxford Archaeology.

Hill, J. D. (1995). *Ritual and Rubbish in the Iron Age of Wessex: A Study on the Formation of a Specific Archaeological Record*. Oxford: British Archaeological Reports.

Hill, J. D. (1996). Hillforts and the Iron Age of Wessex. In T. Champion and J. Collis (eds.), *The Iron Age in Britain and Ireland: Recent Trends*. Sheffield: J.R. Collis, pp. 67–86.

Hill, J. D. (1999). Settlement, landscape and regionality: Norfolk and Suffolk in the pre-Roman Iron Age of Britain and beyond. In J. A. Davies and T. Williamson (eds.), *The Land of the Iceni: The Iron Age in Northern East Anglia*. Norwich: Studies in East Anglia History 4, pp. 185–207.

Hingley, R. (2005). Iron Age 'currency bars' in Britain: Items of exchange in liminal contexts? In C. Haselgrove and D. Wigg-Wolf (eds.), *Iron Age Coinage and Ritual Practices*. Mainz: von Zabern, pp. 183–205.

Hinz, M. (2015). Growth and decline? Population dynamics of Funnel Beaker societies in the 4th millennium BC. In K. Brink, S. Hydén, K. Jennbert, L. Larsson and D. Olausson (eds.), *Neolithic Diversities*. Lund: University of Lund Department of Archaeology and Ancient History, pp. 43–51.

Hodder, I. (1982). Towards a contextual approach to prehistoric exchange. In J. Ericson and T. Earle (eds.), *Contexts for Prehistoric Exchange*. New York: Academic Press, pp. 199–211.

Hodges, H. (1958). A hunting camp at Cullyhanna Lough near Newtown Hamilton, County Armagh. *Ulster Journal of Archaeology* 21, 7–13.

Hodson, F. R. (1964). Cultural grouping within the British pre-Roman Iron Age. *Proceedings of the Prehistoric Society* 30, 99–110.

Holden, E. (1972). A Bronze Age cemetery-barrow on Itford Hill, Beddingham, Sussex. *Sussex Archaeological Collections* 110, 70–117.

Howard, H. (1981). In the wake of distribution: Towards an integrated approach to ceramic studies in prehistoric Britain. In H. Howard and E. Morris (eds.), *Production and Distribution: A Ceramic Viewpoint*. Oxford: British Archaeological Reports, pp. 1–30.

Hughes, G. (2000). *The Lockington Gold Hoard*. Oxford: Oxbow.

Hughes, G., Woodward, A., Barnett, S., Bashford, L. and Bredon, M. (2015). *The Iron Age and Romano-British Settlement at Crick Covert Farm*. Oxford: Archaeopress.

Hunter, F. (2001). The carnyx in Iron Age Europe. *Antiquaries Journal* 81, 77–108.

Hunter, F. (2005). The image of the warrior in the British Iron Age: Coin iconography in context. In C. Haselgrove and D. Wigg-Wolf (eds.), *Iron Age Coinage and Ritual Practices*. Mainz: von Zabern, pp. 43–67.

Hunter, F. (2010). Blair Drummond. *Discovery and Excavation in Scotland* 11, 168–69.

Hunter, F. (2015). Craft in context: Artefact production in later prehistoric Scotland. In F. Hunter and I. Ralston (eds.), *Scotland in Later Prehistoric Europe*. Edinburgh: Society of Antiquaries of Scotland, pp. 225–46.

Hurl, D. (1995). Killymoon: New light on the Late Bronze Age. *Archaeology Ireland* 9, 24–7.

Hustwit, E. (2016). Britishness, Pictishness and the 'death' of the noble Briton: The Britons in Roman ethnographic and literary thought. *Studia Celtica* 50, 19–40.

Hutcheson, N. (2004). *Later Iron Age Norfolk: Metalworking, Landscape and Society*. Oxford: British Archaeological Reports.

Innes, J., Blackford, J. and Rowley-Conwy, P. (2013). Late Mesolithic and early Neolithic forest disturbance: A high resolution palaeoecological test of human impact hypotheses. *Quaternary Science Reviews* 77, 80–100.

Jackson, D. and Dix, B. (1987). Late Iron Age and Roman settlement at Weekley, Northants. *Northamptonshire Archaeology* 21, 41–93.

Jackson, R. (2015). *Huntsman's Quarry, Kemerton*. Oxford: Oxbow.

Jaques, D., Lyons, T. and Phillips, T. (2017). Blick Mead. *Current Archaeology* 326, 18–23.

Jay, M., Montgomery, J., Nehlick, O., Towers, J. and Evans, J. (2013). British Iron Age chariot burials of the Arras Culture: A multi-isotope approach to investigating mobility levels and subsistence practices. *World Archaeology* 45, 473–91.

Jay, M. and Scarre, C. (2017). Tracking the dead in the Neolithic: The 'invisible dead' in Britain. In J. Bradbury and C. Scarre (eds.), *Engaging with the Dead*. Oxford: Oxbow, pp. 7–13.

Johnson, M. and Cameron, K. (2012). *An Early Bronze Age Unenclosed Cremation Cemetery and Pit at Skilmafilly, near Maud, Aberdeenshire*. Scottish Archaeological Internet Report 53, Edinburgh: Society of Antiquaries of Scotland.

Johnson, N. (2017). *Early Bronze Age Round Barrows of the Anglo-Welsh Border*. Oxford: British Archaeological Reports.

Johnston, D. (1997). Biggar Common 1987–93: An early prehistoric funerary and domestic landscape in Clydesdale, South Lanarkshire. *Proceedings of the Society of Antiquaries of Scotland* 127, 185–253.

Johnston, R. (2000). Dying, becoming and being in the field. In J. Harding and R. Johnston (eds.), *Northern Pasts*. Oxford: British Archaeological Reports, pp. 57–70.

Johnston, R. (2005). Pattern without a plan: Rethinking the Bronze Age coaxial field systems on Dartmoor, south-west England. *Oxford Journal of Archaeology* 24, 1–21.

Johnston, S. and Wailes, B. (2007). *Dún Ailinne: Excavations at an Irish Royal Site 1968–1975*. Philadelphia, PA: University of Pennsylvania Museum of Archaeology and Anthropology.

Jones, A. (1999). The excavation of a Later Bronze Age structure at Callestick. *Cornish Archaeology* 38, 1–55.

Jones, A. (2005). *Cornish Bronze Age Ceremonial Landscapes c. 2500–1500 BC*. Oxford: British Archaeological Reports.

Jones, A. (2008). Houses for the dead and cairns for the living: A reconsideration of the Early to Middle Bronze Age transition in south-west England. *Oxford Journal of Archaeology* 27, 153–74.

Jones, A. (2016). *Preserved in the Peat.* Oxford: Oxbow.

Jones, A., Gossip, J. and Quinnell, H. (2015). *Settlement and Metalworking in the Middle Bronze Age and Beyond: New Evidence from Tremough, Cornwall.* Leiden: Sidestone.

Jones, A. and Quinnell, H. (2014). Saucer barrows: Places for ritual within Wessex Early Bronze Age barrow cemeteries. *Oxford Journal of Archaeology* 33, 339–59.

Jones, A. and Thomas, C. (2010). Bosiliack and a reconsideration of entrance graves. *Proceedings of the Prehistoric Society* 76, 27–44.

Jones, A. M., Díaz-Guardamino, M. and Crellin, R. (2016). From artefact biographies to 'multiple objects': A new analysis of the decorated plaques of the Irish Sea Region. *Norwegian Archaeological Review* 49(2), 113–33.

Jones, A. M., Freedman, D., O'Connor, B., Lamdin-Whymark, H., Tipping, R. and Watson, A. (2011). *An Animate Landscape: Rock Art and the Prehistory of Kilmartin, Scotland.* Oxford: Windgather Press.

Jones, A. M. and Sibbesson, E. (2013). Archaeological complexity: Materials, multiplicity and transitions to agriculture in Britain. In B. Alberti, A. M. Jones and J. Pollard (eds.), *Archaeology after Interpretation.* Walnut Creek, CA: Left Coast Press, pp. 151–72.

Jones, C. (1998). The discovery and dating of the prehistoric landscape of Roughan Hill in Co. Clare. *Journal of Irish Archaeology* 9, 27–44.

Jones, C. (2004). *The Burren and the Aran Islands: Exploring the Archaeology.* Cork: The Collins Press.

Jones, C. (2009). Coasts, mountains, rivers and bogs: Using the landscape to explore regionality in Ireland. In G. Barclay and K. Brophy (eds.), *Defining a Regional Neolithic: Evidence from Britain and Ireland.* Oxford: Oxbow, pp. 119–28.

Jones, C. (2016). Dating ancient field walls in karst landscapes using differential bedrock lowering. *Geoarchaeology* 31, 77–100.

Jones, N. and Gibson, A. (2017). Neolithic palisaded enclosures of Radnorshire's Walton Basin. *Archaeologia Cambrensis* 166, 33–88.

Jones, S. and Randal, C. (2010). Death, destruction and the end of the Iron Age at Cadbury Castle, Somerset. In M. Sterry, A. Tullett and N. Roy (eds.), *In Search of the Iron Age.* Leicester: Leicester University School of Archaeology and Ancient History, pp. 165–83.

Jope, E. M. (1961). Daggers of the Early Iron Age in Britain. *Proceedings of the Prehistoric Society* 27, 307–43.

Jope, E. M. (2000). *Early Celtic Art in the British Isles.* Oxford: Clarendon Press.

Kelly, E. (2006). Secrets of the bog bodies: An enigma of the Iron Age explained. *Archaeology Ireland* 20, 26–30.

Kelly, L. (2015). *Knowledge and Power in Prehistoric Societies.* Cambridge: Cambridge University Press.

Kenrick, J. (1995). Excavation of a Neolithic enclosure and Iron Age settlement at Douglasmuir, Angus. *Proceedings of the Society of Antiquaries of Scotland* 125, 29–67.

Kilbride-Jones, H. (1950). The excavation of a composite Early Iron Age monument with 'henge' features at Lugg, Co. Dublin. *Proceedings of the Royal Irish Academy* 53C, 311–32.

Kinnes, I. (1979). *Round Barrows and Ring-Ditches in the British Neolithic.* London: British Museum.

Kinnes, I. (1992). *Non-Megalithic Long Barrows and Allied Structures in the British Neolithic.* London: British Museum.

Kinnes, I., Gibson, A., Ambers, J., Bowman, S., Leese, M. and Boast, R. (1991). Radiocarbon dating and British Beakers: The British Museum programme. *Scottish Archaeological Review* 8, 35–68.

Kinory, J. (2012). *Salt Production, Distribution and Use in the British Iron Age.* Oxford: Archaeopress.

Knight, M., Harris, S. and Appleby, G. (2016). Must Farm: An extraordinary tale of the everyday. *Current Archaeology* 319, 12–18.

Knight, M., Ormrod, T. and Pearce, S. (2015). *The Bronze Age Metalwork of South Western Britain: A Corpus of Material Found between 1983 and 2014.* Oxford: British Archaeological Reports.

Koch, J. (2013). Out of the ebb and flow of the European Bronze Age: Heroes, Tartessos and Celtic. In J. Koch and B. Cunliffe (eds.), *Celtic from the West 2*. Oxford: Oxbow, pp. 101–46.

Koutrafouri, V. and Sanders, J. eds. (2013). *Ritual Failure: Archaeological Perspectives*. Leiden: Sidestone.

Kristiansen, K. (1998). *Europe before History*. Cambridge: Cambridge University Press.

Kristiansen, K. and Larsson, T. (2005). *The Rise of Bronze Age Society: Travels, Transmissions and Transformations*. Cambridge: Cambridge University Press.

Kuijpers, M. (2018). The Bronze Age, a world of specialists? Metalwork from the perspective of skill and material specialisation. *European Journal of Archaeology* 21, 550–71.

Ladd, S. and Mortimer, R. (2017). The Bran Ditch: Early Iron Age origins and implications for prehistoric territories in south Cambridgeshire and the east Chilterns. *Proceedings of the Cambridgeshire Antiquarian Society* 106, 7–22.

Ladle, L. and Woodward, A. (2009). *Excavations at Bestwall Quarry, Wareham, 1992–2005. Vol. 1: The Prehistoric Landscape*. Dorchester: Dorset Natural History and Archaeological Society.

Laidlaw, G. (2017). Excavations of the Late Neolithic site at Scart, Co. Kilkenny. *Journal of Irish Archaeology* 26, 33–56.

Lambrick, G. (1988). *The Rollright Stones*. London: English Heritage.

Lambrick, G. and Allen, T. (2004). *Gravelly Guy, Stanton Harcourt, Oxfordshire: The Development of a Prehistoric and Romano-British Community*. Oxford: Oxford Archaeology.

Lambrick, G. and Robinson, M. (2009). *The Thames through Time: Later Prehistory 1500 BC–AD 50*. Oxford: Oxford Archaeology.

Lamdin-Whymark, H. (2008). *The Residue of Ritualised Action: Neolithic Depositional Practices in the Middle Thames Valley*. Oxford: British Archaeological Reports.

Lanting, J. and Van de Waals, D. (1972). British Beakers as seen from the Continent. *Helinium* 12, 20–46.

Laporte, L. and Tinévez, J.-Y. (2004). Neolithic houses and chambered tombs of western France. *Cambridge Archaeological Journal* 14(2), 217–34.

Last, J. (1998). Books of life: Biography and memory in a Bronze Age barrow. *Oxford Journal of Archaeology* 17, 43–53.

Last, J. ed. (2007a). *Beyond the Grave: New Perspectives on Barrows*. Oxford: Oxbow.

Last, J. (2007b). Covering old ground: Barrows as closures. In J. Last (ed.), *Beyond the Grave: New Perspectives on Barrows*. Oxford: Oxbow, pp. 156–75.

Lawson, A. (2000). *Potterne 1982–5: Animal Husbandry in Later Prehistoric Wessex*. Salisbury: Trust for Wessex Archaeology.

Leach, S. (2015). *Going Underground: An Anthropological and Taphonomic Study of Human Skeletal Remains from Caves and Rock Shelters in Yorkshire*. Leeds: Yorkshire Archaeological Society.

Leary, J., Canti, M., Field, D., Fowler, P., Marshall, P. and Campbell, G. (2013). The Marlborough Mound, Wiltshire: A further Neolithic monumental mound by the River Kennet. *Proceedings of the Prehistoric Society* 79, 137–63.

Leary, J. and Field, D. (2012). Journeys and juxtapositions: Marden henge and the view from the Vale. In A. Gibson (ed.), *Enclosing the Neolithic: Recent Studies in Britain and Europe*. Oxford: British Archaeological Reports, pp. 55–65.

Leary, J., Field, D. and Campbell, G. eds. (2013). *Silbury Hill*. Swindon: English Heritage.

Lelong, O. (2014). Wrappings of power: A woman's burial in cattle hide at Langwell Farm, Strath Oykell. *Proceedings of the Society of Antiquaries of Scotland* 144, 65–131.

Lelong, O. and Pollard, T. (1998). The excavation and survey of prehistoric enclosures at Blackshouse Burn, Lanarkshire. *Proceedings of the Society of Antiquaries of Scotland* 128, 13–53.

Lévi-Strauss, C. (1983). *The Way of the Masks*. London: Cape.

Lewis, J., Leivers, M., Brown, L., Smith, A., Cramp, K., Mepham, L. and Phillpotts, C. (2010). *Landscape Evolution in the Middle Thames Valley: Heathrow Terminal 5 Excavations*, Vol. 2. Oxford / Salisbury: Framework Archaeology.

Lewis, J. and Mullin, D. (2011). New excavations at Priddy Circle 1. *Proceedings of the University of Bristol Speleological Society* 25, 133–63.

Lewis, J. and Mullin, D. (2016). Excavations at a cropmark henge near Bredon, Worcestershire. *Transactions of the Worcestershire Archaeological Society* 25, 17–36.

Lewis, J. and Preston, S. (2012). *Bronze Age and Roman Settlement with Neolithic and Saxon Burials at Itchen Farm, Winchester, Hampshire.* Reading: Thames Valley Archaeological Services.

Lewis-Williams, D. and Pearce, D. (2005). *Inside the Neolithic Mind.* London: Thames and Hudson.

Lloyd Morgan, C. (1887). The stones of Stanton Drew: Their source and origin. *Proceedings of the Somerset Archaeological Society* 33, 37–50.

Loveday, R. (2006). *Inscribed across the Landscape: The Cursus Enigma.* Stroud: Tempus.

Loveday, R. and Barclay, A. (2010). 'One of the most interesting barrows examined' – Liffs Low revisited. In J. Leary, T. Darvill and D. Field (eds.), *Round Mounds and Monumentality in the British Neolithic and Beyond.* Oxford: Oxbow, pp. 108–29.

Luke, M. (2016). *Close to the Loop: Landscape and Settlement Evolution beside the Biddenham Loop, West of Bedford.* Norwich: East Anglian Archaeology 156.

Lynch, A. (2014a). *Poulnabrone: An Early Neolithic Portal Tomb in Ireland.* Dublin: Stationary Office.

Lynch, A. (2014b). Newgrange revisited: New insights from excavation at the back of the mound in 1984–8. *Journal of Irish Archaeology* 23, 13–82.

Lynch, F. (1971). Report on the re-excavation of two Bronze Age cairns in Anglesey: Bedd Branwen and Treiowerth. *Archaeologia Cambrensis* 120, 11–83.

Lynch, F. (1991). *Prehistoric Anglesey*, 2nd edition. Llangefni: Anglesey Antiquarian Society.

Lynch, F. (1993). *Excavations in the Brenig Valley.* Bangor: Cambrian Archaeological Association.

Lynch, F. and Davey, P. eds. (2017). *The Chambered Tombs of the Isle of Man: A Study by Audrey Henshall in 1971–1978.* Oxford: Archaeopress.

Lynch, F. and Musson, C. (2001). A prehistoric and early medieval complex at Llandegai. *Archaeologia Cambrensis* 150, 17–142.

Lynch, M. (2017). The later Mesolithic of the north-west coast of Clare. *Archaeology Ireland* 31, 24–8.

Lynn, C. (1977). Trial excavations at the King's Stables, Tray Townland, County Armagh. *Ulster Journal of Archaeology* 40, 42–62.

Lyons, A. (2011). *Life and afterlife at Duxford, Cambridgeshire.* Norwich: East Anglian Archaeology 141.

MacGregor, G. (2004). *Excavation of an Iron Age Burial Mound, Loch Borralie, Sutherland.* Scottish Archaeological Internet Report 9, Edinburgh: Society of Antiquaries of Scotland.

Macklin, M., Johnstone, E. and Lewin, J. (2005). Pervasive and long-term forcing of Holocene river instability and flooding in Great Britain by centennial-scale climate change. *The Holocene* 15, 937–43.

Madgwick, R., Grimes, V., Lamb, A. and McCormick, F. (2017). Isotope analysis reveals that feasts at Navan Fort, Ulster, drew people and animals from across Ireland. *Past* 87, 15–6.

Madgwick, R. and Mulville, J. (2015). Feasting on fore-limbs. *Antiquity* 89, 629–44.

Maginess, C., O'Dowd, J. and Tierney, J. (2014). Prehistoric campsite and trackway remnants at Ballynaclogh. In J. McKean and J. O'Sullivan (eds.), *The Quiet Landscape.* Dublin: National Roads Authority, pp. 147–54.

Malim, T. (2000). The ritual landscape of the Neolithic and Bronze Age in the middle and lower Ouse valley. In M. Dawson (ed.), *Prehistoric, Roman and Post-Roman Landscapes of the Great Ouse Valley.* York: Council for British Archaeology, pp. 57–88.

Mallory, J. (1984). The Long Stone, Ballybeen, Dundonald, County Down. *Ulster Journal of Archaeology* 47, 1–4.

Mallory, J. (1995). Haughey's Fort in the Navan complex of the Late Bronze Age. In J. Waddell and E. Shee Twohig (eds.), *Ireland in the Bronze Age.* Dublin: Stationery Office, pp. 73–86.

Mallory, J. (2000). Excavation of the Navan ditch. *Emania* 18, 21–35.

Mallory, J. (2013). *The Origins of the Irish.* London: Thames and Hudson.

Mallory, J. and Baban, G. (2014). Excavations in Haughey's Fort East. *Emania* 22, 13–32.

Manby, T. (1974). *Grooved Ware Sites in Yorkshire and the North of England*. Oxford: British Archaeological Reports.

Manby, T., King, A. and Vyner, B. (2003). The Neolithic and Early Bronze Age: A time of early agriculture. In T. Manby, S. Moorhouse and P. Ottaway (eds.), *The Archaeology of Yorkshire*. Leeds: Yorkshire Archaeological Society, pp. 35–116.

Manning, A. and Moore, C. (2003). A Late Bronze Age site at Springfield Park, Chelmsford. *Essex Archaeology and History* 34, 19–35.

Manning, S. (2014). *A Test of Time and A Test of Time Revisited*. Oxford: Oxbow.

Manning, W. and Saunders, C. (1972). A socketed iron axe from Maids Moreton, Buckinghamshire. *Antiquaries Journal* 52, 276–92.

Markey, M., Wilkes, E. and Darvill, T. (2002). Poole Harbour – an Iron Age port. *Current Archaeology* 181, 7–11.

Martin, E. and Murphy, P. (1988). West Row Fen, Mildenhall, Suffolk: A Bronze Age fen-edge settlement. *Antiquity* 62, 353–8.

Masters, L. (1983). Chambered tombs and non-megalithic barrows in Britain. In C. Renfrew (ed.), *The Megalithic Tombs of Western Europe*. London: Thames and Hudson, pp. 97–112.

McAvoy, F. (2000). The development of the Neolithic monument complex at Godmanchester, Cambridgeshire. In M. Dawson (ed.), *Prehistoric, Roman and Post-Roman Landscapes of the Great Ouse Valley*. York: Council for British Archaeology, pp. 51–6.

McClatchie, M., Bogaard, A., Colledge, S., Whitehouse, N., Schulting, R., Barratt, P. and McLaughlin, R. (2016). Farming and foraging in Neolithic Ireland: An archaeobotanical perspective. *Antiquity* 90, 302–18.

McCullagh, R. and Tipping, R. (1998). *The Lairg Project 1988–1996*. Edinburgh: Scottish Trust for Archaeological Research.

McFadyen, L. (2007). Neolithic architecture and participation: Practices of making in early Neolithic Britain. In J. Last (ed.), *Beyond the Grave*. Oxford: Oxbow, pp. 22–9.

McGarry, T. (2009). Irish late prehistoric burial ring-ditches. In G. Cooney, K. Beckers, J. Coles, M. Ryan and S. Sievers (eds.), *Relics of Old Decency: Archaeological Studies of Later Prehistory*. Dublin: Wordwell, pp. 413–23.

McGrail, S. (1997). *Studies in Maritime Archaeology*. Oxford: British Archaeological Reports.

McKinley, J., Leivers, M., Schuster, J., Marshall, P., Barclay, A. and Stoodley, N. (2014). *Cliffs End Farm, Isle of Thanet, Kent*. Salisbury: Wessex Archaeology.

McLaughlin, R., Whitehouse, N., Schulting, R., McCatchie, M., Barrattt, P. and Bogaard, A. (2016). The changing face of Neolithic and Bronze Age Ireland: A big data approach to the settlement and burial record. *Journal of World Prehistory* 29, 117–53.

McOmish, D. (1996). East Chisenbury: Ritual and rubbish at the British Bronze Age-Iron Age transition. *Antiquity* 70, 68–76.

McOmish, D., Field, D. and Brown, G. (2002). *The Field Archaeology of the Salisbury Plain Training Area*. Swindon: English Heritage.

McQuillan, L. and Logue, P. (2008). Funerary querns: Rethinking the role of the basin in Irish passage tombs. *Ulster Journal of Archaeology* 67, 14–21.

Medlycott, M. ed. (2011). *Research and Archaeology Revisited: A Revised Framework for the East of England*. Norwich: East Anglian Archaeology Occasional Paper 24.

Meikeljohn, C., Chamberlain, A. and Schulting, R. (2011). Radiocarbon dating of Mesolithic human remains in Great Britain. *Mesolithic Miscellany* 21, 220–58.

Melton, N., Montgomery, J. and Knüsel, C. (2013). *Gristhorpe Man: A Life and Death in the Bronze Age*. Oxford: Oxbow.

Mercer, R. (1981a). Excavations at Carn Brea, Illogan, Cornwall 1970–73. *Cornish Archaeology* 20, 1–204.

Mercer, R. (1981b). The excavation of a late Neolithic henge-type enclosure at Balfarg, Markinch, Fife, Scotland. *Proceedings of the Society of Antiquaries of Scotland* 111, 63–171.

Mercer, R. (1981c). *Grimes Graves, Norfolk, Excavations 1971–2*, Vols. 1 and 2. London: HMSO.

Mercer, R. (1997). The excavation of a Neolithic enclosure complex at Helman Tor,

Lostwithiel, Cornwall. *Cornish Archaeology* 36, 5–63.

Mercer, R. (2018). *Natives and Roman on the Northern Frontier: Excavations and Surveys in a Later Prehistoric Landscape in Upper Eskdale, Dumfriesshire*. Edinburgh: Society of Antiquaries of Scotland.

Mercer, R. and Healy, F. (2008). *Hambledon Hill Dorset: Excavation and Survey of a Neolithic Monument Complex and its Surrounding Landscape*. Swindon: English Heritage.

Miket, R. (1981). Pit alignments in the Milfield basin and the excavation of Ewart 1. *Proceedings of the Prehistoric Society* 47, 137–46.

Miket, R. (1985). Ritual enclosures at Whitton Hill, Northumberland. *Proceedings of the Prehistoric Society* 51, 137–48.

Miles, D., Palmer, S., Lock, G., Gosden, C. and Cromarty, A. M. (2003). *Uffington White Horse and its Landscape*. Oxford: Oxford Archaeology.

Millett, M. (1992). *The Romanization of Britain*. Cambridge: Cambridge University Press.

Millican, K. (2016). *The Timber Monuments of Neolithic Scotland*. Oxford: British Archaeological Reports.

Milner, N., Conneller, C. and Taylor, B. (2018). *Star Carr 1: A Persistent Place in a Changing World*. York: White Rose University Press.

Mitchell, F. (1992). Notes on some non-local cobbles at the entrances to the passage graves at Newgrange and Knowth, County Meath. *Journal of the Royal Society of Antiquaries of Ireland* 122, 128–45.

Mitchell, F. and Ryan, M. (1998). *Reading the Irish Landscape*. Dublin: Town and Country House.

Mizoguchi, K. (1993). Time in the reproduction of mortuary practices. *World Archaeology* 25, 223–35.

Montgomery, W., Provan, J., McCable, A. and Yalden, D. (2014). Origin of British and Irish mammals: Disparate post-glacial colonisation and special introductions. *Quaternary Science Reviews* 98, 144–65.

Moore, H. and Wilson, G. (2011). *Shifting Sands: Links of Noltland, Westray*. Edinburgh: Historic Scotland.

Moore, T. (2006). *Iron Age Societies in the Severn – Cotswolds*. Oxford: British Archaeological Reports.

Mortimer, R. and Phillips, T. (2012). Clay Farm's evolving landscape. *Current Archaeology* 264, 32–7.

Mount, C. (1994). Aspects of ritual deposition in the Late Neolithic and Beaker periods at Newgrange, Co. Meath. *Proceedings of the Prehistoric Society* 60, 433–43.

Mount, C. (1997). Adolf Mahr's excavation of an Early Bronze Age cemetery at Keenoge, County Meath. *Proceedings of the Royal Irish Academy* 97C, 1–68.

Mounteney, G. (1981). Faunal attrition and subsistence reconstruction at Thwing. In G. Barker (ed.), *Prehistoric Communities in Northern England*. Sheffield: Sheffield University Department of Prehistory and Archaeology, pp. 73–86.

Murray, D. and Ralston, I. (1997). Excavation of a square-ditched barrow and other cropmarks at Boysack Mill, Inverkeillor, Angus. *Proceedings of the Society of Antiquaries of Scotland* 127, 359–86.

Murray, H. and Murray, C. (2014). Mesolithic and Early Neolithic activity along the Dee: Excavations at Garthdee Road, Aberdeen. *Proceedings of the Society of Antiquaries of Scotland* 144, 1–64.

Murray, H., Murray, C. and Fraser, S. (2009). *A Tale of Unknown Unknowns: A Mesolithic Pit Alignment and a Neolithic Timber Hall at Warren Field, Crathes, Aberdeenshire*. Oxford: Oxbow.

Musson, C. (1991). *The Breiddin Hillfort*. York: Council for British Archaeology.

Mytum, H. (2013). *Monumentality in Later Prehistory: Building and Rebuilding Castell Henllys Hillfort*. New York: Springer.

Nebelsick, L. (2000). Rent asunder: Ritual violence in Late Bronze Age hoards. In C. Pare (ed.), *Metals Make the World Go Round: The Supply and Circulation of Metals in Bronze Age Europe*. Oxford: Oxbow, pp. 160–75.

Needham, S. (1988). Selective deposition in the British Early Bronze Age. *World Archaeology* 20, 229–48.

Needham, S. (1991). *Excavation and Salvage at Runnymede Bridge, 1978: The Late Bronze Age*

Waterfront Site. London: British Museum Press.

Needham, S. (1992). The structure of settlement and ritual in the Late Bronze Age of south-east England. In C. Mordant and A. Richard (eds.), *L'habitat et l'occupation du sol à l'Age du Bronze en Europe*. Paris: Editions du comité des travaux historiques et scientifiques, pp. 49–69.

Needham, S. (2000). Power pulses across a cultural divide: Cosmologically driven acquisition between Armorica and Wessex. *Proceedings of the Prehistoric Society* 66, 151–207.

Needham, S. (2004). Migdale-Marnoch: Sunburst of Scottish metallurgy. In I. Shepherd and G. Barclay (eds.), *Scotland in Ancient Europe*. Edinburgh: Society of Antiquaries of Scotland, pp. 217–45.

Needham, S. (2005). Transforming Beaker Culture in north-west Europe: Processes of fusion and fission. *Proceedings of the Prehistoric Society* 71, 171–217.

Needham, S. (2007). 800 BC: The great divide. In C. Haselgrove and R. Pope (eds.), *The Earlier Iron Age in Britain and the Near Continent*. Oxford: Oxbow, pp. 39–63.

Needham, S. (2012). Case and place for the British Chalcolithic. In M. Allen, J. Gardiner and A. Sheridan (eds.), *Is There a British Chalcolithic?* Oxford: Prehistoric Society Research Paper 4, pp. 1–26.

Needham, S. (2016). The lost cultures of the halberd-bearers: A non-Beaker ideology in later third millennium Atlantic Europe. In J. Koch and B. Cunliffe (eds.), *Celtic from the West 3*. Oxford: Oxbow, pp. 41–81.

Needham, S. and Ambers, J. (1994). Redating Rams Hill and reconsidering Bronze Age enclosures. *Proceedings of the Prehistoric Society* 60, 225–43.

Needham, S. and Bowman, S. (2005). Flesh-hooks, technological complexity and the Atlantic feasting complex. *Journal of European Archaeology* 8(2), 93–136.

Needham, S., Parfitt, K. and Varndell, G. (2006). *The Ringlemere Cup: Precious Cups and the Beginning of the Channel Bronze Age*. London: British Museum Press.

Needham, S., Parham, D. and Frieman, C. (2013). *Claimed by the Sea: Salcombe, Langdon Bay and Other Marine Finds of the Bronze Age*. York: Council for British Archaeology.

Needham, S. and Spence, T. (1997). Refuse and the formation of middens. *Antiquity* 71, 77–90.

Newman, C. (1997a). *Tara: An Archaeological Survey*. Dublin: The Discovery Programme.

Newman, C. (1997b). Ballinderry Crannog No. 2, Co. Offaly: The later Bronze Age. *Journal of Irish Archaeology* 8, 91–100.

Newman, P. (2011). *The Field Archaeology of Dartmoor*. Swindon: English Heritage.

Niblett, R. (2001). A Neolithic dug-out from a multi-period site near St Albans, Herts, England. *International Journal of Nautical Archaeology* 30, 155–95.

Nick, M. (2018). The impact of coinage on ritual offerings during the late Iron Age (c. 250–25/15 BC). In N. Myrberg Burström and G. Tarnow Ingvardson (eds.), *Divina Moneta: Coins in Ritual and Religion*. Abingdon: Routledge, pp. 30–48.

Noble, G. (2006). *Neolithic Scotland: Timber, Stone, Earth and Fire*. Edinburgh: Edinburgh University Press.

Noble, G. (2017). *Woodland in the Neolithic of Northern Europe: The Forest as Ancestor*. Cambridge: Cambridge University Press.

Noble, G. and Brophy, K. (2011). Ritual and remembrance at a prehistoric ceremonial complex in central Scotland: Excavations at Forteviot, Perth and Kinross. *Antiquity* 85, 787–804.

Noble, G. and Brophy, K. (2017). Cremation practices and the creation of monument complexes: The Neolithic cremation cemetery at Forteviot, Strathearn, Perth and Kinross, Scotland, and its comparanda. *Proceedings of the Prehistoric Society* 83, 213–45.

Noble, G., Greig, M. and Millican, K. (2012). Excavations at a multi-period site at Greenbogs, Aberdeenshire, Scotland and the four-post timber architecture tradition of Late Neolithic Britain and Ireland. *Proceedings of the Prehistoric Society* 78, 135–71.

Northover, P. (1984). Iron Age bronze metallurgy in central southern England. In B. Cunliffe and D. Miles (eds.), *Aspects of the Iron Age in Central Southern Britain*. Oxford: Oxford University Committee for Archaeology, pp. 126–45.

Nowakowski, J. (2001). Leaving home in the Cornish Bronze Age: Insights into planned abandonment behaviour. In J. Brück (ed.), *Bronze Age Landscapes: Tradition and Transformation*. Oxford: Oxbow, pp. 139–48.

Nowakowski, J. and Quinnell, H. (2011). *Trevelgue Head, Cornwall*. Truro: Cornwall County Council.

Nowakowski, J., Quinnell, H., Sturgess, J. H., Thomas, C. and Thorpe, C. (2007). Return to Gwithian: Shifting the sands of time. *Cornish Archaeology* 46, 13–76.

Ó Donnchadha, B. and Grogan, E. (2010). *M1 Dundalk Western Bypass, Site 116: Balregan 1 and 2 Final Report*. Kilcoole: Irish Archaeological Consultancy.

Ó Drisceoil, C. (2009). Archaeological excavation of a Late Neolithic Grooved Ware site at Balgatheran, County Louth. *County Louth Archaeological and Historical Journal* 27, 77–102.

Ó Faoláin, S. (2004). *Bronze Artefact Production in Late Bronze Age Ireland*. Oxford: British Archaeological Reports.

Ó Floinn, R. (2011). Annagh, Co. Limerick. In M. Cahill and M. Sikora (eds.), *Breaking Ground, Finding Graves*, Vol. 1. Dublin: National Museum of Ireland, pp. 17–47.

Ó Néil, J. (2013). Being prehistoric in the Iron Age. In M. O' Sullivan, C. Scarre and M. Doyle (eds.), *Tara from the Past to the Future*. Dublin: Wordwell, pp. 249–55.

Ó Néil, J., Plunkett, G. and Whitehouse, N. (2007). Archaeological and palaeoecological investigation of a Middle Bronze Age settlement at Ballyarnet Lake, County Derry. *Ulster Journal of Archaeology* 66, 39–49.

Ó Nualláin, S. (1972). A Neolithic house at Ballyglass near Ballycastle, Co. Mayo. *Journal of the Royal Society of Antiquaries of Ireland* 102, 49–57.

Ó Nualláin, S. (1998). Excavation of the small court cairn and associated hut sites at Ballyglass, near Ballycastle, Co. Mayo. *Proceedings of the Royal Irish Academy* 98C, 125–75.

O'Brien, W. (1992). Boulder burials: A Later Bronze Age megalith tradition in south-west Ireland. *Journal of the Cork Historical and Archaeological Society* 97, 11–35.

O'Brien, W. (1999). *Sacred Ground: Megalithic Tombs in Coastal South-West Ireland*. Galway: National University of Ireland.

O'Brien, W. (2004a). *Ross Island: Mining, Metal and Society in Early Ireland*. Bronze Age Studies 6, Galway: National University of Ireland, Galway.

O'Brien, W. (2004b). (Con)fusion of tradition? The circle henge in Ireland. In A. Gibson and A. Sheridan (eds.), *From Sickles to Circles*. Stroud: Tempus, pp. 323–38.

O'Brien, W. (2009). *Local Worlds: Early Settlement Landscapes and Upland Farming in South-West Ireland*. Cork: Collins Press.

O'Brien, W. (2012). Aspects of Fulacht Fiadh function and chronology in Cork. *Journal of the Cork Historical and Archaeological Society* 117, 107–33.

O'Brien, W. (2015). *Prehistoric Copper Mining in Europe 5500–500 BC*. Oxford: Oxford University Press.

O'Brien, W. and O'Driscoll, J. (2017). *Hillforts, Warfare and Society in Bronze Age Ireland*. Oxford: Archaeopress.

O'Connell, A. (2013). *Harvesting the Stars: A Pagan Temple at Lismullin, Co. Meath*. Dublin: National Roads Authority.

O'Connell, M. and Molloy, K. (2001). Farming and woodland dynamics in Ireland during the Neolithic. *Proceedings of the Royal Irish Academy* 101B, 99–128.

O'Connor, B. (2007). Llyn Fawr metalwork in Britain: A review. In C. Haselgrove and R. Pope (eds.), *The Earlier Iron Age in Britain and Beyond*. Oxford: Oxbow, pp. 64–79.

O'Connor, B. (2010). From Dorchester to Dieskau – some aspects of relations between Britain and Central Europe during the Early Bronze Age. In H. Meller and F. Bertemes (eds.), *Der Griff nach den Sternen*. Halle: Tagungen des Landesmuseums für Vorgeschichte Halle, pp. 591–602.

O'Kelly, M. (1958). A wedge-shaped gallery grave at Island, Co. Cork. *Journal of the Royal Society of Antiquaries of Ireland* 88, 1–23.

O'Kelly, M. (1982). *Newgrange: Archaeology, Art and Legend*. London: Thames and Hudson.

O'Kelly, M., Cleary, R. and Lehane, D. (1983). *Newgrange, Co. Meath: The Late Neolithic/Beaker*

Period Settlement. Oxford: British Archaeological Reports.

O'Regan, C. (2010). A monumental discovery in South Derry. *Archaeology Ireland* 24, 22–4.

O'Sullivan, A. (1996). Later Bronze Age intertidal discoveries in North Munster estuaries. *Discovery Programme Reports* 4, 63–71.

O'Sullivan, M. (2004). Little and large: Comparing Knockroe and Knowth. In H. Roche, E. Grogan, J. Bradley, J. Coles and B. Raftery (eds.), *From Megaliths to Metals*. Oxford: Oxbow, pp. 44–50.

O'Sullivan, M. (2005). *Duma na nGiall: The Mound of the Hostages, Tara*. Bray: Wordwell.

O'Sullivan, M., Davis, S. and Stout, G. (2012). Henges in Ireland: New discoveries and emerging issues. In A. Gibson (ed.), *Enclosing the Neolithic*. Oxford: British Archaeological Reports, pp. 37–53.

Olalde, I., Brace, S., Allentoft, M. E., Armit, I., Kristiansen, K., Booth, T., Rohland, N., Mallick, S., Szécsényi-Nagy, A., Mittnik, A., Altena, E., Lipson, M., Lazaridis, I., Harper, T. K., Patterson, N., Broomandkhoshbacht, N., Diekmann, Y., Faltyskova, Z., Fernandes, D., Ferry, M., Harney, E., de Knijff, P., Michel, M., Oppenheimer, J., Stewardson, K., Barclay, A., Alt, K. W., Liesau, C., Ríos, P., Blasco, C., Vega Miguel, J., Menduiña García, R., Avilés Fernández, A., Bánffy, E., Bernabò-Brea, M., Billoin, D., Bonsall, C., Bonsall, L., Allen, T., Büster, L., Carver, S., Castells Navarro, L., Craig, O. E., Cook, G. T., Cunliffe, B., Denaire, A., Dinwiddy, K. E., Dodwell, N., Ernée, M., Evans, C., Kuchařík, M., Francès Farré, J., Fowler, C., Gazenbeek, M., Garrido Pena, R., Haber-Uriarte, M., Haduch, E., Hey, G., Jowett, N., Knowles, T., Massy, K., Pfrengle, S., Lefranc, P., Lemercier, O., Lefebvre, A., Heras Martínez, C., Galera Olmo, V., Bastida Ramírez, A., Lomba Maurandi, J., Majó, T., McKinley, J. I., McSweeney, K., Balázs Gusztáv, M., Modi, A., Kulcsár, G., Kiss, V., Czene, A., Patay, R., Endródi, A., Köhler, K., Hajdu, T., Szeniczey, T., Dani, J., Bernert, Z., Hoole, M., Cheronet, O., Keating, D., Velemínský, P., Dobeš, M., Candilio, F., Brown, F., Flores Fernández, R., Herrero-Corral, A.-M.,

Tusa, S., Carnieri, E., Lentini, L., Valenti, A., Zanini, A., Waddington, C., Delibes, G., Guerra-Doce, E., Neil, B., Brittain, M., Luke, M., Mortimer, R., Desideri, J., Besse, M., Brücken, G., Furmanek, M., Haluszko, A., Mackiewicz, M., Rapiński, A., Leach, S., Soriano, I., Lillios, K. T., Cardoso, J. L., Pearson, M. P., Włodarczak, P., Price, T. D., Prieto, P., Rey, P.-J., Risch, R., Rojo Guerra, M. A., Schmitt, A., Serralongue, J., Silva, A. M., Smrčka, V., Vergnaud, L., Zilhão, J., Caramelli, D., Higham, T., Thomas, M. G., Kennett, D. J., Fokkens, H., Heyd, V., Sheridan, A., Sjögren, K.-G., Stockhammer, P. W., Krause, J., Pinhasi, R., Krause, J., Haak, W., Barnes, I., Lalueza-Fox, C. and Reich, D. (2018). The Beaker phenomenon and the genomic transformation of northwest Europe. *Nature* 555, 190–6. doi: 10.1038/nature 25738.

Oswald, A., Dyer, C. and Barber, M. (2001). *The Creation of Monuments: Neolithic Causewayed Enclosures in the British Isles*. Swindon: English Heritage.

Owen, O. (1992). Eildon Hill North. In J. Rideout, O. Owen and E. Halpin (eds.), *Hillforts of Southern Scotland*. Edinburgh: AOC, pp. 211–71.

Owoc, M. A. (2004). A phenomenology of the buried landscape: Soil as material culture in the Bronze Age of south-west Britain. In N. Boivin and M. A. Owoc (eds.), *Soils, Stones and Symbols: Cultural Perceptions of the Mineral World*. London: UCL Press, pp. 107–23.

Pailler, Y. and Stéphans, P. (2014). Landscape evolution and human settlement in the Iroise Sea (Brittany, France) during the Neolithic and Bronze Age. *Proceedings of the Prehistoric Society* 80, 105–39.

Palmer, S. (1999). Archaeological excavations in the Arrow Valley, Warwickshire. *Transactions of the Birmingham and Warwickshire Archaeological Society* 103, 1–231.

Palmer, S. (2009). Neolithic, Bronze Age, Iron Age, Romano-British and Anglo-Saxon sites excavated on the Transco Churchover to Newbold Pacey gas pipeline in 1999. *Transactions of the Birmingham and Warwickshire Archaeological Society* 113, 1–174.

Pantos, A. and Semple, S. eds. (2003). *Assembly Places and Practices in Medieval Europe.* Dublin: Four Courts Press.

Pare, C. (2000). Bronze and the Bronze Age. In C. Pare (ed.), *Metals Make the World Go Round: The Supply and Circulation of Metals in Bronze Age Europe.* Oxford: Oxbow, pp. 1–38.

Parfitt, K. and Needham, S. (in press). *Ceremonial Living in the Third Millennium BC: Excavations at Ringlemere.* London: British Museum.

Parker Pearson, M. (1999). Food, sex and death: Cosmologies in the British Iron Age with special reference to east Yorkshire. *Cambridge Archaeological Journal* 9, 43–69.

Parker Pearson, M. (2007). The Stonehenge Riverside Project: Excavations at the east entrance of Durrington Walls. In M. Larsson and M. Parker Pearson (eds.), *From Stonehenge to the Baltic.* Oxford: British Archaeological Reports, pp. 125–44.

Parker Pearson, M., Bevins, R., Ixer, R., Pollard, J., Richards, C., Welham, K., Chan, B., Edinborough, K., Hamilton, D., Macphail, R., Schlee, D., Schwenninger, J.-L., Simmons, E. and Smith, M. (2015). Craig Rhos-y-felin: A Welsh bluestone quarry for Stonehenge. *Antiquity* 89, 1131–52.

Parker Pearson, M., Chamberlain, A., Craig, O., Marshall, P., Mulville, J., Smith, H., Chenery, C., Collins, M., Cook, G., Craig, G., Evans, J., Hiller, J., Montgomery, J., Schwenniger, J.-L., Taylor, G. and Wess, T. (2005). Evidence for mummification in Bronze Age Britain. *Antiquity* 79, 529–46.

Parker Pearson, M., Chamberlain, A., Jay, M., Marshall, P., Pollard, J., Richards, C., Thomas, J., Tilley, C. and Welham, K. (2009). Who was buried at Stonehenge? *Antiquity* 8, 23–39.

Parker Pearson, M., Chamberlain, A., Jay, M., Richards, M., Sheridan, A., Curtis, N., Evans, J., Gibson, A., Hutchison, M., Mahoney, P., Marshall, P., Montgomery, J., Needham, S., O'Mahoney, S., Pellegrini, M. and Wilkin, N. (2016). Beaker people in Britain: Migration, mobility and diet. *Antiquity* 90, 620–37.

Parker Pearson, M., Chan, B., Chapman, H., Gaffney, V., Garwood, P., Marshall, P., Aldrian, L. and Neubauer, W. (2017).

Durrington Walls: Was this the start of Britain's Copper Age? *Past* 86, 3–5.

Parker Pearson, M., Pollard, J., Richards, C., Thomas, J., Welham, K., Dunn, P., Stanford, A. and De Luis de la Cruz, I. (2015). *Stonehenge: Making Sense of a Prehistoric Mystery.* York: Council for British Archaeology.

Parker Pearson, M. and Ramilsonina (1998). Stonehenge for the ancestors: The stones pass on the message. *Antiquity* 72, 308–26.

Parker Pearson, M., Sharples, N. and Symonds, J. (2004). *South Uist: Archaeology and History of a Hebridean Island.* Stroud: Tempus.

Parmenter, P., Johnson, E. and Outram, A. (2015). Inventing the Neolithic? Putting evidence-based interpretation back into the study of faunal remains from causewayed enclosures. *World Archaeology* 47, 819–33.

Passmore, D. and Waddington, C. (2009). *Managing Archaeological Landscapes in Northumberland: Till-Tweed Studies,* Vol. 1. Oxford: Oxbow.

Patrick, J. (1975). Megalithic exegesis: A comment. *Irish Archaeological Research Forum* 11(2), 9–14.

Peacock, D. (2013). *The Stone of Life: Querns, Mills and Flour Production in Europe to AD 500.* Southampton: Highfield Press.

Pearce, S. (1983). *The Bronze Age Metalwork of Southwestern Britain.* Oxford: British Archaeological Reports.

Pearson, T. and Topping, P. (2002). Rethinking the Carrock Fell enclosure. In G. Varndell and P. Topping (eds.), *Enclosures in Neolithic Europe.* Oxford: Oxbow, pp. 121–7.

Perkins, D. (2010). The distribution patterns of Bronze Age barrows in north-east Kent. *Archaeologia Cantiana* 130, 277–314.

Peters, F. (2000). Two traditions of Bronze Age burial in the Stonehenge landscape. *Oxford Journal of Archaeology* 19, 343–58.

Petersen, F. (1972). Traditions of multiple burial in Later Neolithic and Early Bronze Age England. *Archaeological Journal* 129, 22–55.

Pétrequin, P., Cassen, S., Klassen, K., Sheridan, A. and Pétrequin, A.-M. eds. (2012). *Jade. Grandes haches alpines du Néolithique européen. Ve et IVe millénaires av. J.-C.* Besançon: Presses Universitaires de Franche-Comté.

Pickstone, A. and Mortimer, R. (2012). War Ditches, Cherry Hinton: Revisiting an Iron

Age hillfort. *Proceedings of the Cambridge Antiquarian Society* 101, 31–59.

Piggott, S. (1938). The Early Bronze Age in Wessex. *Proceedings of the Prehistoric Society* 4, 52–106.

Pilcher, J. (1969). Archaeology, palaeoecology and C 14 dating of the Beaghmore stone circles. *Ulster Journal of Archaeology* 32, 73–91.

Pioffet, H. (2015). *Sociétés et identités de premier Néolithique de Grand-Bretagne at d'Irlande dans leur context nord européen: Characterisation et analyses comparatives des productions céramiques entre Manche, Mer d'Irlande et Mer du Nord.* Rennes: Université de Rennes.

Pitts, M. (2001). Excavating the Sanctuary: New investigations on Overton Hill, Avebury. *Wiltshire Archaeological Magazine* 94, 1–23.

Pitts, M. (2018). Stonehenge without borders. *British Archaeology* 160, 20–35.

Plunkett, G. (2007). Pollen analysis and archaeology in Ireland. In E. Murphy and N. Whitehouse (eds.), *Environmental Archaeology in Ireland.* Oxford: Oxbow, pp. 221–40.

Pollard, J. (1992). The Sanctuary, Overton Hill: A re-examination. *Proceedings of the Prehistoric Society* 58, 213–26.

Pollard, J. (2004). The art of decay and the transformation of substance. In C. Renfrew, C. Gosden and E. DeMarrais (eds.), *Substance, Memory, Display: Archaeology and Art.* Cambridge: McDonald Institute for Archaeological Research, pp. 47–62.

Pollard, J. ed. (2008). *Prehistoric Britain.* Oxford: Blackwell.

Pollard, J. (2009). The materialisation of religious structures in the time of Stonehenge. *Material Religion* 5(3), 332–53.

Pollard, J., Garwood, P., Parker Pearson, M., Richards, C., Thomas, J. and Welham, K. (2017). Remembered and imagined belongings: Stonehenge in the age of the first metals. In P. Bickle, V. Cummings, D. Hofmann and J. Pollard (eds.), *The Neolithic of Europe.* Oxford: Oxbow, pp. 279–97.

Pollard, J. and Robinson, D. (2007). A return to Woodhenge: The results and implications of the 2006 excavation. In M. Parker Pearson and M. Larsson (eds.), *From Stonehenge to the Baltic: Living with Cultural Diversity in the Third Millennium BC.* Oxford: British Archaeological Reports, pp. 159–68.

Pope, R. (2007). Ritual and the roundhouse: A critique of recent ideas on the use of domestic space in later British prehistory. In C. Haselgrove and R. Pope (eds.), *The Earlier Iron Age in Britain and the Near Continent.* Oxford: Oxbow, pp. 204–28.

Pope, R. (2015). Bronze Age architectural traditions: Dates and landscapes. In F. Hunter and I. Ralston (eds.), *Scotland in Later Prehistoric Europe.* Edinburgh: Society of Antiquaries of Scotland, pp. 159–84.

Powell, A. (2005). The language of lineage: Reading Irish court tomb design. *European Journal of Archaeology* 8, 9–28.

Powell, A. (2011). *An Early Iron Age Enclosure and Romano-British Features at High Post, near Salisbury.* Salisbury: Wessex Archaeology.

Powell, A. (2015). Bronze Age and Early Iron Age burial grounds and later landscape development outside Little Woodbury, Wiltshire. *Wiltshire Archaeological Magazine* 108, 44–78.

Powell, A., Barclay, A., Mepham, L. and Stevens, C. (2015). *Imperial College Sports Ground and RMC Land, Harlington.* Salisbury: Wessex Archaeology.

Powell, K., Smith, A. and Laws, G. (2010). *Evolution of a Farming Community in the Upper Thames Valley.* Oxford: Oxford Archaeology.

Powell, T. and Daniel, G. (1956). *Barclodiad y Gawres: A Megalithic Chamber Tomb in Anglesey.* Liverpool: Liverpool University Press.

Powelsland, D. (1988). Staple Howe in its landscape. In T. Manby (ed.), *Archaeology in Eastern Yorkshire.* Sheffield: Sheffield University Department of Archaeology, pp. 101–8.

Prendergast, F., O'Sullivan, M., Williams, K. and Cooney, G. (2017). Facing the sun. *Archaeology Ireland* 31(4), 10–17.

Price, E. (2000). *Frocester,* Vol. 1. Gloucester: Gloucester and District Archaeological Research Group.

Proctor, J. (2002). Late Bronze Age / Early Iron Age placed deposits from Westcroft Road, Carshalton: Their meaning and interpretation. *Surrey Archaeological Collections* 89, 65–103.

Proudfoot, V. B. (1955). *The Downpatrick Gold Find: A Hoard of Gold Objects from Cathedral Hill, Downpatrick*. Belfast: HMSO.

Pryor, F. (1984). *Excavations at Fengate, Peterborough, England: The Fourth Report*. Northampton: Northamptonshire Archaeological Society.

Pryor, F. (1998). *Etton*. London: English Heritage.

Pryor, F. (2001). *The Flag Fen Basin: Archaeology and Environment of a Fenland Landscape*. London: English Heritage.

Pryor, F. (2003). *Britain BC*. London: Harper Collins.

Pryor, F. and Bamforth, M. (2010). *Flag Fen, Peterborough: Excavation and Research 1995–2007*. Oxford: Oxbow.

Pryor, F., French, C., Crowther, D., Gurney, D., Simpson, G. and Taylor, M. (1985). *Archaeology and Environment in the Lower Welland Valley*. Norwich: East Anglian Archaeology 27.

Purcell, A. (2002). Excavation of the Neolithic houses at Corbally, Kilcullen, Co. Kildare. *Journal of Irish Archaeology* 11, 77–97.

Quinnell, H. and Blockley, K. (1994). *Excavations at Rhuddlan, 1969–73*. York: Council for British Archaeology.

Raftery, B. (1984). *La Tène in Ireland: Problems of Origins and Chronology*. Marburg: Vorgeschtlichen Seminar Marburg.

Raftery, B. (1994). *Pagan Celtic Ireland*. London: Thames and Hudson.

Raftery, B. (1995). The conundrum of Irish Iron Age pottery. In B. Raftery, V. Megaw and V. Rigby (eds.), *Sites and Sights of the Iron Age*. Oxford: Oxbow, pp. 149–56.

Raftery, B. (1996). *Trackway Excavations in the Mountdillon Bogs*. Dublin: Department of Archaeology, University College Dublin.

Raftery, B. (2004). Pit 119, Rathgall, Co. Wicklow. In H. Roche, E. Grogan, J. Bradley, J. Coles and B. Raftery (eds.), *From Megaliths to Metals*. Oxford: Oxbow, pp. 83–90.

Ray, K. and Thomas, J. S. (2018). *Neolithic Britain: The Transformation of Social Worlds*. Oxford: Oxford University Press.

Reich, D. (2018). *Who We Are and How We Got Here: Ancient DNA and the New Science of the Human Past*. Oxford: Oxford University Press.

Renfrew, C. (1973). Monuments, mobilisation and social organisation in Neolithic Wessex. In C. Renfrew (ed.), *The Explanation of Culture Change*. London: Duckworth, pp. 539–58.

Renfrew, C. (1979). *Investigations in Orkney*. London: Society of Antiquaries.

Renfrew, C. (2000). The auld hoose speaks: Society and life in Neolithic Orkney. In A. Ritchie (ed.), *Neolithic Orkney in its European Context*. Cambridge: McDonald Institute for Archaeological Research, pp. 1–20.

Reynolds, A. (2009). *Anglo-Saxon Deviant Burials*. Oxford: Oxford University Press.

Reynolds, P. (1979). *Iron Age Farm*. London: British Museum Press.

Richards, C. (1988). Altered images: A re-examination of Neolithic mortuary practices in Orkney. In J. Barrett and I. Kinnes (eds.), *The Archaeology of Context in the Neolithic and Bronze Age: Recent Trends*. Sheffield: Sheffield University Department of Prehistory and Archaeology, pp. 42–56.

Richards, C. (1996a). Henges and water: Towards an elemental understanding of monumentality and landscape in late Neolithic Britain. *Journal of Material Culture* 1, 313–36.

Richards, C. (1996b). Monuments as landscape: Creating the centre of the world in Neolithic Orkney. *World Archaeology* 28, 190–208.

Richards, C. (2004). Labouring with monuments: Constructing the dolmen at Carreg Samson, north-west Wales. In V. Cummins and C. Fowler (eds.), *The Neolithic of the Irish Sea*. Oxford: Oxbow, pp. 72–80.

Richards, C. (2005). *Dwelling among the Monuments*. Cambridge: McDonald Institute for Archaeological Research.

Richards, C. (2013). *Building the Great Stone Circles of the North*. Oxford: Windgather Press.

Richards, C., Jones, A. M., MacSween, A., Sheridan, A., Dunbar, E., Reimer, P., Bayliss, A., Griffiths, S. and Whittle, A. (2016). Settlement duration and materiality: Formal chronological models for the development of Barnhouse, a Grooved Ware settlement in Orkney. *Proceedings of the Prehistoric Society* 82, 193–225.

Richards, C. and Jones, R. eds. (2016). *The Development of Neolithic House Societies in Orkney*. Oxford: Windgather.

Richards, C. and Thomas, J. S. (1984). Ritual activity and structured deposition in later Neolithic Wessex. In R. Bradley and J. Gardiner (eds.), *Neolithic Studies*. Oxford: British Archaeological Reports, pp. 189–218.

Richards, M. (2004). The Early Neolithic in Britain: New insights from biomolecular archaeology. In I. Shepherd and G. Barclay (eds.), *Scotland in Ancient Europe*. Edinburgh: Society of Antiquaries of Scotland, pp. 83–90.

Richards, M. (2008). Stable isotope values. In R. Mercer and F. Healy (eds.), *Hambledon Hill Dorset: Excavation and Survey of a Neolithic Monument Complex and its Surrounding Landscape*. Swindon: English Heritage, pp. 522–7.

Richardson, A. and Johnson, P. (2007). Excavation of a Middle Bronze Age settlement at Knockhouse Lower, Co. Waterford. *Decies* 63, 1–17.

Ripper, S. and Beamish, M. (2012). Bogs, bodies and burnt mounds. *Proceedings of the Prehistoric Society* 78, 173–206.

Rippon, S. (2018). *Kingdom, Civitas and County: The Evolution of Territorial Identity in the English Landscape*. Oxford: Oxford University Press.

Risch, R. and Meller, H. (2015). Change and continuity in Europe and the Mediterranean around 1600 BC. *Proceedings of the Prehistoric Society* 81, 239–64.

Ritchie, A. (1983). The excavation of a Neolithic farmstead at Knap of Howar, Papa Westray, Orkney. *Proceedings of the Society of Antiquaries of Scotland* 113, 189–218.

Ritchie, J. N. G. (1974). Excavation of a stone circle and cairn at Balbirnie, Fife. *Archaeological Journal* 131, 1–32.

Ritchie, J. N. G. (1976). The Stones of Stenness, Orkney. *Proceedings of the Society of Antiquaries of Scotland* 107, 1–60.

Ritchie, J. N. G. (1998). The Ring of Brodgar, Orkney. In C. Ruggles (ed.), *Records in Stone*. Cambridge: Cambridge University Press, pp. 337–50.

Ritchie, K., Allen, M., Barnett, C., Cook, N., Crowther, J., Gale, R., Grant, M., Jones, G., Knight, S., Lievers, M., Mand Wyles, S., McKinley, J., Macphail, R., Mepham, L., Scaife, R., Stevens, C. and Wyles, S. (2008). Environment and land use in the lower Lea valley. *Transactions of the London and Middlesex Archaeological Society* 59, 1–38.

Rivet, A. L. F. and Smith, C. (1979). *The Place-Names of Roman Britain*. London: Batsford.

Robb, J. (2013). Material culture, landscapes of action, and emergent causation: A new model for the origins of the European Neolithic. *Current Anthropology* 54, 657–83.

Roberts, B. (2007). Adorning the living but not the dead. Investigating ornaments in Britain *c.* 1400–1100 cal. BC. *Proceeding of the Prehistoric Society* 73, 135–67.

Roberts, B., Boughton, D., Dinwiddy, M., Doski, N., Fitzpatrick, A., Hook, D., Meeks, N., Mongiatti, A., Woodward, A. and Woodward, P. (2015). Collapsing commodities or lavish offerings? Understanding massive metalwork deposition at Langton Maltravers, Dorset, during the Bronze Age–Iron Age transition. *Oxford Journal of Archaeology* 34, 365–95.

Roberts, B. and Wrathmell, S. (2000). *An Atlas of Rural Settlement in England*. London: English Heritage.

Roberts, D., Last, J., Linford, N., Bedford, J., Dunbar, E., Forward, A., Linford, P., Marshall, P., Mays, S., Payne, A., Pelling, R., Reimer, P., Russell, M., Soutar, S., Valdez-Tullett, A., Valledner, J. and Worley, F. (2017). The early field systems of the Stonehenge landscape. *Landscapes* 18(2), 120–40.

Roberts, I. (2005). *Ferrybridge Henge: The Ritual Landscape*. Morley: West Yorkshire Archaeology Service.

Robertson, D. (2016). A second timber circle, trackways and coppicing at Holme-next-the-Sea, Norfolk. *Proceedings of the Prehistoric Society* 82, 227–58.

Robertson, R. (2016). *Iron Age Hillfort Defences and the Tactics of Sling Warfare*. Oxford: Archaeopress.

Robin, G. (2009). *L'architecture des signes*. Rennes: Presses Universitaires de Rennes.

Robinson, M. (2000). Further consideration of Neolithic charred cereals, fruits and nuts. In

A. Fairbairn (ed.), *Plants in Neolithic Britain and Beyond*. Oxford: Oxbow, pp. 85–90.

Robinson, M. (2014). The ecodynamics of clearance in the British Neolithic. *Environmental Archaeology* 19, 291–7.

Roche, H. and Eogan, G. (2008). The reassessment of the enclosure at Lugg, County Dublin, Ireland. In C. Gosden, H. Hamerow and G. Lock (eds.), *Communities and Connections*. Oxford: Oxford University Press, pp. 154–68.

Rogers, A. (2013). *Female Burial Traditions of the Chalcolithic and Early Bronze Age: A Pilot Study Based on Modern Excavations*. Oxford: Archaeopress.

Rohl, B. and Needham, S. (1998). *The Circulation of Metal in the British Bronze Age: The Application of Lead Isotope Analysis*. London: British Museum.

Roland, T., Caseldine, C., Charman, D., Turney, C. and Amesbury, M. (2014). Was there a '4.2 ka event' in Great Britain and Ireland? Evidence from the peatland record. *Quaternary Science Reviews* 83, 11–27.

Romankiewicz, T. (2011). *The Complex Roundhouses of the Scottish Iron Age*. Oxford: British Archaeological Reports.

Rowlands, M. (1980). Kinship, alliance and exchange in the European Bronze Age. In J. Barrett and R. Bradley (eds.), *Settlement and Society in the British Later Bronze Age*. Oxford: British Archaeological Reports, pp. 15–59.

Rowley-Conwy, P. (2004). How the West was lost: A reconsideration of the agricultural origins in Britain, Ireland, and southern Scandinavia. *Current Anthropology* 45, 83–113.

Rowley-Conwy, P. (2011). Westward Ho! The spread of agriculture from Central Europe to the Atlantic. *Current Anthropology* 52, S431–51.

Rowley-Conwy, P. and Owen, A. (2011). Grooved Ware feasting in Yorkshire: Late Neolithic animal consumption at Rudston Wold. *Oxford Journal of Archaeology* 30, 325–67.

Roy, M. and Heppell, G. (2014). A prehistoric landscape at Lanford Hall, near Heybridge. *Transactions of the Essex Society for Archaeology and History* 5 (4th Ser.), 19–36.

Ruggles, C. (1999). *Astronomy in Prehistoric Britain and Ireland*. New Haven, CT: Yale University Press.

Ruiz-Gálvez Priego, M. (1998). *La Europa atlántica en la Edad del Bronce*. Barcelona: Crítica.

Russell, M. and Cheetham, P. (2016). Finding Duropolis: A new kind of Iron Age settlement. *Current Archaeology* 313, 12–18.

Sahlins, M. (1955). Esoteric efflorescence in Easter Island. *American Anthropologist* 57, 1045–52.

Sahlins, M. (1972). *Stone Age Economics*. Chicago, IL: Aldine.

Salanova, L. (2016). Behind the warriors: Bell Beakers and identities in Atlantic Europe. In J. Koch and B. Cunliffe (eds.), *Celtic from the West 3*. Oxford: Oxbow, pp. 13–40.

Saville, A. (1990). *Hazleton North*. London: English Heritage.

Saville, A. (2002). Lithic artefacts from Neolithic causewayed enclosures: Character and meaning. In G. Varndell and P. Topping (eds.), *Enclosures in Neolithic Europe*. Oxford: Oxbow, pp. 91–105.

Savory, H. (1956). Excavation of the Pipton long cairn. *Archaeologia Cambrensis* 105, 7–48.

Scarre, C. (2015). Parallel lives? Neolithic mortuary monuments and the Channel divide. In H. Anderson-Whymark, D. Garrow and F. Sturt (eds.), *Continental Connections: Exploring Cross-Channel Relationships from the Mesolithic to the Iron Age*. Oxford: Oxbow, pp. 78–98.

Schulting, R. (2010). Holocene environmental change and the Mesolithic–Neolithic transition in north-west Europe: Revisiting two models. *Environmental Archaeology* 15, 160–72.

Schulting, R. and Bradley, R. (2014). 'Of human remains and weapons in the neighbourhood of London': New AMS 14C dates on Thames 'river skulls' exhibiting injuries. *Archaeological Journal* 170, 31–77.

Schulting, R. and Fibiger, L. (2014). Violence in Neolithic North-west Europe: A population perspective. In A. Whittle and P. Bickle (eds.), *Early Farmers: The View from Archaeology and Science*. London: British Academy, pp. 281–306.

Schulting, R., Murphy, E., Jones, C. and Warren, G. (2012). New dates from the north, and a proposed chronology for Irish court tombs. *Proceedings of the Royal Irish Academy* 112C, 1–60.

Schulting, R., Sheridan, A., Clarke, S. and Bronk Ramsay, C. (2008). Largantea and the dating of Irish wedge tombs. *Journal of Irish Archaeology* 17, 1–17.

Schulting, R., Sheridan, A., Crozier, R. and Murphy, E. (2010). Revisiting Quanterness: New AMS dates and stable isotope data from an Orcadian chamber tomb. *Proceedings of the Society of Antiquaries of Scotland* 140, 1–50.

Schulting, R. and Wysocki, M. (2005). 'In the chambered tombs were found cleft skulls …': An assessment of the evidence for cranial trauma in the British Neolithic. *Proceedings of the Prehistoric Society* 71, 107–38.

Schulz Paulsson, B. (2017). *Time and Stone: The Emergence and Development of Megaliths and Megalithic Societies in Europe.* Oxford: Archaeopress.

Scott, D. (2016). The solar lunar alignments of the Orkney-Cromarty and Clava Cairns. *Journal of Skyscape Archaeology* 2, 45–66.

Scott, J. (1989). The stone circle at Temple Wood, Kilmartin, Argyll. *Glasgow Archaeological Journal* 15, 53–125.

Serjeantson, D. (2014). Survey of animal remains from southern Britain finds no evidence for continuity from the Mesolithic period. *Environmental Archaeology* 19, 256–62.

Sharples, N. (1985). Individual and community: The changing role of megaliths in the Orcadian Neolithic. *Proceedings of the Prehistoric Society* 51, 59–74.

Sharples, N. (1991). *Maiden Castle: Excavation and Field Survey 1985–6.* London: English Heritage.

Sharples, N. (2010). *Social Relations in Later Prehistory: Wessex in the First Millennium BC.* Oxford: Oxford University Press.

Sharples, N. (2014). Are the developed hill forts of Southern England urban? In M. Fernández-Götz, H. Wendling and K. Winger (eds.), *Paths to Complexity: Centralisation and Urbanisation in Iron Age Europe.* Oxford: Oxbow, pp. 224–32.

Shee Twohig, E. (1981). *The Megalithic Art of Western Europe.* Oxford: Clarendon Press.

Shee Twohig, E., Roughley, C., Shell, C., O'Reilly, C., Clarke, P. and Swanton, G.

(2010). Open-air rock art at Loughcrew, Co Meath. *Journal of Irish Archaeology* 19, 1–28.

Shennan, S. (2013). Demographic continuities and discontinuities in Neolithic Europe: Evidence, methods and implications. *Journal of Archaeological Method and Theory* 20(2), 300–11.

Shennan, S. (2018). *The First Farmers of Europe: An Evolutionary Perspective.* Cambridge: Cambridge University Press.

Shennan, S., Bevan, A., Edinborough, K., Kerig, T., Parker Pearson, M. and Schauer, P. (2017). Supply and demand in prehistory? Economics of Neolithic mining in NW Europe. *Archaeology International* 2017, 76–81.

Shepherd, D. (2014). Variations on a theme: An account of possible kerbed boulders in the South Pennines and Cumbria. *Time and Mind* 7, 309–20.

Sheridan, A. (1986). Megaliths and megalomania: An account and interpretation of the development of passage tombs in Ireland. *Journal of Irish Archaeology* 3, 17–30.

Sheridan, A. (2003a). Ireland's earliest 'passage tombs': A French connection. In G. Burenhult (ed.), *Stones and Bones.* Oxford: British Archaeological Reports, pp. 9–25.

Sheridan, A. (2003b). New dates for Scottish cinerary urns: Results from the National Museums of Scotland Dating Cremated Bones Project. In A. Gibson (ed.), *Prehistoric Pottery: People, Pattern and Purpose.* Oxford: British Archaeological Reports, pp. 201–26.

Sheridan, A. (2004). Going round in circles? Understanding the Irish Grooved Ware 'complex' in its wider context. In H. Roche, E. Grogan, J. Bradley, J. Coles and B. Raftery (eds.), *From Megaliths to Metals.* Oxford: Oxbow, pp. 26–37.

Sheridan, A. (2010). The Neolithisation of Britain and Ireland: The 'big picture'. In B. Finlayson and G. Warren (eds.), *Landscapes in Transition.* Oxford: Oxbow, pp. 89–105.

Sheridan, A. (2013). Early Neolithic habitation structures in Britain and Ireland: A matter of circumstance and context. In D. Hofmann and J. Smyth (eds.), *Tracking the Neolithic*

House in Europe. New York, NY: Springer, pp. 283–300.

Sheridan, A. (2014). Little and large: The miniature 'carved stone ball' beads from the eastern passage tomb under the main mound at Knowth, Ireland, and their broader significance. In R.-M. Arbogast and A. Greffier-Richard (eds.), *Entre archéologie et écologie, une préhistoire de tous les mileux*. Besancon: Presses universitaires de Franche-Comté, pp. 303–14.

Sheridan, A., Schulting, R., Quinnell, H. and Taylor, R. (2008). Revisiting a small passage tomb at Broadsands, Devon. *Proceedings of the Devon Archaeological Society* 66, 1–26.

Sheridan, A. and Shortland, A. (2004). '… beads that have given rise to so much dogmatism, controversy and rash speculation': Faience in Early Bronze Age Britain and Ireland. In I. Shepherd and G. Barclay (eds.), *Scotland in Ancient Europe*. Edinburgh: Society of Antiquaries of Scotland, pp. 263–79.

Sherlock, S. (2012). *Late Prehistoric Settlement in the Tees Valley and North-East England*. Hartlepool: Tees Archaeology.

Sherratt, A. (1996). Why Wessex? The Avon route and the river transport in British prehistory. *Oxford Journal of Archaeology* 15, 211–34.

Sherratt, A. (1997). *Economy and Society in Prehistoric Europe*. Edinburgh: Edinburgh University Press.

Sidell, J., Cotton, J., Rayner, L. and Wheeler, L. (2002). *The Prehistory and Topography of Southwark and Lambeth*. London: Museum of London.

Simmons, I. (1996). *The Environmental Impact of Later Mesolithic Cultures*. Edinburgh: Edinburgh University Press.

Simpson, D. (1993). Stone artefacts from the Lower Bann Valley. *Ulster Journal of Archaeology* 56, 31–43.

Simpson, D., Murphy, E. and Gregory, R. (2006). *Excavations at Northton, Isle of Harris*. Oxford: British Archaeological Reports.

Skoglund, P. (2017). Axes and long-distance trade: Scania and Wessex in the early second millennium BC. In P. Skoglund, J. Ling and U. Bertilsson (eds.), *North Meets South: Theoretical Aspects on the Northern and Southern Rock Art Traditions in Scandinavia*. Oxford: Oxbow, pp. 199–213.

Smith, A., Allen, M., Brindle, T. and Fulford, M. (2016). *The Rural Settlement of Roman Britain*. London: Society for the Promotion of Roman Studies.

Smith, K. (1977). The excavation of Winkelbury Camp, Basingstoke. *Proceedings of the Prehistoric Society* 43, 31–129.

Smyth, J. (2014). *Settlement in the Irish Neolithic*. Oxford: Prehistoric Society Research Paper 6.

Snoeck, C., Schulting, R., Lee-Thorp, J., Leben, M. and Zazzzo, A. (2016). Impact of heating conditions on the carbon and oxygen isotopic composition of calcined bone. *Journal of Archaeological Science* 65, 32–43.

Sørensen, L. and Karg, S. (2014). The expansion of agrarian societies towards the north: New evidence for agriculture during the Mesolithic / Neolithic transition in Southern Scandinavia. *Journal of Archaeological Science* 51, 256–62.

Speak, S. and Burgess, C. (1999). Meldon Bridge: A centre of the third millennium BC in Peebleshire. *Proceedings of the Society of Antiquaries of Scotland* 129, 1–118.

Speed, G. (2009). *Scorton Quarry, North Yorkshire: Area 2 and 4B*. Barnard Castle: Northern Archaeological Associates.

Spratt, D. (1993). *Prehistoric and Romano-British Archaeology of North-East Yorkshire*. London: Council for British Archaeology.

Standish, C., Dhuime, B., Hawkesworth, G. and Pike, A. (2015). A non-local source of Irish Chalcolithic and Early Bronze Age gold. *Proceedings of the Prehistoric Society* 81, 149–77.

Stanford, S. C. (1982). Bromfield, Shropshire: Neolithic, Beaker and Bronze Age Sites, 1966–79. *Proceedings of the Prehistoric Society* 48, 279–320.

Startin, B. and Bradley, R. (1981). Some notes on work organisation and society in prehistoric Wessex. In C. Ruggles and A. Whittle (eds.), *Astronomy and Society in Britain during the Period 4000–1500 BC*. Oxford: British Archaeological Reports, pp. 289–96.

Stead, I. (1991). *Iron Age Cemeteries in East Yorkshire*. London: English Heritage.

Stead, I. (2006). *British Iron Age Swords and Scabbards*. London: British Museum.

Stead, I. (2014). Snettisham swansong. In C. Gosden, S. Crawford and K. Ulmschneider (eds.), *Celtic Art in Europe: Making Connections*. Oxford: Oxbow, pp. 297–303.

Steffen, C. (2010). *Die Prunkgräber der Wessex- und der Aunjetitz-Kultur: Ein Vergleich der Repräsentationssitten von sozialen Status*. Oxford: British Archaeological Reports.

Stevens, C. and Fuller, D. (2012). Did Neolithic farming fail? The case for a Bronze Age agricultural revolution in the British Isles. *Antiquity* 86, 707–22.

Stewart, D. and Russell, M. (2017). *Hillforts and the Durotriges: A Geophysical Survey of Iron Age Dorset*. Oxford: Archaeopress.

Stewart, R. (2017). The Isle of Portland, Portland chert and Neolithic arrrowheads: Qualities and connections. *Lithics* 38, 57–71.

Stoertz, C. (1997). *Ancient Landscapes of the Yorkshire Wolds*. Swindon: Royal Commission on the Historical Monuments of England.

Stone, J. F. S. and Young, W. (1948). Two pits of Grooved Ware date near Woodhenge. *Wiltshire Archaeological Magazine* 52, 287–304.

Stout, G. (1991). Embanked enclosures of the Boyne region. *Proceedings of the Royal Irish Academy* 91C, 245–84.

Stout, G. and Stout, M. (2008). *Newgrange*. Cork: Cork University Press.

Sturt, F. (2015). From sea to land and back again. In H. Anderson-Whymark, D. Garrow and F. Sturt (eds.), *Continental Connections: Exploring Cross-Channel Relationships from the Mesolithic to the Iron Age*. Oxford: Oxbow, pp. 7–27.

Sturt, F., Garrow, D. and Bradley, S. (2013). New models of North Western Holocene palaeogeography and inundation. *Journal of Archaeological Science* 40, 3963–76.

Suddaby, I. (2013). *Excavation of Post-Built Roundhouses and a Circular Ditched Enclosure at Kiltaraglen, Portree, Isle of Skye*. Scottish Archaeological Internet Report 54, Edinburgh: Society of Antiquaries of Scotland.

Sunter, N. and Woodward, P. (1987). *Romano-British Industries in Purbeck*. Dorchester: Dorset Natural History and Archaeological Society.

Sweet, R. (2004). *Antiquaries: The Discovery of the Past in Eighteenth Century Britain*. London: Hambledon.

Sweetman, D. (1976). An earthen enclosure at Monknewtown, Co. Meath. *Proceedings of the Royal Irish Academy* 76C, 25–72.

Sweetman, D. (1985). A Late Neolithic / Early Bronze Age pit circle at Newgrange, Co. Meath. *Proceedings of the Royal Irish Academy* 81C, 195–221.

Sweetman, D. (1987). Excavation of a Late Neolithic / Early Bronze Age site at Newgrange, Co. Meath. *Proceedings of the Royal Irish Academy* 87C, 283–98.

Szécsényi-Nagy, A., Brandt, G., Haak, W., Keerl, V., Jakucs, J., Moeller-Rieker, S., Köhler, K., Mende, B. G., Oross, K., Marton, T., Osztás, A., Kiss, V., Fecher, M., Pálfi, G., Molnár, E., Sebők, K., Czene, A., Paluch, T., Šlaus, M., Novak, M., Pećina-Šlaus, N., Ősz, B., Voicsek, V., Somogyi, K., Tóth, G., Kromer, B., Bánffy, E. and Alt, K. W. (2015). Tracing the genetic origin of Europe's first farmers reveals insights into their social organization. *Proceedings of the Royal Society B* 282(20150339).

Tabor, R. (2007). A Middle Bronze Age metal-working building and enclosure at Sigwells, Somerset, England. *Past* 57, 9–12.

Tavener, N. (1996). Evidence of Neolithic activity near Marton-le-Moor, North Yorkshire. *Northern Archaeology* 14, 183–87.

Taylor, R. (1993). *Hoards of the Bronze Age in Southern Britain*. Oxford: British Archaeological Reports.

Thomas, A. (2016). *Art and Architecture in Neolithic Orkney*. Oxford: Archaeopress.

Thomas, J. (2010). The village people? Origin and development of 'aggregated' settlement in the East Midlands. In M. Sterry, A. Tullett and N. Roy (eds.), *In Search of the Iron Age*. Leicester: Leicester University School of Archaeology and Ancient History, pp. 1–26.

Thomas, J. (2018). Glenfield Park: Living with cauldrons. *British Archaeology* 158, 17–21.

Thomas, J. S. (1988). Neolithic explanations revisited: The Mesolithic–Neolithic transition in Britain and South Scandinavia. *Proceedings of the Prehistoric Society* 54, 59–66.

Thomas, J. S. (2006). On the origin and development of cursus monuments in Britain. *Proceedings of the Prehistoric Society* 72, 229–41.

Thomas, J. S. (2007a). The internal features at Durrington Walls: Investigations in the Southern Circle and Western Enclosures. In M. Larsson and M. Parker Pearson (eds.), *From Stonehenge to the Baltic*. Oxford: British Archaeological Reports, pp. 145–57.

Thomas, J. S. ed. (2007b). *Place and Memory: Excavations at the Pict's Knowe, Holywood and Holm Farm, Dumfries and Galloway 1994–8*. Oxford: Oxbow.

Thomas, J. S. (2010). The return of the Rinyo-Claction Folk: The significance of the Grooved Ware complex in later Neolithic Britain. *Cambridge Archaeological Journal* 20, 1–15.

Thomas, J. S. (2013). *The Birth of Neolithic Britain*. Oxford: Oxford University Press.

Thomas, J. S. (2015a). House societies and founding ancestors in Early Neolithic Britain. In C. Renfrew, M. Boyd and I. Morley (eds.), *Death Shall Have No Dominion*. Cambridge: Cambridge University Press, pp. 138–53.

Thomas, J. S. (2015b). *A Neolithic Ceremonial Complex in Galloway: Excavations at Dunragit and Droughduil*. Oxford: Oxbow.

Thomas, J. S. (2016). Cattle, consumption and causewayed enclosures. *World Archaeology* 48, 729–44.

Thomas, K. (1982). Neolithic enclosures and woodland habitats on the South Downs in Sussex, England. In M. Bell and S. Limbrey (eds.), *Aspects of Woodland Ecology*. Oxford: British Archaeological Reports, pp. 147–70.

Thomas, N. (2005). *Snail Down, Wiltshire*. Devizes: Wiltshire Archaeological Society.

Thomas, R. (1997). Land, kinship relations and the rise of enclosed settlements in first millennium BC Britain. *Oxford Journal of Archaeology* 16, 211–18.

Thomas, R., Oswin, J. and Brown, L. (2012). A Late Bronze Age / Earliest Iron Age settlement on Bathampton Down, Bath. *Proceedings of the Somerset Archaeological Society* 155, 204–7.

Thompson, S. and Powell, A. (2018). *Along Prehistoric Lines*. Salisbury: Wessex Archaeology.

Thompson, S., Leivers, M. and Barclay, A. (2017). The Larkhill causewayed enclosure. *Current Archaeology* 326, 30–4.

Tierney, J. (2009). Life and death in the Later Neolithic and Early Bronze Age at Ballynacarriga, Co. Cork. *Archaeology Ireland* 23(4), 34–8.

Tierney, J. and Logan, E. (2008). Beaker settlement: Area 13, Ahanaglogh. In P. Johnston, J. Kiely and J. Tierney (eds.), *Near the Bend in the River: The Archaeology of the N25 Kilmacthomas Realignment*. Dublin: National Roads Authority, pp. 29–43.

Tilley, C. (2004). *The Materiality of Stone*. Oxford: Berg.

Tilley, C. (2010). *Interpreting Landscapes*. Abingdon: Routledge.

Tilley, C. (2017). *Landscape in the Longue Durée*. London: UCL Press.

Timberlake, S. (2001). Mining and prospecting for metals in Early Bronze Age Britain: Making claims within the archaeological landscape. In J. Brück (ed.), *Bronze Age Landscapes: Tradition and Transformation*. Oxford: Oxbow, pp. 179–92.

Timberlake, S. (2016). New ideas on the exploitation of copper, tin, gold and lead in Bronze Age Britain: The mining, smelting and movement of metal. *Materials and Manufacturing Processes* 32, 709–27.

Timby, J., Brown, R., Biddulph, E. and Powell, A. (2007). *A Slice of Rural Essex*. Oxford / Salisbury: Oxford Wessex Archaeology.

Tipping, R. (1994a). The form and fate of Scotland's woodlands. *Proceedings of the Society of Antiquaries of Scotland* 124, 1–54.

Tipping, R. (1994b). 'Ritual' floral tributes in the Scottish Bronze Age: Palynological evidence. *Journal of Archaeological Science* 21, 133–39.

Tipping, R. (2010a). *Bowmont: An Environmental Investigation of the Bowmont Valley and the North Cheviot Hills, 10,000 BC–AD 2000*. Edinburgh: Society of Antiquaries of Scotland.

Tipping, R. (2010b). The case for climatic stress forcing choice in the adoption of agriculture in the British Isles. In G. Warren (ed.), *Landscapes in Transition*. Oxford: Oxbow, pp. 66–77.

Tipping, R. (2017). Catastrophism, climate change, Colin Burgess and the Cheviots. In R. Crellin, C. Fowler and R. Tipping (eds.), *Prehistory without Borders: The Prehistoric Archaeology of the Tyne-Forth Region*. Oxford: Oxbow, pp. 191–9.

Tipping, R., Bradley, R., Sanders, J., McCulloch, R. and Wilson, R. (2013). Moments of crisis: Climate change in Scottish prehistory. *Proceedings of the Society of Antiquaries of Scotland* 147, 9–25.

Topping, P. (1989). Early cultivation in Northumberland and the Borders. *Proceedings of the Prehistoric Society* 55, 161–79.

Topping, P. (1992). The Penrith henges. *Proceedings of the Prehistoric Society* 58, 249–64.

Tourunen, A. (2007). No bones about it: Burnt mounds along the N9/N10. *Seanda* 2, 70–1.

Towers, R., Card, N. and Edmonds, M. (2017). *The Ness of Brodgar*. Kirkwall: Ness of Brodgar Trust.

Tresset, A. (2003). French Connection 2: Of cows and men. In I. Armit, E. Murphy, E. Nelis and D. Simpson (eds.), *Neolithic Settlement in Ireland and Western Britain*. Oxford: Oxbow, pp. 18–30.

Tubb, P. (2011). Late Bronze Age / Early Iron Age transition sites in the Vale of Pewsey. *Wiltshire Archaeological Magazine* 104, 44–61.

Valdez-Tullett, A. (2017). Sheep in wealth's clothing: Social reproduction across the Bronze Age to Iron Age transition in Wiltshire, Southern England. *European Journal of Archaeology* 20, 663–81.

Van de Noort, R. (2011). *North Sea Archaeologies*. Oxford: Oxford University Press.

Van de Noort, R., Chapman, H. and Collis, J. eds. (2007). *Sutton Common*. York: Council for British Archaeology.

Vander Linden, M. (2006). *Le phénomène campaniforme dans l'Europe de 3ème millénaire avant notre ère: Synthèse et nouvelles perspectives*. Oxford: Archaeopress.

Vander Linden, M. (2016). Population history in third-millennium BC Europe: Assessing the contribution of genetics. *World Archaeology* 48, 714–28.

Vandkilde, H. (2017). *The Metal Hoard from Pile in Scania, Sweden*. Aarhus: Aarhus University Press.

Vatcher, F. (1961). The excavation of a long mortuary enclosure on Normanton Down, Wiltshire. *Proceedings of the Prehistoric Society* 27, 160–73.

Vejby, M. (2016). Radiocarbon dates from the Loughcrew Cairn H bone slips. *Oxford Journal of Archaeology* 35, 213–21.

Vera, F. (2000). *Grazing Ecology and Forest History*. Wallingford: CAB International.

Vyner, B. (1984). The excavation of a Neolithic cairn at Street House, Loftus, Cleveland. *Proceedings of the Prehistoric Society* 50, 151–95.

Vyner, B. (1988). The Street House Wossit: The excavation of a Late Neolithic and Early Bronze Age palisaded ritual monument at Street House, Loftus, Cleveland. *Proceedings of the Prehistoric Society* 54, 173–202.

Vyner, B. (2011). A new context for rock art: A Late Neolithic and Early Bronze Age ritual monument at Fylingdales, North Yorkshire. *Proceedings of the Prehistoric Society* 77, 1–23.

Waddell, J. (1978). The invasion hypothesis in Irish prehistory. *Antiquity* 52, 121–8.

Waddell, J. (1990). *The Bronze Age Burials of Ireland*. Galway: Galway University Press.

Waddell, J. (1992). The Irish Sea in prehistory. *Journal of Irish Archaeology* 6, 29–40.

Waddell, J. (2005). *Foundation Myths: The Beginnings of Irish Archaeology*. Bray: Wordwell.

Waddell, J. (2010). *The Prehistoric Archaeology of Ireland*, Revised edition. Dublin: Wordwell.

Waddington, C. (2007). Rethinking Mesolithic settlement and a case study from Howick. In C. Waddington and K. Pedersen (eds.), *Mesolithic Studies in the North Sea Basin and Beyond*. Oxford: Oxbow, pp. 101–13.

Waddington, C. (2012). Excavations at Fin Cop, Derbyshire: An Iron Age hillfort in conflict? *Archaeological Journal* 169, 159–236.

Waddington, K. (2013). *Settlements of Northwest Wales: From the Late Bronze Age to the Early Medieval Period*. Cardiff: University of Wales Press.

Waddington, K. (2014). The biography of a settlement: An analysis of Middle Iron Age deposits and houses at Howe, Orkney. *Archaeological Journal* 171, 61–96.

Waddington, K. and Sharples, N. (2011). *The Excavations at Whitchurch 2006–2009: An Interim Report*. Cardiff: Cardiff University Department of Archaeology.

Wainwright, G. (1969). A review of henge monuments in the light of recent research. *Proceedings of the Prehistoric Society* 35, 112–33.

Wainwright, G. (1971). The excavation of a fortified settlement at Walesland Rath, Pembrokeshire. *Britannia* 2, 48–108.

Wainwright, G. (1979). *Mount Pleasant*. London: Society of Antiquaries.

Wainwright, G. and Longworth, I. (1971). *Durrington Walls: Excavations 1966–1968*. London: Society of Antiquaries.

Walker, K. and Farwell, D. (2000). *Twyford Down, Hampshire*. Winchester: Hampshire Field Club.

Wang, Q., Strekoptov, S., Roberts, B. and Wilkin, N. (2016). Tin ingots from a possible shipwreck off the coast at Salcombe, Devon. *Journal of Archaeological Science* 67, 80–92.

Ware, P. (2017). An Iron Age chariot burial: Excavating a square-barrow cemetery at Pocklington. *Current Archaeology* 327, 26–31.

Warner, R. (2000). Keeping out the Otherworld: The internal ditch at Navan and other Iron Age 'hengiform' enclosures. *Emania* 18, 39–44.

Waterman, D. (1997). *Excavations at Navan Fort 1961–71*. Belfast: The Stationery Office.

Watkins, T. (1985). *Rullion Green: Report on the 1985 Season of Excavations*. Edinburgh: Edinburgh University Department of Archaeology.

Watson, A. (2001a). Composing Avebury. *World Archaeology* 33, 296–314.

Watson, A. (2001b). Round barrows in a circular world: Monumentalizing landscapes in Early Bronze Age Wessex. In J. Brück (ed.), *Bronze Age Landscapes*. Oxford: Oxbow, pp. 207–16.

Watson, A. (2004). Making space for monuments: Notes on the representation of experience. In C. Renfrew, C. Gosden and E. DeMarrais (eds.), *Substance, Memory, Display: Archaeology and Art*. Cambridge: McDonald Institute for Archaeological Research, pp. 79–96.

Watson, A. and Bradley, R. (2009). On the edge of England: Cumbria as a Neolithic region. In K. Brophy and G. Barclay (eds.), *Defining a Regional Neolithic: The Evidence from Britain and Ireland*. Oxford: Oxbow, pp. 65–77.

Watson, A. and Keating, D. (1999). Architecture and sound: An acoustical analysis of megalithic monuments in Britain. *Antiquity* 73, 325–36.

Watts, S. (2014). *The Life and Death of Querns*. Southampton: Highfield Press.

Webley, L. (2015). Rethinking Iron Age connections across the Channel and the North Sea. In H. Anderson-Whymark, D. Garrow and F. Sturt (eds.), *Continental Connections: Exploring Cross-Channel Relationships from the Mesolithic to the Iron Age*. Oxford: Oxbow, pp. 122–44.

Webley, L. and Adams, S. (2016). Material genealogies: Bronze moulds and their castings in Later Bronze Age Britain. *Proceedings of the Prehistoric Society* 82, 323–40.

West, M. (2007). *Indo-European Poetry and Myth*. Oxford: Oxford University Press.

Whimster, R. (1981). *Burial Practices in Iron Age Britain*. Oxford: British Archaeological Reports.

White, D. (1982). *The Cremation Cemeteries at Simons Ground, Dorset*. Dorchester: Dorset Natural History and Archaeological Society.

Whitehouse, N. (2006). The Holocene British and Irish woodland fossil beetle fauna: Implications for forest history, biodiversity and faunal colonisation. *Quaternary Science Reviews* 25, 1755–89.

Whitehouse, N., Schulting, R., McClatchie, M., Barratt, P., McLaughlin, T. R., Bogaard, A., Colledge, S., Marchant, R., Gaffrey, J. and Bunting, M. (2014). Neolithic farming on the western European frontier: The boom and bust of early farming in Ireland. *Journal of Archaeological Science* 51, 181–205. doi: 10.1016/j.jas.2013.08.009.

Whitfield, A. (2017). 'Celtic' fields: A reinterpretation of the chronological evidence from Céide Fields, North-western Ireland. *European Journal of Archaeology* 20, 257–79.

Whittle, A. (1997). *Sacred Mound, Holy Rings: Silbury Hill and the West Kennet Palisade Enclosures*. Oxford: Oxbow.

Whittle, A. (2004). Stones that float to the sky: Portal dolmens and their landscape of memory and myth. In V. Cummings and C. Fowler (eds.), *The Neolithic of the Irish Sea*. Oxford: Oxbow, pp. 81–90.

Whittle, A. (2018). *The Times of their Lives*. Oxford: Oxbow.

Whittle, A., Atkinson, R., Chambers, R. and Thomas, N. (1992). Excavations in the Neolithic and Bronze Age complex at Dorchester-on-Thames, Oxfordshire, 1947–52 and 1981. *Proceedings of the Prehistoric Society* 58, 143–201.

Whittle, A., Healy, F. and Bayliss, A. (2011). *Gathering Time: Dating the Early Neolithic Enclosures of Southern Britain and Ireland.* Oxford: Oxbow.

Whittle, A., Pollard, J. and Grigson, C. (1999). *The Harmony of Symbols: The Windmill Hill Causewayed Enclosure, Wiltshire.* Oxford: Oxbow.

Whittle, A. and Wysocki, M. (1998). Parc le Breos Cwm transepted long cairn, Gower, West Glamorgan: Date, contents and context. *Proceedings of the Prehistoric Society* 64, 139–82.

Wicks, K., Pirie, A. and Mithen, S. (2014). Settlement patterns in the late Mesolithic of western Scotland: The implications of Bayesian analysis of radiocarbon dates and inter-site technological comparisons. *Journal of Archaeological Science* 41, 406–22.

Wigg-Wolf, D. (2018). Death by deposition? Coins and ritual in the late Iron Age and early Roman transition in northern Gaul. In N. Myrberg Burström and G. Tarnow Ingvardson (eds.), *Divina Moneta: Coins in Ritual and Religion.* Abingdon: Routledge, pp. 13–29.

Wilkes, E. (2007). Prehistoric sea journeys and port approaches: The south coast and Poole Harbour. In V. Cummings and R. Johnston (eds.), *Prehistoric Journeys.* Oxford: Oxbow, pp. 121–30.

Wilkin, N. (2016). Pursuing the penumbral: The deposition of Beaker pottery at Neolithic ceremonial monuments in Chalcolithic and Early Bronze Age Scotland. In K. Brophy, G. McGregor and I. Ralston (eds.), *The Neolithic of Mainland Scotland.* Edinburgh: Edinburgh University Press, pp. 261–318.

Williams, B. (1978). Excavations at Lough Eskragh, County Tyrone. *Ulster Journal of Archaeology* 41, 37–48.

Williams, G. (1984). A henge monument at Ffynnon Newydd, Nantgaredig. *Bulletin of the Board of Celtic Studies* 31, 177–90.

Williams, G. and Mytum, H. (1998). *Llawhaden, Dyfed: Excavations on a Group of Small Defended Enclosures.* Oxford: British Archaeological Reports.

Williams, M. (2003). Growing metaphors: The agricultural cycle as metaphor in the later prehistoric period of Britain and North-Western Europe. *Journal of Social Archaeology* 3, 223–55.

Williams, R. and Zeepfat, R. (1994). *Bancroft.* Aylesbury: Buckinghamshire Archaeological Society.

Willis, C., Marshall, P., McKinley, J., Pitts, M., Pollard, J., Richards, C., Richards, J., Waldron, T., Welham, K. and Parker Pearson, M. (2016). The dead of Stonehenge. *Antiquity* 90, 337–56.

Wiseman, R. (2018). Random accumulation and breaking: The formation of Bronze Age scrap hoards in England and Wales. *Journal of Archaeological Science* 90, 39–49.

Woodbridge, J., Fyfe, R. M., Roberts, N., Downey, S., Edinborough, K. and Shennan, S. (2014). The impact of the Neolithic agricultural transition in Britain: A comparison of pollen-based land-cover and archaeological 14C date-inferred population change. *Journal of Archaeological Science* 51, 216–24. doi: 10.1016/j.jas.2012.10.025.

Woodman, P. (2015). *Ireland's First Settlers: Time and the Mesolithic.* Oxford: Oxbow.

Woodman, P., Anderson, E. and Finlay, N. (1999). *Excavations at Ferriter's Cove 1983–95.* Dublin: Wordwell.

Woodward, A. (2000). *British Barrows: A Matter of Life and Death.* Stroud: Tempus.

Woodward, A. and Hunter, J. (2015). *Ritual in Early Bronze Age Grave Goods.* Oxford: Oxbow.

Woodward, A. and Woodward, P. (1996). The topography of some barrow cemeteries in Bronze Age Wessex. *Proceedings of the Prehistoric Society* 62, 275–91.

Woodward, P., Davies, S. and Graham, A. (1993). *Excavations at Greyhound Yard, Dorchester 1981–4.* Dorchester: Dorset Natural History and Archaeological Society.

Wrathmell, S. and Nicholson, A. (1990). *Dalton Parlours: Iron Age Settlement and Roman Villa.*

Wakefield: West Yorkshire Archaeology Service.

Wysocki, M., Griffiths, S., Hedges, R., Bayliss, A., Higham, T., Fernández-Jalvo, Y. and Whittle, A. (2013). Dates, diet and dismemberment: Evidence from the Coldrum megalithic monument, Kent. *Proceedings of the Prehistoric Society* 79, 61–90.

Yates, A., Holmes, M., Chapman, A. and Wolframm-Murray, Y. (2012). A Middle Neolithic enclosure and mortuary deposit at Banbury Lane, Northampton: An interim report. *Northamptonshire Archaeology* 37, 19–28.

Yates, D. (2007). *Land, Power and Prestige: Bronze Age Field Systems in Southern England*. Oxford: Oxbow.

Yates, D. and Bradley, R. (2010a). Still water, hidden depths: The deposition of Bronze Age metalwork in the English Fenland. *Antiquity* 84, 405–15.

Yates, D. and Bradley, R. (2010b). The siting of metalwork hoards in the Bronze Age of south-east England. *Antiquaries Journal* 90, 405–15.

York, J. (2002). The life cycle of Bronze Age metalwork from the Thames. *Oxford Journal of Archaeology* 21, 77–92.

Zvelebil, M. and Rowley-Conwy, P. (1986). Foragers and farmers in Atlantic Europe. In M. Zvelebil (ed.), *Hunters in Transition*. Cambridge: Cambridge University Press, pp. 67–93.

INDEX